W9-DCL-155

A History of Portugal and the Portuguese Empire

The Kingdom of Portugal was created as a by-product of the Christian Reconquest of Hispania. With no geographical raison d'être and no obvious political roots in its Roman, Germanic, or Islamic pasts, it long remained a small, struggling realm on Europe's outer fringe. Then, in the early fifteenth century, this unlikely springboard for Western expansion suddenly began to accumulate an empire of its own – eventually extending more than halfway around the globe. *A History of Portugal and the Portuguese Empire,* drawing particularly on historical scholarship postdating the 1974 Portuguese Revolution, offers readers a comprehensive overview and reinterpretation of how all this happened – the first such account to appear in English for more than a generation. Volume I concerns the history of Portugal itself from pre-Roman times to the climactic French invasion of 1807, and Volume II traces the history of the Portuguese overseas empire.

A. R. Disney was educated at Oxford and Harvard universities and has taught history at Melbourne and La Trobe universities. His publications include *Twilight of the Pepper Empire* (1978) and numerous articles, papers, and essays, published variously in the *Economic History Review, Studia, Indica, Mare Liberum, Anais de Historia de Alem-mar,* and other journals and proceedings.

A History of Portugal and the Portuguese Empire

From Beginnings to 1807
Volume 1: Portugal

A. R. DISNEY

La Trobe University

CAMBRIDGE UNIVERSITY PRESS

CAMBRIDGE UNIVERSITY PRESS
Cambridge, New York, Melbourne, Madrid, Cape Town, Singapore,
São Paulo, Delhi, Dubai, Tokyo

Cambridge University Press
32 Avenue of the Americas, New York, NY 10013-2473, USA

www.cambridge.org
Information on this title: www.cambridge.org/9780521603973

First published 2009
Reprinted 2009 (twice)

Printed in the United States of America

A catalog record for this publication is available from the British Library.

Library of Congress Cataloging in Publication data

Disney, A. R. (Anthony R.), 1938–
A history of Portugal and the Portuguese empire / A. R. Disney.
p. cm.
Includes bibliographical references and index.
ISBN 978-0-521-84318-8 (hardback) – ISBN 978-0-521-60397-3 (paperback)
1. Portugal – History. 2. Portugal – Colonies – History. I. Title.

DP517.D57 2009
946.9–dc22   2008039017

ISBN 978-0-521-84318-8 Hardback
ISBN 978-0-521-60397-3 Paperback

Contents

Contents for Volume 2

Abbreviations

AHR	*American Historical Review*
BAR	*British Archaeological Reports*
CEHCA	Centro de Estudos de História e Cartografia Antiga
CIP	Antunes M (ed) *Como interpretar Pombal? No bicentenário de sua morte*
CNCDP	Comissão Nacional para as Comemorações dos Descobrimentos Portugueses
CP	Marques A H de O (ed) *Chancelarias portuguesas. D. Afonso IV*
CRB OM	Boxer C R *Opera Minora*
DA	Turner J (ed) *The dictionary of art*
DHDP	Albuquerque L de (dir) *Dicionário de história dos descobrimentos portugueses*
DHP	Serrão J (ed) *Dicionário de história de Portugal*
DIHP	*Dicionário ilustrado da história de Portugal*
EI	Gibb H A R et al (eds) *Encyclopaedia of Islam*
GE	*Grande encyclopédia portuguesa e brasileira*
HA	Chicó M et al (eds) *História da arte em Portugal*
HAHR	*Hispanic American Historical Review*
HEPM	Baião A, Cidade H and Múrias M (eds) *História da expansão portuguesa no mundo*
HP	Mattoso J (dir) *História de Portugal*
LMS	Jayyusi S K et al (eds) *The legacy of Muslim Spain*
MedHP	Medina J (dir) *História de Portugal dos tempos préhistoricós aos nossos dias*
MHP	Marques A H de O *History of Portugal* vol 1

NHEP	Serrão J and Marques A H de O (dirs) *Nova história da expansão portuguesa*
NHP	Serrão J and Marques A H de O (dirs) *Nova história de Portugal*
PDH	*Portugal – dicionário histórico, corográfico, heráldico, biográfico, bibliográfico, numismático e artístico*
PHP	Peres D (dir) *História de Portugal. Edição monumental*
RHC	Rodrigues F *História da companhia de Jesús na assistência de Portugal*
RHES	*Revista de história económica e social*
SHP	Serrão J V *História de Portugal*

List of Maps

Preface

Fort Jesus, the Portuguese-built stronghold that stands sentinel over the gently shimmering waters of Mombasa harbour with their clustered dhows, first drew me to Portugal's history. As a boy I lived on a farm in western Kenya. Occasionally, when the price of maize was favourable or coffee had had a particularly good year, my father would treat my mother, my sister and me to a holiday on the coast. There, each time, would be the fort – a quietly brooding monument to Mombasa's turbulent past and to the seemingly mysterious role played in it by the Portuguese.

In Oxford, on a cool November day of 1960, my interest in Fort Jesus was unexpectedly re-kindled. Gazing at a display in Blackwell's window, I caught sight of a new book with a bright, glossy dust jacket: *Fort Jesus and the Portuguese in Mombasa* by C. R. Boxer and Carlos de Azevedo. There, splashed across the front, was a photograph of the fort, its mellowed seawalls supporting their serrated Arab battlements, fringed by gently swaying coconut palms, with the little beach nearby. As soon as I could, I scraped together from my modest student allowance the required twenty-one shillings and bought that book. It was the fort, and the book about the fort, that led me in due course to write *A History of Portugal and the Portuguese Empire: From Beginnings to 1807*.

One of the first European kingdoms to establish stable borders, Portugal has had an unusually long and rich history. Emerging in the twelfth century from the confusion of the Iberian Reconquest, it remained for long a relatively small and struggling frontier kingdom – until its fortunes began to change, and its importance to grow, from the early fifteenth century. Underlying this enhancement was the fact that the Portuguese, almost by accident, had begun to accumulate, bit by bit, what would eventually become one of the most remarkable and wide-flung of all the European empires. The aim of the present book is to make available to English-speaking readers a quite comprehensive view of how all this happened, tracing Portugal's story from its earliest beginnings down to the demise of the Old Regime at the start of the nineteenth century.

As its title indicates, this first volume is about metropolitan Portugal only. It consists of fourteen chapters which recount the country's history through a succession of epochs, from pre-historic times to 1807. Each chapter contains a mixture of narrative, description, comment and analysis, which I have endeavoured to integrate in such a way that they form a coherent, readable and intellectually stimulating whole. Further, all chapters are divided into sections with headings. If readers so desire, they can therefore easily single out sections that are of particular interest to them and read these in isolation. Nevertheless, all chapters are designed to form integrated wholes – and in my view it is better to treat them as such.

Chapters 1 to 4 are concerned with Portuguese space and the people who lived in it, in the eras before the existence of Portugal as a discrete political entity. They describe how successive waves of Roman, Germanic and Islamic intruders overlaid an Hispanic base that was already much affected by the impact of Mediterranean 'Orientalising' and northern 'Celticising' influences. Although the experiences of these times do not explain the subsequent emergence of Portugal as a kingdom, and as a nation, they were fundamental in the formation of the Portuguese people and their characteristic culture.

The early inhabitants of Portugal did not know that the land they occupied would one day become a separate kingdom with its own language, traditions and institutions. In Chapter 5, it is argued that the decisive steps that eventually led to this outcome were taken in the mid-twelfth century. It was then that the kingdom of Portugal emerged as a by-product of the Reconquest and the evolution of feudal relationships in the northwestern segment of the Iberian peninsula. A long struggle to make the kingdom viable followed. This involved not only consolidating it against various disruptive forces from within but also defending it from residual Islamic enemies without – and from the seductive attractions of pan-Hispanism.

During the two centuries or so after the creation of the kingdom, Portugal experienced a gradual transition into nationhood. This process is discussed in Chapter 6, which also contains an overview of Portugal at the peak of its rather modest Medieval prosperity in the early fourteenth century. It then goes on to describe the demographic, economic and political crises that together almost destroyed the young kingdom from the late 1330s. An account of Portugal's recovery in the fifteenth century, and of the gradual strengthening of royal government under the early Avis kings, follows in Chapter 7.

In the early sixteenth century, Portugal experienced a remarkable 'Golden Age' – which, however, all too quickly tarnished from that century's middle years. During the Golden Age, some groups and individuals in the kingdom attained considerable prosperity, largely as a consequence of overseas trade and expansion. But the situation gradually changed for the worse as Portugal was overtaken by an array of economic and political problems, culminating in the disastrous defeat of Al-Ksar al-Kabir and the ensuing loss of independence in 1578–80. All this is recounted in Chapters 8 and 9. Then in Chapter 10, I go on to describe how Portugal fared when its crown was united with that of Castile, what eventually caused the union to fail and the manner in which Portugal's separate identity was recovered in 1640.

Chapter 11 is about the nature of the Bragança Restoration, the struggle to sheet it home and the kind of regime its adherents sought to entrench. It also explains how the situation was gradually stabilised in the late seventeenth century. The first half of the eighteenth century, an 'Age of Gold and Baroque Splendour', when Old Regime Portugal was at its apogee, but the seeds of change were also beginning to germinate, is examined in Chapter 12. This is followed by two chapters reviewing in turn the extraordinary ascendancy of Pombal and the associated reform program, the subsequent Marian reaction and the series of events that culminated in the *ano tormentoso* of 1807. That was the year that saw Portugal invaded by Napoleonic troops, causing the royal family and court to withdraw to Brazil – dramatic moves that marked the beginning of the end, if not the end itself, of the Portuguese Old Regime.

I am deeply conscious of the extent to which I have relied on the research of others – particularly of my Portuguese predecessors and colleagues – in the writing of this volume. Only occasionally, when I considered it particularly necessary or desirable, have I gone directly to the primary sources myself. Any reader who wishes to ascertain the precise material on which the volume is based may readily do so by referring to the footnotes, in conjunction with the bibliography. However, I must point out that the latter is limited to works cited in the notes only. It should not therefore be regarded as a comprehensive guide to Portuguese historical writings – though it might perhaps serve as a preliminary indicator. Those who wish to inquire further should consult the bibliographies in the several multi-volume Portuguese histories discussed in the following pages, especially in the *Nova história de Portugal*.

Portugal has a strong tradition of producing quality multi-volume national histories, several of which have been invaluable sources for my own work. This tradition began with the so-called 'Barcelos' history, the monumental seven-volume *História de Portugal*, directed by Damião Peres (1928–35). The Barcelos history, which set new standards of rigorous scholarship at the time, still remains of value today, especially for political developments. However, with

the major upsurge in Portuguese historical writing from the early 1970s, the
need for a new updated synthesis became more imperative. To date, four
massive multi-volume publications have appeared in response to this need.

The earliest of these four works is Joaquim Veríssimo Serrão's *História de
Portugal* (Editorial Verbo, Lisbon, 1977–2001). This publication comprises
fourteen volumes, of which the first six together take the history of Portugal
down to the start of the nineteenth century. Veríssimo Serrão offers the reader a
reliable, well-documented empirical history, written from a generally conservative viewpoint. Next, there is the lavishly illustrated eight-volume *História
de Portugal,* directed by the distinguished Medievalist José Mattoso (Editorial
Estampa, Lisbon, 1993). The first four volumes of the 'Mattoso' history are
relevant to the period before 1807. However, although there is much of value
in this work, the various volume editors have adopted widely different
approaches. This has resulted in considerable loss of overall coherence and left
major gaps.

A third collective history is the *História de Portugal dos tempos pré-
históricos aos nossos dias* (Clube Internacional do Livro, Amadora, 1995).
This was written by various contributors, under the overall direction of the
Lisbon historian João Medina. There are fifteen volumes in the 'Medina' history, the first seven of which take us down to the end of the eighteenth century.
I found volume 7, which deals with the Habsburg period, especially useful, but
again, there are major gaps, notably the late seventeenth century.

The fourth and most important in this sequence of multi-volume national
histories is the *Nova história de Portugal,* directed by Joel Serrão and A. H. de
Oliveira Marques (Editorial Presença, Lisbon, 1986–). At the time of writing,
this projected thirteen-volume collective history is still incomplete. However, of
the first eight volumes – which are the ones relevant here – all except volume six
(on the Habsburg era) and volume eight (on the second half of the eighteenth
century) are now published. This history prioritises 'structures' over political
and narrative history. It is also indisputably the most comprehensive, the most
balanced and the most scholarly of the national histories briefly reviewed above –
and it was a fundamental source for the present work.

Before finishing with the general sources, it might be useful to mention
briefly what is available in English. National histories of metropolitan Portugal
in English that devote substantial attention to the pre-nineteenth-century
period are, it has to be said, rather rare, but there is no doubt which is the
most authoritative. It is A. H. de Oliveira Marques's *History of Portugal*
(2 vols., Columbia University Press, 1972). This history, which includes chapters and sections on the empire as well as the metropolis, again downplays
politics in favour of structures. However, it was written before the post-1974
upsurge in new historical writing and is therefore now somewhat outdated.

H. V. Livermore's *A New History of Portugal* (Cambridge University Press, 1966) still remains useful as a traditional political history.

Apart from the general histories discussed above, a rapidly growing number of more specialist works concerning Portugal's past – monographs, regional studies, case studies, biographies, journal articles and so forth – have appeared in the now almost four decades since the change of regime in the early 1970s. One of the aims of the present volume is to draw on a wide selection of these works to inform a fresh synthesis – an overview, for English-speaking readers, of new scholarship. However, I must stress that in writing this volume no attempt has been made to take into account *every* significant work on Portuguese history of the last generation. Rather the aim has been to utilise a sufficiently representative selection of such works, while also not neglecting meritorious older sources. Again, the present volume is fully documented, so that by referring to the footnotes, in conjunction with the bibliography, the reader may go back to the particular sources on which the book is based.

A question that inevitably arises for historians writing about Portugal in English is how to present and standardise foreign names. In what follows I have, with few exceptions, left non-English European names in the forms in which they are customarily written in their respective languages, rather than Anglicising some and not others. This means a few historical personages appear in a guise that may at first seem unfamiliar to English-speaking readers – such as Prince Henrique rather than Henry the Navigator, or Fernando and Isabel of Spain rather than Ferdinand and Isabella. It seemed to me that this would be a small price to pay for greater consistency, while also enabling Portuguese names to be clearly distinguished from their Castilian equivalents. The relatively few names of individuals and places in Arabic that occur in the text have simply been transcribed into Roman script, without the use of diacritical marks.

In the course of writing this volume, I have incurred many debts of gratitude – to mentors, fellow scholars, university colleagues and friends. I owe particular thanks to the late António H. de Oliveira Marques, a giant figure in Portuguese historiography; Luís Filipe Reis Thomaz, who generously gave me the run of his library at Parede; Maria Augusto Lima Cruz, who so kindly showed me round Braga and took me to see the remarkable ruins of Citânia de Briteiros; the patient and ever-hospitable Artur Teodoro de Matos and Maria de Jesus dos Mártires Lopes; Teotónio de Souza, who so kindly secured for me various books I could not access in Australia; João Zilhão, Alfredo Pinheiro Marques and Jorge Filipe de Almeida, who also all kindly sent me publications; Sanjay Subrahmanyam; Dauril Alden; Jorge Flores and Malyn Newitt. I acknowledge gratefully the indispensable financial support of the Australian Research Grants Commission that enabled me to travel and to undertake research in Portugal itself and released me for time to write. Likewise, I thank La Trobe University for its generous grants of study leave in the past – and for its continued support extended to me as an honorary associate, after my retirement from teaching. Last, but not least, I thank my wife, Jenny, who has listened to me long and patiently and read through the manuscript, offering many suggestions and drawing attention to errors.

Anthony Disney
March 2008

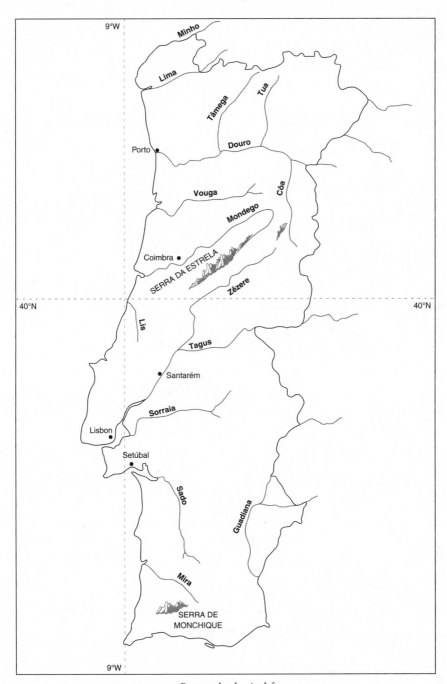

MAP 1. Portugal: physical features.

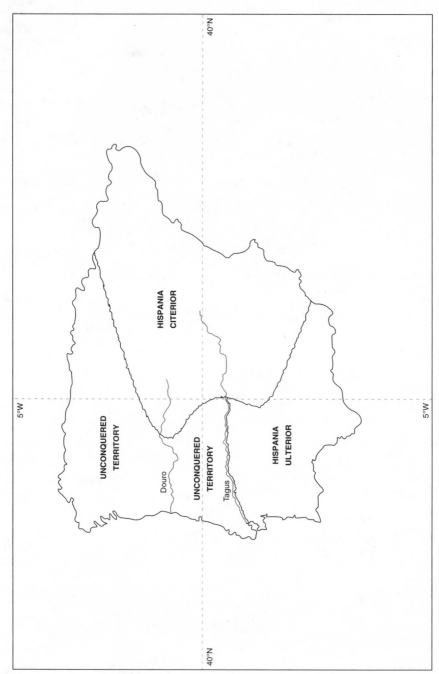

MAP 2. Roman Hispania at approximately the death of Viriatus, 139 BC.

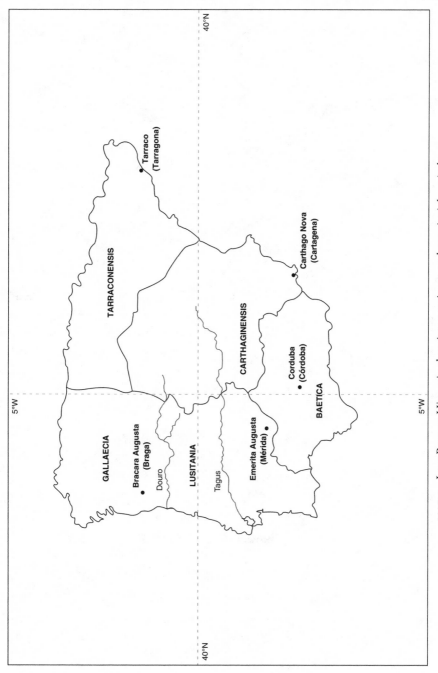

MAP 3. Late Roman Hispania showing provinces and provincial capitals.

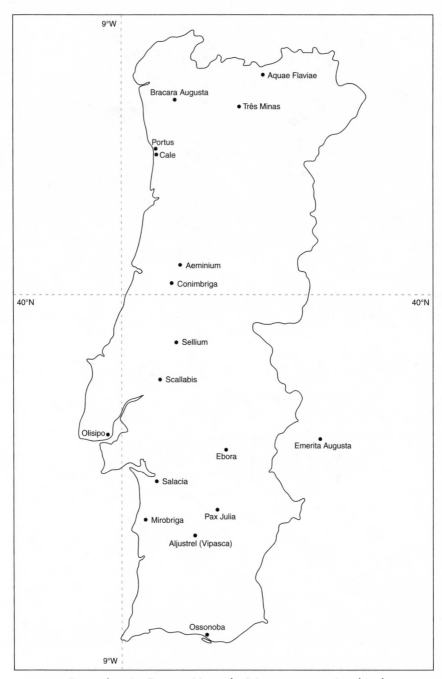

9°W

● Aquae Flaviae

Bracara Augusta
●

● Três Minas

Portus
●Cale

● Aeminium
● Conimbriga

40°N   40°N

● Sellium

● Scallabis

Olisipo●
                                                        ●
                                                Emerita Augusta
                                    ●
                                  Ebora

● Salacia

              ●
            Pax Julia
● Mirobriga
            ●
      Aljustrel (Vipasca)

Ossonoba
●

9°W

MAP 4. Portugal: major Roman cities and mining centres mentioned in the text.

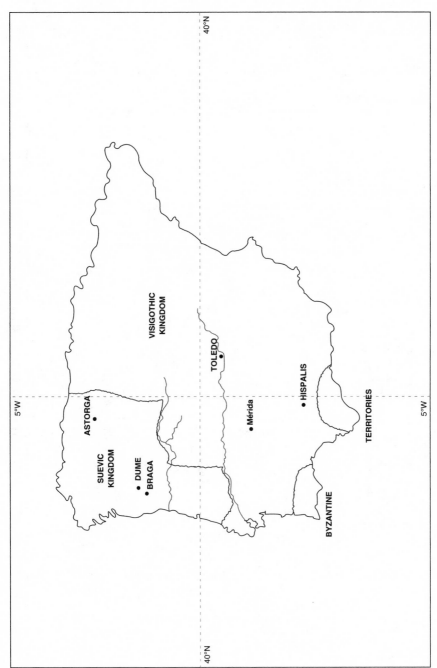

MAP 5. Germanic Hispania: late sixth century AD.

MAP 6. Al-Andalus, mid-eighth century.

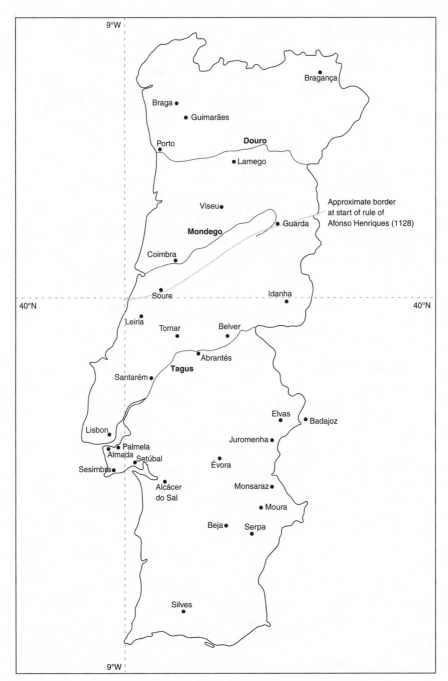

MAP 7. Gharb al-Andalus and the Portuguese Reconquest.

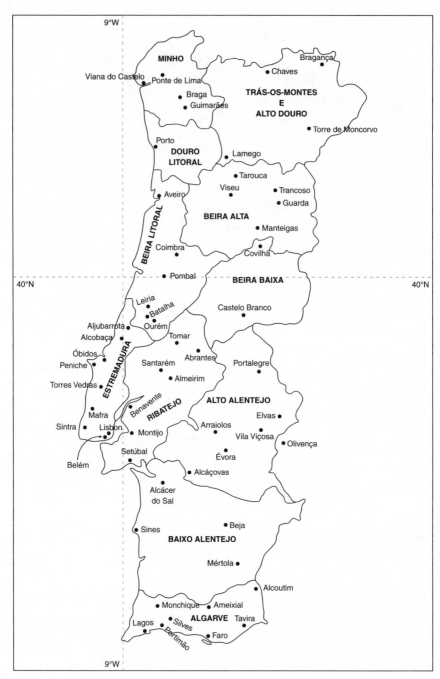

MAP 8. Portugal: traditional provinces and some leading towns.

Introduction: The Geographical Setting

Portugal is a small country of just 92,000 square kilometres – approximately the size of Hungary, a little larger than Austria or marginally smaller than Greece. It occupies less than one sixth of the Iberian peninsula's land surface. On any map of that peninsula, it has the appearance of a neat rectangle, extending for some 560 kilometres from north to south and up to 215 kilometres from west to east. Such compactness, and such symmetry, suggest internal coherence. However, while this is an impression that carries some validity it requires considerable qualification.

For much of its history Portugal was a remote frontier outpost, far from the European centre of gravity. On its northern and eastern flanks lay what would eventually be Spain – the country's only, and overweening, direct neighbour. Close by to the south loomed Africa – for long both a danger and a temptation – while to the west stretched vast expanses of open Atlantic. Thus, clinging to the southwestern extremity of Europe, Portugal was separated from everywhere on the continent except Spain; but its inhabitants nevertheless possessed, thanks to their long Atlantic coastline, the opportunity to make counterbalancing contacts across the sea. In effect, Portugal was closely hemmed in by Spain, Africa and the Atlantic – and each exerted its own profound influence on Portuguese history.

There are no obvious geographical reasons why Portugal should be distinct from the rest of the Iberian peninsula. The border with Spain is marked neither by any formidable natural barriers nor by significant discontinuities of terrain or climate. The principal natural regions of Portugal are all western extensions of their counterparts in Spain – of the mountains of Galicia in the north, of the Spanish meseta in Trás-os-Montes and most of Beira Alta, of Extremadura in the Alentejo and of Andalusia in the Algarve. Therefore, as the Portuguese geographer Orlando Ribeiro has expressed it, 'the idea of Portugal's geographical individuality as a basis for its political separateness ... lacks foundation'.[1] Yet, if the regions of Portugal are natural extensions of Spain, with many similar characteristics, their climate and landscape are also strongly influenced by the presence of the Atlantic. This duality has ensured that Portugal, despite its compact size, does not possess a uniform or even particularly coherent internal geography.

The principal geographical division within Portugal is between the north, which is the part most influenced by the Atlantic, and the south where the climate and landscape are largely Mediterranean. The approximate dividing line between these Atlantic and Mediterranean regions runs diagonally in a northeasterly to southwesterly direction along the southern fringe of the Serra da Estrela, the country's central mountain range, and along the lower Mondego valley. Much of the territory north of this line is mountainous, the rainfall generous and the landscape predominantly green. But to the south, where there are relatively few hills, the climate is hotter and drier and the horizons are long and low. The transition between northern and southern vegetation was originally much sharper than it is now. But the actions of man from Roman times onwards, through cultivation and other forms of development, have increasingly softened it.[2] The divide is now not a rigid one, and some Atlantic characteristics occur as far south as the hills of the Algarve, while Mediterranean elements may be found in certain lowlands and valleys even in Trás-os-Montes.

Furthermore, both northern and southern Portugal are in themselves complex geographical regions with important internal divisions, distinguished from one another by their physical features, climate, demography and cultural traditions.[3] Thus, the western or Atlantic north differs in many respects from the interior north. The Atlantic north comprises roughly that portion of the country enclosed by the River Minho, the lower Mondego valley and the southern fringe of the Serra da Estrela. Here, the climate is heavily influenced by the presence of the ocean: there is high rainfall and consequently lush green vegetation. The Atlantic north includes some of the wettest areas in Europe – and for centuries it has been the most heavily populated and intensively cultivated part of Portugal. It was also the cradle of the Portuguese state.

There is a rich tapestry of sub-regions in this Atlantic north. In the Minho, quintessential Atlantic north, the summers are relatively short and mild, the colours gentle, the numerous valleys often surpassingly beautiful. Here arose the city of Braga, seat of Portugal's oldest archbishopric. Further south, near the mouth of the River Douro, is the city of Porto, the country's second largest. Beyond Porto the sandy coastal plains of Beira Litoral stretch south to the

[1] In DHP vol 3, p 434.
[2] Ribeiro O 1967 p 159.
[3] Ibid, pp 144–55.

Mondego. Inland from this coast, in Beira Alta and in the central cordillera, the land is less productive, population is sparser and the landholdings are larger.

While the Atlantic north has an oceanic climate, that of the interior north is continental. Here in Trás-os-Montes – meaning 'beyond the mountains' – and in eastern Beira Alta, the influence of the ocean is much weaker, winters are colder and summers hotter. The light in this area seems harsh in comparison with the Minho, and the ground itself is harder and more unyielding. The upper River Douro bisects the interior north, then flows eastward towards the Atlantic – often passing through deep valleys and spectacular ravines, being fed en route by numerous tributaries. The interior north has a complex of mini-climates, temperatures often varying sharply between the high country, with its stunted vegetation and crags of granite and shale, and the shaded valleys. It is a land of relatively low population density, isolated village communities and few large towns.

Portugal's 'south' begins approximately along the southern slopes of the Serra da Estrela, or central cordillera, and from the left bank of the Mondego. While the country at no point touches the Mediterranean Sea, beyond this line the climate and terrain become increasingly Mediterranean in character – until the Algarve, that most Mediterranean of all Portuguese provinces, is finally reached. To pass from northern Portugal to the south is to enter a different world. The mountains are largely left behind, giving way to the broad and flat expanses of the tablelands, with their almost uniform landscape. Journeying south along the coast, the transition seems gradual, the traveller traversing successively the alluvial plains of the Mondego, the Tagus and the Sado. The limestone hills of Estremadura that separate the first two of these plains attract much rainfall. However, the soils here are notably thin, supporting only such Mediterranean plants as holm oaks, wild olives and various fragrant herbs. Lisbon itself, sited on the north bank of the Tagus estuary, lies in a transition zone. This is clearly evident in the contrasting landscapes of the two ranges closest to it: the Sintra Hills to the north, which form an Atlantic enclave with lush woods and mossy slopes, and the Serra da Arrábida south of the river, which is thoroughly Mediterranean with its scrub and meadow-lands, its picturesque streams and waterfalls. Ribatejo – the Tagus valley – is low-lying with mostly poor quality gravel soils; but it has flood plains and was destined in time to become a region for cultivating cereals, fruit and vegetables and rearing bulls and horses.

South of these transitional zones, as in most of the interior, the climate and terrain are similar to Spanish Extremadura and Andalusia. This is the Alentejo – a land of hot, stifling summers that covers almost a third of the country. The soils of the Alentejo are generally thin. Moreover, because there are few natural features to encourage precipitation, despite the relative proximity of the Atlantic

Ocean, rainfall is limited. The inhabitants of Alentejo have long engaged in the herding of sheep and the rearing of pigs. Traditionally, many of the landhold-ings were large, ownership was concentrated and the towns remained widely separated. Instead of the pines, oaks and other deciduous varieties of the north, here there are cork oaks and olive groves.

Between the Alentejo and the coast facing Africa is Portugal's southernmost region, the Algarve. Approaching from the north, anyone entering the Algarve first traverses a range of low hills with craggy peaks of metamorphic rock marking the edge of the tableland. Then they descend into the coastal fringe itself. However, despite the sub-tropical brilliance that helps to make this coast one of the most popular tourist regions in Europe today, the southern Algarve is a land of predominantly poor soils and is naturally covered in Mediterranean scrub. The rural population here is greater than in the Alentejo. Traditionally, it has clustered in towns and villages, for easier access to water and for security from sea raiders. In the Algarve, since Roman and then Muslim times, there has been much use of irrigation.

Such, briefly, is the physical setting of what was destined to become Portugal.

I

Hunter-Gatherers to Iron Age Farmers

THE EARLY HUNTER-GATHERERS

The beginnings of a human presence in what is now Portugal are lost in the mists of time, but probably go back at least 500,000 years. The first inhabitants were Lower Palaeolithic hunter-gatherers whose simple stone tools have been found in a number of sites, particularly in the central coastal region. They possessed a lithic culture then common throughout western Europe which was associated with *homo erectus,* a hominid predecessor of modern humans.[1] Many millennia later, probably about 100,000 years before the present, there appeared in Portugal the human sub-species commonly known as Neanderthal. A people of heavy muscular build, the Neanderthals hunted in small groups, and their artefacts now lie scattered in various Portuguese sites. A Neanderthal tooth found at Nova da Columbeira cave in Estremadura is the oldest human fossil so far discovered in Portugal.[2]

Modern humans – the sub-species *homo sapiens sapiens* – arrived in Portugal about 35,000 years ago and spread rapidly throughout the country. They completely supplanted the Neanderthals who, as elsewhere in Europe, became extinct. How and why this happened are teasing questions. Did the Neanderthals, unable to compete, slowly succumb over many generations – or were they deliberately and systematically slaughtered? Was there mixing between the two sub-species, and were the Neanderthals perhaps gradually absorbed into the communities of their rivals? Near Leiria in 1998 a 24,500-year-old child's skeleton was discovered which some scholars believe, on the basis of morphological analysis, is that of a Neanderthal-modern hybrid. If they are correct, it

---

[1] Freeman L G 1975, pp 664, 700–1; NHP vol 1, pp 43–50.
[2] NHP vol 1, pp 55–6.

would be the first real evidence found anywhere indicating Neanderthals and *homo sapiens sapiens* interbred, and perhaps coexisted for several millennia before the latter finally triumphed.[3]

It was towards the end of the period of transition between Neanderthals and modern humans that the most recent Ice Age reached its peak in the last glacial maximum (LGM) some 18,000 years ago. By then northern Europe was covered by an enormous ice sheet, and much of France and Spain were tundra. Portugal's coast was lapped by polar waters, and the shoreline extended up to forty kilometres beyond its present limits. The limestone hills of Estremadura had become almost treeless; but lower, more sheltered areas, such as the Tagus valley and some stretches of the Portuguese coast, were climatically more favoured and still supported mixed forests. Hunter-gatherer groups killed chamois and mountain goats in the colder parts of Portugal and deer, horse, aurochs, wild boar and rabbit in the milder regions. Possibly aquatic foraging took place along the coasts though the evidence is elusive. Human numbers remained small; the population of Estremadura had perhaps reached 500, which was just sufficient to be self-sustaining.

Today, the most striking legacy of this era consists of several thousand Stone Age engravings incised into granite rocks and boulders along a seventeen-kilometre stretch of the Côa River valley, Beira Alta, publicly revealed for the first time in late 1992. These engravings depict mostly animals – especially aurochs, horses and mountain goats – and have been dated variously from between about 25,000 and 10,000 years ago. They constitute the largest and most important concentration of open-air Palaeolithic art so far discovered anywhere.[4] Subsequent finds in the Tagus basin suggest that the phenomenon was actually much more widespread. Such major discoveries made so recently underline how tentative any conclusions about the Portuguese Palaeolithic must for the present remain.

After the LGM Portugal's climate grew rapidly warmer, and by about 11,000 years ago it was already much like today's. In the same period, a new culture known as the Mesolithic gradually evolved, displacing the Palaeolithic cultures which had persisted for so long. Like their predecessors, the folk of the Mesolithic era were hunter-gatherers; but, in the milder conditions of post-glacial times, they were able to draw on a wider range of food resources. Mesolithic people gathered fruit, nuts and seeds, and also relied to a significant degree on fishing and collecting shellfish. These activities could be carried out by family groups, complementing the ancient but less predictable hunt, the

---

[3] Duarte C 1999, pp 7604–9.
[4] Personal communication from Professor João Zilhão; also Carvalho A F de, Zilhão J and Aubrey T 1996, p 29.

traditional preserve of men. To sustain such diversity, a more complex lithic technology was needed – and so to the tools of earlier times were now added a great variety of microliths. These latter were often set in grooved hafts or used as barbs and tips for fishing, spearing or trapping. Mesolithic communities were proto-sedentary, occupying the same sites season by season. They built huts on beaches, estuaries and river banks, leaving behind tell-tale middens. They buried their dead in the foetal position, along with funerary ornaments and offerings of shellfish. Most Mesolithic sites in Portugal are located on the Estremadura, Alentejo and Algarve coasts, or in the Tagus, Sado and Mira river valleys. They date from up to 8,000 years ago; but earlier settlements doubtless existed, long since submerged by rising sea levels.

Mesolithic culture predominated in Portugal for over six millennia. In the past, perhaps too readily influenced by distorted views of tribal peoples formed in the heyday of nineteenth-century European imperialism, prehistorians often underestimated such societies. Today, in the light of work by scholars like Marshall Sahlins and David Clarke, the Mesolithic achievement cannot be dismissed so lightly. Mesolithic folk adapted appropriately and highly success-fully to the particular conditions they faced. In Portugal, these conditions were such that there was little incentive to change. Mesolithic ways therefore long persisted – even while Neolithic culture was developing elsewhere in Europe. But when Neolithic culture did finally take hold in Portugal it wrought change of revolutionary proportions.[5]

THE NEOLITHIC REVOLUTION

By 6000 BC, agriculture and herding were being practised in many parts of western Europe, patches of forest and grassland were being progressively cleared and populations were clustering in favoured locations to form villages. Polished stone tools, including hafted axes and adzes, entered general use, and pottery became widespread. This was the Neolithic revolution. In Portugal, these changes appeared first on the central and southern coasts, slowly spread to the interior and finally reached the north. A transitional period when Meso-lithic and incipient Neolithic communities existed side by side in the country was effectively over by about 4000 BC; then, for some 2,000 years, Neolithic ways predominated. During this era, the cultivation of cereals and legumes and the herding of cattle, sheep and pigs provided the basis for subsistence. Portugal's population increased, and permanent settlements became the norm. In early Neolithic times, these settlements were often located in unprotected

[5] Zvelebil M and Rowly-Conwy P 1986, p 88; Arnaud J M 1993, pp 173, 182.

open country; but later, especially in the south, naturally defensive sites were commonly selected, usually in ridge-top locations. Many communities built striking monuments of stone known as megaliths – characteristic symbols of the Neolithic.

The origins of megalith-building have long been debated. The eastern Mediterranean was once widely assumed to have been its birthplace, and as recently as the 1960s scholars argued that the megalith tradition and technology were brought to the Iberian peninsula by Aegean colonists. But this view is no longer tenable, for radiocarbon dating indicates megalithic chamber tombs in Portugal and Spain pre-date anything comparable in the Aegean by hundreds of years.[6] It now seems likely that megalith-building evolved more or less simultaneously in many different parts of Europe and the Mediterranean, stimulated by social, technological and perhaps ideological developments generated locally. Today some of the earliest and most significant megaliths are to be found in Portugal, where literally hundreds still survive in various forms and sizes. There are tombs covered by mounds of earth and stones, single menhirs, grouped menhirs forming cromlechs, simple dolmens made of large, upright slabs surmounted by capstones and collective passage-graves. Mostly of granite or schist, these megaliths are scattered throughout the country, but are particularly common in Alto Alentejo, the Beiras and Trás-os-Montes. Their appearance coincided with much increased assertiveness over land-ownership as agriculture spread and populations increased. Megaliths may have served as territorial boundaries or indicated the presence of ancestors, so affirming a community's continuity over successive generations. Since building megaliths required labour on a fairly large scale, their presence also implies elite control and organisation. It is also possible that some megaliths had cult significance. Bulls' heads inscribed on rocks in a sanctuary at Montemor-o-Novo suggest a bovine cult perhaps linked to similar cults in the Mediterranean world.[7]

THE METALLURGICAL CULTURES

There was no sudden transformation in Portugal from a Neolithic to an incipient metallurgical culture, but rather a slow, uneven process of adaptation. The soft metals – silver, gold and especially copper – were all known from about 2500 BC. Southern Portugal was one of the first regions in Europe where copper was extracted and then processed into desirable objects. Portugal had been slow to adopt Neolithic technology; but it was quick to enter the Copper Age, a development facilitated by plentiful outcrops of copper ore in the eastern

[6] Blance B 1961, p 192; Renfrew C 1978, pp 94–101.
[7] NHP vol 1, pp 113, 136–7, 141–2, 152–3, 158; Raposo L 1989, pp 37, 39.

Algarve and Baixo Alentejo. Initially, output was small and the items produced were ornamental only; but soon the range of goods expanded to include copper axes, awls, burins, daggers and even primitive saws.

The first metal-workers probably used a process of simple cold hammering, then progressed to annealing. Later, they learned how to smelt, perhaps using methods adapted from ceramics technology – and finally they mastered casting.[8] The necessary skills were doubtless restricted to particular specialists living near the copper mines; but use of the metal soon spread far and wide, and items of copper came to serve as a kind of currency. Bronze objects, particularly axes, first appeared in Portugal between 2000 and 1500 BC, probably introduced from northwest Europe. By the late second millennium BC, tin was being mined in northern Portugal, and with copper readily available in the south, a local bronze industry was able to develop. But most likely before this, during the Copper Age, there had already occurred what Andrew Sherratt calls the SPR (secondary products revolution). This involved a series of major advances in the techniques of resource production and utilisation achieved in the wake of agriculture and herding, including the adoption of animal traction, the riding of horses, the use of cow's milk for human consumption, the production of wool, the development of weaving, the introduction of irrigation and possibly the use of simple ploughs.[9] While as yet there is only fragmentary evidence of developments of this kind in northern Portugal, in Estremadura and the south the signs of a Copper Age SPR are clear.

Roughly coinciding with the rise of copper production, bell beaker pottery, aesthetically one of the most attractive ceramic forms of prehistoric times, appeared in Portugal. Bell beakers – so called because they resembled large, upturned bells – were manufactured especially in the Lisbon and Setúbal peninsulas where over 100 sites are known, among them the fortified settlements of Vila Nova de São Pedro and Zambujal.[10] The demand for bell beaker pottery and prestige goods in copper or bronze inevitably led to increased contacts between communities both within Portugal and beyond. An extensive exchange system therefore gradually developed, encompassing a vast area. This benefited certain strategically-located communities and encouraged the formation of new settlements on key communications routes. Because of its central location and its river systems Estremadura was pre-eminent in this process, and its productiveness may also have made it an exporter of foodstuffs to drier regions. Exactly how goods were transported in this era, and along which routes they travelled, is only dimly understood. Land routes probably followed ridgeways

---

[8] Renfrew C 1978, pp 188–9.
[9] Sherratt A 1981, pp 261–3; NHP vol 1, pp 176–7.
[10] Harrison R J 1980, pp 9–15, 126–40, 160–5.

and can sometimes be tentatively traced by the distribution of artefact finds. Seaborne transport is even more problematic, for no Copper or Bronze Age vessels have been found in Portuguese waters, and there are no depictions of vessels in rock art of the kind so common in Scandinavia.[11] It has, however, been suggested that the Portuguese *saveiro,* a craft of very ancient design with no keel, rudder or mast, which was still being made early in the twentieth century, may have been related to ships used in these times. In any event, exchange of goods both within the present borders of Portugal and with the world beyond was already extensive by the late Bronze Age. Portugal's mineral resources were attracting outside interest and therefore stimulating interchanges, as attested by numerous finds of imported objects originating from both Atlantic Europe and the Mediterranean. Various Bronze Age metal objects have been found in Portugal from as far away as Ireland.

By the Copper Age, Portugal was a society of small, scattered villages and hamlets. J. M. Arnaud has shown that in the south a typical village of the time occupied between one and five hectares and accommodated some 150 to 350 inhabitants. Smaller out-settlements housed perhaps thirty to fifty persons. Dwellings were simple and built of local materials; several coastal settlements studied in the Sines region of Baixo Alentejo consisted of rather flimsy rectangular huts, each containing a semi-circular hearth. While some villages relied on natural protection, constructed defence works were becoming more common. An early example is Monte da Tumba near Alcácer do Sal, which was occupied continuously between about 2500 and 2000 BC and was protected by a wall surrounding a central precinct. Its defences went through several reconstructions, and in the final stage a central tower was erected.[12]

Later, during the early and mid-Portuguese Bronze Age, further expansion took place – especially into low-lying farming country where at first many open and undefended villages were formed. Then, in the late Bronze Age, increasing numbers of hilltop forts known as *castros* began to appear. It is unclear against whom these *castros* were constructed. Perhaps it was pastoral nomads or wandering marauders, though rival settled groups of similar cultural background seem more likely. There is no evidence of intruders from outside Portugal at this time.[13] In any event, a degree of interdependence soon developed between the open settlements, which were primarily centres of production, and the *castros.* Some of the former possessed below-ground storage facilities capable of supplying grain well beyond the requirements of their own inhabitants; others evidently concentrated on artefact production or mining. In the north,

[11] Johnstone P 1980, pp 87–93; Coles J M 1982, pp 291, 295–6; Raposo L 1989, p 41.
[12] NHP vol 1, pp 169–70, 232–3.
[13] Ibid, pp 177–8, 188, 247–8.

the people controlling the *castros* often exploited nearby lowland settlements as their granaries and oversaw the local production and distribution of tin, in return providing protection. Likewise in Alentejo, many *castros* were strategically situated to dominate either adjoining agricultural land or copper mines. Clearly control of the sources of production, and the networks of exchange, were recognised as the means to accumulate wealth and power.

Society in Portugal during the Copper and Bronze Ages grew less egalitarian, as elites managed to reinforce their power and privileges. This increasing social differentiation has stimulated much debate among prehistorians and remains a controversial issue.[14] Who comprised the elites, and on what was their power predicated? It is clear that metal weapons and ornaments were important marks of prestige, and ability to control access to such objects and manage their distribution was therefore vital. This, and the evidence of monumental art and grave goods, point strongly to a warrior leadership. Bronze Age steles depicting stylised warriors, most probably dating from the early first millennium BC, are fairly common in Portugal. The Longroiva stele found in northeast Beira Alta – a granite slab bearing the carved figure of a warrior with halberd, bow and dagger – is a splendid early example. In the Algarve and Alentejo, funerary lids have been uncovered engraved with stylised figures carrying swords, dating from about 1200 to 900 BC, and late Bronze Age menhirs have been found in the north displaying similar warlike objects.[15] This was the era of the bronze carp's tongue sword (so called because of its distinctive design and shape), the bronze spear, the round leather shield, the bronze helmet and perhaps also the horse-drawn chariot. Indeed, it seems that there was among Portuguese Bronze Age elites a marked uniformity of material culture with a broad standardisation of weapons and burial customs, stretching across the entire country from the Algarve to Minho – and all with a strong warrior emphasis. The conclusion seems inevitable that leadership in the Bronze Age was by force of arms and that the highest status was that of the warrior hero. Moreover, the arms which made warrior control possible were overwhelmingly of bronze. This contrasts with the situation among non-elite inhabitants whom the evidence suggests were still largely confined to tools of stone, wood or bone in their everyday labours. Indeed, for most ordinary people, it would probably have seemed quite meaningless to speak in terms of a Bronze Age at all.[16]

Some scholars have detected in grave inventories from as early as the Copper Age, especially in Estremadura and southern Portugal, evidence of new perceptions of the supernatural world and the rites required to manage it. Gone are

---

[14] Coles J M 1982, pp 315–16; Velasco J A S 1994, pp 289–90.
[15] NHP vol 1, pp 220, 233–4.
[16] Coles J M 1982, p 288.

the phallic menhirs and bulls' heads of Neolithic times, and instead there is a proliferation of mysterious 'eye idols' engraved on plaques of schist or bone and portrayed on spotted ceramic vases. Often linked to what appear to be solar or stellar symbols these votive objects may perhaps be images of a Mother Goddess. They were certainly widely present in southern Iberia and were conceptually of Mediterranean origin. Clearly, religious ideas were now entering Portugal from external cultures.

The Copper and Bronze Ages in Portugal were not then just eras of technological advancement when metallurgy was introduced for the first time. More fundamentally they constituted a time when elites differentiated themselves from the rest of the population, and relationships between different settlements and even regions were becoming ever more extensive and complex. Warrior elites appeared, and perhaps even incipient chiefdoms. If Portugal by the late Bronze Age was indeed a society of chiefdoms, then it is possible that the principle of transmitting status by heredity had already been introduced. Authority would then have been based on family lineage. But the evidence for this is as yet inconclusive.[17]

Iron was first introduced in Portugal by Phoenician traders from the eastern Mediterranean and Celtic immigrants from the north. The earliest known iron artefact is an iron-bladed dagger with a bronze handle found near Viseu in Beira Alta in 1983 and tentatively dated at about 700 BC.[18] As a material for making weapons and tools, iron possessed clear advantages over bronze. It was stronger, could be honed to superior sharpness and was plentiful. To work iron and produce quality products, not only was a knowledge of smelting required but the laborious process of forging had to be mastered. Evidence that the latter skill was practised in Portugal in the early Iron Age is meagre. However, iron objects are often under-represented in a culture's archaeology. This is because of the corrosive nature of iron itself, a problem exacerbated in northern Portugal by acidic soils. Portugal was actually an iron-rich region possessing numerous outcrops of accessible ore, especially in the south – and it was there that an iron industry first developed. By the mid-fifth century BC, a range of iron arms, tools and implements was being produced in various locations scattered throughout the country, though such objects are rarely found today in a well-preserved condition. Bronze remained important, was still preferred for ornaments and even continued to be used for some utilitarian items.

The earliest known inscriptions in Portugal also belong to the Iron Age. They occur on funerary steles dating from between the late seventh and fifth centuries BC, found in various cemeteries in the Algarve and Baixo Alentejo.

---

[17] Raposo L 1989, p 48; NHP vol 1, pp 235, 244.
[18] NHP vol 1, p 259.

There are more than fifty known sites; but each contains only a few inscriptions which were clearly confined to a small, privileged elite. The greatest number occurs at Bensafrim near Lagos. There are no other extant epigraphic finds in Portugal from this era apart from some inscribed coins and a few ceramic vases bearing graffiti in the same script as on the steles. All these inscriptions remain undeciphered and have roused much speculation. However, it seems likely that the language was that of a local people whom the Romans later called Conii, while the script – which was partly syllabic and partly alphabetic – was derived from archaic Phoenician.[19]

These southern Portuguese inscriptions are the earliest traces of writing found anywhere in the Iberian peninsula. Modest though they are, they indicate that writing was already being used there for a variety of purposes – a major cultural breakthrough. However, for historians, their usefulness is limited; references to Iron Age Portugal in early Greek and Latin literary works – such as the *History* of Herodotus dating from the mid-fifth century BC, Strabo's *Geography* written near the turn of the first century BC and the *Ora Maritima* of the fourth-century AD Roman poet Rufus Festus Avienus – are far more informative. (Avienus's work is relevant because it contains a description of southern Iberia which draws heavily on a now lost Massilian periplus of the fifth century BC.) They were these authors who for the first time identified for posterity some of the people then living in Portugal, as we shall see shortly.

THE COMING OF THE CELTS

Iron Age Portugal was deeply influenced, even transformed, by successive waves of Indo-European newcomers entering from the north. Not all of these people were strictly speaking Celts; but most of them probably were, and the term Celticisation is generally used to describe the process of acculturation that followed. Social organisation, religious practices, artistic expression, technology and material culture generally were all affected by Celticisation, as well as the ethnic composition of the country's inhabitants.

The Celts were an Indo-European group of people from north-central Europe, who emerged from obscurity in the mid-to-late Bronze Age. Tall and fair, with long hair and curled moustaches, their menfolk made intrepid horsemen and warriors of fearsome repute. During the course of the first millennium BC, they undertook a series of massive migrations to the east, west and south, sweeping over Europe from Ireland to the shores of the Black Sea in

---

[19] Ibid, pp 279–81; Gamito T J 1988, pp 46–7, 49–50, 143–4; Villar F 1990, p 375.

a matter of centuries. Their presence in Portugal is traceable in broad outline through archaeological and linguistic evidence. They arrived in two major waves – the first in the sixth and early fifth centuries BC, and the second in the fourth and third centuries. They came to dominate northern and much of central Portugal; but in the south, which retained its mainly non-Indo-European character down to the Roman conquest, they were less successful.[20] Everywhere, they were never more than a minority and were obliged to share the land with pre-existing, non-Indo-European people.

For the first time, towards the end of this era, some of the people inhabiting Portugal, both Celtic and non-Celtic, were identified in writing by name, at least in a Greek or Latin form. Avienus mentioned the Cempsi, a Celtic or Celticised people who had entered Portugal during the first migratory wave and controlled the Tagus and Sado river valleys. In the northwest were the Celtic Saefes – together with the Oestrimnici who were probably Indo-European but pre-Celtic. The Conii, another pre-Celtic, Indo-European people, lived in the western Algarve. Celtic and Celticised people who moved into Portugal with the second wave in the fourth and third centuries BC are traceable through their stamped decorated pottery. Many stayed in the north; but some went to the Algarve and Alentejo, and these are much better documented. Strabo described the Turduli, a Celticised people who founded a number of cities in southern Portugal, perhaps including Ossonoba (Faro). He thought them wise, gentle and an important civilising influence in the region. The Turduli co-existed peacefully with their neighbours the Celtici, a Celtic people. Both these people also had a presence in the north, with Celtici settled in Minho and Turduli south of the Douro.[21] The Lusitani – of whom we shall hear more shortly – though Indo-European were not necessarily Celtic. At this time, they were in central Portugal, between the Tagus and Douro rivers.

Portugal's northern interior during the Iron Age was a wild and mountainous place. Much of it was infertile with a rigorous climate, difficult communications and severe isolation. The main activity was herding, supplemented by small-scale subsistence agriculture, hunting and gathering. Pigs, which foraged on acorns, were ubiquitous; goats were commonplace and a major source of meat; sheep, cattle and the small northern horse were all reared. The inhabitants ate butter rather than olive oil, and drank beer or water instead of wine – practices that placed them squarely within the north European dietary zone. Cereal crops were grown on a small scale, together with peas, beans and flax. Chestnuts and acorns were gathered, the latter used to make bread. Women

---

[20] Villar F 1990, p 369.
[21] Alarcão J de 1988, pp 36–7; Gamito T J 1988, pp 102–3, 115–21; NHP vol 1, pp 263–6, 289, 298.

cultivated the plots using rudimentary tools, aided by older men and children. Hides and skins were traded and widely used domestically.[22] By contrast, the coastal region between the Douro and Galicia was well watered and productive. Here, the land was already intensively occupied, pre-figuring the patterns of later times. Further south, in Estremadura and Ribatejo, where the climate was mild, the land flatter and communications easier, latifundia already existed by the late Iron Age, with relatively large-scale agriculture and stock-rearing.

The rugged northern and central interior remained the stronghold of the *castros*. By the Iron Age many *castros* were already of considerable antiquity, in some cases their sites continuously occupied for many centuries. The typical *castro* was designed to provide a community refuge in times of danger. Within was a space for livestock and a cluster of huts built of mud-brick on stone foundations and roofed with thatch. The whole was surrounded by one or more stone walls. Most *castros* were located atop hills or in deep valleys remote in their mountain fastness and usually had small, isolated populations. But some *castros* developed into much larger centres similar to the southern *oppida* or towns. Among the most spectacular were Citânia de Briteiros near Guimarães in Minho and Citânia Sanfins northeast of Porto. Citânia de Briteiros was a heavily fortified town containing many dwellings within an elaborate series of concentric walls, with formidable ramparts and concealed entrances. It contained a large circular building that may have been a meeting house.[23] Some *castros* were occupied well into Roman times, and in some instances even into the Middle Ages.

There were no kingdoms in northern Portugal. Society was based on kinship, extended families being the primary units for residential, economic and religious purposes. The dead were buried either within the family house or in its precincts. Family alliances were formed through marriages especially at the elite level, and groups of families with common ancestors formed clans. A clan often seems to have corresponded to the inhabitants of a particular *castro*, or quarter of a larger *citânia*. It would have its own tutelary deities and possessed certain collective rights and responsibilities such as supervising the distribution of land. It was headed by a chieftain whose office may, in some cases at least, have been hereditary.[24] A group of clans together formed what later Latin sources called a *populus* or *gens*, which had its own tribal council. In turn, loose ethnic confederations such as the Lusitani in the central interior and the Callaeci in the northwest traditionally consisted of groups of associated *populi*.

[22] Strabo 1917–32 vol 2, p 75; Braudel F 1981, pp 210–12; DHP vol 3, p 439; NHP vol 1, pp 309–10.
[23] Savory H N 1968, pp 257–8; NHP vol 1, p 305.
[24] Alarcão J de 1988, pp 47–8; NHP vol 1, pp 326–8, 331.

However, this structure seems to have been slowly undermined by the effects of war, raiding and brigandage which became entrenched in the late Iron Age. Leaders elected for particular expeditions or military responsibilities tended to consolidate their authority on the basis of personal prestige.

The proliferation of *castros* in the late Iron Age suggests a troubled and insecure society. An atmosphere of endemic violence prevailed throughout much of the north, especially from the fourth century BC onwards, spurred on by growing population pressure and increasing militarisation. Estremadura, where social tensions had arisen from the extremes of wealth and poverty generated by the latifundiary system, became the target of raiders from the mountains who probably found many local sympathisers. These raiders were Lusitani and Callaeci, fierce and intractable peoples who grew their hair long, slept on the bare ground and were notorious for brigandage.[25] Strabo portrays an Estremaduran economy under serious disruption in the years preceding Roman intervention, with fields often neglected.

There were numerous gods in the Iron Age north, of whom over 100 are known by name. Some were widely worshipped, such as Banda and Nabia, who were introduced by Celtic immigrants and were venerated among the Lusitani and the Callaeci. Others were limited to particular regions or *populi*. Some dwelt in sacred woods, springs or caves; but there were probably no man-made temples. A triad of superior gods existed for priests, warriors and producers, respectively. To the warrior god were sacrificed rams, horses and human prisoners. Stone-carved warrior statues survive from this era with round Celtic shields, short swords and torques, which could be tutelary heroes. Pig and bull statues are also quite common and may represent gods of the flocks and herds.[26]

ORIENTALISATION

Between about 700 and 550 BC southern Portugal and neighbouring Andalusia underwent a series of far-reaching cultural changes, which turned what had previously been relatively simple farming and herding communities into societies more resembling those of the Ancient Near East. The use of iron became widespread, mining operations expanded substantially and wheel-made pottery replaced the handmade variety. *Oppida* developed, a more sophisticated artistic tradition evolved, writing was adopted and new religious cults appeared. These developments are sometimes collectively referred to as Orientalisation

---

[25] Strabo 1917–32 vol 2, pp 71, 73, 75, 77; Savory H N 1968, pp 254–5; Keay S J 1988, pp 23–4.
[26] Strabo 1917–32 vol 2, pp 73–5; Alarcão J 1988, pp 91–2, 94–5; NHP vol 1, pp 332, 334–6.

since they particularly involved absorbing ideas, techniques and attitudes from the Mediterranean. Though mainly a southern phenomenon, Orientalisation in Portugal is traceable through the Guadiana, Sado and Tagus valleys, and all along the Atlantic coast as far north as the present Galician border. The process affected mainly elites, most of the relevant finds being of luxury objects. Among the leading sites is the ancient town of Alcácer do Sal in Baixo Alentejo.[27]

By the late eighth century BC, Phoenician traders from cities such as Tyre, Sidon and Ugarit were regularly visiting the western Mediterranean in search of raw materials and markets. As client states of the Assyrian Empire they acted effectively as its commercial arm and established a string of trade settlements in southern Andalusia, most notably at Gades (Cadiz). These settlements were usually located at river mouths, their landward approaches protected by walls, and the merchants who occupied them apparently did not mix much with the local people. However, they marketed perfumes, unguents, glass, jewellery, quality pottery, furniture, oil and wine, acquiring in return particularly metals and purple dye.[28] In Portugal, evidence of the Phoenician presence is slighter than in Andalusia; but there were apparently Phoenician voyages along the Algarve coast seeking silver, gold, copper and tin, and Phoenician products were also brought into Portugal overland from Spanish Extremadura. Eastern practices like cremation were introduced into the Algarve while rites associated with Astarte, the Phoenician fertility goddess, and other exotic deities also made their appearance.[29]

These interactions continued until, with the overthrow of the Assyrian empire in 612 BC, the Phoenician presence in all parts of the Iberian peninsula rapidly faded. Meanwhile Portugal had become known to the Greeks, although direct contacts were probably very limited. There is no solid evidence that the inhabitants of Iron Age Portugal did any regular business with Greek traders, whose nearest major colonies were far away at Massilia in southern France and Emporion in northeastern Spain. However, Greek objects did reach Portugal, directly or indirectly, for Attic pottery and a few Greek bronzes have been found in Portuguese sites. Much of the Orientalising influence affecting Portugal in this period was diffused from coastal Andalusia, the then heartland of the southwest Iberian cultural region. Here flourished between about 800 and 500 BC the small kingdom of Tartessos, with its capital at Huelva some twenty-five kilometres from the present Portuguese border. The sudden emergence of Tartessos as a sophisticated urbanised polity was described by the Roman historian Justinus and was almost certainly stimulated by Phoenician and Greek

[27] Alarcão J de 1988, p 35.
[28] Gamito T J 1988, pp 46, 54–5, 60, 65; NHP vol 1, p 259.
[29] NHP vol 1, pp 267–8, 279, 281–2.

traders. The Tartessians in turn maintained a vigorous commerce with their own periphery, including mineral-rich southern Portugal.[30] Tartessian objects were imported and widely copied in Portugal and have been found as far north as Douro Litoral. Although much about Tartessos remains mysterious, and more in the realms of rumour and legend than of history, that it was a major Orientalising influence on Portugal seems likely.[31]

From about the mid-sixth century BC Carthage, a North African colony of Tyre, also began to play a significant role in southern Iberian trade. At first the objectives and behaviour of the Carthaginians seem to have differed little from those of their Phoenician predecessors. They traded in much the same places and commodities, with metals, especially silver, remaining the principal attraction.[32] However, over time their involvement gradually intensified and then began to take on political dimensions. Eventually in the late third century BC under the leadership of the Barcid family they crossed the line from commerce to conquest, carving out an Iberian empire of which southern Portugal formed the western wing. Relatively little is known about this enterprise; but Jorge Alarcão points out that a Carthaginian expedition reached as far north as the mouth of the Tagus.[33] There was also a Carthaginian settlement in the Algarve founded by Hannibal in 221–218 BC, which was later called Portus Hannibalis by the Romans, and was perhaps located near the present town of Portimão. Carthaginian finds are frequent along the Portuguese coast from the Algarve to Beira Littoral and even Minho. The most spectacular site is at Garvão in Baixo Alentejo, which appears to be a religious sanctuary. Among objects found at Garvão are gold and silver plaques dedicated to a deity identified as Tanit, the Carthaginian fertility goddess.[34]

There is no doubt that well before the Carthaginian military intervention southern Portugal was already moving towards a partially urban way of life. People were increasingly organised and controlled from *oppida* – centres that were sufficiently large to qualify as true towns, and that dominated the surrounding territory politically and militarily. Life in southern Portuguese *oppida* is well portrayed in Judice Gamito's study of Santa Eulalia, a region of Alto Alentejo situated northwest of the modern city of Elvas.[35] Santa Eulalia contained various Iron Age settlements including two *oppida* – Vaiamonte and Segovia. Vaiamonte, the principal agricultural centre, dominated the best soils

---

[30] Savory H N 1968, pp 214–15, 232–3; Gamito T J 1988, pp 132–9; NHP vol 1, pp 269–72.
[31] HP vol 1, pp 114–5.
[32] Rouillard P 1991, pp 234–5.
[33] Alarcão J de 1988, pp 3–4, 37.
[34] Harrison R J 1988, pp 122, 126; Raposo L 1989, p 60; NHP vol 1, pp 294–5.
[35] Gamito T J 1988, pp 159–68.

and later became an important Roman villa. Segovia, strategically located near the Guadiana river and probably the administrative capital, was the focal point for mining, trade and communications. Though populations were relatively small – Vaiamonte had perhaps 2,300 inhabitants, Segovia about 1,000 – society was highly stratified. Segovia's elite probably dominated the whole area, imposing tribute on the general population in kind and service in return for protection. While the economy of Santa Eulalia was a mixed one combining hunting, agricultural, pastoral, mining and trading activities, it seems the latifundium had already emerged as the principal form of rural enterprise. Some wheat was grown, and probably exported; but the emphasis was on sheep, cattle, pigs and horses. Wool was spun locally, then probably sent on to Alcácer do Sal to be woven into cloth for which that town had become renowned. However, the region's key exports were minerals including copper, iron and possibly tin. Trade was apparently substantial, and luxury goods including Greek and Campanian pottery, jewellery, fine fabrics and wine were imported.

Strabo praised the Algarve and southern Andalusia for their wealth and civilisation, approving their adaptation to Classical Mediterranean norms; but he knew rather less about the southern Portuguese interior that stretched north to the Tagus and which by the late Iron Age was much more Celticised.[36] Both Celticisation and Orientalisation are apparent in the Iron Age religious cults of southern Portugal. There was a heaven and an underworld, and initiates could pass from the one to the other. As in the north a triad of superior deities was worshipped; each had particular functions, and together they represented a synthesis of Celtic and eastern ideas. Bulls, boars, stags and goats all had sacred associations. The bull and the wild boar were linked to Cernunnos, supreme Celtic god of the forest, usually depicted with antlers and wearing a torque. Endovelicus, a Jupiter-type figure who may also be identifiable with Cernunnos, was the god of princes and priests and had a temple at Alandroal, Alto Alentejo. The god of warriors or smiting god, a more shadowy deity, was possibly of eastern origin. Votive offerings to the Celtic-sounding but probably syncretic Ategina, *inter alia* goddess of producers, are relatively common, usually in the form of goat statuettes.[37] Such were the peoples whose lives and world view were about to be so drastically altered by Roman conquest.

---

[36] Strabo 1917–32 vol 2, pp 11–13; NHP vol 1, pp 290–97.
[37] Gamito T J 1988, pp 127–31, 180; Alarcão J de 1988, pp 91–2; NHP vol 1, pp 282–3, 296.

2

The Roman Experience

THE ROMAN CONQUEST

In the late third century BC, it must have seemed that if present-day Portugal was to be absorbed into a Mediterranean empire it would not be that of Rome, but Carthage. Already the Carthaginians had established control over much of the country's south, and they had constructed at Carthago Nova (Cartagena) on the nearby coast of Murcia a major military centre. Rome was suspiciously watchful; but it made no effort to obstruct the Carthaginian moves, apparently accepting that Iberia fell within its arch-rival's sphere of influence.

Rome was unwise to react so passively – for in 218 BC the Carthaginian general Hannibal used Carthago Nova as the base for an unprecedented surprise invasion across the Pyrenees and Alps into the plains of northern Italy, igniting the Second Punic War. His expedition recruited many Lusitanian and other peninsular mercenaries.[1] The details of the epic struggle that followed do not particularly concern us here, except insofar as Rome's response included a counter-invasion of Carthaginian Spain. After a hard-fought struggle, with many changes of fortune, Carthago Nova fell in 209 BC. Three years later, the Romans had expelled the Carthaginians from all their peninsular possessions.

Up till that point Roman involvement in the Iberian peninsula had been slight. But now, finding itself in occupation of the former Carthaginian conquests, Rome simply decided to stay, perhaps enticed by the rich mineral and agricultural resources of the region and the access it provided to cheap labour. By 197 BC, two Roman provinces had been created in Spain – Hispania Citerior (Nearer Spain), which consisted roughly of the Ebro valley, Valencia and Murcia, and Hispania Ulterior (Further Spain) comprising essentially Andalusia,

---

[1] Livy 1919–35 vol 5, pp 127, 169.

but later extending west to the River Guadiana. Early Roman administration of these provinces was predatory: gold, silver and copper; wheat, wine and olives; recruits and slaves – all were siphoned off to Rome. The inevitable result was widespread discontent, then open revolt. Unsubdued peoples from western Iberia soon became involved, raiding Roman territory and in turn provoking punitive reaction. Gradually the Romans came to realise they could only enforce their authority by incorporating the rest of the peninsula into their empire.

Southern Portugal was then rather easily occupied sometime during the first half of the second century BC. This seems to have been achieved more by peaceful persuasion than military conquest, though the details remain obscure; for no contemporary accounts survive, and the archaeology is largely unexplored. The Conii in particular became Roman allies, while both the Algarve and Alentejo were effectively placed under Roman control probably well before 150 BC.[2] However, the rugged interior between the Rivers Tagus and Mondego, and the mountain regions of the north, proved a very different proposition. Here the Romans met determined and prolonged resistance from the Lusitani, Callaeci and other people, and it took about 175 years before the whole country was subdued. Part of the struggle against the Lusitani is quite well known because it is described by Strabo and Appian. It probably began as early as 194–193 BC when a Roman army clashed with Lusitanian raiders returning home with booty after a pillaging expedition into Hispania Ulterior.[3]

The Beiras, bisected by the forbidding granite massif of the Serra da Estrela, formed the inner homeland of the Lusitani. A hardy people living in fortified hilltop villages in the *castro* tradition, the Lusitani were primarily shepherds who also practised some small-scale agriculture. Their's was a poor country, and so they had grown accustomed to raiding the more prosperous plains that surrounded them, as far afield as Andalusia. Mounted on nimble mountain horses, their wild and unkempt hair flowing, their round shields attached to their shoulders by thongs, and armed with dirk, javelin or bronze-tipped spear, they made an extraordinarily elusive and effective fighting force. Their leaders won respect from the Romans and forced their way into the Classical histories. The first individuals in Portugal whose names were recorded, and preserved for posterity albeit in Romanised form, are Lusitanian war-leaders of the mid- to late second century BC who appear in the pages of Strabo and Appian. Among them are Punicus who raided deep into Roman territory in 155 BC destroying and looting, Caesarus who inflicted heavy casualties on the Roman general Mummius in 153 BC, and Caucaenus who raided the Roman Algarve, captured

[2] Alarcão J de 1988, pp 3–4; NHP vol 1, pp 346–7.
[3] Livy 1919–35 vol 10, pp 3–5.

Conistorgis (as yet unidentified) and even crossed the straits to pillage North Africa in 151 BC.[4] Frustrated by his inability to subdue the Lusitanians by conventional campaigning, the Roman general Servius Galba tricked and massacred a large group of them under cover of negotiations in 150 BC. One of the few survivors of this killing-field was a young warrior named Viriatus. Embittered by Roman treachery, he would subsequently become the outstanding leader of Lusitanian resistance.

Viriatus is traditionally portrayed as a highland shepherd from the Serra da Estrela, but may have been a native of the Estremaduran lowlands. In any event, he was a guerrilla leader of exceptional ability who possessed the kind of charisma needed to inspire the Lusitani. For seven years, between 146 and 139 BC, he waged a bold and relentless war inflicting a series of humiliating defeats on the Romans, often with heavy casualties – until they finally procured his assassination through bribery.[5] Viriatus has long been hailed as the first truly heroic figure in proto-Portuguese history. It is an image to which the highland peoples of his time may well have subscribed; but those living in the more settled and Romanised parts of southern Portugal and Andalusia, the frequent victims of Lusitanian raids, could hardly have shared it.

After the death of Viriatus, the determination of the Lusitani to take the war deep into enemy territory diminished, and their tactics became more defensive. In 138–137 BC, the Romans occupied the Tagus valley and campaigned along the coast as far north as Galicia. Little is known of events over the next half century, but it seems the Lusitani were contained rather than subdued, until in 80 BC the outbreak of civil war between rival Roman forces in Spain gave them an opportunity to reassert themselves. Quintus Sertorius, the governor of Hispania Citerior and a more than competent soldier, was associated with a group that had recently been ousted from power at Rome. He decided to attempt a comeback using his province as a base, and duly rebelled. Official armies were soon sent from Rome to deal with Sertorius; but many of the local natives, including the Lusitani, flocked to his standard. Fighting continued for eight years, much of it in Portugal; but gradually the rebel forces were worn down. Sertorius himself was murdered in 72 BC, after which his movement quickly collapsed.[6]

The death of Sertorius marked the beginning of the end of serious resistance to Rome. Over the next few decades, especially during the successive governorships in Hispania Ulterior of Julius Caesar and Gnaius Pompeius (61–44 BC), most territory between the Tagus and the Douro was successfully occupied.

[4] Appian 1912–13 vol 1, p 233 and vol 4, pp 225, 227; Strabo 1917–32 vol 2, pp 71, 73, 107.
[5] Appian 1912–13 vol 1, pp 233–57.
[6] Alarcão J de 1988, pp 9–10; NHP vol 1, pp 348–9.

Although intermittent resistance continued, the majority of the Lusitani submitted at this time, and in the war between Caesar and Pompeius that followed some of them served as mercenaries in the rival Roman armies. In the end persistent close contact with Roman affairs seems gradually to have brought the remaining Lusitani into the empire less by force of arms than by gradual acculturation. After that the only part of Portugal still outside the Roman fold was the mountainous north. This was dealt with by Augustus who arrived fresh from victory in the Roman civil wars and oversaw a series of systematic campaigns in the area in 24–19 BC. By the latter date Rome considered the conquest complete.

The extraordinary length of time it took the Romans to pacify northern Portugal can be attributed partly to its remote location at the far outer fringe of the then known world. Long and difficult communications confronted Roman armies operating in the more rugged parts of the country, and only when Roman bases had been constructed in or close to these areas, and permanent garrisons established, did the situation become manageable.[7] The skill and determination of the Lusitani and other mountain peoples in conducting guerrilla-type warfare, and the outstanding qualities of some of their leaders, such as Viriatus, helped slow the conquest. Moreover, the Lusitani were sometimes able to take advantage of divisions and conflicts among the Roman invaders themselves. However, when the period of Rome's civil wars eventually came to an end, and Augustus established his principate, the resistance of peoples like the Lusitani and Callaeci was quickly crushed.

TOWNS AND ROADS

After the Augustan pacification, Portugal remained within the Roman Empire for nearly 450 years – time for a long, complex process of Romanisation to take place. Scholars argue over the extent to which Portugal was ultimately transformed by this process, with Classicists generally accepting Romanisation as more thorough than the more sceptical archaeologists. But all would agree that change occurred first and most profoundly in the south. This was to be expected, for the inhabitants of the south had long been in contact with the Mediterranean world, were already part of its trading system and were relatively well-prepared for adjusting to Roman ways. Moreover, with its pleasant climate and relatively developed economy the south attracted more Italian colonists than other regions. The central coast was probably also quite strongly Romanised and had some colonists. However, the central and northern

---

[7] Strabo 1917–32 vol 2, p 77.

hinterlands remained poor and sparsely peopled – and even the northern coast though more heavily populated was too remote, unfamiliar and Atlantic-orientated to draw in many settlers. Romanisation was therefore much slower and less thorough in these regions than in the south.

Above all Romanisation meant adopting the traditions and practices of Roman civic life, and urbanisation occurred rapidly in Portugal during the first and early second centuries AD. The names of most important Portuguese towns today, and many smaller places as well, are directly derived from their Roman equivalents or from Latinised forms of pre-Roman names. Some Roman cities in Portugal were new foundations, such as Pax Julia (Beja) and probably Bracara Augusta (Braga). However, most were developed from pre-existing *oppida,* including Olisipo (Lisbon), Ebora (Évora), Salacia (Alcácer do Sal), Scallabis (Santarém), Aeminium (Coimbra), Ossonoba (Faro), Sellium (Tomar) and the twin towns of Portus and Cale (Porto). In their Romanised forms, these towns were very different from their Iron Age predecessors – in the design and construction of their buildings, in layout and in overall conception. While a few Roman towns, such as Mirobriga and Conimbriga, were eventually abandoned or sank into obscurity, most have persisted to this day. The Roman network of cities in Portugal is the basis of its modern counterpart.

The critical period for the creation of Roman cities in Portugal was the principate of Augustus (25 BC–AD 14), though some municipalities were perhaps founded a little earlier. The building of a Roman city usually followed a familiar pattern. A central forum, market, theatre, baths, probably an aqueduct and perhaps an amphitheatre would be constructed. Peristyle houses for the prosperous and temples to various gods and the imperial cult appeared, while an area for industries and crafts was developed. Such major undertakings obviously required careful planning, knowledge of sophisticated architectural principles and access to financial and technical resources. Moreover, the local population had to learn how to live in the Roman fashion, a process best encouraged by the presence of Roman or Romanised colonists.[8]

A feature of the urban network in Roman Portugal was the relative neglect of coastal sites. To the Romans the coast of Portugal had few attractions. Much of it seemed bleak and windswept, was devoid of useful offshore islands and carried little strategic significance – a frontier to nowhere. Accordingly, nearly all important administrative centres were located at key river crossings, well to the east. Emerita Augusta (Mérida), the major administrative centre for most of what is now Portugal, was so far east that it was actually in Spanish Extremadura. None of the three key western Portuguese cities of later times – Lisbon,

---

[8] Alarcão J de 1988, p 40.

Coimbra and Porto – were administratively very important, though each had a certain strategic significance, all being located at good, defensive sites on major river crossings. While no precise population figures are known for any Roman towns in Portugal, Alarcão has cautiously suggested large centres like Beja and Lisbon may have had 30,000 to 40,000 inhabitants each, and smaller ones like Conimbriga about 10,000 to 15,000.[9] Numerous villages established in earlier centuries continued to be occupied in the Roman era and were also gradually Romanised. They included many northern *castros,* though some of these did not survive into Roman times, but were destroyed or abandoned during the conquest.

While virtually all the significant towns of Roman Portugal were already in existence by the end of the Augustan era, urban development continued quite vigorously for about another century. This process was particularly evident during the prosperous years of the Flavian emperors (69–96 AD) when many public buildings, and sometimes entire city centres, underwent major reconstruction. A vast new forum and a magnificent complex of public baths with domed hot rooms and a monumental garden were built in this period at Conimbriga.[10] Likewise the famous temple at Évora dates from the late first or early second century AD. After this period, urban development in Portugal slowed, and the next major upsurge in construction did not take place until the fourth century AD, when it came in response to fears of barbarian invasion. At that time, many cities were provided for the first time with walls, and consequently urban space became more constricted. Cities took on an increasingly Medieval appearance, a trend reinforced by the gradual adoption of Christianity and the abandonment of temples in favour of churches.[11]

The cities of Roman Portugal were linked by roads which were built for military, commercial and administrative purposes. A great south-north road ran from Lagos on the Algarve coast to Odivelas, where it joined the road from Beja, before going on through Alcácer do Sal and Setúbal to the mouth of the Tagus. From Lisbon on the northern side of the river it continued up the Tagus valley to Santarém, headed north through Conimbriga and Coimbra, crossed the lower Douro at Porto, proceeded to Braga and then headed eastward via Chaves into Galicia. At the same time, there was a strong tendency for lines of communication to run west to east, with roads either converging on Mérida or passing further south into Andalusia. While knowledge of the Roman road system in Portugal is still very incomplete, there is no doubt it was remarkably extensive.[12]

---

[9] NHP vol 1, p 396.
[10] Keay S J 1988, p 139.
[11] Alarcão J de 1988, p 43.
[12] Ibid, pp 49–61.

VILLAS AND MINES

As towns became more stagnant and inward-looking in the later days of the empire, often declining in both population and wealth, so that other quintessentially Roman institution – the villa or country estate – grew in importance. Villas had made their appearance in Portugal much earlier, in the late first century BC. The earliest were fortified, were probably built by colonists from Italy and were heavily concentrated between the mines of Baixo Alentejo and the river port of Mértola. This suggests that they may have been founded partly to provide protection for precious metals convoys. However, the basic function of villas was economic, not military. They were a device for exploiting agricultural and pastoral resources on a relatively large scale, and this was as true of Portugal as anywhere else. The typical Portuguese villa consisted of a principal residence with appropriate out-buildings surrounded by wheat fields, olive groves, vineyards, orchards and ubiquitous flocks and herds. Some villas developed quarries or produced bricks, tiles and other ceramics. Some, notably on the Algarve coast and in the Tagus and Sado estuaries, concentrated on salting fish and making *garum*.[13] By the first century AD, villas were to be found in many parts of Portugal. They were particularly suited to Alentejo where climatic conditions, topography and predominantly poor soils made intensive small-scale agriculture impracticable. Already in the Iron Age there were some latifundia functioning there and in Estremadura, and in these cases villas simply took over pre-existing operations. However, the Romans brought various improvements in the techniques and practices of agriculture, such as fallowing, fertilising and crop rotation and probably new seeds and improved animal stock. Also introducing Portugal to the efficient harnessing of water, they developed sophisticated hydraulic works, dug wells, constructed dams and built irrigation systems, while many of their larger villas were provided with thermal baths.[14]

By the final years of the second century AD, elite landowners were residing much less in the cities, choosing instead to remain on their villas. Spending on civic monuments declined and money was diverted to embellishing private country seats, which became ever more luxurious. An outstanding villa of this era was Milreu, located near modern Faro. Originally built in the first century AD on a simple peristyle plan, the Milreu residence was substantially enlarged and re-modelled in the late third and fourth centuries. It had many rooms, with a grand thermal bath on its southern side, and was magnificently decorated with mosaics. A large temple was built adjoining the house, which was later

[13] Ibid, pp 64, 71, 87–8.
[14] Ibid, p 72; Gamito T J 1988, pp 159, 163–4.

converted into a church.[15] How much land was attached to a major villa of this kind is uncertain, though it seems likely thousands of hectares would have been required to sustain it. The late Roman villa in Portugal supported and sustained a whole community, from the patrician master and his family to the mass of dependent workers, at least some of whom were slaves. At the same time, the villa was far from being the only type of rural enterprise. The much more modest *casal* was also widespread, especially in the central and northern regions. A *casal* was a family farm, usually worked with little if any help from slave or wage labour. Then there was the small, intensively cultivated subsistence plot so characteristic of the densely populated areas of the northwest. Such plots were usually located within two to three kilometres of a village – the distance it was practicable to walk to daily work. That pattern has persisted into modern times.[16] A southern tradition of latifundia and a northern tradition of minifundia were already taking shape in the Roman era.

While Roman Portugal possessed an overwhelmingly agricultural and pastoral economy, from the viewpoint of the imperial government it was the mining industry that really mattered. The peninsula was one of the most important metal-producing regions in the empire. A major share of production came from Portugal, including iron, copper, tin, lead and above all gold and silver. Precious metals were the first resource exploited by the Romans in the wake of the conquest and always received priority. Alluvial gold was panned in the Tagus, Douro and Mondego river valleys; but the principal source of gold was Três Minas (Vila Pouca de Aguiar) in Trás-os-Montes, where shaft mining was conducted. Most mines in Roman Portugal were run by private operators; but the Três Minas gold mines were administered directly by the Roman state, under military supervision. Operations at Três Minas involved deep shaft mining and a complex hydraulic system with dams, channels and sluices. A mostly slave labour force of about 2,000 was used.[17] The other key mines were at Vipasca near Aljustrel in Baixo Alentejo, which had been in production since the Bronze Age, and yielded mainly silver and copper. Two remarkable Roman legal documents inscribed on bronze tablets were discovered at Vipasca in 1876 and 1906. They reveal much about the administration and society of these mines, showing Vipasca belonged to the emperor and was administered by a special imperial procurator. However, it was not state operated, but divided into a myriad of shafts and open cuts leased to private operators on a 50:50 share basis. The work was performed by a mixture of free, convict and slave labour, with children used in the narrower shafts.

[15] Alarcão J de 1988, pp 65–7, 88; Keay S J 1988, 197.
[16] NHP vol 1, pp 420–4.
[17] Alarcão J de 1988, pp 74–80; NHP vol 1, pp 413–14.

Though both the Três Minas and Vipasca mines predated the Roman conquest, they were exploited by the Romans on a far greater scale than previously
and integrated by them into the international economy. They were at their most
productive in the 200 years between the time of Augustus and the early third
century AD. Such mining operations played a significant part in the process of
acculturation. They attracted immigrant labour, encouraged geographical
mobility, facilitated ethnic mixing and brought on Romanisation. At the same
time, they were often environmentally destructive, creating slag heaps and consuming vast quantities of timber and charcoal, resulting in deforestation – a
process that probably contributed to the eventual decline of the industry in the
third century AD.[18]

FREE AND SLAVE

Roman rule brought much more geographical mobility to the inhabitants of
Portugal and increased their interaction with outsiders. Merchants and professionals travelled freely between one region of the peninsula and another, or
from the peninsula to other parts of the empire. Labourers seeking opportunities for employment migrated to more prosperous areas – like the group from
Clunia (Coruña del Conde) in Castile, attracted into what is now eastern
Portugal by the mining industry.[19] Soldiers routinely served in different locations and often eventually settled far from their places of birth. Slaves were
shifted to where their labour was required. All this in turn contributed to the
gradual breaking down of tribal differences and accelerated Romanisation.

The population of Portugal had probably reached about a million by the
settled years of the late first century AD.[20] It comprised a society formally
divided between free persons on the one hand and slaves on the other. The
vast majority of the free formed an amorphous sub-elite in town and country of
which relatively little is known beyond the glimpses afforded by government
regulations, the deeds of trade guilds or occasional epitaphs. But the small,
privileged elite has left a more visible profile.

Roman policy was to win over indigenous leaders wherever possible.
Accordingly, in Portugal many natives received Roman citizenship in the first
century AD, especially under Emperor Claudius (AD 41–54). As Roman towns
appeared, each produced its own group of leading citizens. They came partly
from native families of substance and partly from the families of local Italian
colonists, and they shared the principal municipal offices among them. While

---

[18] Edmondson J C 1987, pp 73, 77–81.
[19] NHP vol 1, p 408.
[20] Ibid, p 396.

the basis of their wealth and prominence was usually landed property, many focussed their ambitions on their city. It was customary at least until the late second century AD for these men to demonstrate their prominence by sponsoring municipal public works such as temples, theatres, baths and monuments, as proclaimed in many an inscription. Some of the more ambitious sought careers at higher levels of the imperial bureaucracy, eventually moving to the provincial capital or even to Rome itself. A few, through lavish public spending, patient imperial service and probably the aid of influential connections, eventually attained equestrian or even senatorial status, the highest in the Roman hierarchy. This usually meant living in Rome, so that individual senators or equestrians only rarely figure in records in Portugal.[21] However, any citizen who could meet the stringent wealth and service qualifications, regardless of ethnic or geographical origins, was eligible.

As in most Ancient Mediterranean societies, the slave system was fundamental to Roman Portugal. The brief Carthaginian empire in southern Iberia had already brought a foretaste of slavery, and enslavement was the fate of many Lusitanian and other captives during the subsequent Roman conquest when men, women and children were sold to wherever in the empire demand dictated. In Portugal itself by the first century AD perhaps a third of the population consisted of slaves. The supply came from a variety of sources, including prisoners-of-war from the frontier regions, and children sold by poor or debt-ridden parents; but many people were also born slaves. The law consigned the offspring of all slave mothers to slavery.[22]

Slaves were used for a wide range of purposes in both public and private employment. Many laboured in the fields, while others worked in the mines, in domestic service, in trades and in various forms of municipal or imperial service. Skilled or well-educated slaves, usually Greeks with professional backgrounds, often served as tutors, physicians, accountants, business managers or artists. Technically slaves were chattels with few rights under the law. They could not own property or have a legally recognised family and were obliged to live and work as their owners dictated. But they usually received remuneration of some kind and were permitted to purchase their freedom. Freedmen or women, while still in various ways obligated to their former owners with whom they usually maintained close relationships, could otherwise live and work as they pleased. Some held responsible managerial positions and occasionally rose into the elite within a generation or two, aided by good fortune and judicious marriages. Inscriptions show freedmen in Portugal active in commerce, mining and the professions.[23]

---

[21] Ibid, pp 402–3.
[22] Keay S J 1988, pp 75–6.
[23] Ibid 77–8; NHP vol 1, pp 405–6.

ROMAN ADMINISTRATION AND THE IDEA OF PORTUGAL

After the Augustan settlement, Rome administered Portugal largely by consent, despite the bitter fighting that had occurred during the conquest. The people of western Iberia came to respect the city of Rome as the symbol of universal order, with the emperor as its supreme embodiment. This attitude lasted right through to the fifth century AD, even if the emphasis slowly shifted during the later empire from Rome the city to the emperor personally.

Roman administration in Portugal functioned broadly at three levels – provincial, district and city. Originally, Hispania (the Iberian peninsula) had been divided into two provinces called Citerior and Ulterior, each under its own governor backed by legions. However, the gradual extension of Roman rule eventually made further divisions necessary, and so Augustus decided to split Ulterior into the new provinces of Baetica and Lusitania. Baetica comprised essentially modern Andalusia; Lusitania, which is our principal concern here, included most of southern and central Portugal plus some of southwestern Spain, and its capital was the newly founded Mérida. Northern Portugal was never part of Lusitania, but was assigned to Citerior, now renamed Tarraconensis. These arrangements remained in force until the Emperor Diocletian in AD 284–8 detached the northwest of Hispania from Tarraconensis to form the province of Gallaecia, with its capital at Braga. Diocletian also created a new official called a *vicarius* who was to oversee military and civilian administration for the whole of Hispania from his headquarters at Mérida.

At sub-provincial-level, Hispania was divided up into various judicial and administrative districts called *conventus*. The system may have been introduced by Augustus, but more probably belongs to the time of Vespasian (69–79 AD). Lusitania contained three *conventus* which were called Pacensis, Scallabitanus and Emeritensis, and their capitals were at Beja, Santarém and Mérida, respectively. Tarraconensis had seven *conventus,* but almost all of northern Portugal was in just one of these – Bracarensis – with its headquarters at Braga. Each *conventus* had its own assembly made up of representative notables from the cities that lay within its territories. The third administrative unit was the *civitas* (city), which always consisted of an urban centre plus its surrounding territory. Alarcão has identified up to twenty-four *civitates* in Portuguese Lusitania, but in Portuguese Gallaecia there was for long only one. This was Braga, which consequently had an exceptionally large jurisdiction. The reason was probably the more fragmented nature of society north of the Douro and the absence of well-developed pre-conquest *oppida*.[24] Under

---

[24] Alarcão J de 1988, pp 17–28, 30–3.

these circumstances, the Romans were obliged to administer much of the region by direct military rule or through tribal chieftains.

It is obvious that the Romans gave Portugal an administrative structure far more developed and comprehensive than anything it had remotely experienced before. Roman rule, by bringing Portugal firmly into the fold of the most powerful and extensive polity yet known in the European world, was also able to overlay ancient divisions with one universalising political culture. Nevertheless, there is no evidence that either the Romans or the inhabitants of western Hispania ever recognised what is now Portugal as a discrete entity. The political map of Roman Hispania was very different from that of the peninsula in the Middle Ages and provided no prefiguring of modern Portugal. While most of Portugal is located within the old province of Lusitania, that province extended well east of the present international frontier, and its capital and prime focus were actually inside Spanish Extremadura. Portugal north of the Douro was always consigned to a separate province – first Citerior, then Tarraconensis and finally Gallaecia. Roman Lusitania cannot therefore be equated with Portugal.

If Portugal is not the direct successor of Lusitania, can it be said to correspond to any other political division or combination of divisions within Roman Hispania? A close correspondence has sometimes been claimed between Portugal and the territory encompassed by the three Roman *conventus* of Pacensis, Scallabitanus and Bracarensis. However, the conventual borders only really coincide quite closely for Pacensis in the south.[25] Nor is there any obvious reason why such a grouping of *conventus,* two from Lusitania and one from Gallaecia, should form the basis of a coherent territorial or national unit. Nothing suggests such an entity was ever envisaged or even unconsciously prefigured under the late empire. The idea of Portugal as a political entity appears to owe nothing directly to Roman administration, but is rather a consequence of later circumstances we shall have to examine in another chapter.

The formative impact on Portugal of the Roman experience was nevertheless extraordinarily powerful. By the end of Roman rule, the basic demographic and socio-economic patterns of the future nation were already evident – patterns that would display tenacious continuity, despite many vicissitudes, well into the future. The location of towns had been largely decided, and contrasting land tenure systems had become entrenched in the south and north. A literate culture had developed, and the people had grown accustomed to Roman law and justice. Within the territory's borders people spoke in a form of vulgar Latin which would one day develop into Portuguese. Great advances

[25] MHP, pp 13–16; Alarção J de 1988, pp 1, 32; NHP vol 1, p 384.

had occurred in technology and material life. Architecture had been introduced and Roman artistic norms accepted. In short, Portugal had become part of a much wider culture and value system.

THE GODS

Until the formal adoption of Christianity, Roman Portugal had a smorgasbord of gods co-existing in relative mutual harmony. Pre-Roman indigenous deities like Banda, Nabia and Endovelicus long continued to be worshipped but gradually took on Romanised form with their votive offerings expressed in Latin. Native and Roman gods with similar attributes often blended. Thus, Trebaruna, the warrior deity commonly worshipped among the Lusitani, was eventually identified with the Roman goddess Victoria. Native household deities were easily transformed into their Roman tutelary equivalents, the *Lares* and *Penates*. Pre-Roman gods of particular places continued to be worshipped as *genii locorum,* or local protecting spirits. Meanwhile, gods of the traditional Roman pantheon entered Portugal in the baggage trains of the conquerors and soon became established in the larger cities. From there they gradually extended their influence into surrounding populations, perhaps mainly through markets, games or other gatherings. Jupiter, the father of the gods of Rome, was the most widely worshipped. As Jupiter Optimus Maximus (best and greatest) his altars have been found not only in towns but in many smaller settlements, even in the less Romanised interior of central and northern Portugal. This ubiquity suggests one of the prime symbols of Rome's supremacy was successfully assimilated.[26]

Often initially linked to Jupiter-worship, though clearly more overtly political, was the imperial cult. The practice of emperor-worship was introduced at Rome at the end of the first century BC to legitimate the authority of Augustus. In Portugal, statues and altars to Augustus and his family began to appear soon after pacification and were quickly installed in most important towns.[27] Augustus was formally deified after his death, and similar treatment was accorded to his successors. In Portugal, the imperial cult flourished especially during the first and second centuries AD and proved a strong unifying influence enhancing the prestige of empire. However, emperor-worship could be effective only as long as the emperors themselves remained credible. That credibility was undermined first by a sequence of short-term, blatantly military emperors in the late third century who ruled by force, and then by the rise of Christianity.

---

[26] Alarcão J de 1988, pp 94–5, 100; NHP vol 1, pp 442, 445, 447–9, 452.
[27] Alarcão J de 1988, pp 106–7; NHP vol 1, pp 445–7.

The religious inclusiveness of the empire allowed the steady infiltration of oriental cults. In southern Portugal, a tradition of absorbing such cults already existed even before the conquest, and this was reinforced under Roman rule by increased commercial and cultural contacts. The mother goddess Cybele, who was originally from Asia Minor but had become an important figure in the Roman pantheon, acquired many worshippers in the Algarve. The Egyptian deities Serapis and Isis were also worshipped, the latter as far north as Braga. By soon after AD 200 the mystery cult of the ancient Iranian god Mithras had reached Portugal, probably brought there by legionaries.[28] The great rival of Mithraism at the time was Christianity.

While the origins of Christianity in Portugal are obscure, Christian communities had certainly appeared there by the early third century. At first, converts were largely confined to freedmen, slaves, and others of lowly status, although a slow trickle soon began to join from the elite. During that century there were bishops in at least five Portuguese towns (Braga, Chaves, Faro, Évora and Lisbon); but little is known of them or their dioceses. The Emperor Constantine's conversion to Christianity in AD 312 greatly boosted the prestige of the new faith and increased the number of its adherents, especially in the towns. Churches slowly became familiar features in the Portuguese landscape, and Christian cemeteries appeared. Christianity, which offered no compromise to paganism, also brought a new exclusiveness to the religious scene. In AD 392, Emperor Theodosius I, who had already declared Nicene Christianity (Catholicism) the official state religion, banned paganism altogether, and the old religious inclusiveness was lost forever.[29] By that time the barbarian invasions that ended Roman rule in Portugal were less than twenty years away – and major change was imminent.

---

[28] Alarcão J de 1988, pp 103–5.
[29] MHP, p 16; Keay S J 1988, pp 188–9, 199–200; NHP vol 2, p 37.

3

The Germanic Kingdoms

At the beginning of the fifth century AD, Hispano-Roman life in Lusitania and Gallaecia had been undisturbed by outside intruders for four centuries. It is true that in the late third century, Frankish raiding parties had come uncomfortably close to the two provinces and had plundered nearby Tarraconensis (AD 270–5). Lusitania and Gallaecia had shared in the widespread disruption of those times and had been prompted to fortify some of their unwalled towns. Nevertheless, when the fifth century began, neither province had ever been the target of a serious barbarian attack.[1]

This was now all about to change. In the autumn of AD 409, a loose confederation of Vandals, Suevi and Alans broke through the Pyrenean passes from Gaul into Hispania virtually unopposed. Three years earlier, these barbarian peoples had breached the Rhine frontier, then wrought systematic havoc in Gaul. They were now seeking fresh territory to pillage, and an intact and prosperous Hispania seemed ripe for the picking. No detailed account of what followed in the critical period between late 409 and 411 has ever been found; but Hydatius and Orosius, fifth-century Gallaecian chroniclers, provide the broad outline. The intruders apparently crossed and re-crossed the two provinces plundering, killing and destroying as they went. Many communities lying in their path sought safety in the nearest walled city or even retreated to one of the ancient *castros*. Plague, famine and the oppressive demands of tax collectors, more insistent than ever in such troubled times, compounded the misery.[2] In Lusitania and Gallaecia, the authority of the Roman emperors simply

---

[1] Tranoy A 1981, pp 400, 441; Alarcão J de 1988 pp, 14, 43.
[2] Orosius P 1964, pp 356–8; Hydace 1974 vol 1, pp 115–17.

evaporated. It would never be restored, although many of the Hispano-Roman inhabitants appear not to have understood the fundamental nature of what was occurring, nor to have accepted that the changes were permanent.

Throughout most of the Iberian peninsula the collapse of Roman power came with stunning speed. By 411, the barbarian invaders were dominant almost everywhere apart from Tarraconensis. There were, of course, scattered pockets of territory into which they had not yet penetrated and strongholds where local populations held out. But these places the newcomers could safely ignore for the moment, and so in AD 411 they decided to divide up their conquests for permanent settlement. The procedure used is uncertain, though both Orosius and Hydatius say that the occupied provinces were distributed by lot. This suggests an exclusively internal arrangement among the four confederate peoples without reference to the Romans. However, circumstantial evidence points to a possible treaty with the provincial government in Tarraconensis. In any event, it is clear that in 411 Lusitania and Carthaginensis went to the Alans, Gallaecia was allotted to the Suevi and Hasding Vandals, Baetica fell to the Siling Vandals and Tarraconensis remained Roman.[3]

The settlement of 411 brought some relief from lawlessness and terror. Orosius tells us that the barbarians 'detesting their swords, turned to their ploughs', while Hydatius makes no mention of further outrages in western Hispania for the next five years.[4] Nevertheless, the respite was brief, for in 416 the Visigoths, a much more numerous barbarian people, entered Hispania and re-ignited the violence. The Visigoths had been settled in southern Gaul as Roman *foederati,* but had recently come under pressure from the Franks and were running low on food and other supplies. The Roman authorities in Gaul had therefore decided to steer them south, requesting they deal with the Alans and Siling Vandals and offering provisions as an inducement. The Visigoths under King Wallia (416–19) duly invaded Hispania and swiftly crushed the Alans in Carthaginensis and the Siling Vandals in Baetica, killing their respective kings and eliminating them entirely as autonomous political forces. Their mission accomplished, they returned to Gaul in 418.

Soon after these events, the Hasding Vandals reached the conclusion that the rugged mountain terrain of northern Gallaecia allotted them in 411 was inadequate for their support and decided to move south in search of better country. Their route lay through Suevic territory in southwest Gallaecia, and they may have tried to force the Suevi to join them. In any event, they were soon at war with the Suevi, much of the local populace and even briefly with a Roman force that belatedly re-entered Gallaecia in 419–20. After devastating the Braga

---

[3] Thompson E A 1976: 22–4; NHP vol 2, pp 29–31; Collins R 1995, pp 17–18.
[4] Orosius P 1964, p 358.

region and apparently sustaining heavy losses the Hasding Vandals passed on into Lusitania and Baetica, allegedly sparking another upsurge of violence and inflicting widespread destruction.[5] Eventually in 429 they moved into North Africa from where, apart from occasional brief raids into southern Lusitania, they did not trouble the peninsula further. Of the four barbarian confederates who had crossed the Pyrenees twenty years before only the Suevi now remained.

There is little in the respective backgrounds of these barbarian nations to explain their remarkable success in occupying Hispania. The Suevi and Vandals were Germanic tribal peoples who had been known to the Romans since at least the first century BC. For almost five centuries, they had lived on the northwestern fringes of the empire without causing much concern. Both were pastoral but non-nomadic peoples whose main wealth consisted of cattle, but who also practised some agriculture. The Alans had rather different origins, being Iranian nomads who had recently reached Germany following a long migration via southern Russia. When they formed their loose confederacy and crossed into the empire all four nations were apparently suffering from food shortages in their homelands and may also have been responding to pressure from the Huns.[6] Be that as it may, the Suevi, Vandals and Alans moved into Gaul and then on to the Iberian peninsula not simply as marauding armies, but as uprooted migrants, bringing their women and children with them. Their immediate objectives were provisions and loot generally; but they were also looking for new territory on which to settle long term. Their numbers were quite substantial, but not overwhelming. About 30,000 Suevi entered Hispania in 409–11, including at most 8,000 warriors. In all, the four barbarian nations amounted to perhaps 200,000 people. They were certainly far fewer than the Hispano-Romans whose territory they were entering.[7] Moreover, their military technology was inferior to that of the Romans and their commissariat primitive. It seems highly unlikely such invaders could have defeated a fully manned, well-equipped and competently-led Roman army.

But the invasion of 409 occurred at a time of serious military disorganisation within the empire. In western Hispania, the barbarian confederates were never seriously confronted simply because there were no effective Roman forces at hand with which to fight them. In earlier times, a more vigorous reaction could have been expected; but successive political crises, and a gradual weakening of central control within the Roman state during the fourth century, had largely destroyed the capacity for decisive imperial action. Authority had become

[5] NHP vol 2, p 44.
[6] Goffart W 1980, p 28.
[7] Thompson E A 1965, pp 111–15, 144–5; NHP vol 2, pp 27–8.

increasingly decentralised. In Hispania local landed elites, city magistrates and the bishops between them had assumed responsibility for most day-to-day government. The eastern and western empires had split in 395, and in the west frequent military coups and endemic wars between rival emperors had followed. Most Roman troops in Hispania had been withdrawn to participate in these struggles. The professional Roman military which had saved the empire from earlier barbarian invasions in the late third century was now preoccupied with fighting to control the centre. It had little in common with provincial elites and gave decreasing priority to their defence. When the barbarians crossed the Pyrenees there was no unified Roman command in Hispania, and the guarding of the passes had been left to unreliable allied auxiliaries. They allowed the invaders in and probably joined them in plundering.[8] Given that the empire was then under great pressure on many frontiers, and Italy itself was facing invasion (Rome was sacked by Visigoths in 410), there were no central reserves available to reinforce the Hispanic provinces. A credible campaign by Roman forces to restore control in Portugal was therefore impossible, and such resistance as was offered was organised locally.

THE SUEVIC KINGDOM

The Suevi established their capital in or near Braga in southwestern Gallaecia. From there kings Hermeric (409?–38) and Rechila (438–48) progressively extended their dominion until it covered the entire peninsula except for Tarraconensis and eastern Carthaginensis. Hermeric began the process by launching a series of raids into those parts of Gallaecia which had previously been Hasding Vandal territory. Much of this country was remote and rugged, and the local inhabitants resisted stoutly. A brief peace was therefore arranged, but the Suevi soon broke it.[9] These tactics – sudden attack followed by negotiations to consolidate gains, an uneasy peace, then renewed attacks – were used repeatedly during the next few decades, as the Suevi gradually expanded their operations beyond Gallaecia. Rechila led his forces deep into Lusitania and then Baetica, sweeping aside opposition and imposing Suevic rule. In 439, he took Mérida and in 441 Hispalis (Seville), in Baetica. By the end of that decade, the Suevi were well established in both these provinces and probably also in western Carthaginensis. They had also begun raiding Tarraconensis where they formed a tactical alliance with local *Bacaudae*. After Rechila's death his son Rechiarius (448–56) concluded a peace with the Roman authorities in Tarraconensis, which apparently left Gallaecia, Lusitania and Baetica in Suevic hands. Tarraconensis itself and

---

[8] Collins R 1995, p 16.
[9] Hydace 1974 vol 1, p 131.

probably most of Carthaginensis remained Roman. But within three years Rechiarius broke the peace, re-invaded Roman territory and carried off many of the inhabitants.[10] The Suevi were now at the pinnacle of their power, and for a brief moment it seemed they might subjugate the whole of Hispania.

Lack of written sources means historians are as handicapped in trying to explain the rapid ascendancy of the Suevi as they are in accounting for the initial barbarian conquests. However, it is evident that when their three confederates were all for various reasons eliminated from the scene, the Suevi were free to pursue their ambitions without competition. Probably their ranks were swelled by Hispano-Roman collaborators and by remnants of the Alans and Vandals. Beyond that, their success is once again more convincingly explained in terms of the weaknesses of their adversaries and victims than by any particular strengths of their own. The imperial forces were powerless to counter their aggression, though from the start of the 440s a succession of new Roman commanders were sent to Tarraconensis. In 446 Vitus, the most active of these generals, took the field; but he was soon defeated, after which no further attempt was made to drive out the Suevi. The fundamental reason remained lack of troops. By the late 440s, the Romans had lost most of their recruiting grounds in Hispania, previously a key source of mercenaries. Maintaining military forces in Tarraconensis became more difficult than ever and offensive capacity minimal. Moreover contemporary Tarraconensis was seriously troubled by *Bacaudae* revolts, pre-occupying local Roman commanders with problems of internal security. This helps explain the repeated but generally feeble attempts to reinforce Tarraconensis from outside Hispania and the increasing reliance on Visigothic *foederati*. The army in what was left of Roman Hispania was simply fading away.[11] By the early 460s, the imperial commanders in Tarraconensis were no longer appointed by the emperor, but by the king of the Visigoths. In fact, if not in name, Rome had lost control of its last Iberian territories.

At the local level, some Hispano-Roman and native communities did resist the Suevi – and at times resisted successfully, especially where walled towns, *castros* or other retreats were available to them. It is impossible to be sure how widespread defiance was, but it was probably quite common in the mountainous parts of Gallaecia and northern Lusitania. It was less apparent from the lowland villas, perhaps because they were generally more difficult to defend, and there is little evidence of organised opposition from great landowners. Therefore, while resistance in some places was determined and prolonged, it was also piecemeal and lacked coordination.[12] No great leader emerged in

[10] Ibid, pp 143, 153, 154–5; Collins R 1995, p 22.
[11] Thompson E A 1976, pp 16–18, 25–31.
[12] Tranoy A 1981, p 442.

either Gallaecia or Lusitania to galvanise the native inhabitants against the Suevi, as Viriatus had done against the Romans in the second century BC. Nevertheless, invading Tarraconensis in 455 was a fatal miscalculation for the Suevi – for it provoked an angry response from Rome's ally in southern Gaul, the Visigothic king Theoderic II. Acting in the emperor's name, Theoderic entered Hispania at the head of a powerful army and overwhelmingly defeated the Suevi at a place called Campus Paramus near Asturica (Astorga) in 456. Subsequently, Visigothic forces took and sacked Braga. They desecrated the Catholic churches (the Visigoths being Arians), but refrained, somewhat to the surprise of Hydatius, from massacring the local inhabitants or raping Catholic nuns. Rechiarius was captured and executed, and the main Suevic strongholds in Gallaecia were occupied by Theodoric's troops, as were parts of Lusitania, Carthaginensis and Baetica.[13]

The great defeat of 456 terminated both the short-lived Suevic ascendancy in Hispania and the first dynasty of the Suevic kings; but it did not put an end to the autonomous Suevic kingdom in Gallaecia. Soon after the execution of Rechiarius, Theodoric's troops were withdrawn, and a certain Maldras, who may have been Hispano-Roman or even a Visigoth, briefly exercised power.[14] Subsequent recovery was slow and painful, power became fragmented among rival war-leaders and banditry increased. Suevic raids into Lusitania also soon resumed. Olisipo was twice occupied, and Conimbriga was attacked and destroyed in the 460s. Because Hydatius's chronicle abruptly ends in 496, the sequence of events thereafter becomes hazier, and the late fifth and sixth centuries are the most obscure and poorly documented periods in Portugal's history. But apparently by 500, a revived Suevic kingdom centred on Braga had re-asserted control over much of Gallaecia, and intermittently over northwestern Lusitania. It continued to function, though with increasing precariousness owing to Visigothic encroachments, into the late sixth century. Eventually in 585, there was a disputed succession, and the Visigothic king Leovigild decided to intervene. He deposed Audeca, last of the Suevic kings, and annexed the kingdom. Apart from one brief and feeble uprising the annexation met with no resistance, and if any serious autonomist sentiment persisted it has left no trace.[15] After a history of over 150 years the Suevic kingdom had ceased to exist.

When the Suevi first entered Hispania they were probably pre-literate and had only limited experience of the Roman world. Little is known of how their kingdom was organised and governed, though it seems likely that they maintained the old Hispano-Roman administrative structure, particularly for

[13] Thompson E A 1976, pp 3–6; NHP vol 2, pp 52–3.
[14] MHP, p 24; Collins R 1995, p 23.
[15] Collins R 1995, p 49.

purposes of tax collection. The Suevic crown was apparently hereditary, passing from father to son. The kings presided over a court. They also maintained a treasury, developed a chancery and issued their own coinage, doubtless with the aid of Hispano-Roman officials. Nevertheless, neither written laws nor any other official documents from the Suevic regime have survived.[16]

Historians have found little that was attractive about the Suevi. They have been dismissed as mere marauders, a people who allegedly spent the entire period of their ascendancy engaged in plunder.[17] Yet such summary condemnation begs important questions. The Suevi in Hydatius's time were quick to violence, often treacherous and thoroughly uncultured by Hispano-Roman standards; but they contrived for about a quarter century to dominate most of Hispania. After that their small northwestern kingdom persisted in an increasingly Hispano-Romanised form for another century and a quarter. These achievements suggest a people of greater substance than their detractors have been willing to concede. Unfortunately, the lack of written records makes an informed evaluation of the Suevic era now quite impossible.

THE VISIGOTHS

Like the Vandals and Suevi, the Visigoths were a Germanic people. Their origins are obscure, but they may have been living in or near Scandinavia at the start of the Christian era. Later, they moved southeast and came into contact with the Romans on the Danube frontier. The imperial authorities allowed them to settle in Dacia, where in the late fourth century they were converted to Arian Christianity. Shortly afterwards, provoked by ill-treatment, they revolted. They caused great disruption, defeated and killed the Emperor Valens and then passed on into northern Italy from where in 410 they sacked Rome. A few years later the western emperor settled them in southern Gaul as *foederati,* and from there they soon became involved in Hispania. After his victory over the Suevi at Campus Paramus Theoderic II took control of Baetica and southern Lusitania. Later, his successor King Euric (466–84) against relatively feeble resistance occupied most of the remainder of the peninsula, including Tarraconensis. This brought the existence of Roman Hispania formally to an end – at about the same time as the last western emperor was deposed in Rome (476).[18]

Most of central and southern Portugal remained within the Visigothic kingdom until the Muslim conquest 250 years later. The only probable exception

---

[16] DHP vol 4, p 101; NHP vol 2, pp 47–8.
[17] Thompson E A 1976, p 6.
[18] Thompson E A 1977, pp 5–6; Collins R 1995, pp 23–4.

was part of the Algarve coast for about seventy years between the 550s and 620s. During this period, much of southern Andalusia was re-incorporated into the Eastern Roman Empire, and it is likely the western fringe of this domain extended into southern Portugal.[19] If so, the coastal Algarve would have experienced the cultural influence of Byzantium, the circulation of imperial coinage and close ecclesiastical links with Constantinople and North Africa. Of course, northern Portugal remained part of the isolated, remnant kingdom of the Suevi until it too was absorbed into the Visigoths' pan-Hispanic realm in 585. In a manner that suggests some parallels with the Roman conquest centuries before, the extension of Visigothic control over Portugal was therefore a stage-by-stage process that ultimately took over a century to complete.

The Visigothic kings maintained their headquarters successively at Toulouse, Tortosa, Narbonne, Barcelona and finally Toledo – all distant from what is now Portuguese territory. Only for a very brief period (549–54) did a king actually reside as far west as Lusitania, and even then it was at Mérida, within the borders of modern Spain. The Visigothic court was therefore a remote presence for the inhabitants of the future Portugal, occasional campaigns or visits by kings notwithstanding. In Lusitania effective Visigothic rule before the reign of King Leovigild (569–86) was probably restricted to the Mérida region, part of Alentejo and the Tagus valley only; but it became established more firmly in both Lusitania and Gallaecia in the late sixth century. By about that time the Visigothic monarchy appears to have possessed a fairly well-organised administrative structure, with each province governed by a *dux* (duke), and a *comes* (count) responsible for each major town. The Visigothic kings were meticulous law-makers and with the aid of Hispano-Roman officials issued successive legal codes. The earliest known are the code of Euric (466–84) and the breviary of Alaric II (484–507), which provided for the kingdom's Visigothic and Hispano-Roman populations respectively.[20] Revised codes were later issued by Leovigild and several of his successors. However, exercising central control was always difficult given poor communications and the diffusion of power locally. Leovigild himself, usually regarded as the most successful of the Visigothic warrior kings, was eventually faced with a serious revolt by his son who tried briefly to establish an autonomous kingdom in Baetica and southern Lusitania in 579–83.

To enhance the prestige of the monarchy, Leovigild and his successors adopted quasi-Byzantine ceremonial including use of a throne, a royal cloak of purple bordered in cloth of gold and an elaborate diadem.[21] Royal authority

---

[19] Thompson E A 1969, pp 320–3; NHP vol 2, pp 64–5.
[20] Collins R 1995, pp 24–5.
[21] Thompson E A 1969, p 57; NHP vol 2, pp 68–9.

was enforced by civil and military judges, and the law prescribed stern punishments, such as mutilation and execution by burning, beheading or hanging. After the conversion of Leovigild's successor Reccared in 587 from Arianism to Catholicism the Visigothic kings received strong backing from the Catholic bishops, and the church became a staunch upholder of centralised royal authority. To the best chronicler of his time, the Santarém-born John of Biclarum, Reccared was the *rex christianissimus*, the new Constantine. From about the middle of the seventh century, successive Visigothic rulers began to claim the sanctified status of *rex et sacerdos* – priest-king. The triumph of Catholicism both reflected and then helped to accelerate the blurring of distinctions between Visigoths and Hispano-Roman natives.[22] Nevertheless, as an institution the Visigothic kingdom remained somewhat insecure. There were frequent political crises, particularly when a king died without an obvious adult successor.

SOCIETY AND ECONOMY

Relationships between the Suevi and the Hispano-Romans were naturally often tense, especially in the early years; but they were not unremittingly hostile. From the late fifth century an uneasy modus vivendi between the two peoples gradually took hold, as the Suevic kingdom sought to institutionalise itself. Ethnic intermarriages apparently occurred with increasing frequency as time passed. Groups of Suevi settled in various parts of Gallaecia, in particular in the Braga and nearby coastal regions, from the early fifth century. The terms of their occupation of the land are not known, but their numbers were certainly small. The general population remained overwhelmingly Hispano-Roman, and many parts of both Gallaecia and Lusitania were never effectively under Suevic control at all. The Visigoths after Campus Paramus maintained garrisons continuously in Lusitania and intermittently in Gallaecia; but as a people they too came west in very limited numbers. Precisely how many eventually settled in Lusitania and Gallaecia is uncertain. However, it has been suggested that there were only about 150,000 Visigoths in the whole of Hispania by the early sixth century. This would have amounted to perhaps 2 per cent of the total population – and in Portugal the percentage was certainly less.[23]

Until the late sixth century, Visigoths and Hispano-Romans were formally treated as two distinct communities within the Visigothic realm with separate laws and law-courts, and separate Arian and Catholic churches. Intermarriage between the two peoples was prohibited, though in practice it could not be entirely prevented and was eventually legalised by Leovigild. However, after

[22] NHP vol 2, pp 74, 79.
[23] Ibid, p 62.

the conversion of the Visigoths to Catholicism ethnic differences steadily faded. There was now one church and one legal system. Distinctive Visigothic dress was abandoned, and some Visigoths even adopted Latin names. These developments suggest an accelerating trend towards Hispano-Romanisation even though right down to the Muslim conquest a discrete but increasingly ill-defined Visigothic identity continued to be officially recognised. The extent to which spoken Gothic was still used by the late seventh century is impossible to determine. However, neither the Suevic nor the Gothic tongue had any significant influence on the development of Portuguese.[24]

The structure of society in western Iberia under the Germanic kings did not differ greatly from what it had been in later Roman times. The fundamental division remained between an elite of nobles, owning great estates and other properties, and a mass of dependent tenants (*coloni*), freedmen (*liberti*) and slaves. In between were small landowners and certain specialist groups such as merchants and free artisans. Some elite Hispano-Romans had fled overseas at the time of the barbarian invasions. But the vast majority stayed on and continued to enjoy their privileged status. Neither the Suevi nor the Visigoths sought to destroy the old nobility, still less the existing social system.

In the fifth century, many Hispano-Roman leaders, clinging to their Roman identity and outlook, probably saw their Suevic conquerors as uncouth and uncultured. Such people were slow to accept that the empire had retreated from western Hispania forever. Some sought outside help against the unwanted intruders – like Bishop Hydatius who in 431–2 led a delegation to the Roman commander in Gaul, vainly seeking his intervention. Yet they also negotiated with the Suevi and arranged various peaces and truces. In the end, the old elite collaborated pragmatically with the newcomers and apparently survived well enough. Some late Roman landowning families, like the Cantabri of Conimbriga, are still traceable in Germanic times, apparently as rich and powerful as ever, the status of their slaves and tenants unchanged.[25] Of course, Suevic and Visigothic families were progressively added to elite ranks – at first most likely on the basis of *hospitalitas*, an arrangement whereby two thirds of a designated estate were transferred to a new Germanic owner, the balance being retained by the previous incumbent. However, the Visigoths generally settled in Spain, and it seems transfers of this kind were less common in Portugal.

Tenant farmers, though technically free and enjoying some legal protection, were tied to the land and incurred the same obligations as in late Roman times, such as tithe, corvee and military service. Freedmen were in a distinct legal category at least until the mid-seventh century and were normally obliged to

---

[24] Thompson E A 1969, pp 58–9, 216–17, 311–14; MHP, p 11; NHP vol 2, p 62.
[25] Thompson E A 1969, pp 114–18; NHP vol 2, p 100.

work for their former owners, now transformed into patrons.[26] But much less is known about sub-elite free persons generally in this society than about slaves, for slaves featured prominently in the laws of the Visigothic kingdom and in the deliberations of church councils. Slave labour was as fundamental to the economy in Suevic and Visigothic Portugal as it had been in Roman times, and the slave population was large and varied. Most slaves did field work, toiled in mines or workshops or were employed in domestic service. Others filled minor administrative jobs, practised professions and trades or served as concubines.

The demand for slave labour was always high on rural properties, both great and small. The abbey of Dume near Braga required at least 500 slaves to work its lands, while an average rural church in the seventh century was said to need about ten.[27] Since children were allotted the status of their mothers, many people were born into servitude. However, slaves were also purchased from slave traders who were active throughout the Mediterranean world and on the margins of the European kingdoms. Some slaves were prisoners-of-war or persons condemned to bondage by the courts for any one of a range of offences, from failure to pay debts to cowardice in battle. Also, free persons could sell themselves or their children in times of want – an act deemed irreversible.

Under the law slaves possessed few basic human rights. They could be bought and sold, put to hard and humiliating labour, deprived of their possessions and severely disciplined. Visigothic law allowed slaves to be given up to 300 lashes and have their heads shaved. They could also have their noses, lips, ears or tongues cut off and suffer castration. Owners could kill their slaves with impunity until a law of King Chindasuinth (642–53) withdrew this privilege.[28] The church both acquiesced in slavery and directly benefited from it. In the tradition of St Paul, Christian leaders called on owners to treat their slaves humanely – and on slaves to obey their masters. Slaves could be freed by the courts. They could also be manumitted by their owners, usually through testamentary provisions. To what extent the harsh laws underpinning slavery were actually applied is unclear; but there seems no doubt that the framework already existed for a system every bit as oppressive as that which later prevailed in Europe's American colonies.

Women were divided into more or less the same class and status groups as men, from noblewoman to slave. But Visigothic society was in essence a warrior society, and women were formally valued less highly than men. Under the law the fine for killing a woman was less than that for a man of comparable

---

[26] Claude D 1980, pp 159–87; NHP vol 2, p 105.
[27] NHP vol 2, pp 103, 105.
[28] Thompson E A 1969, p 269; NHP vol 2, pp 104–5.

status. At the same time, in some respects women received more favourable treatment under Visigothic law than under the Roman system, particularly in matters of property and inheritance rights.[29]

Our knowledge of the economy of western Iberia in this age is limited. However, while compared with the Roman period the Germanic era was hardly one of outstanding economic progress, nor was it as negative or regressive as has sometimes been supposed. Of course, there was significant disruption wrought by the violent disorders of the early and mid-fifth century. Nevertheless, in many areas economic activity apparently continued much as before. Most cities still functioned, and trade and other forms of exchange remained active, particularly along the major rivers. Coins were minted and widely circulated within both the Suevic and Visigothic kingdoms. Ports such as Santarém and Porto provided international trade links and were utilised, as they had been for centuries, by Syrian, Greek and Jewish merchants bringing in imports, including silks, slaves, spices and even relics. The construction industry was quite active, though very few contemporary buildings survive today, Visigothic basilicas at Évora and Egitania perhaps being the best known. Mosaics, paintings and statues were not now produced, though symbolic friezes were.[30]

Rural areas suffered more during the troubles of the fifth century than did towns. Recent archaeological evidence is beginning to show the extent of destruction in Baetica where hundreds of rural properties had ceased to function by the late fifth century. In Gallaecia and Lusitania, the magnitude of destruction has not yet been clearly established, but was probably less severe than in Baetica. Traditional Roman life certainly continued in many parts of the countryside, and in Gallaecia we have evidence of villas operating normally even in the mid-fifth century.[31]

The same forms of landholding existed in the future Portugal after the barbarian conquest as before. In Alentejo and along the central coast and major river valleys there were large to medium-sized rural properties. These belonged variously to the crown, the king personally, the Hispano-Roman and Germanic elites and clerical landlords such as the monastery of Dume. Tenant farms operated by *coloni* were common, and in parts of the northern interior collective holdings existed. Some small private holdings were occupied by the descendants of Germanic veterans, while much land still remained wooded and uncultivated. Little advance in agricultural technology occurred in Germanic times, and the existing range of Hispano-Roman crops and livestock was not significantly changed. However, ancient irrigation works in the south and parts

[29] NHP vol 2, pp 105, 106.
[30] Ibid, pp 95–9, 106–9.
[31] Tranoy A 1981, p 441; NHP vol 2, p 34.

of the Tagus valley were maintained, and the distribution of water was regulated. Mining of iron, silver, gold and lead continued.

CHURCH, FAITH AND PHOBIAS

One of the few Hispano-Roman institutions that came through the era of barbarian invasions and Germanic kingdoms with its authority enhanced was the Roman Catholic church. By the late sixth century, the Catholic church had become entrenched among the most powerful and enduring organisations in western Iberian history. But this triumph was not achieved without a struggle. The Suevi were pagans when they arrived in Hispania, and King Rechiarius was not converted to Catholicism until 450. Then a few years after Rechiarius's death his successor fell under the influence of an Arian missionary called Ajax and adopted Arianism. The Visigoths were already Arians. Therefore, the crucial religious question for most of the sixth century was whether Catholicism or Arianism would ultimately prevail. It was only in about 555 that the Suevi were definitively re-converted to Catholicism, and the Visigothic kings remained Arian for another generation, until the conversion of Reccared in 586. Arianism was formally anathematised at a great church council held in Toledo in 589.[32] By then Catholicism was the faith not only of the vast majority of Reccared's subjects but also of virtually all Western Christendom.

Under the Germanic kings, the church was primarily an urban institution organised through a network of episcopal cities. Each city boasted an imposing cluster of ecclesiastical buildings and precincts including a central church, baptistery, chapels, cemeteries and bishop's palace. There were two metropolitan sees, located respectively at Mérida (for Lusitania) and Braga (for Gallaecia), their suffragan bishoprics grouped around them. Under Mérida were Faro, Beja, Évora, Mértola and Lisbon as well as several bishoprics in Spain. Braga oversaw thirteen dioceses in northern Portugal and Galicia, its jurisdiction extending south to the Tagus until 563, thereafter only to the Douro. The pre-eminence of Toledo over the whole of Visigothic Iberia, with the right to hold general councils and officiate at royal coronations, was established in 681.[33]

Most rural areas, especially in the north, were only superficially Christianised and for long remained essentially mission country. However, a parish system gradually developed, and resident priests came to replace occasional mission preachers. A strong ascetic tradition influenced by models from the Middle East and North Africa developed and monasteries appeared. The specific origins of Portuguese monasticism are somewhat obscure. Though

---

[32] Oliveira M de 1968, p 46.
[33] Collins R 1995, pp 71–2; NHP vol 2, pp 83–5.

Hydatius mentioned communities of nuns in Braga in the early fifth century, the first surviving monastic rule dates from a century later. It was introduced by St Martin of Braga, a missionary born in the Balkans who arrived at the Suevic court in the mid-sixth century and re-converted the king to Catholicism. Martin, who subsequently became bishop of Braga, was familiar with the hermit traditions of Egypt and Palestine, upon which he drew in founding the monastery at Dume in 586. The rule he composed became the model for various other religious houses and was widely used in the peninsula until the eleventh century. Another monastic rule especially influential in Gallaecia was drawn up in 651 by a subsequent bishop of Braga, St Fructuosus.[34] A distinctive feature of St Fructuosus's rule was that it required a written covenant or 'pact' between the monks, as a collective body, and their abbot, rather than individual acts of submission. This became known as 'pactualism'.

After Reccared's conversion the Catholic bishops aligned with the crown – and church and state worked together more closely. Fifteen successive church councils were held at Toledo during the last century of Visigothic rule, meeting at the king's behest and in his royal presence. Provincial councils were also held at Braga – and the tradition of bishops being co-opted into crown service, and of church councils legislating on certain secular as well as religious matters, became firmly established. In both the Suevic and Visigothic kingdoms bishoprics came to be filled as often by incumbents of Germanic as of Hispano-Roman origin. However, if the Catholic church in the future Portugal was much strengthened during Germanic times, it also encountered some serious challenges. Among these were the spread of Arianism, the stubborn persistence in remoter areas of paganism and the widespread influence of so-called 'Priscillianism'.

Arianism was the greatest of these threats until the conversion of Reccared, because it was espoused by the king and the dominant power group. In many cities, Arian churches and bishops were installed in competition with their Catholic counterparts, and bitter struggles were fought over theology and for the control of real estate and saints' relics. Leovigild, the last Arian king, pressured several Catholic prelates, including a bishop of Mérida, into embracing Arianism, though claims he instigated a systematic persecution of Catholics seem exaggerated. After his death Arianism rapidly declined – and even before Reccared's conversion there was a steady haemorrhage of Arians to the Catholic fold.[35]

Paganism remained a problem mainly because much of Gallaecia had been only superficially evangelised. As late as the early eighth century many prehistoric or Roman customs – such as placing lighted lamps near stones, trees or

[34] NHP vol 2, pp 83, 86–7.
[35] Thompson E A 1969, pp 107–9; Collins R 1995, pp 50–3.

other features of the landscape, reading auguries, marrying on the feast day of Venus or even venerating ancient megaliths – still persisted.[36] Martin of Braga directed much of his attention to combating such practices. However, the inadequacy of church resources, the ruggedness of the country and the deeply entrenched nature of pagan traditions meant that the struggle was long and difficult.

Priscillianism was a serious challenge particularly in Gallaecia, where it rapidly infiltrated virtually all levels of Hispano-Roman society. Priscillian was a Gallaecian nobleman who had aroused the ire of church authorities in the twilight of Roman rule by advocating a radical reform program. He urged the zealous study of sacred texts, both Biblical and apocryphal, and espoused a form of asceticism involving celibacy and rigorous retreats. Some of his views – such as vegetarianism and his insistence on equality of males and females – seemed to the hierarchy startlingly radical. He was eventually charged before the emperor with malignant sorcery, and duly condemned and executed, along with several companions, in about 386. After his death, Priscillian's remains were brought back to Gallaecia where they became the object of widespread veneration. Even some local bishops were sympathetic to his cult, and for decades popular sentiment resisted all efforts to suppress it. The Suevic conquest did not help, the new regime showing little interest in such seemingly arcane matters. It took fully two centuries before the church could be reasonably confident Priscillianism had been eradicated – and, even then, the echoes lingered. Indeed, Priscillian's remains may lie buried beneath the cathedral at Compostela itself, which was quite possibly a Priscillianist pilgrimage centre, until it became accepted as the shrine of St James in the ninth century.[37]

A contributory reason to the eventual decline of Priscillianism was the growing prestige of St Martin of Tours. Relics of this saint had been brought to Gallaecia at the time of Martin of Braga, whose own missionary campaign had been much boosted by their presence.[38] This was an era when saints and martyrs in general were the objects of much devotion. Individual saints carried varying degrees of renown, and at least thirty-six of them from the Visigothic period have been identified from Gallaecia alone.[39] The help of saints was sought to combat all that was fearful, from the plague to the machinations of demons, and every city sought to acquire one as its own particular patron. Once recognised, such figures would be furnished with splendid basilicas from which their relics were reverently paraded in elaborate processions, especially

---

[36] Barlow C W 1969, pp 71, 74–5; NHP vol 2, pp 90–2.
[37] Chadwick H 1976, pp 8–10, 168–9, 170–1, 229–30 and passim; Tranoy A 1981, pp 426–8.
[38] Oliveira M de 1968, pp 38–42; MHP, p 24; NHP vol 2, pp 81–3.
[39] NHP vol 2, p 88.

at times of crisis. Mérida's patron saint was St. Eulália, whose reputation was at its peak in the sixth and seventh centuries. Eulália's remains were so valued that, years after the occupation of the city by Muslim invaders, an eighth-century Christian raiding-party rescued them and carried them north to safety. Later, Eulália became the patron saint of Asturias, and today her relics still rest in Oviedo cathedral.[40]

The converse of saints were the demons. Demonic forces were much feared in popular imagination, and the dangers they posed were recognised in Visigothic law. The most celebrated Christian tract written in sixth-century Portugal was Martin of Braga's *De correctione rusticorum,* which comprised in large part a call to arms against demons whom resolute Christians could put to flight with the aid of prayer, the creed and the sign of the cross.[41] At the same time, in the eyes of some Christians, more visible but hardly less abhorrent enemies of the faith were the Jews. If demons were seen as fallen angels whom God had expelled from heaven, then Jews were held to be stubborn unbelievers who had forfeited their right to live within a godly, Christian society. Such views gained ground within the ruling church hierarchy after the conversion of the Visigothic court to Catholicism.

The Jewish communities of Lusitania and Gallaecia dated back to at least Roman times, when they already faced periodic hostility and some discrimination. Although they do not appear to have attracted much attention from the Suevic and early Visigothic rulers, from the early sixth century attitudes towards them gradually hardened, and anti-Semitic legislation was approved by both royal and ecclesiastical councils. Jews were forbidden to hold public office, build synagogues, make converts or own slaves. But they were still grudgingly tolerated – until King Sisebut (612–21) introduced a policy of forced baptisms. A little later King Chintila (636–9), with church approval, decreed the expulsion of all Jews from his realm. This was probably the first time such a draconian policy had been espoused anywhere in western Europe. However, it could not have been effectively implemented, for subsequent rulers adopted new repressive measures. In 654, key Jewish practices, such as circumcision and celebration of the Passover, were prohibited. Then bans were extended to *all* Jewish rites. In 694, a decree reduced the Jews to slavery, ordered their children under six transferred to Christian families and confiscated their property.[42] These measures were parallelled by corresponding enactments in church councils and by virulent anti-Semitic propaganda – even though the popular anti-Semitic hysteria of later centuries had not yet developed.

[40] Hilgarth J N 1980, pp 34–6; Collins R 1995, pp 95–100.
[41] Barlow C W 1969, pp 71–82; Hilgarth J N 1980, pp 24, 41–2.
[42] Thompson E A 1969, pp 156–7, 186; Collins R 1995, pp 133–6.

The reasons for this persecution are not entirely clear. However, the final years of the Visigothic kingdom were beset with myriad problems, including famine and plague in the 680s, which led to a heavy death toll and serious economic disruption. Labour shortages resulted in harsher treatment of *coloni,* increasing reliance on slavery and greater social tensions. Persecution of Jews may have been partly a response to these difficulties, spurred on as much by the crown's interest in acquiring confiscated assets as by increased religious sensibilities. Perhaps by the 690s the Visigothic regime had also come to suspect Jews of collaboration with the menacing Muslim armies now known to be advancing through North Africa. But whatever the case, and despite repeated persecutions, western Iberian Jewry survived – and eventually found some respite in the more tolerant atmosphere of early Islamic times.

4

Gharb al-Andalus

THE MUSLIM CONQUEST

In the spring of 711, a mainly Berber expeditionary force commanded by Tariq ibn Ziyad, a subordinate of the Umayyad governor of North Africa, crossed the Straits of Gibraltar and landed in Baetica. On hearing the news Rodrigo, the Visigothic king (710–11), who was campaigning far to the north, summoned his host to assemble at Cordoba and hastened south. Tariq awaited Rodrigo near Algeciras, and the two armies eventually met, probably in July 711, in southern Baetica somewhere in the vicinity of Medina-Sidonia. In the fateful battle that followed, Tariq's forces were overwhelmingly victorious. Rodrigo was killed – either in the battle itself or soon afterwards – along with most of his noble entourage and household troops. Tariq thereupon rapidly advanced into the heart of the peninsula, encountering little opposition. In 712, the Umayyad governor, Musa ibn Nusayr, realising the scale of Tariq's success, himself crossed the strait to take personal command, bringing another army with him. Toledo was quickly occupied, its Visigothic count and most of the inhabitants having fled. By 716 Musa, his son Abd al-Aziz and Tariq between them had subdued virtually all core strategic and population centres in Visigothic Iberia. Though one or two cities had to be reduced by siege, resistance was uncoordinated and ultimately ineffectual.[1]

Why the Visigothic kingdom was overwhelmed so swiftly is not easy to explain. The most detailed sources that survive are all Muslim; but they are essentially anecdotal, and none was written before the tenth century. A Christian source known as the 'Chronicle of 754', though much closer to the events

---

[1] Levi-Provençal E 1950–3 vol 1, pp 8–34; Taha A D 1989, pp 84–102; Collins R 1989, pp 23–36; Kennedy H 1996, pp 10–13.

themselves, is frustratingly terse. However, what these writings do seem to suggest is that when Tariq invaded Iberia the Visigothic leadership was just emerging from a bitterly contested succession in which Rodrigo, then duke of Baetica, had managed to seize the throne backed by his supporters among the nobility.[2] In achieving this Rodrigo had driven the family and adherents of his predecessor, King Wittiza (693–710), from Toledo, and they may have responded by setting up a rival claimant elsewhere. There is numismatic and some slight documentary evidence that Achila, apparently a son of Wittiza, tried to establish himself in the northeast of the kingdom at about this time. If this is so, it is possible two competing Visigothic kings were vying for control of the realm when Tariq invaded – though it is also possible Rodrigo's rivals had recently submitted to him. In any event it seems that after the death of Wittiza a civil war had occurred within the Visigothic kingdom and that the animosities it generated were still fresh. This could explain why at the fatal battle near Medina-Sidonia a significant part of Rodrigo's army apparently held back and perhaps even joined Tariq. Such behaviour alone would have sealed the king's fate. Moreover, Rodrigo's death without any obvious successor, the destruction of his noble following and household troops and the fall of his capital all in rapid succession would have wrought great confusion. Add to this the speed with which the Muslim armies moved, their capable leadership and the reinforcements they received from North Africa, and the Visigothic collapse begins to look more understandable.

Yet it is also apparent that the invasion of Tariq in 711 was not so sudden and unexpected as sometimes depicted. For some years, Visigothic leaders had known and worried about the rapid westward advance of the Arabs across North Africa, their expulsion of the Byzantines in the 690s and their subjugation of the Berbers between 698 and 710. There are also indications that the battle between Tariq and Rodrigo was not the first clash of Christians with Muslims on peninsular soil, but the culmination of an ongoing process. The 'Chronicle of 754' tells of previous Muslim raids into Visigothic territory 'devastating many cities'. It also alleges that the conquest of southern and central Iberia was notably violent and accuses Musa of perpetrating much killing, looting and destruction and creating widespread panic. This was very likely during the opening phase of the conquest when a major objective of the invaders was booty. Certainly Musa later took back with him to Syria a vast amount of looted property.[3] Nevertheless the subjugation of the peninsula was achieved largely by using the standard tactics of earlier Arab conquests. Before being attacked cities were given the option of immediate voluntary

[2] Wolf K B (ed) 1990, pp 130–1, 132–5; Kennedy H 1996, pp 6–9.
[3] Wolf K B (ed) 1990, pp 131, 132–3.

capitulation. If they agreed, their inhabitants would have to pay tribute like all other unbelievers; but their persons were protected, and they were allowed to retain their homes, property, faith and local autonomy unmolested. If cities refused to surrender and were then taken by force, adult male captives were liable to be executed, and women and children could be enslaved. Under these circumstances, it seems most places submitted promptly, so that after the initial violence the occupation was accomplished relatively peacefully. Nevertheless, many fearful people fled to the mountains or other refuges probably expecting the invaders to withdraw after satisfying their desire for plunder. Of course, some Christians actively collaborated with the Muslim armies – probably including members of Wittiza's family and following – so that what was happening may have seemed to confused natives as much a civil war as an invasion. Meanwhile, Berber immigrants soon began arriving and commenced occupying land abandoned by those who had fled.[4]

After the capitulation of the Visigothic heartland the subjugation of outlying regions like the future Portugal was only a matter of time. It was eventually Musa himself who invaded Lusitania, probably in 713. Most cities of the Algarve and Baixo Alentejo quickly submitted to him, though Mérida, a stronghold of Rodrigo's supporters, surrendered only after a siege lasting several months. Abd al-Aziz then occupied Alto Alentejo and Estremadura, while Musa took the Beiras. By the time both leaders had left for Damascus in or before early 715, their work in western Iberia was all but complete. Portugal had been effectively incorporated into the Umayyad empire, along with nearly all the rest of the Iberian peninsula.[5] By-passing some remote mountain country in Asturias and the Pyrenees, where Christian remnants held out, the Muslim advance passed on into France where it was eventually checked. In an astonishingly short period of less than five years the direction of Iberian history had been radically changed. Yet Islamic rule had come for the long term; it would take over five centuries for all Portuguese territory to be restored to Christian control.

ISLAMIC RULE

Muslims called their conquests in Iberia 'al-Andalus' or the country of the Vandals. Muslim Portugal formed the greater part of 'Gharb al-Andalus' (western al-Andalus). For most of its history Gharb al-Andalus remained roughly coterminous with the old Roman province of Lusitania, Gallaecia being more or less abandoned from an early stage to unsubdued Christian remnants. While

---

[4] Collins R 1989, pp 41–2; Taha A D 1989, pp 93–4; Kennedy H 1996, p 15.
[5] NHP vol 2, pp 121–2.

this division coincidently followed the administrative formula of late Roman times, more fundamentally it reflected ageless geographical realities. The far north with its rugged terrain, cool, damp winters and difficult communications, particularly in Trás-os-Montes and eastern Beira Alta, was never attractive to Muslim settlers. But southern and central Portugal – warmer and drier country, relatively well developed and closer to Cordoba – was a different matter. Muslim immigrants colonised this area willingly and later defended it tenaciously. However, unlike Roman Lusitania, Gharb al-Andalus was not a formal province and never comprised a distinct unit for administrative purposes. Within the context of Muslim Iberia it was politically and culturally a rather peripheral region; but it was also undifferentiated administratively from the rest of al-Andalus and developed no historical tradition of its own. Therefore, historians faced with the task of providing a framework for the history of Gharb al-Andalus tend to look in the first instance to the history of al-Andalus more generally.

For about a generation after the conquest al-Andalus was treated as a dependency of Umayyad North Africa. It was ruled by a military governor appointed from Kairouan, but under the ultimate authority of the caliph in Damascus. However, in the 730s this long, tenuous chain of command was weakened first by a Berber revolt in the Maghrib, then by a bitter feud between peninsula-based and Syrian Arabs in al-Andalus itself. Links were further strained in the late 740s when the Umayyad caliphs were overthrown and replaced by the Abbasids, a Persian dynasty. The Abbasids founded a new capital at Baghdad, more distant than ever from al-Andalus. The ousted Umayyad family was systematically hunted down and slaughtered. However, one young prince escaped and took refuge in al-Andalus. In Cordoba in 756 he proclaimed himself emir of an independent Umayyad state, and his authority was soon accepted throughout al-Andalus. He became known to history as Abd al-Rahman I (756–88).

From the time of Abd al-Rahman I until the late tenth century the emirs at Cordoba were, with few exceptions, able and successful rulers. Internally they had to balance many competing interests – tribal, ethnic and religious – while simultaneously defending the realm against external enemies. Initially the most menacing enemy was the Abbasid caliphate in Baghdad; but this danger soon passed, and the Christian rulers of the north constituted a much more lasting threat. The outstanding Umayyad rulers of al-Andalus during this period were Abd al-Rahman III (912–61) and al-Hakem II (961–76). In 929 Abd al-Rahman III adopted the title of caliph both as a symbol of the growing importance of al-Andalus in the Islamic world and more specifically to combat the pretensions of rivals such as the Banu Ubaid in Kairouan who a few years before had proclaimed their own caliphate. Abd al-Rahman III made Cordoba a magnificent capital, glittering

with splendid mosques and palaces. He was a great patron of art and scholarship, and his court was reputed the most sophisticated in tenth-century Europe.
Al-Hakem II likewise was a highly cultivated ruler whose reign was famously
peaceful and prosperous.[6]

Under the rule of Cordoba al-Andalus was divided up into a number of
districts called *kuwar* (sing. *kura*) each administered by a *wali* (governor).
Kuwar corresponded roughly to Roman conventus, or in some cases established episcopal sees. *Walis,* who were appointed by the emir, were responsible
for military affairs, revenue and law and order in their *kuwar.* Muslim justice
was swift and was dispensed by *qadis* (Islamic judges). However, Christians
and Jews had their own judges for cases exclusive to their particular communities. In Gharb al-Andalus *walis* were often selected from the local aristocracy,
though attempts were also made to shift individuals around to avoid their
becoming too entrenched. A *wali* resided in the capital of his *kura,* which
was usually an important established city, though not necessarily the administrative centre of Visigothic times. In Gharb al-Andalus at its greatest extent
there were ten *kuwar,* the most important based on Beja, Silves, Alcácer do Sal,
Santarém, Lisbon, Idanha and Coimbra. *Kuwar* in turn were subdivided into
madina – units comprising one or more towns with their associated territories,
roughly equivalent to the Roman civitates. Finally, there were numerous villages
called *dayas* that accommodated workers attached to large landholdings, and
villages of autonomous peasant communities called *qaryas.* In due course these
became known as *aldeias* and *alcarias* respectively and as such have passed into
modern Portuguese vocabulary. Probably each village had its own council.[7]
While this outline suggests a centralised administrative system, in practice
al-Andalus was as plagued by centrifugal forces as any Medieval polity. In
Gharb al-Andalus centrifugalism was enhanced by distance from Cordoba
and by the fact that the emirs were primarily sedentary rulers who did not
follow the peripatetic tradition of the Visigothic kings.[8]

Because al-Andalus was subject to periodic raids from the Christian north
and to coastal attacks by Viking sea-raiders, Cordoba appointed military
governors to guard the marches or frontier regions. There was a march for
Gharb al-Andalus initially administered from Medinaceli, but later from Badajoz. Cities were generally fortified, and a network of castles and *atalaias*
(watch-towers) was maintained. In each city, there was an inner precinct called
the *alcaçova,* which contained an *alcácer* (citadel), cisterns, administrative
buildings and the houses of important military and civilian functionaries.

---

[6] LMS, pp 37–8; Kennedy H 1996, pp 100–6.
[7] LMS, p 745; NHP vol 2, pp 154, 184–90.
[8] Collins R 1995, pp 181, 184–5.

In cities exposed to the frontier, like Lisbon and Santarém, the *alcaçova* was much larger and more prominent than in places like Beja situated in more secure locations.[9] At first garrison troops were recruited mainly from the local Muslim citizenry; but slave soldiers were also used, and increasingly from the tenth century Berber mercenaries from North Africa. Offensive action against the Christian north was usually carried out by strike columns of light cavalry which conducted *razias* (raids) into enemy territory burning, looting and seizing captives for enslavement. Full-scale campaigns of conquest were rare, for they required follow-up with settlements, garrisons and a permanent administration.

After the death of al-Hakem II in 976 the fortunes of the caliphs of Cordoba rapidly declined. Al-Hakem was succeeded by his twelve-year-old son, who became a puppet in the hands of his formidable chief minister, al-Mansur. From 980 till his death in 1002 al-Mansur, a ruthless autocrat but also a military commander of great ability, completely dominated affairs in al-Andalus. He won a series of crushing victories against the Christian north, unprecedented since the conquest, and succeeded in subjugating most of the Maghrib. However, to maintain his dictatorship he effectively dismantled the Umayyad state bureaucracy and replaced it with his own followers. He also relied heavily on Berber fighters imported from Morocco. These North Africans later became involved in a series of bloody revolts and attacks on the local Andalusi population, especially in key cities, giving rise to widespread Berberophobia. In short, by emasculating the caliph's authority al-Mansur contributed decisively to the subsequent disintegration of al-Andalus in the early eleventh century.[10]

The death of al-Mansur and the collapse of caliphal power brought political chaos to al-Andalus on a scale not previously experienced. A period known as the *fitna* or anarchy ensued – and its violent internal struggles fractured al-Andalus, at one stage, into as many as sixty petty kingdoms or *taifas*. Most *taifas* were short-lived, though a few became semi-permanent. Gharb al-Andalus was eventually split into the two large *taifas* of Badajoz and Seville plus the four smaller ones of Faro, Mértola, Silves and Huelva. Of these, by the mid-eleventh century only Badajoz and Seville survived, having absorbed all their lesser neighbours between them. Most of southern and central Portugal was in the *taifa* of Badajoz, which was ruled by the Banu-al-Aftas, a wealthy Berber family with extensive lands in the Lisbon and Santarém regions as well as round Badajoz itself.[11] Though the capital of this *taifa* lay outside the present borders of Portugal it was, at its greatest extent, the nearest approach in the Islamic era to an autonomous state in Portuguese space. Consequently some scholars, however

---

[9] NHP vol 2, pp 192–8.
[10] LMS, pp 41–6; Shatzmiller M 2000 pp 33–4.
[11] NHP vol 2, p 132.

improbably, have seen it as a precursor of modern Portugal.[12] Broadly speaking it comprised all the country in Muslim hands south of the Douro river, except for the Algarve and southern Alentejo, which were in the *taifa* of Seville. During the early and mid-eleventh century there was frequent conflict between these two *taifas*. In the end, the *taifa* of Badajoz lasted for some seventy years, during which its court, especially under the poet-ruler Umar al-Mutawakkil, displayed a certain cultured sophistication.

After the death of al-Mansur the northern Christians quickly regained their self-confidence and – ominously for the *taifas* – resumed their attacks on Muslim territory. Ill-equipped to resist, the *taifa* princes began buying off Christian leaders with a form of tribute or protection money called *párias*. Soon in this way vast sums of gold were being paid to the kings of Leon-Castile and other powerful Christian figures, and the arrangement became institutionalised to such an extent that the eleventh century in Iberia has been called the age of párias.[13] The system eventually broke down after Toledo fell to the Castilians in 1085, prompting the remaining *taifa* rulers to appeal for intervention to the Almoravids, a militant Islamic group that had recently seized power in Morocco. In 1086, the Almoravids crossed the Straits of Gibraltar in force and quickly defeated the king of Leon-Castile near Badajoz. But Yusuf ibn Tashufin, the leader of these tough tribesmen from the western Sahara, then decided to depose the ineffectual *taifa* princes and incorporate their realms into his own emirate. This was done, and for a time the Almoravids appeared to re-animate peninsular Islam. However, the revival proved relatively short lived. By the 1120s, the Almoravids were losing their power base in Morocco, and within a few years were obliged to abandon al-Andalus.[14]

SOCIAL AND ECONOMIC FABRIC

The Muslim population of Gharb al-Andalus was of Arab, Berber and converted Hispano-Roman origin, and it grew rapidly after the conquest. The Arabs were mostly Yemeni and formed a small elite minority. The Berbers, who provided most of the immigrants, came from the Djabal and Rif regions of the Maghrib, some being sedentary Barani, but most nomadic Butr tribesmen.[15] The first influx arrived in the immediate aftermath of the conquest, and more followed at various times over the next two centuries. They settled mainly in the Algarve and other areas south of the Tagus. Probably they never

---

[12] Saraiva A J 1979, pp 14–21.
[13] Mackay A 1977, pp 15–20.
[14] Reilly B F 1992, pp 79–91; Fletcher R 1992, pp 105–12; Kennedy H 1996, pp 181–4.
[15] EI vol 1, p 490; LMS, p 13; Kennedy H 1996, p 4.

totalled more than a few thousand, and though some brought their women and families with them, the majority were young bachelors who subsequently married local women. Most Arabs and Berbers of the eighth century still maintained traditional tribal loyalties. Many tribes were represented among the immigrants to Gharb al-Andalus, and initially some attempt was probably made to settle particular groupings in discrete locations. Disputes and violent clashes among the tribes and between Arabs and Berbers were not uncommon; but over time, with ethnic blurring and interlinking of tribal and family networks, such conflicts greatly decreased.[16] Eventually, the majority of Muslims in Gharb al-Andalus comprised converts from Christianity and their descendants. These neo-Muslims were called *muwallads* and came from all levels of society.

In theory both Islamic law and tribal tradition held all believers to be equals; but in practice social differentiation quickly became the norm throughout al-Andalus, though it was more flexible than in the Christian north. The main distinction was between the *hassa* (Muslim aristocracy) and the *amma* (mass of common people). The *hassa* began as an aristocracy of office and never entirely lost this character, though it tended over time to become increasingly hereditary. In Gharb al-Andalus most *hassa* lived in the towns where they controlled the local administration. The *hassa* also owned vast tracts of land, and many supported themselves off rents and dues. It was from the provincial *hassa* that in times of weak central government ambitious local leaders arose and carved out for themselves petty principalities beyond the control of Cordoba. The great majority of the *amma* were tied to the land. There were frequent outbreaks of discontent suggesting existence at this level had changed little since Roman times. The *amma* included many *malados* – freedmen or other dependent labourers – but there were also slave-labourers, for the slave system was as entrenched in al-Andalus as it had been in Roman and Visigothic times. Slaves were acquired as war booty or through purchase. Slave raiding into Christian territory north of the Douro was common; but supplies also came from northern and central Europe and from black Africa, adding to the already considerable ethnic diversity of al-Andalus. Slaves were employed variously in agriculture, domestic service and harems and eventually constituted an important component of the caliphal army.[17]

Muslim Iberia was a strongly city-orientated society. No centre in Gharb al-Andalus was as grandiose as Cordoba or Seville, but towns such as Lisbon, Beja, Coimbra and Silves were all places of substance containing several thousand inhabitants. These cities housed a middle class of merchants, small landholders, scholars and lesser officials, increasingly distinct from both the elite

---

[16] EI vol 1, p 490; LMS, p 683; NHP vol 2, pp 138–40.
[17] Glick T F 1979, p 132; Collins R 1995, pp 192–3; NHP vol 2, p 181.

hassa and the *amma*. While contemporary sources do not recognise these people as constituting a separate social grouping, they were of considerable importance by the tenth century. The social categories assigned to women in al-Andalus generally parallelled those of men. But society was strongly patriarchal, and women, as everywhere in the Islamic world, were largely confined to family roles. However, a few privileged individuals at the various courts, such as mothers, wives and concubines of the Umayyad caliphs, enjoyed richer lives and sometimes controlled considerable property. A few became highly cultured, wrote poetry, studied religious and legal texts and copied the Quran. However, the majority of court women were slaves and servants maintained for pleasure or domestic service – though even for them advancement was sometimes possible, for Andalusi rulers quite often married their slaves.[18]

In the early years of Muslim rule the vast majority of the population was still Christian. However, over time Christian numbers steadily declined, both through conversions to Islam and emigration to the Christian-held north. Christians who stayed on and submitted to Muslim rule but did not themselves adopt Islam came to be called Mozarabs. Their social structure remained largely as it had been before the conquest – there was an hereditary nobility, an intermediate class consisting mainly of merchants, smallholders and artisans, a dependent class of tenants, sharecroppers and vassals tied to the land, and slaves. When the Mozarabs eventually became the minority is disputed; but an analysis by Richard Bulliet on adoption of Arabic first names in al-Andalus suggests Muslims were a majority before the mid-eleventh century.[19] Jews were present, but their numbers were always small, perhaps never exceeding 1,000 in Gharb al-Andalus.[20] They were tolerated on the same basis as Christians and therefore enjoyed much greater freedom than they had in late Visigothic times.

The economy of Gharb al-Andalus was overwhelmingly agricultural and pastoral. Only a small segment of the land – mostly along the Algarve coast – was suitable for intensive cultivation, so that the countryside generally remained rather thinly peopled. Villages were scattered and a much higher proportion of the population was town-based than in the Christian north. Most farming land was controlled by large or medium landowners who either worked their properties directly using slave or dependent free labour, or let them out to tenants. Most land confiscated or abandoned at the conquest was given to Muslim immigrants; otherwise Christian landowners retained their properties, though they were required to pay *haraj* (land tax) and an annual capitation tax. While the scale of land grants to Muslims remains unclear,

---

[18] LMS, pp 711–19; NHP vol 2, p 224.
[19] Bulliet R 1979, pp 115–20, 130.
[20] NHP vol 2, p 144.

significant concentrations of Arab and Berber settlement existed, particularly around Beja in the Alentejo.[21] However, because Muslims were exempt from the *haraj*, the regime's leaders had reason not to transfer more land to them than was strictly necessary. Land formerly belonging to the Visigothic crown reverted initially to the caliph at Damascus and later to his successor at Cordoba. Large landowners were usually absentees who lived in towns, sometimes as far away as Cordoba.[22] The greatest of them controlled many dependents and slaves and owned literally hundreds of properties scattered through different parts of al-Andalus. In the early period of al-Andalus's history, the vast majority of dependent labourers and tenants were Christian; but in time increasing numbers became *muwallads*. In either case their condition remained largely unchanged since Visigothic times.

Most farmers in Gharb al-Andalus grew cereal crops, particularly in the Tagus valley between Lisbon and Santarém. Hard wheat, sorghum and rice were probably all introduced during this period. The cultivation of olives was increased while viticulture was maintained – for fresh grapes, non-alcoholic syrups and fruit juices, as much as for wine. The Middle Eastern tradition of growing fruit, vegetables and herbs was firmly established and a wide range of new products introduced. These latter apparently included apricots, peaches, various citrus fruits, lettuce and spinach. Pastoral activities continued much as before, with the grazing of cattle and sheep ubiquitous; poultry-keeping was widespread, and Christians also reared pigs. Mining of gold, silver, copper and tin continued. The fishing industry, which had flourished since before Roman times, especially in the Algarve, remained important; but it was now more Atlantic-orientated, boosting ports such as Lisbon. There was little manufacturing apart from some woollen textile production in the Beja region. However, significant advances occurred in agricultural technology, especially in relation to water control. Irrigation networks established by the Romans were improved and expanded, new pumping systems were installed to raise water and new techniques introduced for digging wells. Though water mills already existed, they were now improved and extended much more widely. A particularly important advance was the introduction of the hydraulic wheel or *noria,* an ingenious device probably of Syrian origin. *Norias* were mostly animal-powered, but sometimes water-driven. They were commonly used to irrigate land with canal or well water, greatly increasing productivity.[23]

The Muslim cities of Portugal were relatively small. They included Coimbra, Lisbon – which sometime during the Muslim era probably became the largest

---

[21] Collins R 1995, pp 162, 166; NHP vol 2, p 123.

[22] MHP, p 68; NHP vol 2, pp 152–3, 154.

[23] Glick T F 1979, pp 235–8; NHP vol 2, pp 163–4, 166, 168.

town in Portugal – Beja, Santarém, Alcácer-do-Sal, Évora and a cluster of places in the Algarve, such as Silves and Faro. All these towns were established on pre-Roman or Roman foundations. But they were now substantially rebuilt and in some cases, such as Lisbon and Beja, significantly enlarged. Each had its bustling *almedina* or commercial precinct, as well as its *alcaçova*.

MUSLIM FAITH AND CULTURE

In Gharb al-Andalus, where people were identified according to religious loyalties, Muslims naturally occupied a privileged position. Today there is little material evidence of Muslim religious practice left in Portugal, most mosques having been either destroyed or converted into churches during the Christian Reconquest. Yet religion was at the heart of Islamic culture. Every town and village of significance throughout Gharb al-Andalus had its mosque or oratory. These were usually small, square buildings, possibly boasting a minaret. Many were cared for by a single individual who acted as muezzin calling the faithful to prayer. But in large towns religious structures were generally more imposing. The great mosque at Lisbon reportedly had six naves and seven rows of columns at the time of its capture by Christian crusaders in 1147.[24] Everyday religious practice was probably more or less uniform everywhere. The traditional five pillars of Islam – witness, prayer, almsgiving, fasting and the hajj – were fundamental and helped draw all Muslims together into a sense of community. Individual piety was further expressed by reciting the Quran, fasting outside the prescribed times, praying beyond regular requirements and performing acts of humility such as walking barefoot. Perhaps the most striking feature of Andalusi religiosity was devotion to the hajj. Despite the great distance, expense and many hazards involved, a remarkably high number of determined Andalusi Muslims made the pilgrimage to Mecca.[25]

The Muslims of al-Andalus were Sunnis and took pride in their orthodoxy. Their ulama adhered to the Maliki school – they followed the teachings of the theologian and jurist Malik ibn Anas of Medina (d. 795) – and it was not unusual for proponents of other schools to be summarily expelled from al-Andalus. Under Abd al Rahman III, Malikism became entrenched as the official doctrine of the caliphate. Originally a somewhat inflexible tradition, during the tenth century in al-Andalus it became for a while more receptive to outside ideas and willing to accommodate new *hadith*. Then in the late eleventh century, it reverted to more rigid norms, making the official Islamic faith of al-Andalus more formalistic and uncompromising. However, at about this time a form of popular Sufism

[24] *Conquista de Lisboa* 1989, p 78; NHP vol 2, pp 201, 225.
[25] LMS, pp 879–88.

associated with the teachings of the Persian mystic al-Ghazali (d. 1111) was growing in influence at all levels of Andalusi society. Sufism was sometimes linked to political unrest, and in southern Gharb al-Andalus in 1144 a militant Sufi ascetic called Ibn Qasi led a major revolt, proclaiming himself Imam. His actions hastened the fall of the then faltering Almoravid regime.[26]

Academic knowledge was diffused in Gharb al-Andalus through mosques, libraries and Islamic schools. The copying and distribution of manuscripts were widespread, and the level of urban literacy was probably quite high. Islamic scholarship and art flourished in cities like Lisbon and Beja, and in the eleventh century *taifa* courts at Mértola, Badajoz and Silves. Quranic scholars, jurists, philosophers, mathematicians, biographer-historians, poets and musicians gathered under the patronage of such princes as Umar al-Mutawakkil at Badajoz in the late eleventh century. Poetry – religious, romantic or chivalric – was especially favoured. It was not only composed and recited in refined forms at courts but also beloved at the popular level where verse was often put to music – a practice pre-figuring the Medieval Christian *cantigas*.[27]

Arabic was the language of administration and of learning in Gharb al-Andalus, but was also widely spoken – not only by Muslims but also by members of all communities. Andalusi Christians often took Islamic names, and for many Mozarabs Arabic became the normal or even sole language of communication. The contrast between the triumph of Arabic in Gharb al-Andalus, and the much feebler impact of Gothic following the Germanic invasions is very striking. Ultimately, of course, the everyday use of Arabic disappeared in the aftermath of the Reconquest; but its influence on Portuguese was strong and lasting. Up to a thousand Arabic words have been traced in modern Portuguese, mostly relating to foods, plants, agricultural technology, commerce, administration and the military. Many place-names in Portugal are also of Arabic origin, particularly in the Algarve and in the Lisbon and Beja regions, where Arab and Berber settlement was most intense.[28]

CHRISTIANS AND JEWS UNDER ISLAM

For the adherents of any institutionalised religion, keeping the faith under an infidel government is a very different proposition from life within a state controlled by co-religionists. So it was for the Christian church in Gharb al-Andalus. The terms under which the church submitted to Iberia's Muslim conquerors in the eighth century were not unreasonable. Christians were allowed freedom of

---

[26] Ibid, pp 697–8, 895–8.
[27] NHP vol 2, p 220.
[28] Ibid, pp 151, 209.

worship. They kept many of their churches and were occasionally even permitted to build new ones. Their episcopal and parish organisations remained intact, and their monasteries were seldom molested. Initially the Christian community retained its own secular administration for internal purposes, though for how long is uncertain. The caliphal government seems to have demanded some control over the appointment of bishops; but this was hardly a new departure since Visigothic kings had done the same.

Nevertheless, various changes occurred which were clearly detrimental to Christianity. In the principal cities mosques soon took pride of place over churches, replacing many of them. Sometimes Christians were forbidden to live outside designated suburbs. They could not ring church bells, and priests lost the official high status they had previously enjoyed. Christians could become Muslims; but the reverse was forbidden, Muslim converts to Christianity being liable to execution for apostasy. Muslims could have Christian brides and concubines, but Christian men were not allowed to marry Muslim women. Taxes were discriminatory. In rural Gharb al-Andalus these conditions probably did not greatly worry ordinary Christians. Even in towns, they seldom amounted to actual persecution – at least before the late eleventh century. But they were symptomatic of ever-present underlying pressures that were as much political as religious, disadvantaging the church's long-term interests. Arabic displaced Latin as the language of administration and education, and Islamic cultural norms became dominant. Inevitably for ambitious native Christians seeking personal advancement these realities were a strong incentive to abandon Christianity for Islam, and a steady flow of defections resulted, mainly in towns.[29]

In the face of these pressures the vast majority of Christians no doubt tried to adjust and survive as best they could; but the institutional church was soon struggling to maintain itself. Though episcopal organisation remained at least partly functional as late as the twelfth century, very little is known about the Christian leadership. No names of incumbent bishops from the Muslim era have survived for Faro, Beja, Évora or Lisbon, though there was certainly a bishop of Lisbon at its reconquest in 1147, and several bishops of Coimbra are known from the ninth and tenth centuries.[30] Monasteries and nunneries continued to function in Muslim territory north of the Mondego in the ninth through eleventh centuries; but virtually nothing is known about them in the south, though they were tolerated in principle throughout al-Andalus. Two famous centres of Christian pilgrimage in southern Portugal – the tomb of St. Vincent at the Cape which now bears his name and the sanctuary of the

[29] Collins R 1995, pp 204–5, 212, 215.
[30] Almeida F de 1967 vol 1, pp 77–8; NHP vol 2, p 203.

Virgin Mary at Faro – survived and were respected by Muslim authorities. A few individual Christians offered zealous defiance deliberately courting martyrdom, such as St. Sisnando, who was executed at Évora in 851. But fanatical behaviour was discouraged by the church hierarchy, while most *qadis* imposed the mandatory death sentence on such zealots only with great reluctance.[31]

As time passed the church in al-Andalus became more isolated and inward-looking. Probably this was inevitable given the authorities' suspicion of any ecclesiastical contacts with outside Christian powers. But the sense of isolation was also aggravated by the unorthodox views of certain local church leaders themselves, particularly concerning the remarkable doctrine of Adoptionism. The notion that Jesus was the son of God only by adoption was first propounded by Bishop Elipandus of Toledo in the late eighth century and was soon accepted by various prominent clerics in Gharb al-Andalus, including a bishop of Braga. However, the doctrine was condemned by Rome. A seemingly obscure Christological controversy, the dispute over Adoptionism shows that elements within the Mozarab church sought compromises which might bridge theological differences with Islam and Judaism; but they found no echo in the wider church outside the peninsula.[32]

The isolation of the church in al-Andalus also meant that the religious practices of the Mozarabs grew more conservative, yet simultaneously more influenced by mainstream Arab culture. The Mozarab liturgy remained stubbornly Visigothic, expressed in the archaic peninsular Latin of the time of the Muslim conquest. Church leaders understood the importance of maintaining Latin and resisting the encroachments of Arabic, but did so with increasing difficulty. The Bible and other sacred texts were eventually translated into Arabic, and the Mozarab population became more and more immersed in Arab ways. At the final triumph of the Reconquest, some Mozarab communities were so Arabized that they needed interpreters to communicate with their victorious co-religionists.[33] However, bilingualism was more common, and most Mozarabs within their own community probably spoke Lusitano, a Latin-derived dialect with strong Arabic input. It was primarily through Lusitano that Arabic vocabulary entered modern Portuguese.[34]

As we shall see, the sometimes uneasy modus vivendi maintained between the Muslim authorities and the church rapidly deteriorated after the intervention of the Almoravids at the end of the eleventh century. Both the Almoravids – and the Almohads who followed them – rejected the tolerant policies

---

[31] Almeida F de 1967 vol 1, pp 74–5; Collins R 1995, pp 211–12; NHP vol 2, p 202.
[32] Almeida F de 1967 vol 1, p 74; LMS, p 173.
[33] LMS, p 702.
[34] NHP vol 2, p 209.

maintained by earlier Muslim regimes in al-Andalus and set out instead to impose cultural and religious uniformity. These attitudes were reinforced by a growing Muslim siege mentality as the Christian Reconquest gained momentum. Churches were systematically demolished and Christians driven out or deported to the Maghrib so that eventually, when the last remnants of Gharb al-Andalus were retaken by Christian forces, no organised church remained. A grand experiment in inter-communal coexistence on European soil had finally ended in failure.

Completing the religious mosaic in Gharb al-Andalus was a small community of Jews. Under the emirate and then the *taifas* this community was better treated than in late Visigothic times. However, Jews, like Christians, suffered from the late eleventh century first under the Almoravids and then even more under the Almohads. In consequence their numbers probably declined, though there were still synagogues in many larger towns in the twelfth century, including Lisbon, Santarém, Beja, Évora and Silves.[35]

THE CHRISTIAN RECONQUEST OF THE NORTH

When Musa left al-Andalus for Syria his armies had already occupied virtually all the Iberian peninsula except for a few remote areas in the far north, including the mountains of Asturias. It was here in about 722 that a Christian force led by a certain Pelayo won a small victory against the Muslims at a place called Covadonga. Possibly, as the late ninth century 'Chronicle of Alfonso III' claims, Pelayo was King Rodrigo's noble sword-bearer and stood for the old Visigothic order; but more probably he was a local leader of the mountain peoples who traditionally resisted all invaders. Whatever the truth, after Covadonga the Muslim authorities made no serious attempt to subdue Pelayo, who was duly proclaimed king by his following, and whose small remote kingdom became a nucleus of Christian resistance and future reconquest.[36] Within a century, Covadonga had been transformed by Christian imagination into a miraculous happening in which Muslim missiles were turned back by the intervention of the Virgin Mary.[37]

In Portugal, the Reconquest – the long, drawn-out process whereby al-Andalus was gradually recovered from Islam by Christian forces advancing from the north – took over five centuries to complete from the time of Covadonga to the surrender of the last Muslim enclave in 1249. Religious differences always underlay the Reconquest; but the early Christian rhetoric was nevertheless as

---

[35] Ibid, p 205.
[36] Collins R 1995, pp 225–6; NHP vol 2, p 257.
[37] Wolf K B (ed) 1990, pp 164, 167.

much political as credal. In the Asturian chronicles of the ninth and tenth centuries, the struggle was presented as 'just' because it was waged to reclaim a stolen Visigothic inheritance. But in practice more mundane motives were often foremost, including the desire for booty and protection money.

These basic drives, and the fact that cultural interaction with the Muslim world was considerable, not infrequently led to deals and understandings that blurred the lines of faith. There were long interludes of relative peace, broken by periods of heightened conflict. As Fernández-Armesto has shown, the sense of a long, continuing struggle between good and evil – Christianity and Islam – was strong at the Leonese court around the year 1000.[38] But it was not until the late eleventh century that religious fanaticism might be considered the dominant driving force of the Reconquest – and even then, it was far from being the only spur. The territorial ambitions of Christian leaders, sometimes involving intense competition, was another factor of growing importance.

The emergence of the kingdom of Portugal was a long-term by-product of Christian expansion that had its roots in Asturias. After Covadonga the eighth century Asturian kings consolidated their realm, incorporating neighbouring Galicia and the Basque country. Pelayo's successor, Alfonso I (739–57), declared his descent from Leovigild, effectively laying claim to the Visigothic inheritance. Soon Asturian raiders were penetrating as far south as the Douro valley, laying waste the countryside and plundering Muslim-held towns, including Portucale, Braga, Chaves and Viseu. Unable to hold these places, Alfonso is said to have forced their Christian inhabitants to move north, leaving a deserted buffer zone separating Christian and Muslim territory known as the *ermamento*. The extent of the *ermamento*, whether it arose more from forced or spontaneous depopulation, and indeed whether it existed at all, are contested issues among historians.[39] However, it seems that while many people did migrate from the region to safer areas, others remained, and in the late eighth century the *ermamento* was a virtually autonomous no-man's land outside the control of either side.[40] But in the ninth century, when the emirate in Cordoba was weak and troubled by internal revolts, the Asturian kings were able to move in and establish a presence in the area.

Parts of northern Portugal, notably Minho and Trás-os-Montes, began to be incorporated into the kingdom of Asturias from about the 850s. Subsequently, Alfonso III (866–911) extended his control over most territory north of the Douro – and even into some areas between the Douro and Mondego, regions in which Cordoba apparently showed little interest. The processes of settling

[38] Fernández-Armesto F 1992, pp 130–7.
[39] SHP vol 1, pp 58–60.
[40] Mattoso J 1985, pp 15–17.

these lands and establishing an administrative framework were then pressed forward in the late ninth century. Two important landmark achievements were the seizure of the towns of Portucale in 868 and Coimbra in 879. Vímara Peres, the captor of Portucale, was appointed its count with responsibility for most of Entre Douro e Minho, the area between the Minho and Douro rivers. He was granted generous benefices, and his family remained pre-eminent in the region until 1071.

Under the Peres family, Portucale became a flourishing town and already had its own bishop by the end of the ninth century. Braga, the old capital of Gallaecia, was much decayed; but efforts were now made to restore it, though it was over a century before its bishop returned. A monastery and fortress were also now constructed at the villa of Guimarães, which developed into the spiritual shrine and principal military stronghold of the Peres family. The counts of Portucale worked hard to repopulate Entre Douro e Minho by attracting to it Christian settlers from the north as well as Mozarabs from the south.[41] Meanwhile, counts were also appointed to other important centres in the re-occupied territories, including Chaves and Coimbra. Coimbra was the key to the Mondego valley, but was close to the frontier and therefore vulnerable to Muslim attack. Having been substantially Islamised, it for long retained a predominantly Mozarab population. To Count Hermenegildo Guterres of Coimbra, and his descendants, cultural tolerance and good relations with Cordoba were therefore particularly important.[42]

The counts of Portucale and Coimbra have traditionally been regarded as playing significant if perhaps unwitting roles as precursors of the Portuguese kingdom. In particular, the counts of Portucale have attracted attention because of their association with the place that gave the kingdom its name. The word 'Portucale' (Portugal) is derived from the Latin Portus Cale. In Roman times, Cale was a settlement on the left bank of the Douro near its mouth, where the river met the road coming up from the south. There was also a small port on the right bank, and there the Suevi later built a fortress, around which the town grew. Located in fertile country and at a major communications junction, it eventually became Porto, Portugal's second city; but in the ninth and tenth centuries it was usually called Portucale. The term 'Portucale' was also sometimes applied to the entire region between the Minho and Mondego rivers – eventually giving its name to the kingdom of Portugal itself.[43]

Meanwhile, after the death of Alfonso III in 910, the kings of Asturias had shifted their court down to Leon on the Spanish meseta, and the kingdom

[41] MHP, p 47; NHP vol 2, pp 249, 274, 276.
[42] Mattoso J 1985, pp 22–3.
[43] SHP vol 1, pp 61–2; NHP vol 2, p 259.

itself had become known as Leon. The move signalled increasing Christian self-confidence and greater commitment to the permanent occupation of re-conquered land. Coincidently the accession of Abd al-Rahman III in al-Andalus helped to stabilise for the time being the western border between Christian and Muslim territory on the line of the Mondego; but when conflict returned in the era of al-Mansur, it was the Muslim side that took the initiative. The period of al-Mansur's supremacy (980–1002) constituted a terrifying interlude for the Christian north. Repeated raids into Leonese territory wrought widespread destruction and resulted in the capture and enslavement of large numbers of Christian prisoners.[44] In 987 al-Mansur retook Coimbra, then captured and destroyed the city of Leon. King Vermudo II (982–99) was forced to submit and marry his daughter to al-Mansur.[45] In 997, al-Mansur launched a great raid into what is now northern Portugal and Galicia where he captured and burned the pilgrim city of Compostela. Though he spared the shrine of St. James, he carried off the cathedral's bells and doors to Cordoba, where they were melted down to make chandeliers for the great mosque. Large tracts of the Christian north were ravaged over the next few years, and the border with al-Andalus was pushed back to the Douro.

However, despite the widespread panic and mayhem caused by al-Mansur, his campaigns were more predatory and prestige-building than imperial. Al-Mansur was a master of the *razia* in the classic Muslim tradition; but he showed little interest in permanently extending al-Andalus beyond the Douro or in sponsoring Muslim re-settlement. Consequently the impact of his campaigns, though momentarily stunning, soon faded. Moreover, after 1008 conflict between Andalusis and the imported Berber soldiery enveloped al-Andalus, bringing its spectacular military revival to a rapid end. Within a decade or two of al-Mansur's death, the nightmare of his career for the Christians was over, and their advance had resumed.[46]

Leon meanwhile was becoming overshadowed by the growing size and importance of Christian Castile. In 1035 Castile was transformed from a semi-autonomous county on the eastern frontier of Leon into an independent kingdom which rapidly assumed leadership within Christian Iberia. Fernando I 'the Great' of Castile (1037–65) married the sister and heiress of the king of Leon, and the latter kingdom was absorbed into its larger neighbour. Fernando was now the pre-eminent Christian figure in Iberia, and he styled himself emperor, claiming a general overlordship. A consequence of Fernando's ascendancy was a shift in the focus of Christian power from the north of the peninsula towards Castile.

[44] LMS, pp 42–4, Fernández-Armesto F 1992, pp 134–5.
[45] LMS, p 13.
[46] NHP vol 2, pp 260–4.

On the other side of the frontier, al-Andalus in the early eleventh century had dissolved into a patchwork of *taifa* principalities with much reduced capacity to resist military pressure. Consequently, all the Christian losses sustained in the time of al-Mansur were soon recovered. In 1064, the Christians re-occupied Coimbra and then went on to extend the frontier to the Tagus. Fernando entrusted reoccupied Coimbra to one of his confidential aides, the Mozarab Sisnando Davidis. Sisnando had been educated at the *taifa* court in Seville and was thoroughly familiar with Islamic culture. A tolerant broadminded governor, he was respected by the Muslims and Mozarabs under his charge and ruled Entre Douro e Mondego with considerable sensitivity until his death in 1091.[47] Nevertheless, the reconquered lands of northern Portugal remained politically fragmented. The counts of Portucale and Coimbra, whose domains were separated by the Douro, were rivals often at loggerheads. Like other counts they focussed on their own territories and interests, and their careers betray no consciousness of a nascent Portuguese nationhood. As late as the eleventh century there were still no leaders who identified with 'Portugal'.

[47] Mackay A 1977, pp 22, 24; DIHP vol 2, p 224.

5

The Medieval Kingdom

THE *CONDADO PORTUCALENSE*

Portugal's emergence as an independent kingdom during the twelfth century, and its attainment of more or less its present borders by the mid-thirteenth century, seem from a long-term perspective somewhat surprising. Geographically-speaking Portugal is not a particularly coherent expanse of territory, consisting as it does of markedly different northern and southern regions which have more in common with neighbouring parts of Spain than they do with each other. Nor had 'Portugal' ever been a recognised political entity before. There was no language common and exclusive to its people, no awareness of a distinctive shared tradition. It is difficult to identify any convincing long-term reason to explain Portugal's rather sudden appearance. On the other hand, the formation of the kingdom does make sense in the context of certain medium- to short-term political developments closely linked to the twelfth-century Reconquest – and to these we must now turn.

As the territory under Christian rule expanded, so the problems faced by the kings of Leon-Castile in trying to control outlying regions like Portucale and Coimbra became more acute. The counts of these two entities, which were still frontier regions exposed to Muslim attacks, acquired important and self-enhancing military functions which helped them consolidate their personal power. They also accumulated vast estates and lucrative perquisites of office and took care to entrench their families through strategic marriages, and by arranging whenever possible for succession by adult male relatives rather than minors or women. In these ways, they achieved both dynastic continuity and a considerable degree of local autonomy.

Eventually the crown of Leon-Castile became alarmed at the extent of comital autonomy and in the mid-eleventh century began to take steps to reassert its authority. Fernando the Great formally dismissed the counts of Portucale and Coimbra and tried to replace them with men directly responsible to himself. In 1071, the count of Portucale, faced with a calamitous loss of his prestige and fortune, responded by revolting, but was defeated and killed by Fernando's successor, King Garcia. In consequence, the family of Vímara Peres, after almost two centuries of local pre-eminence, was removed as a political force. In 1088 the count of Galicia likewise revolted and was similarly suppressed. These events effectively spelled the end for the time being of semi-independent comital territories.[1]

The success of the kings of Leon-Castile in restoring their authority in the territories of Portucale and Coimbra owed much to support deliberately sought and received from the middle and lesser nobility known in this period as *infanções*. These were mostly rural landowners of Minhoto descent, who either lived in Minho itself or had settled further south, though some were of Galician or Mozarab background. Their lands were usually of modest size but geographically concentrated, enhancing their local linkages. This contrasted with the counts, lords of much vaster but more scattered domains, who were frequently absentee and often seemed remote. In by-passing the counts and turning for support to the *infanções* the kings of Leon-Castile inadvertently helped the latter in the long term to become more aware of their collective interests and intensified the process of seigneurialisation.[2]

Also contributing significantly to the emergence of Portugal as a viable political entity was a growing population of sturdy commoners. Some of these commoners were descended from local inhabitants preceding the Christian re-occupation; but probably most were settlers from relatively crowded Minho and Galicia. Because of its access to these well-populated regions Portugal enjoyed a considerable advantage over other expanding Christian regions, particularly Castile, which lacked equivalent manpower reservoirs.[3] From Minho and Galicia came most of the Christian settlers who rapidly repopulated the Douro valley, Trás-os-Montes and Beira Alta in the ninth and tenth centuries and reinforced the Mozarabs of the Coimbra region in the eleventh century. These settlers formed self-reliant communities, urban or rural, which were administered by local *concelhos* (councils). The councils were often granted charters. The growth of such communities gradually increased cultural and linguistic coherence.[4]

After suppressing the counts, the kings of Leon-Castile tried to check the centrifugal tendencies of their outlying territories by appointing governors with less capacity to act independently. In 1093 Alfonso VI appointed Raymond of

---

[1] Mattoso J 1985, pp 30–1, 34–5.
[2] Mattoso J 1992, pp 93–5; NHP vol 2, pp 329–30.
[3] Glick T F 1979, p 46.
[4] Mattoso J 1985, pp 15, 16, 19; Mattoso J 1992, pp 94, 96–7.

Burgundy, a foreigner with no local roots or political connections, to govern the whole region from Galicia to the Gharb al-Andalus border. Alfonso himself had strong Burgundian links, having married Constance, sister of the duke of Burgundy, in 1073. Raymond had come to Iberia, like other French and Burgundian knights in the late eleventh century, to participate in the Reconquest. He had been welcomed at Alfonso's court and in 1087 had married Alfonso's only legitimate daughter, Urraca. Doubtless the king hoped such a man, brought into his own family, would prove a loyal lieutenant. Raymond's appointment was also backed by the Cluniac monks who had recently become an influential force in Leon and whose mainspring was in Burgundy.

Raymond was soon followed to Alfonso VI's court by Henri of Burgundy, another northern noble destined to play a crucial role in the emergence of an independent Portugal. Raymond and Henri were not cousins as often assumed: Raymond's father was the count of Burgundy while Henri was a younger son of the duke of Burgundy and a nephew of Queen Constance. Nevertheless, the two were linked by a family marriage, Raymond's sister being the wife of Henri's older brother. Both were also related to the Capets, the royal family of France.[5] In about 1095 Alfonso appears to have decided that the territory he had handed over to Raymond was too big, and he therefore divided it into two. This move was crucial for the subsequent emergence of an independent Portugal, for it separated Portucale and Coimbra administratively from Galicia – in other words it effectively split what had once been ancient Gallaecia along the line of the Minho river.

This division marked the culmination of a long evolutionary process. The southern frontier of ancient Gallaecia had been the Douro river; but much of the territory north of that river had fallen to the Muslims in the early eighth century. What was left under Christian control continued to be called Gallaecia, but comprised only a small portion of its ancient namesake. However, as the Reconquest progressed Gallaecia's southern frontier was again gradually extended, until by the tenth century the name was applied to the whole area as far south as the Mondego. The practice then developed of confining the name Gallaecia, now in the form 'Galicia', just to the northern confines of this region. At the same time the area between the Minho and Douro became known as the territory of Portucale and that between the Douro and the northern frontier of Gharb al-Andalus the territory of Coimbra.[6] But because by the 1090s the territory of Coimbra had greatly shrunk as a result of Almoravid advances, what remained was simply bracketed with Portucale to form a single unit called the *condado Portucalense* or earldom of Portugal. In about 1095, Alfonso VI granted this entity to Henri, as both an hereditary fief and a life governorship,

[5] HP vol 2, p 24.
[6] NHP vol 2, pp 266, 271–3.

while Raymond kept Galicia. The arrangement was sealed by Henri's marrying Teresa, Alfonso's bastard daughter.

The combining of Portucale and Coimbra into a single earldom under the name of the former was a crucial step, for here was the nucleus of the future Portuguese kingdom. Henri administered the earldom as a faithful vassal of the kings of Leon-Castile until his death. He was never a formally independent ruler and as long as Alfonso VI lived always acknowledged him as overlord. Henri spent much time at the Leonese court; but he nevertheless pursued policies deliberately designed to strengthen his earldom's autonomy, such as backing the primatial claims of the see of Braga against those of Toledo and Compostela. When Alfonso VI eventually died in 1109, and sporadic civil war broke out in Leon-Castile over the succession, Henri quietly discontinued his feudal obligations – becoming, to all intents and purposes, a ruler in his own right.

Henri died in 1112 when his son Afonso Henriques was still a minor. Control of the earldom then devolved upon his widow Teresa, who immediately fell under strong pressure to re-marry. To understand what happened next we must briefly return to Raymond and Urraca, and their young son, Alfonso Raimundes. Raymond had died a few years before Henri, and Urraca had then married the king of Aragon. A condition of this union was that the throne of Leon would go to the oldest son of the new marriage, but that Alfonso Raimundes would receive Galicia as an autonomous kingdom. Alfonso Raimundes's upbringing was accordingly entrusted to Pedro Froilaz de Trava, a Galician nobleman, and soon the Trava family dominated the young prince's following. To maximise their protégé's inheritance the Travas wished to re-attach the *condado Portucalense* to Galicia and to this end sought to persuade the widowed Teresa to marry one of their own number.

For Teresa to marry a Trava would have subsumed the *condado Portucalense* within the kingdom of Galicia and completely reversed the policy of autonomy doggedly pursued by Henri since the 1090s. It would also have threatened the locally entrenched political and social dominance of the earldom's *infanções* who made clear their wishes that Teresa either remain single or marry one of themselves.[7] Initially Teresa resisted the overtures of the 'Galician' party, but then gradually succumbed to the influence of the Travas. First her daughter was married to a Trava, and then she herself apparently became the lover of Pedro Froilaz's son, Fernando Peres de Trava, whom she may have secretly married. By 1121 this ambitious Galician was effectively the governor of Portugal, and this finally brought to a head the issue of the *condado Portucalense*'s status. One after another the heads of the earldom's leading

7 HP vol 2, pp 44, 46–7; NHP vol 3, pp 21–2.

noble families – the Sousas, the Mendes, the Ribadouros and others – left Teresa's court. They were followed by the bishops of Porto and Coimbra. By 1127 a movement of open revolt had begun against Teresa and the Travas – at the head of which was Afonso Henriques.

Why Afonso Henriques decided to move against his mother is nowhere clearly stated; but it is likely he closely identified with at least some of the discontented nobility. His upbringing had been entrusted to the Mendes family, lords of Riba de Ave, with whom he lived through his childhood and youth. In 1122, when about thirteen years of age, he was apparently taken by Dom Paio Mendes, archbishop of Braga, to Zamora cathedral for his initiation into knighthood. Therefore when the contest between the 'Galician' and 'Portuguese' parties in the *condado Portucalense* reached its climax in 1127 Afonso Henriques was a young man who had lived virtually all his life among the *infançōes* and surely shared their values. He was then only eighteen, but earlier that year had demonstrated both his warrior mettle and political adroitness by defending Guimarães against Alfonso VII of Leon and subsequently securing his withdrawal in return for an acceptable form of submission.

The decisive battle between the forces of Afonso Henriques and Teresa took place at São Mamede near Guimarães on 24 June 1128. The former were completely victorious, and the Travas were quickly expelled. Teresa herself withdrew to Galicia where she died in 1130. São Mamede was a resounding rejection of the Galician option – a rejection clearly backed by the bulk of the *infançōes,* for the first time acting as a coherent interest group and demonstrating a willingness and capacity to pursue collective goals. Only from such action could awareness of 'a common destiny' in turn be born.[8] But while São Mamede set a course firmly towards independence, it should not be understood as representing a patriotic movement in the modern sense. The nobles who fought alongside Afonso Henriques did so not to defend some idealised 'nation', but to protect their own interests. They were ensuring unwelcome outsiders did not assume control of a territory they had come to regard as theirs by right.

AFONSO HENRIQUES AND THE FOUNDING OF THE KINGDOM

Afonso Henriques emerged from São Mamede the autonomous ruler of a large segment of western Iberia stretching from the river Minho to the Gharb al-Andalus border. He pointedly declined to call himself count, adopting instead the more illustrious titles of *infante* or *principe,* implying royal descent and perhaps also the expectation of a royal inheritance.[9] Nevertheless, like other

---

[8] Mattoso J 1992, p 98.
[9] HP vol 2, p 58.

contemporary Iberian rulers he continued to acknowledge that his authority derived from the king-emperor of Leon-Castile to whom he owed fealty, and at this stage he did not take the crucial step of assuming the title of *rex* (king). However, in about 1131 he shifted his court from Guimarães to Coimbra. This was a strategically important move because it distanced him from the northern nobility whose strongholds dominated Minho and the lower Douro and Vouga regions, allowing him instead to focus on the southern frontier. Those who had brought Afonso Henriques to power were left to enjoy their lands and rights undisturbed, and their loyalty was consequently retained. At the same time, in the region from Coimbra southwards, which lacked an established seigneurial nobility, Afonso Henriques could impose his will more firmly. Moreover Coimbra was a better base from which to prosecute the Reconquest, an enterprise essential to the enhancement of Afonso Henriques's credibility. In Coimbra he could reap the benefits of association with the monastery of Santa Cruz, recently founded by the Augustinian canons – an institution which soon became the intellectual collaborator, spiritual guardian and eventually pantheon of the Burgundian dynasty. In Coimbra Afonso Henriques and his regime were also more directly in contact with the Mozarabs and the traditions of the south.

Afonso Henrique's eventual decision to proclaim himself king was not surprisingly linked to his successful expansion southwards into former Gharb al-Andalus. The catalyst was the battle of Ourique (1139), his most celebrated victory over a Muslim force. The battle itself is wreathed in much mystery. No one really knows where it took place, though various possibilities have been suggested ranging from northern Estremadura to Baixo Alentejo, or even across the border in Castile. Ourique may have been part of a campaign of conquest – or may have stemmed from a mere *razia*. Whatever the case, its reputation quickly grew and attained major symbolic importance. Allegedly it was fought on 25 July, the feast of St. James, patron of the Reconquest. In any event, not long after the battle and as a direct consequence of it Afonso Henriques began to style himself *rex*. He was never actually crowned; instead tradition has it he was triumphantly raised on his shield by his following in the manner of a Germanic warrior chief. When he died almost half a century later, a symbolic shield was hung above his tomb in the Santa Cruz monastery. The association of this treasured object with the founding of the kingdom was long maintained; even in the fifteenth century, many believed that when a Portuguese king died the shield came crashing to the ground.[10]

Once established as king within his own territory Afonso Henriques still had to gain recognition from his fellow rulers. The attitude of Alfonso VII, who had

[10] Ibid, p 62.

been crowned king-emperor in 1135 and to whom Afonso Henriques himself had sworn fealty as recently as 1137, was particularly crucial. Of course, assuming a royal title did not necessarily constitute repudiation of feudal vassalage. The rulers of Aragon and Navarre were already recognised kings, yet remained feudatories of the king-emperor. The latter could reasonably argue that the more kings among his vassals the greater his own prestige. It suited both Alfonso and Afonso Henriques to reach an agreement, and this was duly done at Zamora in 1143 with Cardinal Vico, the papal legate, mediating. No text of the deal has survived; but Afonso Henriques must have obtained at least Alfonso's tacit consent to style himself *rex*. Probably in return he promised not to encroach eastward into territory the king-emperor considered his own, and to focus his attention instead on the southern frontier with Gharb al-Andalus. If so the concession was important – for the frontier between the two Christian realms was ill-defined, and the counts of Portugal had long-standing claims within Galicia which both Henri in his final years, and later Teresa, had sought to maximise. Seigneurial relationships in the region were complex and juridical disputes common. At one stage Henri's fiefs had stretched far enough east to include Astorga and even Zamora, and after São Mamede – in 1130 and again in 1135 – Afonso Henriques had made incursions into Galicia, on the second occasion founding a castle at Celmes.

The agreement of 1143 eased frontier tensions for some time. However, in 1157 the situation again became unstable when Alfonso VII died and the imperial title lapsed. Alfonso's dominions were divided between his two sons who became kings of Leon and Castile respectively. For a brief period one son – Fernando II of Leon – tried to assert suzerainty over Portugal. A border war inevitably resulted; but it ended in 1166 when Fernando agreed to abandon his claims to overlordship and to marry Afonso Henriques's daughter. The agreement signified the definitive acknowledgment within the peninsula of Portugal's status as a fully independent kingdom.

There remained the question of papal recognition for which Afonso Henriques had begun lobbying at Rome since before his meeting with Alfonso VII at Zamora. In December 1143, he tried to bring matters to a head by declaring himself both a knight of St. Peter and a vassal of the Holy See. As such he promised to pay the papacy an annual tribute of four ounces of gold, if the pope recognised his kingship and acknowledged his independence of any secular overlord. The initial papal response was equivocal. His Holiness accepted the tribute, but recognised Afonso Henriques only as *dux* (duke) of a *terra* (territory), and not *rex* (king) of a *regnum* (kingdom).[11] It was not until 1179

---

[11] HP vol 2, p 72; NHP vol 3, p 29.

that a bull of Alexander III finally addressed Afonso Henriques as *rex* and clearly recognised Portugal as a kingdom under the suzerainty and apostolic protection of St. Peter. By that time military success against Gharb al-Andalus had extended Portugal's borders south to the Tagus, and a vast program of re-settlement in conquered territory had begun.

EXPANDING SOUTH

For his kingship to be credible it was vital for Afonso Henriques not only to gain formal recognition, but to expand his realm – and serious expansion could only occur southwards into Gharb al-Andalus. The moral and legal justification seemed clear: all rulers of twelfth-century Christian Iberia considered al-Andalus to be occupied territory usurped from the former Visigothic crown, which it was their shared right and duty to recover. This view, which had strong papal endorsement, meant that Afonso Henrique's expansion drive merged with the Reconquest.[12]

It would be easy to misconstrue the meaning of the term 'Reconquest' in reference to Portugal. As such an entity had never previously been imagined, still less actually existed, it could not have been consciously 'reconquered'. When Afonso Henriques embarked on his strategy of expansion he did not do so with some preconceived notion of occupying precisely that part of the peninsula which ultimately came to comprise Portugal. Rather his prime objective was to enlarge the relatively small territory that he possessed between the Minho and Mondego rivers, as opportunity offered, in order to create a viable kingdom. Naturally his southward thrust was directed down the Atlantic side of the peninsula – to which, moreover, it was confined by tacit agreement with his Christian neighbours. But for long precisely where the line separating Portuguese from Leonese and Castilian conquests should be drawn remained unclear, making clashes highly probable.

The later Reconquest – given the prevalence in Western Christendom at the time of crusading sentiment and rhetoric, and the increasing involvement in the peninsula of foreigners who lacked any tradition of economic and cultural interaction with al-Andalus – appears more ideologically driven than earlier. But the contrast can easily be exaggerated. Although there was more peaceful interchange between the two sides during the earlier Reconquest, in both eras the enemy was ultimately defined by creed. However, only in its later phases did the Reconquest take on the full trappings of a holy war, sanctified by papal blessings and endowed with the same redemptive qualities as pilgrimages or crusades to the Holy Land itself.

[12] NHP vol 3, pp 25–6.

It took 110 years from Afonso Henriques's assumption of the kingship for the Portuguese Reconquest to be completed. At first, in the 1140s, the frontier was pushed forward to the Tagus. Most of the fighting during this phase occurred in Estremadura and Ribatejo, though there were occasional thrusts further south. Santarém, the key strategic town in the lower Tagus valley, having changed hands five times in the first half of the twelfth century, fell to Afonso Henriques in 1147. Lisbon was captured the same year – amid considerable carnage and with the aid of foreign crusaders. By the end of that decade the reputation of Afonso Henriques as a formidable warrior king was well established. With the Tagus frontier more or less secured the struggle then passed on into the open spaces of western and central Alentejo. In 1158 Alcácer do Sal was taken on the third attempt, and a string of important towns and districts followed over the next few years including Évora, Serpa, Moura, Monsaraz, Cáceres, Beja and Juromenha. However, in 1169 an attempt by Afonso Henriques to seize Badajoz failed, effectively bringing this phase of the Portuguese Reconquest to an end.

The failure at Badajoz had important consequences for Portugal. Probably Afonso Henriques was hoping to incorporate into his realm all of the former province of Lusitania. If he and his redoubtable mercenary captain, Geraldo the Fearless, had captured the city in 1169, then such aspirations would have certainly been achievable. But Fernando II of Leon could not allow Badajoz, key stronghold of the vital region between the Tagus and Guadiana rivers, to fall to Afonso Henriques. He therefore marched to the aid of the city's Muslim defenders and forced the Portuguese to abort the siege when all but the *alcaçova* had been taken.[13] Meanwhile Afonso Henriques became immobilised by a serious leg injury and fell into the hands of Fernando, who for some time held him captive. The failure at Badajoz meant that Portugal south of the Tagus came to be confined approximately within its present national borders while the contested city in due course became Castilian.

After the Badajoz campaign Afonso Henriques, now sixty years of age, began to delegate increasing responsibilities to his son Sancho. The challenge to the young prince was great – for Muslim military power in al-Andalus had undergone a sudden and vigorous revival because the *taifa* princes, who had reappeared after the demise of the Almoravids, under Christian pressure had again appealed to North Africa for military assistance. This time the response came from a tribal confederation of the southern Atlas Mountains called the Almohads, which had recently been galvanised by a reforming fundamentalist zealot, Ibn Tumart the Mahdi.[14] In 1171 an Almohad army crossed to the peninsula,

[13] Bishko C J 1975, pp 414–15.
[14] LMS, pp 68–9; Fletcher R 1992, pp 118–20.

stemmed the Christian advance and promptly subjugated the discredited *taifa* rulers. Confronted by this dynamic new force the Portuguese Reconquest slowed, then went into reverse. Through the 1180s and 1190s the Almohads made sweeping advances into Christian territory, recovering all the towns lost in Alentejo during the previous two decades except Évora and driving the Portuguese back to the Tagus frontier. But in the long term they could not sustain their momentum. In 1212 at Las Navas de Tolosa, far to the east beneath the Sierra Morena, they were crushingly defeated by a Christian army led by the kings of Castile, Aragon and Navarre, with a Portuguese contingent also participating.

Las Navas de Tolosa was the most decisive battle of the later Reconquest and spelled the beginning of the end for al-Andalus. After the battle Christian rulers all along the frontier resumed their advances. Gharb al-Andalus contained the most isolated and vulnerable of the surviving Muslim enclaves whose fall was only a matter of time. Against a disintegrating opposition Portuguese forces soon re-occupied Alentejo, taking Elvas in 1230. The seizure of the Algarve swiftly followed and was completed by 1249, so rounding off the Christian Reconquest of what had become Portugal. However, Portuguese possession of the Algarve was refused recognition by the king of Castile. Not until the treaty of Alcanices in 1297, after much patient diplomacy backed by papal mediation, was Portugal's entitlement to the area conceded. The Burgundian kings had finally extended their territory to the southern limits of the peninsula, incorporating a region which might so easily have passed to their larger Christian neighbour. The notion that the Algarve was distinct from the rest of the country long persisted, and from the time of Afonso III (1245–79) Portuguese monarchs always styled themselves not just kings of Portugal, but of Portugal and the Algarve.

How can the success of the Portuguese Reconquest be explained? One point to stress is that it was not achieved in isolation. The Portuguese Reconquest was part of a peninsula-wide movement of which it constituted the western flank. Alongside this flank was a central Leonese-Castilian sector, and then an eastern Aragonese-Catalan-Navarrese sector. The leaders of these various sectors were to an extent in competition. They sometimes obstructed or fought each other for a greater share of re-occupied territory and occasionally made tactical alliances with Muslim rulers. But they were united in their ultimate goal of freeing the peninsula from Islamic rule, and to this end they often co-operated. Fernando II may have intervened against the Portuguese in favour of the Muslim garrison at Badajoz in 1169; yet two years later, when Afonso Henriques was closely besieged in Santarém by the Almohads, Fernando hastened to his aid.

The later Reconquest attracted far more Christian participants from outside the peninsula than earlier phases. In 1095 Pope Urban II had appealed to

Western Christendom to free the holy places in Palestine from Islamic rule – and the First Crusade followed. As a consequence anti-Muslim sentiment grew throughout Europe, coincidently boosting international support for the Reconquest. Urban exempted the Iberian Christians from the Palestine crusades urging them instead to free their own peninsula from Islam. By the late eleventh century a trickle of northern European knights was beginning to flow south to aid in this task, attracted as much by the prospect of acquiring fiefs in conquered territory as by the opportunity of raising their swords for the faith. Some, like Raymond and Henri, won the favour of various peninsular monarchs and attained local prominence.

By the twelfth century Portuguese kings were opportunistically using the services of whole crusader expeditions which often called at the kingdom's ports en route to Palestine. This was a mixed blessing because the crusaders sometimes behaved brutally, plundering and committing atrocities like Viking raiders of old. But their interventions could be decisive, as was notably the case at Afonso Henriques's siege of Lisbon, an operation that dragged on for four months through the summer and autumn of 1147 and would probably have failed but for the presence of several thousand English, German and other northerners.[15] These men, who had landed by chance at Porto, were persuaded to participate in the campaign by the local bishop. After the siege some of them remained in Portugal, including an English priest, Gilbert of Hastings, who was appointed bishop of re-occupied Lisbon. Visiting crusaders are known to have rendered significant military assistance to Portuguese kings on at least five other occasions between 1140 and 1190.

Important as the passing crusaders sometimes were, they constituted an essentially ad hoc and unpredictable phenomenon. However, this was not the case with the military orders, another by-product of the Eastern crusades that achieved widespread prominence in Europe during the twelfth century. The two principal international orders were the Templars and the Hospitallers, and they arrived in Portugal in 1128 and 1130 respectively. Their members were recruited mainly from younger or bastard sons of the European nobility. They were disciplined, well-organised and committed for the long term. Particularly from the time of the Almohads they played a major role in the Portuguese Reconquest and ultimately in the resettlement process. They took responsibility for many frontier castles. In the 1150s the Templars were charged with defending Lisbon and Santarém and in 1160 commenced building their great castle at Tomar. The Hospitallers established their principal castle at Belver on the Tagus near Abrantes. During the second half of the twelfth century Portuguese

---

[15] MedHP vol 3, p 107.

chapters of the Spanish Orders of Santiago and Alcántara were also formed. The rule of Calatrava, which had strong Cistercian associations, was adopted by a brotherhood originally assigned by Afonso Henriques to defend Évora, which later became the exclusively Portuguese Order of Avis. All these military orders played major roles in resisting the Almohads and then renewing the Christian advance. By the reign of Afonso II (1211–23), whose physical disabilities prevented him from personally participating in military activity, their leaders had effectively taken over direction of the Reconquest. The campaigns in the Algarve during the time of Sancho II (1223–45) and the final triumph under Afonso III were particularly the work of the knights of Santiago and Avis.

There is no doubt that al-Andalus, on the other side of the frontier, was a much weaker entity in the twelfth and thirteenth centuries than it had been earlier, and for this the periodic interventions of Berber armies ultimately could not compensate. Despite their initial impact, even the Almohads proved unable to consolidate their gains so that the Christians soon resumed their advance. A decisive change had occurred in the balance of power which was already becoming apparent by the late twelfth century and was starkly confirmed by Las Navas de Tolosa. As the Christians' awareness of their strength increased, so did their determination to push on to final victory. Meanwhile, religious fanaticism had hardened on both sides – among Muslim Rabitic zealots fired by notions of jihad, and among Christians fuelled by the ideology of crusade – though in each case the inspiration lay primarily outside the peninsula.

The balance of internal manpower and material resources between Christian north and Muslim south on the eve of the Portuguese kingdom's birth is difficult to determine. However, as Oliveira Marques has pointed out, at the start of Afonso Henriques's reign the rulers of Gharb al-Andalus still controlled nearly all the larger towns and many of the most important castles in Portugal. Coimbra and Braga were the only substantial centres then held by the Portuguese Christians, and Coimbra had been definitively re-occupied only in 1116.[16] On the other hand in Entre Douro e Minho the Christians possessed a considerable reservoir of rural manpower from which could be drawn both fighting men and settlers. As the Reconquest advanced the Mozarab population boosted this advantage further. Then the capture of Santarém and Lisbon, followed soon afterwards by Palmela, Almada and other towns in the mid-twelfth century, shifted the balance decisively in the Christians' favour.

Vision and warrior determination were provided at the leadership level by the first two Burgundian kings. Afonso Henriques in particular had to fight to make his rule credible and ensure the kingdom's survival. Many young nobles,

---

[16] NHP vol 3, p 11.

aspiring to lands and other spoils, were eager to follow where their prince led. Though later kings were not in the same class as warriors as Afonso Henriques and Sancho I, well-qualified subordinates helped fill the breach. As early as the 1160s Geraldo the Fearless, the brilliant and daring mercenary captain who served Afonso Henriques, played a major role in the Alentejo campaigns. Then from the late twelfth century the commanders of the various military orders effectively led the struggle – men such as Paio Peres Correia of the knights of Santiago, whose operations in the Guadiana valley in the 1230s and 1240s became the stuff of legend. The tradition that such figures came to represent also bred a mindset that outlived the Reconquest itself and for long nurtured the image of Islam as the old, enduring enemy – both within and beyond the peninsula.

THE FATES OF THE CONQUERED

As Afonso Henriques and his successors expanded the kingdom's frontiers they acquired Mozarab and Muslim subjects, residents of the re-occupied territories. The Mozarabs were generally speaking content to transfer their allegiance to the conquerors, despite the cultural adjustments required of them; but to Muslims subjugation to Christian rule was naturally less welcome. Many who could flee did so, swelling the population of remaining Gharb al-Andalus and then moving on to southern Spain or Morocco. Others less fortunate died during the fighting, or were simply slaughtered – how many is impossible to say, though significant massacres certainly occurred when both Lisbon and Santarém fell, for which foreign crusaders bore much of the blame.[17] Nevertheless Muslims remained in Christian Portugal, located principally in the centre and south where they became known as *Mudéjars*. Among them were a few landowners and skilled artisans; but the overwhelming majority were poor rural labourers, unskilled urban dwellers or slaves too dependent or poverty-stricken to emigrate.[18]

Mudéjars were tolerated in Christian Portugal as a subject minority for some 250 years. From the time of Reconquest their changed status was soon apparent. When towns were taken their Muslim inhabitants were obliged to live outside the walls. The mosques which had formerly dominated the centres of most towns were either demolished or converted into churches, though smaller mosques were still permitted in outer suburbs. Afonso Henriques and his successors granted protection to Muslims – but imposed on them capitation tax, tithes and other special charges, just as the Muslim conquerors had done to their Christian subjects five centuries before. Urban Muslims were concentrated

---

[17] LMS, pp 705–6.
[18] NHP vol 2, pp 337–8.

in their own ghettoes known as *mourarias* while rural Muslims remained more dispersed. Overall numbers steadily declined, and a century after the Portuguese Reconquest was completed fewer than twenty *mourarias* still survived. These were located in Lisbon, Santarém, Alenquer and various towns south of the Tagus.[19]

Muslims in post-Reconquest Portugal provided a limited unskilled labour force, but had little economic significance and presented no threat to the Christian majority. For many years the *mourarias* were left unmolested and were permitted considerable internal autonomy. But eventually in the mid-fourteenth century policies hardened. Pedro I (1357–67) segregated Muslims from Christians and required them to wear only Muslim dress and display the sign of the crescent. But they kept their mosques and were permitted to teach children the principles of the Quran in Arabic, until Portuguese was made compulsory by João I (1385–1433). There was never any systematic campaign to force Muslims to change their faith, though most eventually did become Christians and merged into the general population. When the final order for expulsion came in 1496 few *Mudéjars* remained.[20]

Meanwhile Jews appear to have adjusted quite successfully to conditions in post-Reconquest Portugal. Jews were generally protected by the Medieval Portuguese kings who valued them for their professional skills and financial know-how. The Jewish community succeeded in retaining its special identity, its numbers gradually increased and the *judiarias* became both more numerous and far more prosperous than the *mourarias*.

SETTLING AND DEVELOPING

In the approximately 150 years between the end of the eleventh century and the conquest of the Algarve, the size of the territory ruled by first the counts and then the kings of Portugal more than doubled. The Portuguese Reconquest was therefore not simply a military enterprise, but a process of absorbing, settling and developing whole new regions. The king could not guarantee his hold on these regions or secure their prosperity by relying on the pre-existing Mozarab and *Mudéjar* populations alone, and a vigorous policy of immigration and resettlement was therefore necessary. Foreign veterans encouraged to remain in Portugal by Afonso Henriques or subsequent kings provided one minor source of settlers. Various northern crusaders, including some Englishmen, remained in or near Lisbon after its conquest in 1147. Sancho I later encouraged French and Flemish colonists to settle in Ribatejo and at Sesimbra.

---

[19] Tavares M J P F 1982, pp 83, 86.
[20] Ibid, pp 88–9.

However, the overwhelming majority of colonists were Portuguese from north of the Douro, particularly from Minho where unoccupied cultivable land was increasingly scarce.[21]

In the eleventh century, when Entre Douro e Mondego was attracting settlers, it was common to acquire holdings by *presúria* – by simply occupying vacant or supposedly abandoned land and later obtaining confirmation of possession from comital or royal officials. Much of the freehold land of Medieval north and north-central Portugal, including many seigneurial holdings, was acquired in this way. However, *presúria* was much less common south of the Mondego and is seldom found in Estremadura and Ribatejo. It was almost unknown in Alentejo where natural conditions favoured large estates worked by dependent labour. In these regions settlement, which got under way from about the mid-twelfth century, was promoted directly by the crown and various lesser seigneurs, both lay and ecclesiastical.

There were two devices commonly used for promoting settlement. One was the creation of seigneuries with their associated rights and immunities collectively termed *coutos*. But Afonso Henriques granted them in limited numbers only and tried to confine them mainly to regions north of the Douro. South of the river he preferred to encourage a non-seigneurial regime – though even there a few traditional seigneuries were granted, particularly in exposed areas along the eastern frontier.[22] The second device was to encourage the formation and growth of communities of free commoners. These communities were called *concelhos,* though the term came increasingly to refer to the local councils that represented and administered them rather than the communities themselves. A formal charter was bestowed on each *concelho* spelling out its rights and privileges. Whether the charter was granted to a pre-existing or new community the principal aims were to attract more colonists, foster economic growth and strengthen frontier defences. Afonso Henriques granted about forty charters of this type, most of them in Estremadura, Ribatejo or Beira Alta. In these areas the Christian conquests of the mid-twelfth century had made available extensive lands for re-settlement and brought important towns under Portuguese control. Immigrants eagerly moved in, resulting in the founding of many new *concelhos.* Charters were likewise granted by later kings, particularly Afonso III and Dinis who sought to consolidate the kingdom after the final demise of Muslim Gharb al-Andalus. More *concelhos* were created in northern Portugal where they helped to provide a counterbalance to the entrenched power of lay and ecclesiastical seigneurs.[23]

---

[21] NHP vol 2, pp 318–19.
[22] HP vol 2, p 66.
[23] Ibid, pp 79–80; NHP vol 3, pp 567–84.

When the focus of action shifted south in the final century of the Reconquest both traditional seigneurs and *concelhos* were overtaken as instruments of settlement by large religious corporations. This process gained momentum with the arrival in Portugal from France of the white monks or Cistercians, the era's most dynamic monastic order. Afonso Henriques granted the Cistercians a swathe of undeveloped territory in Estremadura, where in 1157 they founded Portugal's greatest abbey at Alcobaça. In Alentejo the crown reserved for itself the towns and their immediate environs, but granted out most other lands to the nobility, monasteries, churches and, above all, the military orders.[24] In 1169 the Templars, who had earlier been given extensive lands in the Zêzere valley, were promised a third of all the territory they could conquer in Alentejo. By the mid-thirteenth century the Templars and Hospitallers between them controlled large parts of Beira Baixa, Ribatejo and northern Alto Alentejo. Much of southern Alto Alentejo belonged to the Order of Avis. Further southwest, especially in Baixo Alentejo, were huge holdings granted to the Order of Santiago, balanced to the southeast by smaller territories possessed by the Templars and Hospitallers. All this meant that collectively the military orders were easily the greatest territorial beneficiaries of the Portuguese Reconquest.

When Afonso Henriques became king the economy of Portugal was relatively backward, even by the modest standards of twelfth-century Europe. Activity north of the Douro was overwhelmingly rural. Here the land was divided among numerous seigneuries, their lords ranging from traditional noble families to Benedictine monasteries. Tenants laboured on a patchwork of smallholdings. Wheat, millet, vines and various fruits were widely cultivated while raising livestock, especially cattle, sheep and pigs, was fundamental. The money economy was little developed – as late as the time of Teresa, Henri's widow, there was no mint in Portugal, and such coins as circulated came from Leon or from the Muslim states to the south.[25] Tribute, captives or loot from the Reconquest sometimes yielded useful returns, but were too unreliable to underpin long-term prosperity.

Religious corporations played a key role in the development of larger-scale agriculture in the centre and south of the country, and in this the Cistercians, the twelfth century's model farmers, led the way. Through a system of multiple granges worked by lay brothers, and closely linked to the central abbey, the Cistercians were able to maintain agricultural and stock-rearing enterprises of a sophistication and on a scale previously unknown in Portugal. By 1193 their abbey of Tarouca in Beira Alta had seventeen granges, and Alcobaça probably

---

[24] MHP, pp 81–2.
[25] Ibid, p 57.

more. Later, the military orders adopted comparable economies of scale and sometimes employed notably advanced methods of production such as the irrigation system introduced by the Templars into the Zêzere valley. Surplus production was sold into urban markets.[26] Meanwhile, Portuguese cities became steadily more prosperous as the war with Islam receded. Urban populations grew, and with the encouragement of successive kings commercial activity intensified. By the early thirteenth century signs of a Portuguese international maritime trade were appearing. Merchants from Lisbon, Porto and soon even the Algarve could be found doing business as far afield as Flanders, France or England.

CASTLES, CHURCHES AND RELIGIOUS INSTITUTIONS

Re-occupied territory had to be defended – and in the Reconquest era this was most effectively done by maintaining an extensive network of castles. Before the creation of the kingdom castles were already common in northern Portugal where they formed essential adjuncts to seigneurial power. Often located on strategic hills or mountainsides, and sometimes on the sites of former *castros,* they dominated the landscape and controlled the communications routes. Most comprised just a simple keep, made irregular in shape to fit the contours of the terrain. As well as refuges in times of trouble they served as centres for local administration. By Afonso Henriques's reign they were too far from the frontier to have much relevance to the Reconquest; but they were needed on the borders with Leon, and they long served as strongholds for the northern nobility.

During the twelfth and thirteenth centuries the castles exposed to the war against Islam were those located on or south of the River Mondego. These were often sited to defend a particular town or strategic location – such as Leiria castle, constructed in 1135 at the confluence of the Lis and Lena rivers, which was intended to protect Coimbra and the Mondego valley. Usually such castles formed links in fortified chains built strategically along natural lines of defence. An earlier chain had defended the Douro; another now protected the Mondego and the fringes of the Serra da Estrela, and later still another the Tagus valley. After the final expulsion of the Muslims from Portuguese soil, castles continued to be fundamental to Portugal's defence; but the emphasis shifted to protecting the eastern frontier against the growing threat from Castile.[27]

Unlike the simple castles of the north, those of central and southern Portugal had massive central keeps surrounded by rectangles of crenulated walls. They usually incorporated square corner towers and were constructed of thick stone.

---

[26] HP vol 2, pp 251–2.
[27] DIHP vol 1, p 268; HP vol 2, pp 168–70; NHP vol 3, p 26.

Often there was a protective ring of barbicans, while *atalaias* in the surrounding countryside provided warnings of an enemy approach. Such castles were essential in frontier warfare and gave a distinct edge to defenders over attackers. Before gunpowder, which was not widely used in Portugal until the fifteenth century, castles could be expected to fall only after long and expensive sieges, unless taken by surprise or by some clever stratagem. This helps to explain the relatively slow progress of the Reconquest. Of course, defensive castles were only as effective as those who manned the ramparts. In Portugal, until well into the late twelfth century, this task fell mainly to militias maintained by the *concelhos*. When an attack was expected all men of fighting age in the threatened area could be called on to give service. However, the military orders eventually assumed primary responsibility for defending more threatened regions, and the local militias were gradually relegated to a support role, especially after the coming of the Almohads.[28]

The Portuguese kings of the twelfth and thirteenth centuries accorded high priority to restoring the church in re-conquered territory, which they considered fundamental to the consolidation process, and new settlers were seldom prepared to put down roots without a visible church presence.[29] Appropriate buildings were needed for Christian worship and to serve as cultural and religious symbols. Priests were required to administer the sacraments, recite Mass and generally care for the faithful. An ecclesiastical infrastructure had to be put in place and income provided to support it. Initially, some of the church's material needs were met from what the defeated had left behind. Converted mosques located within the walls of occupied towns often provided the first places of Christian worship; other mosques were demolished and the sites and materials re-used for churches. Where Mozarab churches still existed they were welcomed into a re-organised parish system, but otherwise new churches were built from scratch. Whatever their origins, in the twelfth and thirteenth centuries churches increasingly dominated the landscape of former Gharb al-Andalus, alongside the castles. The architecture was predominantly Romanesque, a style which had its Portuguese beginnings in the north where widespread use of granite gave it a certain austereness. Romanesque continued in Portugal longer than in most parts of western Europe; though in the early thirteenth century the Cistercians constructed Alcobaça abbey in soaring Gothic, the new style spread only slowly.

As the Reconquest advanced a diocesan framework gradually took shape. In many cases, this meant simply reviving bishoprics that had existed in Visigothic times. Mozarab bishops were still functioning in some former Muslim cities

---

[28] Lomax D W 1978, pp 99–101; DIHP vol 1, pp 267–8; HP vol 2, pp 237–9.
[29] Lomax D W 1978, p 97; NHP vol 2, pp 225–6; NHP vol 3, pp 229–30.

when they were recaptured, though in others they had apparently disappeared. Even before Afonso Henriques became king, the sees of Braga, Coimbra and Porto were restored; Lisbon, Lamego and Viseu received bishops in 1147, Évora in 1165, Guarda (replacing Visigothic Idanha) around 1203 and Silves in 1253. This resulted in a total of nine Portuguese sees.[30]

While the reinstatement of these bishoprics was relatively straightforward, grouping them into archdioceses proved far more difficult. Portugal itself had never before been a recognised ecclesiastical entity. The ancient metropolitan see of Braga had covered the same territory as late Roman and Visigothic Gallaecia – which included, but went beyond, northern Portugal. Lusitania had fallen within the archdiocese of Mérida; but the officially-recognised successor of this archbishopric was Compostela, a city now located in the neighbouring kingdom of Leon-Castile.

Afonso Henriques and his successors not unreasonably argued that all Portugal's bishoprics should be placed under Braga, the Portuguese archdiocese. However, Compostela claimed jurisdiction over all sees which had formerly been part of the archdiocese of Mérida, including those in Portugal – and was backed by the king of Leon-Castile. In 1199 Pope Innocent III pronounced that Braga comprised ancient Gallaecia plus all conquests southwards to the Mondego. This gave it the Portuguese bishoprics of Porto, Coimbra and Viseu and five sees in neighbouring Galicia and Leon. However, Compostela retained its metropolitan jurisdiction over Lisbon, Évora, Lamego and Guarda, while the ninth Portuguese see – Silves – was assigned to the archdiocese of Seville. This division was unacceptable to both Portugal and Leon-Castile and led to endless disputes and bickering. Not until 1393 was the bishop of Lisbon raised to archiepiscopal status and the Portuguese dioceses previously attached to Compostela transferred to his authority. In other words, it took fully 200 years before ecclesiastical jurisdictions were finally adjusted to coincide with national borders.

As though this controversy was not enough, Braga was also involved in another long and acrimonious jurisdictional dispute – this time with Toledo. It stemmed from a papal decision in 1088 to recognise the archbishop of Toledo as primate of all Spain, a status he had held before the Muslim conquest when Toledo was the capital of the Visigothic kings. As primates, the archbishops of Toledo claimed the right to confirm and consecrate bishops in all other Iberian sees. But this was contested by the archbishops of Braga who, with strong support from the Portuguese kings, argued they had always come directly under the authority of Rome, and Rome only. So politically sensitive was the issue that in 1218 Pope Honorius III reserved his judgement while enjoining silence on

---

[30] Oliveira M de 1968, pp 130–1.

both parties. There the matter rested indefinitely; but in practice Toledo was always prevented from exercising its claims in Portugal. These jurisdictional issues were important symbolically and practically, with both dignity and patronage at stake. Within a pan-Iberian context they pitched Portuguese separatism against Spanish centralism, raising fundamental issues of sovereignty.[31]

However, for most Portuguese Christians, such episcopal disputes were remote. Their contact with the church occurred at the parish level, and the late eleventh and twelfth centuries were times of rapid parish expansion. Detailed studies of the process are still lacking, but establishing new parish boundaries was the responsibility of local bishops. In the north, more parishes were being founded in Trás-os-Montes while in well-populated regions such as Minho many existing parishes were splitting and multiplying. Further south, especially in re-occupied towns, there was also much growth. By about 1220 Lisbon had eight parishes within its walls and fifteen outside, and many other new parishes were taking shape in Alentejo and the Algarve.[32] The institutional church struggled to keep pace with this growth. In towns the parish clergy were often quite well educated and adequately paid; but in rural areas many were ignorant and poor. Though formally appointed by their bishop, many clergy were in practice selected by powerful lay or ecclesiastical patrons.

During the later Reconquest important changes also occurred in Portuguese monasticism. International orders from beyond the Pyrenees – Benedictines, Cluniacs, Augustinian canons, Cistercians – in turn entered the country, and before them the old peninsular traditions from the times of St Martin of Braga and St Fructuosus gradually gave way.[33] The spread of Cluniac observance in northern Portugal in the late eleventh century meant a gradual phasing out of small community monasteries and their replacement by larger institutions with greater resources and more splendid liturgy. Many leading noble families of the *condado Portucalense* – the Maias, Ribadouros, Sousas and others – were keen to endow and be associated with these establishments. The Cluniacs also exerted their influence in favour of the Roman rite, a key element in Pope Gregory VII's reforms – though its introduction was resisted by Portuguese conservatives. The Augustinian canons, who founded Santa Cruz at Coimbra in 1131, placed less emphasis on liturgy and were somewhat more sympathetic to local tradition. They were not only closely linked to Afonso Henriques and his successors, but found strong support among the middle nobility south of the Mondego. The Cistercians, who reached Beira Alta in the 1140s and then spread south, always settled in sparsely inhabited regions, as at Tarouca and Alcobaça. Their immense

---

[31] Ibid, pp 132–4; NHP vol 3, pp 226–8.
[32] HEPM vol 1, p 54.
[33] Mattoso J 1992, pp 198–223; HP vol 2, pp 183–5; NHP vol 3, pp 230–1.

abbeys, their obvious economic productiveness, their ability to organise labour and perhaps even their social remoteness appealed to the old elite – and not only kings, but illustrious nobles like the Sousas chose to be buried at Alcobaça.

The impact of these various monastic orders went well beyond the strictly religious, extending to the economic, political and cultural spheres. José Mattoso has even suggested that the Cluniac presence in the 1070s was instrumental in giving the *infanções* the crucial sense of shared history that transformed them into a politically conscious dominant class. Without such awareness the *infançoes* would never have collaborated in the creation of the kingdom itself – and in the absence of their collaboration Afonso Henriques's enterprise could not have succeeded.[34]

CROWN, SEIGNEURS AND ECCLESIASTICAL RIGHTS

For most of the twelfth century the central institutions of the Portuguese monarchy remained somewhat rudimentary. The king was accompanied in his ceaseless travels by his royal *cúria* or consultative council. This was composed of his leading vassals and members of his personal retinue – men who owed him counsel and military support. The *cúria* also acted as a central judicial tribunal. A tiny band of functionaries including the *mordomo,* the *alferes* and the chancellor comprised the king's executive. The *mordomo* supervised the king's estates while the *alferes* was the royal standard bearer and military commander; but both offices in time became largely honorific. The chancellor kept the king's great seal and with the aid of a handful of subordinates drafted laws, oversaw the royal judiciary and supervised fiscal administration. By the late twelfth century the chancellor was the most powerful administrative officer in the kingdom, with a major role in formulating policy. Many chancellors, including Mestre Alberto (1142–69), Mestre Julião Pais (1183–1215) and Estevão Anes (1245–79), served for long terms. Most were priests, some eventually became bishops and most were also trained jurists. Only with the development of the new office of confidential secretary (*escrivão da puridade*) under King Dinis (1279–1325) did chancellors begin to lose some of their functions and therefore their power.[35]

Late-twelfth-century Portuguese kings were acutely aware of the extent to which both their revenues and their capacity to govern had been compromised by enormous grants to major vassals, particularly religious corporations. Therefore in the reigns of Sancho I and Afonso II the first systematic attempts were

---

[34] Mattoso J 1992, pp 107–9.
[35] NHP vol 2, pp 278–80; Mattoso J 1995 vol 2, pp 97–107, 112–13; Gomes R C 1995, pp 24, 29–30.

made to claw back some of these concessions. The initial impetus probably came from Chancellor Julião Pais, and the primary instrument was the law. Pais was an able Bologna-trained lawyer, who brought to his task a strong belief in the supreme authority of royal justice. With the backing of the king he sought to strengthen central government through defining legislation. In 1211, at the earliest recorded meeting of the Portuguese *cortes,* Afonso II declared the king's law to be supreme within its sphere, implicitly denying that the church had any jurisdiction over the state in temporal matters. At the time this was a somewhat precocious view; but it was unambiguously re-asserted by Chancellor Mestre Vicente (1224–36?) who pronounced that a Portuguese king within his realm exercised the same sovereign powers as an emperor under Roman law – and derived his authority directly from God, not via the pope.[36] This doctrine was espoused by all subsequent Portuguese kings of the Medieval period. Meanwhile in 1220 the crown had initiated a series of formal inquiries to determine who had a right to what lands and to ascertain if and where royal interests had been usurped. With the exception of the Doomsday surveys in England, these were apparently the earliest inquiries of this type conducted anywhere in Europe.[37]

Not surprisingly, powerful forces within the kingdom felt threatened by the crown's determined moves to assert its authority – and prominent among them were the great religious corporations. By the early thirteenth century, these bodies controlled vast lands and other resources, often with significant seigneurial immunities, depriving the crown of much revenue. Moreover, the church challenged royal authority in other ways, particularly through its sweeping claims to tax exemptions and judicial 'benefit of clergy'. Church leaders also wielded immense spiritual authority, given teeth by the power to excommunicate and impose interdicts.

Differences between church and state, still muted under Afonso Henriques, became more acute in the reign of Sancho I, who moved to halt the alienation of land to ecclesiastical interests. Sancho's less generous stance was partly a con-sequence of changed internal conditions, which could not easily have been foreseen. When the Almohads advanced to the Tagus the resources of the kingdom shrank, while costs increased. Renewed border fighting with the Leonese, then a series of devastating famines and epidemics followed by social unrest, compounded the difficulties. Under the circumstances tensions between the crown and seigneurial interests, both lay and ecclesiastical, intensified, and Sancho soon became involved in bitter conflicts with the bishops of Coimbra and Porto over crown intervention in ecclesiastical affairs.[38]

---

[36] Mattoso J 1995 vol 2, pp 85–8, 90.
[37] DIHP vol 1, pp 23–4; NHP vol 3, pp 100–3.
[38] NHP vol 3, pp 89–90.

In 1211 Sancho I was succeeded by his son, Afonso II. Though handicapped by ill-health – he probably suffered from leprosy – Afonso strove to assert royal authority. But he soon found himself challenged by a formidable alliance of northern nobles, who, alarmed at the erosion of seigneurial rights, revolted under the leadership of the Mendes de Sousa family. This rebellion constituted a serious threat to Afonso, particularly since much of his own army was absent, taking part in the Las Navas de Tolosa campaign. The rebels were aided by Alfonso IX of Leon, while the now independent king of Castile supported Afonso II. Most of the Portuguese prelates rallied to Afonso, who had carefully avoided offending them – for the hierarchy, all things being equal, preferred the stability of royal government to the uncertainties of seigneurial fragmentation.

After the Mendes de Sousa rebellion had been quelled, Afonso II earnestly resumed his father's centralising policies. So relations between crown and church rapidly deteriorated, their mutual animosity much fanned by the king's notorious temper. Afonso wanted the Portuguese church to pay taxes and the clergy to submit to his courts, but met predictable resistance on both counts. His main antagonists were the bishop of Coimbra and, especially from 1219, the formidable Dom Estevão Soares da Silva, archbishop of Braga. A scholar, aristocrat and former close friend of the king, Dom Estevão championed ecclesiastical liberties with the tenacity of a Becket, and his opposition gradually wore Afonso down. By 1223, sick and dying, Afonso sued for peace; but by then the papacy had intervened and demanded the removal of ministers who had allegedly led the king astray. Afonso II was dead before reconciliation could be finalised; so it was granted instead – on humiliating terms – to his fourteen-year-old son and successor, Sancho II (1223–48). Sancho was placed under the tutelage of Dom Estevão, who was to be paid a large indemnity for losses sustained during the dispute. The policy of consolidating royal power, pursued by successive monarchs for over thirty years, was halted in its tracks.[39]

Throughout his troubled twenty-five year reign, Sancho II was confronted by a restless nobility, whose discontent was exacerbated by increasing numbers of landless younger and bastard sons. To occupy them, it was necessary to renew the Reconquest vigorously; but Sancho was incapable of showing the required personal leadership. Responsibility for campaigning was therefore left increasingly to the military orders, royal prestige declined, seigneurial power grew stronger and private castles multiplied. When Sancho reached adulthood in the late 1220s he tried to insist on the crown's rights – and the familiar cycle of confrontation with church leaders, complaints to Rome, and papal intervention resumed. A beleaguered monarch who could not control his realm, Sancho II

---

[39] DIHP vol 1, pp 23–4; HP vol 2, pp 115–16; NHP vol 3, pp 90–9.

was eventually denounced to the pope by the bishops of Lisbon and Porto as incompetent to reign. Deserted by many leading nobles and clerics, he was duly declared deposed by Innocent IV in 1245, and his younger brother invited to replace him. A brief civil war sufficed to install the new king, who took the name of Afonso III (1248–79). The failure and deposition of Sancho II represents one of the lowest points in the fortunes of the house of Burgundy.

AFONSO III AND KING DINIS

With Afonso III Portugal acquired a competent ruler who soon set about restoring order, ably assisted by his trusted chancellor, Estevão Anes. Their efforts were helped by improving conditions within the kingdom. The Reconquest itself was completed in 1249, internal colonisation intensified, many additional charters were granted and economic growth accelerated. Relations with the church by the mid-thirteenth century were less strained. Royal and ecclesiastical jurists had agreed that state and canon law were each supreme in their own spheres – even if argument still sometimes flared over marginal cases.[40] The crown's promotion of itself as temporal legislator, guardian of law and order and fount of justice were now less controversial. Meanwhile the number of crown officials increased, making possible somewhat more efficient administration of both the realm and the royal patrimony. In 1254, Afonso convened at Leiria the kingdom's first *cortes* – a royal *cúria* to which were summoned not only nobles and higher clergy but also representatives from the towns. However, when in 1258 the king tried to establish a commission to inquire into alleged usurpations of crown lands and rights, conflict again flared with the church. Afonso was eventually constrained to pull back. Like his father before him, he made a deathbed submission to the papacy. Having been reconciled, he was buried in the Cistercian abbey at Alcobaça.

Afonso III's successor was his teenage son Dinis whose forty-six-year reign (1279–1325) was the longest of all the Burgundian kings. Under Dinis seigneurial values remained strong, opposition to the crown from great subjects was easily roused and open revolt was an all too frequent reality. Both Dinis's brother and son on separate occasions led rebellions against him. Nevertheless, that the king had the authority and responsibility to exercise certain key functions throughout his realm, seigneurial rights notwithstanding, was becoming more widely if somewhat grudgingly recognised. The institutional framework of royal government was continuing to grow, and nowhere was this more evident than in the gradual extension of the king's justice. Already in the time of Afonso II there was a crown judge presiding over a central court, whereas

[40] Mattoso J 1995 vol 2, p 91.

previously there had merely been a personal adviser to the king on judicial matters. By Afonso III's reign the court's work was such that a second judge had to be appointed, and under Dinis the number increased to four. In the early fourteenth century these royal judges were formally known as *ouvidores* – literally, those who hear. Royal justice was also applied to the provinces where a network of judicial districts (*julgados*) was created, each presided over by a royal judge (*juiz*). Seigneurial courts continued to function, but they were increasingly overshadowed by their royal counterparts.[41]

A man of tireless energy, Dinis travelled extensively within his kingdom issuing laws, dispensing justice, encouraging agriculture and trade, nurturing towns and building castles. He conducted systematic investigations into land titles, as a result of which various claims were found to be invalid and were disallowed. A concordat was concluded with the pope which guaranteed religious orders their property but forbade them for the time being from acquiring more. Dinis also moved to limit the power of the military orders, which had earlier acquired so much land in the course of the Reconquest. He was not hostile to the orders as such; indeed, while some contemporary European rulers sought to destroy them, Dinis generally protected them. But he aimed to nationalise their Portuguese establishments, subject them to crown control and utilise their resources. As a first step, in 1288 he secured a papal bull empowering him to appoint an independent master for the Portuguese knights of Santiago. A few years later the Templars were disbanded by papal edict. Dinis then incorporated their Portuguese members and property into a new national order – the knights of Christ (1319), which in time became the most celebrated of all Portugal's military orders.

When Dinis died in 1325 the kingdom of Portugal had been in existence for almost 200 years. Covering an area of approximately 92,000 square kilometres, it was comparable in size with Scotland or Normandy. Dinis himself was the sixth king in an unbroken line that had begun with Afonso Henriques. These Burgundian kings had reigned on average for over thirty years each, providing considerable continuity. Of course, in 1325 Portugal still retained many characteristics of a feudal state. No definitive resolution had yet been found to the chronic conflict of a centralising crown with a church and nobility determined to retain their special rights and privileges. But institutions appropriate to a monarchic form of government had nevertheless begun to take shape, and the long-term political momentum seemed to favour the crown. As a kingdom Portugal was probably functioning about as well as any other in western Europe.

---

[41] NHP vol 3, pp 107–9, 553–4.

6

The Fourteenth Century

BECOMING A NATION

There is no doubt that by late Medieval times Portugal was already a fully autonomous kingdom. But how and to what extent did its people, inhabitants of a country that had been born of the politics of feudalism and the Reconquest, also go on to attain an awareness of their collective identity, a sense of nationhood and a commitment to being Portuguese?

These have long been absorbing questions for Portuguese historians, giving rise to much thought and discussion.[1] But one fact, already implicit in our story so far, seems undeniable: the kingdom was an essential prerequisite for the nation, and the latter could not have developed without the pre-existence of the former. That having been acknowledged, it can nevertheless be said that by the early fourteenth century one of the key cultural ingredients of Portuguese nationhood was already in place. This was the national language, with an early form of Portuguese being spoken and written throughout the country. Portuguese was a composite tongue that took its structure and most of its vocabulary from the Galician-Portuguese used in the northwest of the peninsula at the time of Afonso Henriques; but it also borrowed significantly from Lusitano and other Mozarab dialects, thereby absorbing hundreds of Arabic words.[2] During the thirteenth century it was increasingly used in official documents, and by the reign of King Dinis it had become the exclusive language of secular government, leaving Latin to the church.[3] Portugal was among the first European states to accomplish this change.

---

[1] Peres D 1992, pp 7–39; Mattoso J 1998 passim.
[2] NHP vol 2, p 209, vol 3, pp 604–5.
[3] NHP vol 3, pp 610–11.

Portuguese was now also widely used in literary compositions. It was the preferred language for the *cantigas* which were so popular at courts and great houses up and down the country from the mid-thirteenth to the mid-fourteenth centuries, and which seemingly owed much to both the traditional poetry of the Muslim south and the ballads of Provence. King Dinis himself and his bastard son, Pedro Afonso, count of Barcelos, were numbered among the keenest aficionados of *cantigas,* which they both loved to compose.[4] There were other forms of vernacular literature – including noble and celebratory genealogies and translations from foreign works on subjects ranging from astrology to veterinary science. Until his death in 1354 Count Pedro Afonso was a particularly generous supporter of such works, and it was he who patronised the first historical chronicle in Portuguese, the *Crónica Geral de Espanha* of 1344.[5] Another significant cultural milestone was the chartering by King Dinis in 1290 of Portugal's national university. Though this institution shifted back and forth between Lisbon and Coimbra several times during the next half-millennium, and was for long modest in both size and reputation, it provided – along with various monastic and cathedral schools – an opportunity for Portuguese to acquire learning without ever leaving the kingdom.

Such developments certainly contributed to the slow but steady growth of a sense of Portuguese identity. However, whether national consciousness had progressed enough by the early fourteenth century to prevent Portugal's reabsorption into some larger Iberian entity, were political circumstances to propel the young kingdom in that direction, was yet to be tested. Much still depended on the attitude and behaviour of the king, and on his family relationships with other royal houses in the peninsula. These relationships were almost invariably close and were constantly being reinforced. King Dinis all but venerated his grandfather, Alfonso X 'the Wise' of Castile (1252–84), treating that monarch's court as a model for his own. Marriage links between the various peninsular royal families were very common. Every Portuguese king from Sancho I to Afonso IV chose his partner from either the royal house of Castile or that of Aragon, while Castilian kings frequently took as brides Portuguese princesses. The possibility of dynastic unification – which would inevitably threaten Portugal's independence and separate identity, given the much larger size of its neighbour – was therefore always lurking. Indeed, from time to time it seemed imminent.[6]

Nor was pan-Hispanism confined to royal courts and dynastic dreaming. While consciousness of a separate Portuguese identity was indeed steadily

[4] MHP, pp 101–4; DIHP vol 1, pp 98–9; Ackerland S R 1990, pp 106–46.
[5] Ackerland S R 1990, pp 25, 33–4, 40–6, 62, 65; NHP vol 3, pp 660–1.
[6] SHP vol 1, pp 397–412.

growing in the fourteenth century, many educated clerics – the most sophisticated group within the kingdom – continued to think in terms of a pan-
Hispanic world. Nobles still pledged their loyalty to the king as feudal overlord
rather than symbol of the nation, while the practical and sentimental attach-
ments of most commoners were overwhelmingly local rather than national.[7] As
always the physical frontier with Castile remained thoroughly permeable:
numerous nobles had interests and loyalties on either side of it, important
ecclesiastical jurisdictions transcended it and in the north Portuguese and
Galicians shared much in common.

Thus a sense of Portuguese identity and a tradition of pan-Hispanism for
long coexisted, if perhaps a little uneasily. It was only in the final decades of the
century that the two drifted, in response to political exigencies, into violent
conflict. That conflict, which took some 250 years to resolve conclusively,
would prove one of the defining issues of early modern Portuguese history –
and its late-fourteenth-century manifestation will form the climax to this chapter. However, before we move on to that climax we need to establish a context.
To do this we shall first review the condition of Portugal as it was earlier in the
century. Then we shall describe the impact of one of the most terrible visita-
tions in human history – the great 'plague' of the late 1340s.

THE ECONOMIC BASE

In the early fourteenth century, Portugal was at the peak of its rather modest
Medieval prosperity and stability. Its population stood at about 1.5 million –
more than at any time in the past. The distribution pattern remained quite
uneven with the most heavily populated region being the old northwest, especially Minho and Douro Litoral. Next came Estremadura, where recent growth
had been particularly high. But the mountainous country of the northeastern
and central interior was sparsely inhabited, while in Alentejo, where few people
lived outside the towns, there were perhaps only two or three persons per
square kilometre.[8]

Though the vast majority of Portuguese lived by subsistence agriculture and
herding, almost all the land was owned not by those who worked it, but by
institutions and elite individuals with seigneurial rights – the crown, various
religious bodies, the nobility and a few better-off commoners. The greatest
single seigneur was the king. Royal lordships were most extensive in the
Alentejo where they probably amounted to over half the land, and even in
Trás-os-Montes, stronghold of the northern nobility, they comprised perhaps

---

[7] HP vol 2, pp 295–6, 546.
[8] Ibid, pp 333–4; NHP vol 4, pp 16–18.

a quarter. Large crown reserves known as *reguengos* had been accumulated in the course of the Reconquest, and some of these still formed consolidated tracts administered by the crown's own agents. However, most *reguengos* had long since been broken up and the segments granted out to various ecclesiastical and lay beneficiaries.[9] Great religious corporations in particular had gained much from this process, the Order of Santiago alone acquiring some 25 per cent of Alentejo. Collectively the nobility also controlled vast tracts of land; but their individual seigneuries tended to be smaller and more fragmented.[10]

A great landowner of this time was likely to maintain one or more demesnes directly administered by his stewards. They were called *quintas* or *granjas* and usually contained a large residence, though they did not necessarily constitute a continuous tract of land. *Quintas* typically included woodland and wasteland as well as cultivated fields and paddocks.[11] The largest were concentrated in Alentejo and Ribatejo, and to a lesser extent Estremadura. Few existed in the heavily populated, highly fragmented Minho region or other parts of the northwest. Although some big properties were possessed by nobles, more of them – and the most choice – belonged to the military orders, the great abbeys and the bishops. The era of powerful lay magnates controlling huge, consolidated fiefdoms was yet to come.

Despite the existence of *quintas,* most seigneurs at this time did not exploit their lands directly, but split them up into smaller units, which they then let out to tenants. Income was secured through rents and seigneurial dues, which were paid in money and/or kind. The basic unit of production was the *casal,* which had its roots in the Roman period. A *casal* was a farm large enough to support an average peasant family and typically comprised a mixture of arable, pasture and woodland. This meant *casais* were frequently made up of scattered patches. They were often very small, sometimes even less than a hectare, especially in the northwest. Moreover, over time there was a tendency for *casais* to be further sub-divided. On the other hand, it was common for peasant families to hold multiple sub-divisions and often more than one *casal.* The outcome was an extraordinarily complex patchwork of minifundia, except in those areas of Alentejo and Ribatejo where conditions favoured large estates.[12]

By the early fourteenth century most tenants held their land by a form of tenure known as *emphyteusis.* This gave security of occupancy variously for life, for several lives or in perpetuity. Tenants paid their seigneur a fixed rent and were usually obliged to make improvements. In the early years of the

---

[9] NHP vol 3, p 400; NHP vol 4, p 74.
[10] NHP vol 3, pp 194–8; NHP vol 4, pp 81–2.
[11] NHP vol 3, pp 400–1; NHP vol 4, p 76.
[12] NHP vol 3, p 402; NHP vol 4, pp 79–81.

kingdom many such contracts had been mere verbal agreements; but from the mid-thirteenth century they had to be formally registered in the royal chancery and confirmed by *cartas de foro* – certificates of tenancy. One such certificate from the reign of Afonso IV may serve as an illustration. On this occasion the king gave two *casais* in the Valongo district near Porto to a certain Domingos de Vouga, his wife and their successors. They were to pay annually to the royal steward precisely specified quantities of grain, wine, flax, vegetables, poultry and butter, plus a small sum of money. If the king visited the area in person, they had to provide various additional items, including a cow. They were required to work and improve the properties and were forbidden to alienate them to the church or anyone of a higher social status than themselves.[13] On accepting such contracts tenants came under the legal jurisdiction of both their immediate seigneur and the king.

It is remarkable just how little the basic features of Portugal's rural economy in the early fourteenth century had changed since Roman times. With bread and wine still for all classes the staples of life, the average *casal* was a self-contained mixed farm with grain field, vines, vegetable patch and a few fruit trees.[14] Wheat was the principal crop, despite being relatively unsuited to conditions in much of Portugal. Vine cultivation was ubiquitous, and wine was frequently specified in land contracts as a commodity in which tenants were to pay their dues. A wide range of European vegetables was grown, including cabbage, spinach, lettuce and broad beans. In northern Portugal apple orchards were common and chestnut trees were valued for both timber and chestnut flour. Flax was produced for the domestic textile industry. In the south figs were grown, while cork oaks and holm oaks provided timber. Cork itself was used to construct various products ranging from floats to bottle stoppers and was already a significant export.[15]

Virtually all subsistence farmers possessed pigs, poultry, sheep and goats. Many also kept a few precious cattle, which were used variously for traction, to supply household milk, butter and cheese and to provide fertiliser. But commercial herding was largely confined to large properties in southern and central Portugal where cattle were reared for beef and hides and in some areas horses were bred. The Cistercian monks of Alcobaça possessed the largest flocks of sheep and produced the finest wool in Portugal. Transhumance was practised, shepherds taking their flocks north to the Serra da Estrela in summer and south to the Alentejo in winter.[16]

---

[13] CP vol I, pp 163–4.
[14] Marques A H de O 1971, pp 26–7; Coelho M H da C 1983, pp 92–4.
[15] NHP vol 3, pp 404–5, 417.
[16] Ibid, pp 417, 437.

After agriculture and livestock-raising, the most important primary industries in fourteenth-century Portugal were aquatic. Portuguese streams provided trout and other freshwater species, while river mouths and estuaries abounded in shellfish, continuously exploited since before history. In early Medieval times, the maritime fishing industry of the Algarve, famous under the Romans, had greatly declined, crippled by market loss, then Viking depredations and the raids of sundry corsairs. But Portugal's coastal waters remained rich in tuna, hake, shark and sardine, and after the completion of the Reconquest the industry revived. A significant shift in population from the interior to the coast occurred, and a string of thriving fishing ports sprang up, most clustered near the mouths of rivers from the Lima to the Guadiana.[17] Whaling was also undertaken, and Portuguese seafarers began to accumulate the skills and experience that later made possible the country's remarkable seaborne expansion.

By contrast with earlier eras late Medieval Portugal was not a significant producer of minerals, with the important exception of salt. The dry climate of the south and the high salinity of Portugal's off-shore waters allowed this product to be retrieved at various coastal sites, most notably Setúbal.[18] Portugal was consequently able to develop a fish-preserving industry and was also a major exporter of salt to northern Europe.

TOWNS AND THE BEGINNINGS OF COMMERCIAL CAPITALISM

Though at the death of King Dinis Portugal remained an overwhelmingly rural country, it possessed a much larger and more prosperous network of towns than at the time of Afonso Henriques. Much of this network, acquired during the Reconquest, was in the former Muslim south, and differences in cultural background, as well as geographical environment, meant that southern towns were usually quite unlike their northern counterparts. The characteristic construction material of the north was granite whereas southern houses were built of mud and plaster. Northern towns were usually small, heavily walled and in appearance Romanesque. Central and southern towns were often larger, and their planning and architecture reflected the traditions of Gharb al-Andalus.[19] Newer centres dating from post-Reconquest times were inclined to be emphatically Christian and often laid out – as in the case of Alcobaça – in parallel streets.[20] But the contrast between the traditional north and traditional south long persisted and is still a basic reality today.

---

[17] Ibid, pp 443–6.
[18] DIHP vol 2, p 197; NHP vol 3, p 452.
[19] Ribeiro O 1992, p 31.
[20] Ibid, p 386.

By the early fourteenth century, throughout all regions of Portugal towns were playing a greater economic role than in previous times. Urban growth had been quite remarkable in the case of Lisbon, which in about 1300 covered some sixty hectares, or almost four times its area when captured in 1147. It had far outstripped all other centres and was firmly entrenched as the most important city in the kingdom.[21] At the same time new towns and suburbs were appearing in many places. In the north Guarda had been founded in 1197, and Guimarães, Braga and Ponte de Lima were all expanding significantly. In central Portugal Coimbra had more than doubled its area since its conquest. Further south Óbidos, Torres Vedras and Abrantes were all developed by the crown, Tomar and Castelo Branco by the Templars. In Alentejo and the Algarve well-located former Muslim cities like Évora and Faro prospered under Christian rule; others, including Serpa, Monsaraz and Mértola, declined.

As Portugal's network of towns grew, so did its trade. Goods passed by land between Portugal and Spain through numerous points of entry, with a regularity impossible during the centuries of Christian-Muslim struggle.[22] At the same time, improved maritime security and the country's strategic location athwart the regular sea route between northern Europe and the Mediterranean meant its ports were increasingly utilised by international shipping. A steady growth in the volume, variety and range of Portuguese seaborne trade resulted – a development of great significance for the kingdom's future. Portugal's exports included wine, fruit, salt, timber, cork and hides, for all of which the principal markets were in northern Europe. Meanwhile, persistent shortfalls in Portuguese grain production meant that the kingdom's long tradition of dependence on imported cereals had already begun. Most other imports, such as quality textiles, were for elite consumption. Overall, the result was an adverse Portuguese balance of trade and a net outflow of gold and silver, for much of this period.

Fourteenth-century Portuguese kings all welcomed foreign merchants, for they generated customs revenue and sometimes provided loans. Italians, particularly the Genoese, probably handled the bulk of Portugal's maritime trade, as well as supplying credit and banking services. In 1338, Afonso IV granted the Genoese a charter of liberties, which was later renewed several times.[23] Of course, there were also Portuguese businessmen, some of whom were now quite active on the international stage – and by the 1290s they already enjoyed formal protection in France and England. Portuguese could be found doing

---

[21] NHP vol 3, p 394.
[22] HP vol 2, p 207; NHP vol 3, pp 488–9.
[23] Diffie B W 1960, p 54; Rau V 1968, pp 13–17; Marques A H de O and Dias J J A 1994, pp 191–2.

business in various coastal and river towns of France, England, Flanders and southern Germany. In Bruges, where a permanent *feitoria* was established, the presence of the Portuguese was so evident that a street was named after them.[24]

THE ORDERING OF SOCIETY: THEORY AND PRACTICE

Portuguese society in the early fourteenth century was conceived of as formally divided into three 'orders' – the *clero* (clergy), *nobreza* (nobility) and *povo* (commoners). Of course, this was an idealisation; actual society was far more untidy, with each of the recognised orders encompassing too many disparate groups to possess much coherence. There was also significant blurring at the borders between the three orders, while many people did not fit easily into any of them. Nevertheless, contemporary literature shows the concept of orders was widely taken for granted, and it received some degree of recognition in law. Used with due caution, it still provides an appropriate analytical framework for an overview of society in this era.

In the early fourteenth century the first order – the *clero* – comprised about 10,000 persons divided almost equally between the secular clergy and the regulars.[25] There was a tiny elite made up of nine archbishops and bishops, the abbots and priors of the leading monasteries and the masters of the military orders. These were great men in their own right who enjoyed generous incomes, kept court, dispensed patronage and often lived in as much opulence as powerful lay magnates. Usually they were well born; but sometimes their social origins were quite modest, for it was not impossible for men to attain prominence in the fourteenth-century church through a combination of luck, ability and good connections. There was a large gap between this elite and the middle-ranking secular clergy, which comprised cathedral canons, chaplains and the like. Finally, there were the lower secular clergy, the great bulk of whom, especially in rural areas, lived material lives that differed little from the common people around them.

At the core of the regular clergy were the old monastic orders with their emphasis on prayer and contemplation and their often aristocratic associations. But there were now also the newer mendicant orders, which deliberately chose to work in the lay world and were deeply committed to evangelisation and pastoral care. The Dominicans and Franciscans – the mendicant friars most active in Portugal – both arrived in the country in about 1216, and both quickly earned respect for their high standards of devotion and austerity. Their focus was urban and their key activities preaching and teaching. Overall, they

[24] Albuquerque L de 1989, pp 14, 18–19, 21–2, 26–7; NHP vol 3, p 515.
[25] NHP vol 4, p 223.

maintained relatively few religious houses: in the early fourteenth century the Dominicans possessed only nine, while the Franciscans had twenty-three. Eight of the latter belonged to the Poor Clares – the female second Order of St. Francis. But Portuguese mendicant establishments were usually much larger than their monastic equivalents, averaging about forty to fifty religious each. This was three to four times more than in a typical Benedictine house.[26] Friars generally, and the Franciscans in particular, were a significant force in fourteenth-century Portugal, their influence extending to the highest levels of society. Many elite persons including members of the royal family, even Afonso IV himself, sought enrolment in the third Order of St. Francis.[27]

Although the clergy in fourteenth-century Portugal enjoyed theoretical precedence in the hierarchy of orders, the nobility were politically more powerful and certainly far more numerous. Nobles comprised up to 10 per cent of the population, perhaps 150,000 people. They ranged from great magnates to desperately poverty-stricken lower nobility with little more than a name, and much pride, to distinguish them from commoners.[28] Contemporary genealogies recognised three main sub-divisions within the *nobreza*. In descending order of status, these were *ricos homens, infanções* and *cavaleiros*. The term *rico* was derived from 'reiks' – one of the few Gothic words to be absorbed into Portuguese – meaning 'great' or 'powerful'. *Ricos homens* were the elite among the nobility, a select group whose members were distinguished for their illustrious lineages and extensive seigneurial holdings.[29] *Infanções* and *cavaleiros* were likewise blood noblemen, but possessed less prestige, and usually far more modest means. In a formal sense, *infanções* in the early fourteenth century constituted a kind of middle nobility; but in practice there was little to differentiate them from many *cavaleiros*. *Infanções* usually held at least small seigneuries, while the distinguishing mark of the *cavaleiro* was that he underwent initiation into knighthood, though this was now becoming little more than a formality. Moreover, by the early fourteenth century, the terms *infanção* and *cavaleiro* were already falling into disuse. Middle and lower-ranking *nobres* were now more often than not referred to as *fidalgos,* a term that simply meant anyone of noble descent.

For most practical purposes, the crucial distinction within the fourteenth-century Portuguese nobility was not between *cavaleiros* and *infanções,* or even between *infanções* and *ricos homens;* it was between the rural nobility and the nobility of the court. The former, which was heavily concentrated in the

[26] Ibid, p 223.
[27] Oliveira M de 1968, p 147; Mattoso J 1992, pp 330–3.
[28] NHP vol 4, p 241.
[29] DIHP vol 2, p 174; Mattoso J 1995 vol 1, p 133.

northwest, derived its income overwhelmingly from the land. Rural nobles viewed the world from the somewhat narrow perspectives of their own, often modest *quintas*. Such men were satirised by court troubadours for their alleged lack of refinement – though not all provincial nobles fitted so rude a stereotype. Some strove to maintain seigneurial courts that reflected in miniature the court of the king himself.[30]

Nevertheless by the early fourteenth century, the reality for many nobles was that they lacked the landed resources to live in the style expected of them. An aspiring nobleman's lifestyle did not come cheaply: it was necessary to support a following, maintain a plentiful table, dress well and generally comport oneself in a manner befitting one's status. The well-rounded nobleman also had to be literate, possess appropriate knowledge, support the church, patronise artists and build and eventually occupy a suitably splendid tomb. To obtain the necessary supplementary income to pay for all this, many were now seeking royal patronage, for which attendance at the king's court was vital.[31] The growth of the court nobility was therefore both a consequence and a contributory cause of more centralised royal government.

Rita Costa Gomes has identified in all a total of 118 noble families associated with the Portuguese court in late Medieval times. Of these some thirty maintained a continuing or frequently recurring court presence, the most important being the Meneses, Albuquerques, Castros, Sousas, Pachecos, Pereiras, Cunhas and Silvas.[32] A high proportion of these nobles came from old established families, although their ranks also included some new names – in most cases raised to prominence as a reward for services rendered. While the traditional warrior function of the nobility was now in decline, it nevertheless continued to provide avenues of advancement for some. Younger sons and bastards in particular might still hope to advance their prospects by serving the king with their swords.

Nobles from other parts of the peninsula also waited in attendance at the Portuguese court. These foreign courtiers sought protection and patronage from the king of Portugal, usually because they were out of favour with their own king. A number of them, such as the Castros from Galicia, in due course acquired court positions of considerable importance. Conversely, Castile attracted various Portuguese nobles who tended to see their larger neighbour as an exemplary kingdom, ordered and governed in a manner more favourable to the interests of their order than Portugal itself.[33] There were therefore

---

[30] Mattoso J 1995 vol 1, pp 192–3.
[31] Ibid vol 3, pp 220–4.
[32] Gomes R C 1995, pp 64–5.
[33] Thomaz L F R 1989, pp 168–9.

always Portuguese dissidents and exiles at the court of Castile, just as their Castilian counterparts resided at the court of Portugal. The ease with which nobles circulated between the various royal courts suggests many saw themselves as part of a peninsula-wide elite, not just a national one. This self-perception was doubtless reinforced by inter-marriage between noble families on either side of the border. In any event, fourteenth-century Portuguese kings found managing the nobility was closely linked to conducting relations with Castile.

The last of the three orders that composed traditional Portuguese society, and easily the largest, was the *povo*. This order included all Christians who worked for a living. As Oliveira Marques has noted, work was considered obligatory for the *povo*; but it was also a right from which members of the first two orders were excluded, at least in theory.[34] Three formal divisions within the *povo* were recognised, the first being *cavaleiros-vilãos* (commoner knights). This term had been applied during the Reconquest to men of non-noble birth who fought at their own cost on horseback; but by the early fourteenth century it had fallen into disuse. Those who comprised the elite within the *povo* were now increasingly referred to as *cidadãos honrados* (reputable citizens) and were distinguished not for any military function, but for their wealth and civic standing. They included large urban and rural property-owners, merchants of substance, doctors of civil law and medicine and various royal and municipal office-holders. *Cidadãos honrados* enjoyed special privileges and immunities and had much in common with the lower nobility. Their leaders dominated the councils of the larger cities – and as the cities grew during the course of the century, the *cidadãos honrados* developed into an urban-based economic and political force of considerable importance. Effectively they were an upper bourgeoisie. After a generation or two the more successful among them often acquired noble status.

The second formal division within the *povo* comprised the *peões*. This term originally meant foot-soldiers, but had lost most of its military significance. *Peões* were men of independent but modest means. Some possessed small free-hold farms, usually composed of several *casais*, while others were lesser public functionaries. The largest group among them were the *mesteirais* – skilled artisans, shopkeepers and the like who worked for themselves, or sometimes for a seigneur, and constituted a kind of lower middle to upper working class. Lacking the immunities and privileges of the *cidadãos honrados*, the *mesteirais* provided much of the tax revenue. The third and final division within the *povo* consisted of *jornaleiros* or day-labourers. *Jornaleiros* included

[34] NHP vol 4, p 262.

agricultural field workers, stockmen, apprentices and servants. All worked for wages and were most obviously distinguished from *peões* by their lack of independent means. In a labour market that favoured employers they had few rights and little opportunity for self-improvement. However, as we shall see shortly, new circumstances from the mid-fourteenth century changed this situation critically.

It needs to be reiterated that real society in late Medieval Portugal was considerably more complex than the notion of three 'orders' outlined here suggests. For one thing, the concept of orders as traditionally conceived gives scant recognition to women, who barely feature beyond their husbands' or fathers' shadows. High-status women led protected and secluded lives, seldom venturing out except under escort. Unless they were widows, or their husbands were temporarily absent, few played an overt role in affairs beyond the domestic arena. Noble brides were obviously needed to perpetuate lineages and seal family alliances. However, many girls, especially younger daughters, were surplus to these requirements. They therefore remained spinsters under the protection of male relatives or became nuns – traditionally Benedictine or Cistercian, but now increasingly Franciscan. An ideal of female spirituality developed in which renunciation became a virtue, and Christ as spiritual husband replaced the possibility of an earthly one.[35]

Non-elite women, whether married, widowed or single, had to work. One consequence was that they tended to manage their own and their families' affairs more actively than their elite sisters, often exercising a considerable degree of independence. Countrywomen laboured with their husbands on the land; townswomen were often involved in petty retail trade, perhaps keeping stalls or hawking everyday commodities from door to door.[36] Women were also involved in all stages of textile manufacture, and many worked as domestic servants or wet nurses. That females contributed to the urban economy was recognised in municipal regulations, for women were accorded a place in religious processions, especially at Corpus Christi. Even prostitutes had an acknowledged role – though Afonso IV wanted them segregated and thought they should wear identifying insignia.[37]

Of course, Jews remained outside the traditional orders; but within their own community there existed a business and professional elite, and a sub-elite whose members earned their living as small shopkeepers, artisans and labourers. There were also marginalised Christians who did not make it even into the lowest ranks of the *povo*. Some of these were considered deserving poor, people

[35] Mattoso J 1992, pp 219–33, 344.
[36] Coelho M H da C 1987, pp 46, 50–5.
[37] Marques A H de O 1971, p 179.

who through misfortune had fallen on hard times and merited charity. Others, marked out as vagabonds, criminals or sundry undesirables, were simply rejected from recognised society.[38] Nevertheless all, from the grandest noble-man to the meanest outcaste, were to be touched before the century was out by one of the greatest natural calamities of human history. It is to this and its extraordinary impact that we must now turn.

THE BLACK DEATH AND ITS AFTERMATH

Portugal's steady growth and internal colonisation in the twelfth and thirteenth centuries were largely the consequence of the later Reconquest, a peculiarly Iberian circumstance. But prevailing conditions in Europe more generally also helped. Between the ninth and the early thirteenth century the European pop-ulation had been gradually increasing almost everywhere, a trend linked to rising agricultural production made possible by a long period of mild climatic conditions. Then near the end of the thirteenth century the climate in much of Europe suddenly became colder. Harvests declined significantly, marginal lands had to be abandoned and regular food surpluses became a thing of the past. Many areas began to experience periodic famines. These famines were partic-ularly widespread and devastating between 1315 and 1322, when almost the entire region north of the Alps was affected.[39] Although there was some improvement again in the late 1320s, those born and reared during the famine years may have been weaker than normal, and therefore more susceptible to disease.[40] In any event, cooler conditions predominated until the early six-teenth century and were a defining characteristic of the transition from Medi-eval to Modern times.

Initially Portugal was less affected by these changes than northern Europe. It continued to enjoy a relatively benign climate and suffered only occasionally from poor harvests. However, by the late 1320s Portugal too had begun to feel some impact, for there is evidence agricultural production had declined, at least in the Mondego valley.[41] Whether this was the start of a new trend or just a short-term aberration will never be known; for it was soon overtaken by the sudden, unprecedented catastrophe of the Black Death.

Until recently almost all historians accepted that the Black Death was bubonic plague, with the pneumonic and septicaemic forms of plague also sometimes present. However, Susan Scott and Christopher Duncan have now

[38] Tavares M J P F 1983, pp 29–54.
[39] Gottfried R S 1983, pp 22, 26–7.
[40] Jordan W C 1996, pp 7–8, 184–7.
[41] NHP vol 3, pp 160–3; NHP vol 4, pp 19–20.

shown this understanding to be mistaken. The Black Death was almost certainly a viral haemorrhagic fever, its symptoms somewhat similar to Ebola. Spread directly from person to person, neither rats nor fleas had anything to do with its transmission.[42] The pandemic was the most destructive ever experienced, moving quickly down the trade routes from the Levant and entering Europe via Sicily and perhaps several other points by land and sea. It reached Portugal in September 1348, most likely first through the port of Lisbon. Soon it had spread to virtually all corners of the kingdom, striking with catastrophic virulence. Places where people lived in proximity to one another such as in city tenements, monasteries and nunneries particularly suffered. The immediate impact on rural areas was probably less than on towns, though the limited evidence is far from conclusive. In any event, by the time the visitation subsided early in 1349 a huge number of people – perhaps a third of the kingdom's population – had been swept away.[43]

The terrible toll taken by the Black Death was later compounded by at least seventeen lesser outbreaks over the next 150 years – an average of one every eight or nine years. In addition a minimum of twenty-two significant famines and eleven earthquakes are known to have struck Portugal between 1309 and 1404.[44] There were also civil wars in 1319–24, 1355, 1383–5 and 1438 and five separate Castilian invasions between 1369 and 1385. Cumulatively, the disruption to everyday life engendered by these misfortunes must have been crippling, allowing little opportunity to recover from the Black Death.[45] While there are no precise figures it seems likely that Portugal's population declined from about 1.5 million in the early fourteenth century to under 900,000 in 1450.[46] Not without reason, Portuguese Medieval historians like Oliveira Marques have portrayed the fourteenth and early fifteenth centuries as an age of crisis.[47]

One of the consequences of the Black Death and subsequent calamities was a widespread feeling of insecurity. Acutely aware of the transitoriness of human life, people sought to make their peace with God and took thought for the saving of their souls. There was an upsurge in public acts of piety and in devotion to the Virgin Mary and those saints whose interventions were considered most efficacious. A sharp increase in endowments to *albergarias* from the 1340s was symptomatic of greater attention to charitable giving. On the

[42] Scott S and Duncan C J 2001, pp 107–9, 356–63; Scott S and Duncan C J 2005, pp viii, 171–84, 204, 225–6, 249, 274. See also Twigg G 1984, pp 200–22.
[43] NHP vol 4, pp 20–9.
[44] DHP vol 4, pp 163–4.
[45] MHP, pp 108–9; NHP vol 4, pp 20–9, 30, 32, 502–3.
[46] HP vol 2, pp 334–5; Marques A H de O and Dias J J A 1994, p 176.
[47] Homem A L de C, Andrade A A and Amaral L C 1988, pp 117–19.

other hand there was also a tendency to look for scapegoats. Jews, whose numbers in Portugal had been steadily rising, were now frequently targeted.[48]

From the authorities' point of view the most disturbing aspect of the crisis was its impact on the work force. After the Black Death there was an acute and prolonged labour shortage that affected all sectors of the economy. In turn this led to a new mood of self-assertion among *jornaleiros,* and the working poor generally, who suddenly found market conditions had shifted in their favour. Workers became geographically more mobile, feudal ties weakened and there was an accelerating trend towards free labour. In pursuit of more acceptable working conditions and higher wages people shifted in increasing numbers from rural areas into towns. So the urban population, which had declined immediately after the great plague, in the longer term increased substantially. Many towns, including Évora, Porto, Setúbal, Santarém, Braga, Beja and above all Lisbon, were obliged to build new walls to accommodate this growth. During the fourteenth century Lisbon's area almost doubled – and in the same period urban poverty increased significantly. A resentful proletariat came into being, conscious of its marginalised status.[49] The rootless drifted into vagrancy and lawlessness, and wandering bands of beggars and bandits multiplied.

But it was in rural Portugal that the economic crisis had its most devastating impact. Labour shortages and shrinking production were widespread, with abandoned smallholdings common features of the landscape, especially in Entre Douro e Minho, Trás-os-Montes and the Mondego valley. In some areas over a third of pre–Black Death *casais* remained deserted as late as the mid-fifteenth century.[50] Not surprisingly, landowners everywhere experienced great difficulty in attracting and retaining the tenants and labourers they needed. The area of cultivated land decreased, grain output declined and even some vineyards were neglected. Marginal areas reverted to wasteland or grazing, and the nobility expanded their game preserves. The price of wheat in Portugal remained depressed until the late fifteenth century, acting as a disincentive to growers – and an increasing proportion of cultivated land was instead given over to vines and olives.[51] The country's ability to meet its basic requirements for grain therefore further deteriorated, and dependence on foreign imports of wheat increased.

The authorities reacted to these developments with coercive legislation. Already by July 1349 the first laws designed to prevent workers abandoning

---

[48] Marques A H de O 1971, pp 270–1; NHP vol 4, pp 372–3, 397–8; Vasconcelos e Sousa B 1990, p 42.
[49] Godinho V M 1962, p 70; NHP vol 4, pp 32, 181–3.
[50] NHP vol 4, pp 29–30.
[51] MHP, pp 111–12.

their customary occupations and migrating to the towns were being enacted, and measures were soon introduced to try to halt the decline in cereals production. This was the beginning of a protracted struggle. A confused and fearful landed elite, its interests profoundly at stake, strove to limit the damage to agriculture and claw back dwindling seigneurial incomes. Workers resisted – sometimes violently. The late fourteenth century was therefore an era of mass unrest and periodic protests, sometimes in the countryside, but especially in Lisbon and Porto. As the economy contracted it was not only landed incomes that were adversely affected; traditional state revenues also diminished, perhaps by as much as 50 per cent during the century after 1367.[52] Against this background the crown and many nobles began to take a more serious interest in trade. Trade fared better than agriculture in the changed conditions after the Black Death, relatively soon reentering a period of expansion. Afonso IV and Pedro I both appreciated that the best opportunities for growth in royal revenue now lay in taxing or even directly participating in trade, which it was therefore in their interests to encourage. By the reign of Pedro's son, King Fernando (1367–83), the crown was a merchant and shipowner of considerable substance.

With Portuguese international trade recording promising growth in the late fourteenth century those linked into it were able to prosper. Commercial ties strengthened with both Italy and northern Europe. Foreign merchants – including Genoese, Venetians, Catalans and Englishmen – were especially attracted to Lisbon by its safe harbour, its strategic location and its demand for Baltic wheat and sundry manufactures. In Portugal they could conveniently acquire both typical Mediterranean products like wine, olives and cork and Atlantic commodities such as salt and fish.[53] Meanwhile, from the late fourteenth century local Portuguese merchants increased their participation in overseas trade, partly in response to improved market opportunities and partly as a consequence of systematic support from the crown. They concentrated particularly on exporting and retailing, because these were areas where non-Portuguese were officially restricted. Pedro I and King Fernando encouraged Portuguese shipbuilding, granting concessions to cut timber in crown forests. The Portuguese business community steadily increased its wealth and was influential enough by the 1370s to have effectively gained representation in the *cortes*.[54]

Most Portuguese merchants in this period still traded individually, employed agents and despatched goods on consignment. When they banded together they did not, as far as is known, create companies, but merely formed short-term associations for particular ventures. Nevertheless, Portuguese commercial

[52] DHP vol 2, p 255.
[53] Rau V 1968, pp 14–18; NHP vol 4, pp 151–2, 154.
[54] Albuquerque L de 1989, pp 32–5, 37.

practice was becoming more sophisticated, merchants had begun to utilise bills of exchange and marine insurance had been introduced, bringing greater confidence to the shipping industry.[55] What Oliveira Marques describes as revolutionary new accounting methods were spreading, with book-keeping becoming more arithmetic, less ponderous and far more systematic than previously.[56] Moreover, this was achieved while still using Roman rather than Arabic numerals, the latter not being widely adopted in Portugal until the fifteenth century. Overall, Portugal's trading future at the end of Fernando's reign looked quite promising. But the political storm clouds were meanwhile gathering steadily – and, before the century was out, would envelop Portugal in a military and constitutional crisis that threatened its very survival.

AFONSO IV AND PEDRO I

When Afonso IV came to the Portuguese throne in 1325 he was thirty-four. Personally brave, and sternly Franciscan in values, he was more of a soldier than King Dinis and less interested in such facets of courtly culture as literature and music. Shortly before he became king Afonso had fought a destructive civil war against his father that lasted on and off for four years (1320–4). The principal causes were personal: Afonso's frustration at his exclusion from power and a growing suspicion that Afonso Sanches, Dinis's favourite illegitimate son, was manoeuvring to challenge his succession. But once Dinis was dead Afonso quickly settled accounts with Afonso Sanches and assumed firm control. Portugal's relations with Castile were now the main external preoccupation – and they began on a promising note, a treaty of friendship being signed between Afonso IV and Alfonso XI of Castile in 1327. Nevertheless, tension grew between the two kings over a range of political and family matters, and in 1336 each invaded the other's territory. Hostilities continued until a Marinid assault on Andalusia brought a hurried rapprochement, Afonso leading his army to the Castilians' aid and participating personally in the great Christian victory at Rio Salado in 1340. After Rio Salado Afonso made friendly relations with Castile the mainstay of his foreign policy.

Meanwhile within the kingdom tensions between crown and nobility remained a nagging problem. When Afonso came to power he had enjoyed the backing of most northern and central nobles, who had supported him in the civil war against Dinis, and he continued for some time to enjoy their approval. However, these men had fought Dinis to protect their traditional seigneurial rights and incomes, and their loyalties were fickle.[57] The fourteenth century

---

[55] Ibid, pp 74–5, 171–4.
[56] NHP vol 4, p 65.
[57] Ibid, pp 491–4; Mattoso J 1992, pp 293–308; HP vol 2, pp 483–4.

was never an easy time for landed nobles. With the Reconquest completed, traditional opportunities for expansion and for acquiring windfall plunder were no longer available. Many nobles were finding their rural incomes insufficient and were seeking a remedy at court through royal patronage. But the crown's resources were limited and could only partially meet the demand. Noble discontent was therefore endemic and never far from the surface. As Afonso IV grew older and more sedentary, he became remote particularly from the northern nobility, whose values he had shared in his youth. Moreover by the final years of his reign the Black Death was already casting its terrible shadow, exacerbating the economic fears and grievances of many seigneurs. Finally, in 1355, when Afonso was sixty-four years of age, a group of northern nobles revolted under the leadership of the heir, Prince Pedro. Although the revolt was relatively short lived and had little material impact, it was nonetheless long remembered for the personal melodrama that accompanied it. This melodrama was to have serious long-term political consequences.[58]

In about 1340, Pedro had become infatuated with Ines de Castro, a ravishingly beautiful Galician noblewoman who was his wife Constanza's lady-in-waiting and also his cousin. After Constanza's death Pedro lived openly with Ines who bore him four children. He may have tried to secure a papal dispensation to marry her – but if so, he failed.[59] Meanwhile, Afonso IV grew alarmed at the influence exercised over his son by Ines's relatives. Finally, after being warned that Ines's brother was trying to persuade Pedro to lay claim to the Castilian crown, Afonso decided the Castros were a threat to his foreign policy and could not be tolerated. He therefore either directly procured, or at least encouraged, Ines's assassination. It was carried out by a group of young nobles in January 1355.

Although for most of the young nobles who backed Pedro's uprising in 1355 Ines's murder was merely the pretext for action, to Pedro himself it was the prime cause.[60] Pedro inherited the crown two years later – and immediately made the punishing of Ines's killers his highest priority. He pursued them relentlessly, and most were eventually caught and executed. Pedro also built for Ines a magnificent tomb of white marble in the north transept at Alcobaça abbey, to which her remains were brought from Coimbra, passing along a processional route lit for the entire distance by mourners bearing tapers. Her effigy was given a crown as though she had been a queen. Later, Pedro himself was buried in a matching tomb in the south transept. These two monuments, built at a time when mortuary sculptors in Portugal were striving to

[58] Ferreira A 1987, pp 94–111.
[59] SHP vol 1, pp 275–6; NHP vol 4, p 505.
[60] DIHP vol 1, p 24; NHP vol 4, p 505.

create recognisable likenesses, have long been admired for their poignancy and beauty.[61]

Pedro had some attractive personal qualities: he was a good communicator who related well to people of all conditions, and he loved riding, hunting and merry-making.[62] Although occasionally vindictive, he usually displayed a genuine concern for justice. Pedro's reign was afflicted with the same economic and social problems that had troubled his father's; yet, unlike Afonso IV, he avoided serious conflict with the nobility. Probably he achieved this in part through personal charm; but a more fundamental reason was his strong personal identification with noble values and disinclination to pursue centralising policies which conflicted with seigneurial interests.

Pedro's attitude towards the nobility was nevertheless self-interested and short-sighted. He consistently rewarded and promoted relatives and favourites. These included the two bastard sons Ines de Castro had borne him, whom he declared legitimate – though without the formal approval of the church. Together with Ines's brother, Dom Álvaro Peres de Castro, they received generous patrimonies. Another favourite courtier, Dom João Afonso Telo, was made count of Barcelos. Then for his six-year-old son Dom João, offspring of his later mistress Teresa Lourenço, Pedro secured the mastership of Avis, a move that helped significantly towards reintegrating the landholdings of the military orders into the royal patrimony.[63] Perhaps more by chance than design, Pedro also increased crown control over the temporal affairs of the Portuguese church – for the prelates were no longer able to defend their interests in the aggressive manner of earlier times. Finally, in his relations with Castile, Pedro acted more prudently than his father had feared, carefully refraining from meddling in the internal politics of that country. At his death he left a relatively settled kingdom, with its nobility humoured, and at peace with its neighbour – for the time being.

FERNANDO AND THE CASTILIAN WARS

Pedro I was succeeded in 1367 by his only legitimate son, Fernando. Though far from the incompetent he has sometimes been painted, Fernando was impulsive, self-indulgent and prone to serious errors of political judgement. This last weakness was particularly evident in his Castilian policies, resulting in disaster after disaster during the course of his troubled reign. Luso-Castilian relations reached their first crisis under Fernando in 1369, when King Pedro the Cruel of

---

[61] Lopes F 1994, p 200; NHP vol 4, pp 441–2.

[62] Lopes F 1994, pp 7–8, 61–3.

[63] Livermore H V 1966, pp 90–1; DIHP vol 2, pp 93–4; NHP vol 4, p 507; HP vol 2, pp 485–90.

Castile was defeated and killed in battle by his bastard half-brother, Enrique of Trastámara. After his victory Enrique declared himself king; but Fernando was the closest legitimate male relative of the vanquished Pedro, some of whose former adherents sought refuge at the Portuguese court where they urged Fernando to avenge their fallen leader. Several Castilian border towns declared for Fernando, and a number of Portuguese nobles, seeing possibilities for self-enhancement, urged him to intervene. Fernando concluded he had a God-given opportunity to unite the crowns of Castile and Portugal in his own person, and in the summer of 1369 he duly proclaimed himself the rightful king of Castile. He then crossed the border and occupied Galicia against only slight resistance.[64] But Enrique, bolstered by French support, quickly mounted a counter-invasion of Portugal, forcing the Portuguese into precipitate retreat. Fernando urgently sought peace and in 1371 signed the treaty at Alcoutim. By this he renounced all claims to the Castilian throne in exchange for a few border concessions and agreed to marry Leonor, Enrique's daughter.

Having extracted himself somewhat bruised from this fiasco, it was not long before Fernando's political troubles again began to multiply. Like his father he was surrounded by favourites to whom he gave titles, land grants and high offices. Among them were Pedro I's former intimate João Afonso Telo and various Castros, particularly Ines de Castro's brother, Dom Álvaro Peres de Castro, who now received the earldoms of Viana and Arraiolos.[65] Many of these favourites were foreigners, and they inevitably roused the suspicion and hostility of a restless urban populace as well as the resentment of nobles excluded from the inner court circle. Nevertheless, with extraordinary political irresponsibility, within a year of Alcoutim Fernando married João Afonso Telo's niece, Leonor Teles de Meneses (usually called simply Leonor Teles).[66] Obviously, this decision nullified his agreement to marry Leonor of Castile and rapidly led to renewed hostilities with Enrique. At court it fed the fires of resentment by further entrenching the Teles de Meneses faction. It also brought to prominence a new Galician favourite – Leonor Teles's own eminence grise, João Fernandes Andeiro. An unusually able and ambitious fidalgo, Andeiro was soon playing a prominent role in court affairs.

Meanwhile, John of Gaunt, duke of Lancaster, another significant new-comer on the stage of peninsular politics, was about to make his presence felt. English interest in Portugal had been growing for sometime, its catalyst the Anglo-French Hundred Years War (1327–1453). In that struggle both sides had found use for peninsular allies, while the freelance soldiers it bred were

[64] Russell P E 1955, pp 151–2.
[65] Ibid, p 504.
[66] DIHP vol 1, p 245; NHP vol 4, p 510; Tavares M J P F 1992, pp 59–71.

easily attracted to the peninsula's own internal conflicts. France regarded Enrique of Castile as its protege, which in turn meant Portugal gravitated towards the English camp. It was a position reinforced by the growing importance of Anglo-Portuguese trade after the Black Death. Fernando's volte-face regarding Alcoutim was linked to his relations with England and the fortuitous appearance from that quarter of John of Gaunt as a serious contender for the Castilian throne. Gaunt's claim was derived from Pedro the Cruel's daughter Constanza, whom he had married in September 1371.[67] To many legitimists the claim seemed credible, and Fernando resolved to support it in return for an English military alliance. The plan was for Gaunt to invade Castile from Gascony while Fernando mounted a simultaneous invasion from Portugal. But Gaunt was forced to postpone his campaign, enabling King Enrique to concentrate his forces against Fernando. In the summer of 1372 a Castilian galley fleet blockaded the Tagus. Meanwhile Enrique himself crossed the border and captured a string of Portuguese cities as he advanced swiftly towards the capital. By early 1373, having taken and sacked the outer suburbs of Lisbon, he besieged the inner city. Ill-prepared, Fernando had little alternative but to sue for peace. At a treaty signed in Santarém he renounced Gaunt and declared himself again an ally of Trastámara Castile. All Castilian exiles at his court were expelled, various Portuguese castles were surrendered to Enrique for three years and Lisbon itself was briefly occupied by Castilian troops.[68]

These two Castilian wars were very destructive. In 1369–71, Enrique's forces devastated much of Trás-os-Montes and Minho, including Braga; then in 1372–3 it was the turn of Lisbon, Coimbra and many other towns in the north and centre of the kingdom.[69] The coinage was repeatedly debased, prices soared, plague returned in the early 1370s and famine reappeared. Vagabondage, crime and popular unrest mounted, while smallholders, traders, artisans and urban workers formed associations to protect their interests. In both 1371 and 1372 protests were voiced in the *cortes,* and popular disturbances broke out in various towns. In Lisbon they were led by Fernão Vasques, a mere tailor.

Fernando proved more adept in responding to these events than he had been in evolving a foreign policy. He took vigorous measures to restore the kingdom's defences and to re-energise its economy. A special levy was imposed to fund major improvements to castles and fortifications, and more particularly to pay for the construction of a strong wall to protect the newer suburbs of Lisbon. The prudence of this latter step would within a few years be amply demonstrated. In 1375 he also issued a comprehensive land management code

[67] Russell P E 1955, pp 165–9, 173–5.
[68] Ibid, pp 191–9; SHP vol 1, pp 286–7; NHP vol 4, pp 515–18; Tavares M J P F 1992, pp 48–9.
[69] Tavares M J P F 1992, pp 48–9.

called the *Lei das Sesmarias,* aimed at curbing the exodus of rural manpower and increasing agricultural production by regulating the expropriation and re-allocation of under-utilised land. Rural workers with property below a speci-fied value were required to remain on the land, together with their sons and grandsons. They were to be given the oxen they needed, but would have to work for fixed wages.[70]

By the late 1370s a new crisis in foreign relations was beginning to loom. The English lacked a navy to combat Castilian galleys which, in alliance with the French, were raiding their coasts. Portugal possessed galleys, and the Eng-lish offered Fernando a closer alliance to secure their services. Also at about this time the Great Schism of 1378–1417 broke out, forcing rulers everywhere to choose between rival popes. Portugal recognised Urban VI, the Roman pope also supported by England. Clement VII, the pope at Avignon, was backed by France and Castile – and the rivalry between the Anglo-Portuguese and Franco-Castilian blocs was reinforced accordingly. Enrique of Castile died in 1380, leaving his kingdom to a young and untried son, Juan I. Gaunt saw this as an opportunity to renew his bid for the Castilian throne, while Fernando sensed a chance to recover his earlier losses. The two therefore struck a new deal, under the terms of which Gaunt agreed to lead an army into Castile from Gascony and to send a smaller force to Portugal under his brother Edmond, earl of Cambridge, to co-ordinate operations with Fernando.

Cambridge's army duly reached Lisbon in July 1381. However, handicap-ped by indifferent generalship, poor discipline and inadequate transport, it did little beyond alienating much of the Portuguese populace. Juan raided Portugal, taking a few border towns and castles; but neither he nor Fernando were really in a position to sustain a prolonged campaign. Then, quite suddenly, in August 1382 they made peace. The terms of their agreement were remarkably favour-able to Portugal. Fernando formally recognised Juan as king of Castile, while Juan undertook to withdraw completely from Portuguese territory, release all his prisoners, return captured galleys and transport Cambridge's army back to England. The peace was sealed with the betrothal of Beatriz, daughter and only surviving child of Fernando and Leonor Teles, to Juan's son. Later, after Juan's own wife died, it was agreed Beatriz would instead marry Juan himself.[71]

The Castilians were eager to make peace in 1382 for very clear reasons. They were, of course, wary about a possible invasion by Gaunt; but their principal concern was not with anything the English might do, but a new and quite fortuitous political development that had arisen within Portugal itself. Information had reached Castile that Fernando was seriously ill, and

[70] SHP vol 1, pp 351–3; DIHP vol 2, p 224; NHP vol 4, p 274.
[71] NHP vol 4, pp 519–23; DIHP vol 1, p 66.

probably dying. Given that Beatriz was then Fernando's only legitimate child, securing her hand in marriage became extremely attractive to King Juan – for it offered him the prospect of soon acquiring the crown of Portugal by inheritance.[72] This made it imperative to terminate hostilities immediately and work to minimise anti-Castilian sentiment among the Portuguese. Juan moved none too soon: within a year Fernando was dead, only thirty-seven years of age, probably a victim of tuberculosis.

DYNASTIC CRISIS: A CASTILIAN USURPER OR A PORTUGUESE BASTARD?

The passing of Fernando in October 1383 was followed by the greatest dynastic crisis in Portugal since the kingdom had come into being. At the time Beatriz, the dead king's heir, was just eleven years old. For long a hapless pawn in her father's erratic foreign policy, she had been promised in turn to Enrique II's bastard son, his legitimate son (the future Enrique III), Cambridge's six-year-old son and Juan I's son, before finally marrying Juan himself, only months before Fernando's death. The marriage contract stipulated that she and Juan reign jointly over Portugal until their son (presuming they had one) reached the age of fourteen, at which point he would inherit the kingdom; but if the marriage produced no such heir, the throne would pass directly to the kings of Castile. Meanwhile Leonor Teles was to govern as regent.[73]

The now probable union of the crowns of Portugal and Castile would have marked the consummation of a long-held dynastic ambition. However, it did not necessarily require the integration of the kingdoms themselves, and the marriage treaty stipulated that they should continue to be governed separately. The appointment of a regent while Beatriz remained in Castile complied with this condition.[74] In 1383, there was little hostility to Beatriz personally, whose legitimate rights were generally acknowledged. But the selection of Leonor Teles to serve as regent was a different matter. The choice was widely seen as contrived by Leonor's favourite, João Fernandes Andeiro, who by the early 1380s had become indisputably the dominant figure at court, having ousted the Castros.[75] Moreover Andeiro was rumoured to be Leonor's secret lover and the father of her infant son, who had lived for just four days in July 1382. Outside the regent's immediate circle his influence was intensely resented. Leonor herself was despised for her alleged scandalous behaviour and tainted by her

---

[72] Russell P E 1955, pp 335–9; HP vol 2, pp 493–4.
[73] HP vol 2 pp 523–4.
[74] NHP vol 4, pp 522–3.
[75] Ibid, p 522.

identification with foreigners. Increasingly regarded as a tool of the king of Castile, she became popularly known as *a aleivosa* – the traitor. Within months of her assuming the regency, political tensions within Portugal were displaying every sign of imminent descent into violent conflict.

One of the leading opponents of Leonor's regency was the late King Fernando's half-brother João of Avis, bastard son of Pedro I and Teresa Lourenço. Now in his twenties, João was intelligent, wealthy and widely respected. Nevertheless, in 1382 at the instigation of Leonor Teles and Andeiro, Fernando had ordered him arrested on a trumped-up charge of treason – and he may well have been executed, but for the personal intervention of Cambridge.[76] Understandably in these circumstances João felt threatened by Leonor's appointment as regent, while Leonor distrusted João. On taking office Leonor resolved to make João military commander in Alentejo, presumably to remove him as far as possible from Lisbon. In response João and a small band of co-conspirators among the nobles and *cidadãos honrados* decided they must take immediate action before it was too late. On 6 December 1383 they broke into the palace and murdered Andeiro. Meanwhile Álvaro Pais, João's key supporter in Lisbon, roused the city. For a while uncontrolled violence reigned. One victim was Dom Martinho, the pious and learned bishop of Lisbon, unfortunate enough to be both a Castilian and a Clementist, who was flung to his death from the tower of the cathedral. The mob also turned its wrath on certain Lisbon Jews, and a pogrom was narrowly averted by João's personal intervention.[77] Realising she had lost control, Leonor Teles fled to Santarém.

By the end of 1383 João of Avis had assumed de facto control of Lisbon; but both he and his supporters felt exceedingly vulnerable. The legality of their coup was obviously doubtful and had sparked widespread upheaval. Already an indignant Juan had crossed the border at Guarda and was slowly advancing on the capital.[78] João contemplated fleeing to England, but in the end was persuaded to stay. Álvaro Pais proposed an arranged marriage between João and Leonor as a way out for the conspirators; but when approached, Leonor rejected this improbable suggestion out of hand.[79] Instead she fled to Juan who promptly confined her in a Castilian castle. With Leonor out of the picture and Juan now heading the forces ranged against João and his supporters, it is possible to see how the two opposing sides could become labelled 'legitimist' and 'patriot' respectively. On the patriot side – that of João – was a disparate coalition of some great and many lesser nobles, the Urbanist clergy, bureaucrats

[76] Russell P E 1955, pp 323–4.
[77] Lopes F 1990 vol 1, pp 27, 34–5.
[78] DIHP vol 2, pp 168–9; NHP vol 4, pp 523–4.
[79] Serrão J 1981, p 41.

from earlier reigns and most of the bourgeoisie. Popular sentiment, especially in the cities, being strongly anti-Castilian, was overwhelmingly for João, and the south in general was also patriot. But in the north, the stronghold of the old seigneurial nobility, there was much legitimist support for Juan. Many noble houses were split, and castellans of neighbouring fortresses often found themselves on opposing sides.

By December 1383, it had become urgent for João's supporters to formalise his position, and an extraordinary meeting of the Lisbon *câmara* was therefore called to proclaim him regent and protector of the realm. This it eventually did – but only after much hesitation and under extreme pressure from a large, expectant crowd.[80] In early 1384, Juan approached Lisbon, having already secured the submission of sundry towns and castles. He soon occupied Santarém and in February arrived before the capital. Probably he expected João's supporters to crumble before him; but instead he found stubborn resistance. He also discovered that the walls of Lisbon, thanks to repairs ordered by Fernando a decade earlier, were in sound condition to withstand the siege that now commenced. Among those attracted to João's banner was Nuno Álvares Pereira, a young nobleman of unusual military talent. He was a bastard son of a prior of the Hospitallers and a nephew of João's close associate Rui Pereira. Soon he was given command of patriot forces in Alentejo where in April 1384 he won the battle of Atoleiros, then began systematically mopping up pro-Castilian strongholds. Meanwhile Juan became hopelessly bogged down outside the walls of Lisbon, and in September, his army exhausted and decimated by plague, he was forced to raise the siege and turn tail for Castile. The siege of Porto by a combined army of Castilians and Portuguese legitimists under the archbishop of Santiago de Compostela similarly ended in failure.[81]

These developments much enhanced João's prestige, enabling him to attract more noble supporters, raise funds and take the offensive. Increasing numbers of towns and castles declared for him, and soon he felt confident enough to summon a *cortes*. This was assembled at Coimbra in April 1385, its principal task to determine the succession to the throne. Initially some of those present argued for Beatriz; but they were few, and quickly overridden. A rather larger group supported Dom João de Castro, the elder son of Pedro and Ines. But his candidature was impracticable because he had fled to Castile where Juan had detained him. That left only João of Avis.

João's case was persuasively argued before the *cortes* by Dr João das Regras, a respected Bologna-trained lawyer and former chancellor to both Pedro I and Fernando. Regras's supposed arguments were outlined at length in the

---

[80] NHP vol 4, pp 525–8; HP vol 2, p 495.
[81] SHP vol 1, pp 297–8; NHP vol 4, pp 128–9.

chronicle of Fernão Lopes half a century later and may be summarised roughly as follows.[82] The scandalous behaviour of Leonor Teles meant that the legitimacy of her daughter Beatriz was doubtful. The legitimacy of Pedro's two sons by Ines de Castro had been formally denied by the church, and both had also forfeited their claims by fleeing to Castile. Juan had lost any rights he may have possessed by violating the terms of the Luso-Castilian treaties, invading Portugal and detaining the regent Leonor Teles. He had also offended the church by recognising the anti-pope at Avignon. For all these reasons the throne was now vacant, and it was right and proper for the *cortes* to choose a new king. On 6 April 1385, João of Avis was duly and unanimously proclaimed João I, king of Portugal.[83]

ALJUBARROTA

The choice of the *cortes* notwithstanding, in the spring of 1385 João I's throne was far from secure. The legitimists remained strong in the north, and Juan was preparing a new invasion; João knew he must fight, and he desperately needed allies. With this in mind, even before his election he had sent emissaries to England to seek recruits and urge Gaunt once again to revive his claim to the crown of Castile. With difficulty, his agents engaged a small Anglo-Gascon force which reached Portugal while the *cortes* was still in session. Once proclaimed, João moved quickly to secure a formal alliance with Richard II, and the outcome was the treaty of Windsor signed in May 1386. Under the terms of this treaty each king agreed to provide the other with military and naval assistance on request and to grant reciprocal trading rights to their respective citizens in each other's territory. Richard also promised to support João against any enemy who tried to overthrow him, and João sent Richard a squadron of galleys. The treaty of Windsor was the foundation stone of the long-lasting Anglo-Portuguese alliance.[84]

Nuno Álvares Pereira meanwhile had been appointed constable of the king's army, and in 1385 both he and João campaigned in the north where they took a string of legitimist towns, including Braga. Early in July a large Castilian raiding party was defeated at Trancoso in Beira Alta; then a few weeks later Juan crossed the border with the main Castilian army. Juan, whose force numbered perhaps 20,000 men including many legitimist Portuguese and a contingent of French men-at-arms sent by Charles VI, planned to crush the patriots with overwhelming force. He advanced towards Lisbon along the well-worn

---

[82] Lopes F vol 1 1990, pp 393–424.
[83] SHP vol 1, pp 305–9; NHP vol 4, pp 525–30; Tavares M J P F 1992, pp 67–85.
[84] Russell P E 1955, pp 363–78, 414–16, 527–8.

invasion route down the Mondego valley. João, on Nuno Álvares's advice, decided not to retreat behind the walls of his capital, but to stand and fight.

On 14 August 1385 João's army of about 7,000, including the small contingent of men-at-arms and archers recruited in England, occupied defensive positions on a ridge called Aljubarrota, overlooking the Leiria-Lisbon road. The van was commanded by the constable, the main body by the king. A division of Portuguese knights and bowmen was on the right flank and the Anglo-Gascons on the left.[85] The Castilian army arrived after a long and tiring march, and its more experienced leaders quickly saw that to launch a frontal attack would invite disaster. Juan therefore ordered that no assault should be attempted that day; but hotheads within his army could not or would not contain themselves, and soon began to engage. By late afternoon, against the better judgement of its commanders, the whole Castilian army had become drawn into a general advance on well-prepared Portuguese positions.

In the course of the fourteenth century one of the most important changes in European military technology was the introduction of the crossbow. This complex and expensive weapon required special skills of its user, but properly used was stunningly effective. Crossbowmen represented a new kind of warfare in which men fought at a distance. They could be deadly against knights in armour who traditionally engaged in personal combat. Nuno Álvares Pereira was well aware of these facts and at Aljubarrota employed his precious crossbowmen to deadly effect.[86] In a battle lasting barely an hour Juan's army was utterly defeated. Fighting in the van, many of the Portuguese legitimist leaders were mowed down – an outcome with major long-term political consequences. The rest of the invading host simply disintegrated; Juan himself was forced to flee, his campaign ending in ignominious failure. Aljubarrota proved one of the most consequential victories in Portuguese history. It confirmed the rule of João I and the house of Avis, demonstrated Portugal's emphatic rejection of the idea of Iberian union and constituted a defining moment in the evolution of national consciousness.[87]

Afterwards, near the place where the battle had been won, and in fulfilment of his vow on the day it was fought, João ordered an abbey be raised. Builders worked on its construction for almost 150 years, and even then it was never completed. Nevertheless, the unfinished monument – which was called Batalha (battle) abbey – is unquestionably a magnificent example of late Gothic architecture and one of the few truly outstanding buildings ever created in Portugal. It was and is a fitting symbol of the new dynasty and the triumphant reassertion of the kingdom's independence.

[85] Ibid, pp 385–6.
[86] NHP vol 4, pp 59–63; HP vol 2, pp 526–7.
[87] SHP vol 1, pp 310–11; NHP vol 4, pp 530, 536.

7

The Making of Avis Portugal

THE COMING OF JOÃO I: A BOURGEOIS REVOLUTION?

The celebrated historian and essayist António Sérgio once described the dramatic events of 1383–5 as a 'bourgeois revolution' in which maritime commercial interests triumphed over the nobility.[1] In other words, he considered there was a clash of classes, and that victory fell to the class that allegedly inspired Portugal's great seaborne discoveries of the fifteenth century – the urban bourgeoisie. Joel Serrão later developed a rather more sophisticated variant of this model, based on deeper research. He concluded that it was the urban proletariat that initially seized the initiative and that the bourgeoisie only assumed prominence at a later stage. To Joel Serrão there were therefore two distinct and successive revolutionary phases: the proletarian phase in 1383 and the bourgeois in 1385.[2]

Other historians have reacted to these interpretations with varying degrees of scepticism. Verríssimo Serrão avowed that there was simply no class struggle at all in 1383–5, no pitting of the people against nobles and clergy.[3] However, Oliveira Marques took a more nuanced view, arguing that undercurrents of social tension were indeed present, but that to interpret what happened as simply a struggle between city interests and the traditional nobility was an oversimplification. The reality was more fluid and more complex.[4]

The relevance of this last observation may become clearer if we review briefly what the chronicler Fernão Lopes had to say. Lopes certainly believed that after Andeiro's murder the role of the Lisbon crowd was crucial in gaining

[1] Sérgio A 1979, pp 31, 32.
[2] Serrão J 1981, pp 48–53.
[3] SHP vol 1, p 300.
[4] NHP vol 4, p 525.

for João control of the city. Called out into the streets by Álvaro Pais, a prominent *cidadão honrado*, burgess and former chancellor of King Fernando, the crowd – which was composed mainly of artisans (*mesteirais*) and day-labourers (*jornaleiros*) – held much of the initiative during December of 1383. It was the crowd's spokesmen who pressured João into staying on rather than fleeing to England, and it was also they who thrust on him the offices of regent and defender of the realm. When the burgesses controlling the Lisbon *câmara* hesitated to confirm João's appointment they were brow-beaten into compliance by a vociferous mob led by a tanner.[5] In April 1384, João appears to have duly rewarded the city's artisans by granting each craft the right to send two representatives to sit in the *câmara*. This led to the establishment of the so-called 'house of twenty-four' (*casa de vinte e quatro*) – for long the representative body of the Lisbon craft guilds. Later, in the reign of Afonso V, the craft guilds were granted similar representation in Porto and several other centres.

Nevertheless, as time passed the influence of the working class on affairs of state steadily receded – while city merchants and lawyers continued to be heard, with Lisbon's representatives in the *cortes* regularly expressing the concerns of these groups.[6] This was especially so during the first half of João I's reign, when the *cortes* was convened at least twenty-eight times.[7] However, it did not necessarily follow that there was a significant increase in bourgeois input into royal policy; for already in late Burgundian times burgesses of major coastal towns were being listened to and their services utilised, and many of the lawyers and merchants who rose to prominence under João I had previously held office under Pedro I or King Fernando.

João's political situation in 1383–5 meant that he inevitably relied to a significant degree on the backing of the burgesses and other *cidadãos honrados*, especially those of Lisbon. He needed their subsidies to fund the war effort and for subsequent reconstruction – and their support was also useful in his struggle with discontented landed nobility. But that this state of affairs amounted to a 'bourgeois revolution' may be seriously doubted. The new regime was influenced by far more than just city pressure groups – which the king himself readily ignored, when it suited him. Moreover, the underlying trend in royal government was still towards more centralisation, which impacted on bourgeois interests as well as those of the nobility. Witness such measures as the replacement of municipal magistrates by royal judges and the transformation of municipal excise duties (*sisas*) into permanent state taxes, both of which, understandably, were opposed by the city bourgeoisie.

---

[5] Lopes F 1990 vol 1, pp 24–30, 33–5, 40–3, 46–9, 52–4; Serrão J 1981, pp 43–4.
[6] Lopes F 1990 vol 1, p 55; NHP vol 4, p 525.
[7] Sousa A de 1990 vol 1, pp 291–344.

The kingdom that emerged from the crisis of 1383–5 was one in which traditional elites still remained powerful, although certain shifts had occurred within their ranks. The upper bourgeoisie in the cities had increased its influence, but had by no means replaced landowning interests. The proletariat, which briefly made its voice heard, was unable to maintain its new-found influence for long. Finally, as we shall see later, the crown soon resumed its struggle to consolidate its own authority.

SETTLING THE DYNASTY: WAR, PEACE AND ROYAL MARRIAGES

After Aljubarrota King Juan had retreated to Castile under cover of a truce. But he continued to style himself king of Portugal and clearly intended to return as soon as circumstances permitted. João knew he must urgently strengthen his defences and that he needed allies. So he turned again to John of Gaunt, whose claim to the crown of Castile he offered to support. Gaunt, with the formal approval of the English government, raised an army and sailed for Spain, landing at La Coruña in late July 1386.[8] He quickly occupied the pilgrim centre of Santiago de Compostela, then set up court at Orense. He and João met that November near the Portuguese-Galician border and signed a pact. João agreed to bring 5,000 men to Gaunt's aid in Castile, while Gaunt undertook to stand by João against any enemy who sought to dethrone him. The duke also promised that when he became king of Castile he would cede to João a strip of territory along the border about eighty kilometres wide, to increase Portugal's security. Finally, it was decided João was to marry Philippa – the twenty-nine-year-old daughter of Gaunt and his first wife, Blanche.[9]

João and Philippa were duly wed in the cathedral at Porto on 10 February 1387, amidst much festivity and rejoicing. Their marriage proved felicitous and most fruitful, Philippa bearing the king five sons and a daughter, who survived into adulthood: Duarte, Pedro, Henrique, Isabel, João and Fernando – and all of them, particularly the first three, were destined to make significant contributions to Portuguese history. Philippa also exerted a strong personal influence at court. She learned Portuguese and nurtured the close relationship between Portugal and England, well after its initial raison d'être had passed. She and her following introduced a range of English customs and refinements, and she apparently even managed to restrain the king from siring more bastards.[10] However, militarily the alliance with John of Gaunt bore little fruit. An Anglo-Portuguese force invaded Leon in the summer of 1387; but it received

[8] Russell P E 1955, pp 400–21.
[9] Ibid, pp 438–41; Lopes F 1990 vol 1, pp 217–18.
[10] Martins J P de O 1958 vol 1, p 15.

minimal local support and failed to make headway. The French sent aid to Juan, and it soon became clear that Gaunt could not win Castile without substantial reinforcements. He therefore decided to negotiate and in mid-1388 struck a deal. In return for a large cash payment and a substantial annual pension, he renounced his claim to the Castilian throne and recognised Juan. Then he withdrew his army, abandoning João and implicitly accepting Juan as king of Portugal. His shameless treatment of an ally and son-in-law who had supported him so staunchly in his own enterprise did the duke of Lancaster little credit.

Despite Gaunt's departure, the English alliance remained in force, the treaty of Windsor having been confirmed by Richard II. The Luso-Castilian truce was also renewed, for Juan was not yet ready to fight. But in October 1390 Juan himself suddenly died and was succeeded by Enrique III, who was still a minor. The prospect of invasion from Castile therefore receded, even though Enrique maintained his father's claims. Meanwhile in 1396 Dom Dinis de Castro, surviving illegitimate son of Pedro I and Ines de Castro, made a bid for the Portuguese crown; but his modest invading force of Castilians and Portuguese emigres was easily defeated.[11] A Luso-Castilian stalemate followed, with neither kingdom in a position to wage offensive war, and it became increasingly obvious that acceptance of the status quo by both sides was now inevitable. Peace negotiations duly began, but progressed with painful slowness. In 1402, a ten-year truce was arranged, but only in 1411 did the parties agree to a definitive peace. Then at last, after twenty-five years of debilitating struggle, the house of Avis could count itself secure.

But it was years before relations between the royal families of Portugal and Castile returned to their old intimacy. João I remained ever wary of dynastic entanglements with a neighbour he still viewed with suspicion. Fear of Castile had underlain his decision to seek the hand of Philippa, Gaunt's wholly English daughter, rather than that of Catherine, the duke's other daughter, who was half-Castilian. Many at court had favoured Catherine; but her potential claims to the Castilian crown might again have dragged Portugal into conflict with its neighbour.[12] Throughout his reign João took pains to strengthen his family links outside Castile, whenever he could. In 1405 he married off Brites, his bastard daughter, to the English earl of Arundel. As his legitimate children matured the same strategy was continued, even after the peace with Castile in 1411. Duarte married Leonor, sister of Alfonso V of Aragon, in 1428. Isabel married Philippe le Bon, duke of Burgundy, and Pedro married a daughter of the Aragonese count of Urgel. Links were also forged with the Holy

---

[11] Russell P E 1955, pp 514–15, 519–25, 537–9, 547; NHP vol 4, pp 535–46.
[12] Russell P E 1955, p 438.

Roman Empire and the kingdom of Hungary. The result was that as time passed a credible Castilian claim to the throne of Portugal became more and more unlikely.

CHANGE AND CONTINUITY IN THE NOBLE ESTATE

Any suggestion that the Portuguese nobility was solidly opposed to the movement of 1383–5 cannot be sustained on the evidence.[13] First, far from displaying class solidarity, the Portuguese nobility was deeply split over what was happening in these years. Neighbour opposed neighbour, families were divided and individual noblemen changed sides during the course of the struggle, whether from expediency or conviction. Overall, more nobles supported than opposed João, particularly among younger sons, and all the military orders except the Hospitallers rallied to him. Nor is there much support for the claim that after 1385 there was a 'new' nobility. Certainly following João's victory some twenty additional noble families of obscure origin appeared at court, suggesting rather more social mobility than usual, but hardly a fundamental change in the make-up of the second estate. Most established noble families survived the traumas of 1383–5 quite successfully, though sometimes only through younger sons or collateral relatives. Recent prosopographical research indicates that the major families of the court nobility in the mid-fourteenth century maintained their position virtually without interruption into the mid-fifteenth century and beyond.[14]

João I faced the same dilemma in regard to the nobility as had so tried his Burgundian predecessors. How could royal authority be sustained in the teeth of local particularisms, or the royal estate be protected against persistent encroachments? Nobles who espoused João's cause naturally expected to keep their rights and privileges intact – and indeed looked for additional generous land grants and rewards.[15] Initially it was difficult to resist such pressures, because of both high expectations and the extraordinary facility with which dissatisfied nobles could move between the courts of Portugal and Castile. Every one of the eight principal families associated with the Portuguese court in the late Middle Ages – the Meneses, Albuquerques, Castros, Sousas, Silvas, Cunhas, Pachecos and Pereiras – also maintained important links to the Castilian court.[16] Indeed, prominent families were frequently split between the two, including even that of the great constable Nuno Álvares Pereira. Before

[13] Sérgio A 1979, pp 31–5; Russell P E 1955, pp 359–60.
[14] Tavares M J P F 1983b, pp 82–3; Gomes R C 1995, pp 64–5, 104–5.
[15] Moreno H B 1988, pp 3–4.
[16] Gomes R C 1995, pp 66–89.

becoming João's right-hand man, Nuno Álvares had been attached to the circles of Leonor Teles and the young Beatriz, and two of his brothers fought on the Castilian side at Aljubarrota. Under such circumstances João had little alternative but to yield to his noble supporters' expectations and distribute lands and titles generously. Some of the lands came from estates of men killed in the fighting or were obtained by dispossessing legitimists; but the rest were drawn directly from the royal patrimony. The greatest beneficiary was Nuno Álvares Pereira himself. He received the earldoms of Barcelos, Ourém and Arraiolos and the lordships of Braga, Guimarães, Chaves and fifteen other towns. According to the chronicler Fernão Lopes, the constable eventually accumulated such vast holdings that some contemporaries alleged they amounted to half the kingdom.[17]

As soon as he felt sufficiently secure João I set about halting this alarming haemorrhage. From at least 1393, with the help of centralist lawyers like João das Regras, the systematic resumption of crown lands was commenced, mainly by applying strict inheritance laws. João also insisted that only the king could have vassals, forcing magnates who had made grants of land in vassalage to their own followers to cancel them. Moreover, duties in the form of *sisas* were now imposed on land transfers. The inevitable result was widespread noble discontent, which was strongly voiced in the *cortes* of 1397. After failing to get satisfaction at this assembly a number of nobles shifted their allegiance to the king of Castile, and a steady trickle of defectors followed suit – some of whom handed over border castles to the Castilian crown. Even Nuno Álvares Pereira allegedly contemplated leaving the kingdom. However, with so much to lose, it is hard to imagine him actually doing so – and he allowed himself to be persuaded to stay.[18]

Throughout the late 1390s, João I persisted tenaciously with his centralising policies. Noble discontent peaked at about the turn of the century. Then, with the voluntary departure of many aggrieved nobles and the exiling of others, it gradually subsided. Two important developments in the second decade of the fifteenth century each played a major role in bringing about this change: peace with Castile and expansion into Morocco from 1415. Meanwhile, João I had begun systematically endowing his own children. Indeed, one of his principal justifications for resuming royal lands was to obtain resources for precisely this purpose.[19] The important consequence was that during the first half of the century the Portuguese higher nobility came to be dominated by a small group of great magnates, who were nearly all of royal origin. The process began in

---

[17] Lopes F 1990 vol 2, pp 332–3.
[18] Ibid, pp 335–6.
[19] Ibid, p 333.

1401 when Afonso, the king's bastard son, was married to the daughter and heiress of Nuno Álvares Pereira. The marriage agreement involved Nuno Alvares's title of count of Barcelos and a significant share of his lands being transferred to Afonso. From João's viewpoint this had the value of neutralising the house of Nuno Álvares by linking it firmly to his own. Later, João gave substantial endowments and illustrious titles to each of his legitimate sons as they came of age. From 1408 Pedro received a series of lordships mainly in the centre-north of the country and Henrique in the south. Then in 1415 these two were made respectively duke of Coimbra and duke of Viseu. In 1418 Prince João was made master of Santiago, and in 1420 Henrique administrator of the order of Christ. Both these offices involved control of substantial resources.[20] The policy of nurturing a few powerful noble houses headed by magnates of royal descent was continued by King Duarte and later by Afonso V.

KING DUARTE AND THE REGENCY OF PRINCE PEDRO

João I's policies to protect the royal patrimony were eventually given definitive expression by King Duarte in the *Lei Mental* of 1434. This important law was a systematisation of practices to which the new king himself was closely linked, having been involved in his father's administration since at least 1411. The *Lei Mental* defined the royal patrimony as inalienable. Grants made from it were always conditional and could not be sub-divided. They were inheritable by oldest sons or grandsons only, and not by female or collateral male relations. The *Lei Mental* was fundamental because it established a clear framework of rules, and it remained in place for 400 years. However, it did not end the struggle between crown and nobility over land, which continued for most of the fifteenth century. Often, powerful nobles found ways round the restrictions – mainly by securing exemptions. In the very year of the *Lei Mental*'s inception the greatest nobleman in the country, other than the royal *infantes* – Dom Afonso, count of Barcelos – was exempted. Others clambered for the same concession.[21]

Duarte died prematurely in September 1438, apparently of 'plague', and was succeeded by his six-year-old son, Afonso V. The late king's will had named his widow, Leonor of Aragon, as regent.[22] This arrangement pleased many nobles, being confident Leonor could be induced to reverse recent policy and hand out generous grants of lands, offices and titles. But another group of nobles was disturbed at the prospect of Leonor's rule, and there were

---

[20] NHP vol 4, p 546.
[21] Moreno H B 1988, p 9.
[22] Moreno H B 1979–80 vol 1, pp 3–6.

mutterings that the *cortes,* not the late king, had the right to designate a regent. This view was soon subscribed to by the overwhelming majority of *concelhos.*[23] Moreover as a non-Portuguese, a woman and a figure with suspiciously close foreign links – particularly to the royal house of Aragon and to nobles in Castile who had recently usurped control of that kingdom – Leonor was considered an unacceptable choice by many. Hostility to her was especially strong in Lisbon and most other major towns.[24]

In late 1438 an uneasy compromise was reached with Leonor, brokered by Prince Henrique, whereby she would share the regency with the boy king's oldest uncle, Prince Pedro. But this arrangement soon proved unworkable, and in 1439 the Lisbon *câmara,* backed by Prince João, demanded that Pedro rule as sole regent. This position was shortly afterwards endorsed by the *cortes.* Pedro, after a brief show of reluctance, acquiesced and was promptly inducted into office.[25] Leonor was outraged; but her principal ally, the count of Barcelos, was isolated in the country's north and could do little to help her. She and her household first took shelter in Crato castle and then, when Pedro moved against that fortress, fled to Castile. Over the next few months, Leonor's supporters were systematically removed from office. In many cases, their properties were also seized, most being re-distributed to members of Pedro's personal following.[26] For the next few years Leonor plotted Pedro's overthrow from across the border, until death removed her in 1445. By then her exiled supporters and dependents had been reduced to the direst circumstances; but Pedro's attitude towards them remained staunchly unforgiving.[27]

Prince Pedro exercised the regency from 1439 to 1446. During these years, he administered the kingdom with integrity; but as time passed his support-base dwindled and his difficulties mounted. The death in 1442 of his younger brother and firm ally Prince João was a particularly telling blow. Then his backing in the *concelhos* began to fall away, perhaps because he seemed to be encroaching on jealously-guarded local rights and privileges.[28] The opposition was meanwhile rallying round the person of Afonso, count of Barcelos, and grew steadily, despite a brief reconciliation in 1442, when Pedro granted Afonso the title of duke of Bragança. The real test came after Afonso V attained his majority at the age of fourteen in 1446. At first Pedro seemed to weather the change successfully: he retained the title of regent and apparently strengthened

---

[23] Ibid, pp 7–12, 663–4.
[24] Ibid, pp 11–16, 21–4, 58–9; Thomaz L F 1994, pp 102–3.
[25] Moreno H B 1979–80 vol 1, pp 37–40, 55–9.
[26] Ibid, pp 92–3, 100–35.
[27] Ibid, pp 161, 187, 238–9.
[28] Ibid, p 264.

his influence at court by securing the marriage of his daughter, Isabel, to the young king himself. However, those whom Pedro had driven out of Portugal were now returning and beginning to clamour for retribution. Afonso V was too weak and inexperienced to resist the pressure for long – and Pedro's enemies, headed by Bragança and his eldest son, the count of Ourém, finally succeeded in having the regent dismissed in July 1448.[29]

After his dismissal Pedro withdrew to his ducal stronghold in Coimbra. This encouraged his enemies, and almost immediately Bragança began ousting the former regent's appointees in northern Portugal. Then in September 1448, the king was persuaded to annul all the grants and appointments that Pedro had made during the course of his administration and place them under review.[30] This was a direct challenge to Pedro, and he had to confront it. Attempts were made to mediate, first by Prince Henrique and later by Queen Isabel, but were unsuccessful. When a new *cortes* met that November it quickly became obvious that support in that body for the ex-regent had almost wholly evaporated. He was peremptorily ordered to disarm; but instead, early in 1449, he marched at the head of his ducal army towards Lisbon, where he probably hoped to secure popular backing.[31] Meanwhile, Afonso V, prodded by Bragança, Ourém and others, made preparations to crush his uncle. By this time Pedro was a spent and largely abandoned force, his army outnumbered by at least five to one and steadily dwindling through desertion. He was duly defeated and killed at the battle of Alfarrobeira near Lisbon on 20 May 1449, an arrow piercing his heart.[32]

In the chronicle of Rui de Pina, written about half a century after the prince's death, Pedro is already portrayed as an intelligent, principled regent. He has had his advocates ever since – most recently, and perhaps most ardently, Alfredo Pinheiro Marques.[33] There is little doubt Pedro was indeed a well-informed and cultivated man for his times. He had received a good education and was widely travelled – in England, the Netherlands, Germany, Hungary, Aragon and Castile.[34] Humberto Baquero Moreno, who has written the most exhaustive and authoritative review of events leading up to Alfarrobeira and analysed hundreds of individuals who made up the opposing forces, considers that as regent Pedro also stood for strong, centralised government.[35] But Pedro was nevertheless always obliged to operate within the constraints of a political

[29] Ibid, pp 247–9, 252, 259–61.
[30] Ibid, pp 327–8.
[31] Ibid, pp 333–45.
[32] Ibid, pp 420–1, 425–8; DIHP vol 1, p 34; Marques A P 1994, pp 69–73, 542–3.
[33] Marques A P 1994, pp 47–80.
[34] Rogers F M 1961, pp 31–58.
[35] Moreno H B 1979–80 vol 1, pp vii, 264, 665–6.

system that depended on personal loyalties and that was profoundly influenced by seigneurial tradition. This meant any attempted centralisation had to be based on the person of the de facto ruler. So it was that crown offices under Pedro, be they judicial, fiscal, military or other, were entrusted overwhelmingly to members of his own household. *Corregedores,* castellans, *escrivães,* even the *procuradores* representing some of the towns in the *cortes,* all came from his following, as did most of those who received confiscated estates.[36] Such a situation was doubtless unavoidable. Where else could Pedro have found men he could trust? But by the same token, as soon as his regency ceased his appointees were bound to be replaced by persons loyal to whatever new leadership followed.

Pedro's centralising efforts as regent did not therefore bring significant progress towards the creation of a modern nation state. Nor did the conditions under which he held office allow him to uphold unswervingly the interests of the crown against those of the nobility. For Pedro held power by virtue of support from his royal brothers, some of the nobility and most of the representatives of the *concelhos* in the *cortes.* To shore up that support he had no choice but to grant concessions, especially to great magnates. During the regency his actions contributed to an increase in the wealth and power of some of these magnates – particularly his brother Henrique, duke of Viseu, and his half-brother Afonso, count of Barcelos, whom he made duke of Bragança. Pedro's commitment to the crown's interests may have been sincere enough; but he could do little in practice to curb the great nobles.[37]

REGRESSION UNDER AFONSO V

Afonso V (1438–81) occupied the Portuguese throne for almost forty-three years – far longer than any other monarch of the house of Avis, apart from João I. Yet the internal history of Portugal during this period has been widely neglected. This is unfortunate, for the reign represents an important phase in the transition from Late Medieval to Modern times. Afonso himself was a man of complex and intriguing personality. Deprived of paternal guidance at a very young age, he was brought up at a court riddled with rivalry and intrigue. Under the regent Pedro's direction he nevertheless received a Humanist education, probably from Italian tutors. He acquired a love of books and music and was the first Portuguese king to form a royal library.[38] Yet the values manifested in both his public policies and private behaviour during his long

---

[36] Ibid, pp 264–306, 510–11.
[37] NHP vol 4, p 555.
[38] SHP vol 2, p 102.

reign – his fascination with crusading, his fawning over the higher clergy, his assiduous pandering to the landed nobility and their feudal privileges, his ambition to become emperor of all the Spains and his desperate but thwarted determination towards the end of his life to be a hermit in the Holy Land – seem stubbornly Medieval in a world that was inexorably modernising. As Armindo de Sousa has aptly concluded, between Afonso V's imagined world and the world in which he actually lived there was, or at least seemed to be, 'an abyss of centuries'.[39]

During Afonso's reign royal lands, offices, pensions and other benefits were transferred from the crown to the nobility more liberally than at any other time since the early years of João I. Noble power increased correspondingly, though it was power heavily concentrated in the hands of just a few great magnates. The leading beneficiaries were Prince Henrique and successive dukes of Bragança. But Henrique died childless in 1460, and from then on the house of Bragança was by far the richest and most powerful in Portugal, exceeded only by that of the king himself. Successive dukes of Bragança were also the acknowledged champions of noble rights. Other great magnates likewise prospered, the extent of their success demonstrated most obviously in the rapid proliferation of illustrious titles. The designations marquis, baron and viscount were introduced for the first time during this period, added to the existing titles of duke and count. Fernando, the king's younger brother, was made duke of Beja in 1453. The duke of Bragança's oldest son became duke of Guimarães, and his other two sons marquis of Montemor-o-Novo and count of Faro respectively. There were two other marquises, nine new counts (making a total of twenty-five, compared with only six at the death of Duarte), the baron of Alvito and one viscount. So depleted had become the royal estate by the time Afonso V died in 1481 that his successor, João II, complained he had been left only the king's highways.[40]

Under Afonso V the policy of avoiding dynastic entanglements with Castile was gradually abandoned. The first breach occurred in 1447, when a daughter of Prince João married Juan II of Castile. This was followed in 1455 by the marriage of Afonso V's younger sister to the weak and vacillating Castilian king, Enrique IV. This was a more fateful union, for it produced a daughter, Juana. Shortly before his death in 1474 Enrique bequeathed his kingdom to Juana – and called on Afonso V, who was by then a widower, to marry her and assume the government of Castile.[41] However, Juana's succession was disputed by Enrique's sister Isabel, who had married Fernando of Aragon – which couple

[39] In HP vol 2, p 508.
[40] MHP, p 179; NHP vol 4, pp 557, 559.
[41] Mendonça M 1991, p 102.

later become famous as 'the Catholic kings'. Their supporters declared Juana was the daughter not of Enrique, but of one Beltrán de la Cueva, a Castilian nobleman, and that Isabel was therefore the rightful queen of Castile.

Why the ageing Afonso then threw caution to the winds and invaded Castile as Juana's champion is somewhat puzzling – especially given the bitter lesson of the earlier Castilian wars. Perhaps he was simply convinced of the justice of his niece's cause, moved by family honour and persuaded by Castilian exiles. Be that as it may, in May 1475 he entered Castile at the head of a small army and proceeded to Palencia. There he went through a marriage ceremony with Juana, having meanwhile applied for a papal dispensation. However, it soon became clear that the vast majority of Castilians did not want a Portuguese king. The Castilian nobility preferred Isabel, while her husband, Fernando, proved a particularly resourceful opponent. The decisive battle was fought at Toro in 1476, a confused encounter which ended with the Portuguese withdrawing and Isabel's forces claiming victory. Crucially, Afonso had lost face. He made a desperate but forlorn attempt to engage the support of Louis XI of France, who was known to be concerned about the union of Castile and Aragon. When this failed, and no dispensation was forthcoming from the papacy, Afonso could do little more for Juana's cause. Frustrated and disillusioned, he was forced to negotiate and in 1479 signed a treaty with the Catholic kings at Alcáçovas.[42] Under its terms he renounced all claims to the Castilian throne and recognised Isabel, while the luckless Juana was sent to a nunnery. There were no more attempts to unite Portugal and Castile under a Portuguese monarch by military force.

JOÃO II, NOBLE CONSPIRACIES AND ROYAL POWER

Afonso V died in 1481 and was succeeded by his son, João II (1481–95). Although only twenty-six at the time, João was well experienced in affairs of state, having been closely involved in decision-making by his father. He possessed a deep and very Portuguese religiosity and was a man of intense emotions; but he had also been well educated, perhaps in part by the Italian Humanist Justo Baldino, and was an accomplished Latinist.[43] A strong belief in the majesty of kingship, a deep sense of responsibility to his subjects and a commitment to doing justice were among his guiding principles. Determined, hard-working and politically shrewd, João brought a new steel to royal government. Fernando and Isabel of Spain with somewhat grudging admiration referred to him simply as 'the man', and Machiavelli allegedly used him as a

---

[42] Elliott J H 1963, pp 6, 7–9, 11–12; SHP vol 2, pp 91–5.
[43] Mendonça M 1991, p 75.

model for the archetypal Renaissance ruler portrayed in *The Prince*.[44] Those of
João's own subjects who in the early years of his reign thought to challenge him
soon learned to change their tune – or suffered the consequences.

Although João II's reign was relatively short, it was also one of the most
pivotal in Portuguese history. This was partly because of remarkable progress
in Portuguese overseas expansion, to which João had a strong personal commitment. But it was also because within Portugal itself the power of the crown
grew significantly. João's determination to assert royal authority – and to do so
vigorously – was already evident at his first *cortes*, which convened at Évora in
1481 in an atmosphere of tense expectancy. Everyone knew João was of
tougher mettle than his father, and the magnates feared what he might do.
The representatives of the *concelhos* took the opportunity to submit a long list
of grievances, many of which concerned alleged abuses committed by greater
nobles within their patrimonies. The representatives called for royal justice to
be enforced by crown officials in all such jurisdictions. These demands were not
new: João himself had heard similar grievances at earlier sessions of the *cortes*
in 1475 and 1477, when acting as regent for his father. He was also acutely
aware that under Afonso V the great magnates had prevented effective action
being taken. Things would be different this time.[45]

While affirming his respect for the traditional rights of the nobility, João
declared that all grants of land, lordships and jurisdictional privileges now
required confirmation, before which they would be carefully scrutinised. He
also insisted that magnates and other leading subjects must swear their allegiance to him in a manner that acknowledged him as their unequivocal superior. It was no longer acceptable to acknowledge him as merely first among
equals, as in the feudal tradition.[46] Accordingly, a great oath-taking ceremony
was held at Évora in 1481. João sat on his throne – in regal splendour holding
his sceptre – while the assembled magnates and representatives of the *cortes*
remained humbly standing. One by one they advanced, knelt, placed their
hands in those of the king and solemnly pledged their allegiance. Each oath
was then recorded, signed and witnessed. At the conclusion the royal orator
spoke, asserting a subject's duty to be 'total obedience' and describing the king
as comparable to an Ancient Persian monarch or a Roman emperor.[47] This
performance, and the principles it represented, roused bitter resentment among
some nobles – including Dom Fernando, third duke of Bragança, the most
powerful magnate in the country. João was well aware of the potential threat

---

[44] Ibid, p 165.
[45] Moreno H B 1970, p 48; Sousa A de 1990 vol 1, pp 420–5; Mendonça M 1991, pp 128–39.
[46] Mendonça M 1991, pp 208, 247–8.
[47] Pina R de 1950, pp 16–17; Mendonça M 1991, pp 206–7.

posed by Bragança, who was said to be capable of raising a private army of 3,000 cavalry and 10,000 foot. So powerful did Bragança appear to be that João was supposed to have once quipped to him, 'the royal patrimony is divided more or less equally between you and me'.[48]

Given João's determination to be a king in fact as well as name, a showdown at some stage with Bragança was almost inevitable. It was not long in coming. By 1482 the duke and his supporters had already decided João had to go and had begun to conspire for his removal. Apparently they received some encouragement from the Catholic kings, Fernando and Isabel; but their security was lax, and late that year their conspiracy was betrayed by one of the duke's retainers. João moved swiftly, arresting Bragança and such other suspects as he could find. The duke was duly arraigned on twenty-two counts of treason, including obstructing royal justice and negotiating with the Catholic kings to seize control of Portugal. He was tried by a specially-constituted court, convicted and publicly beheaded at Évora on 20 June 1483. Among his co-conspirators were his brothers, the marquis of Montemor-o-Novo and the count of Faro, who fled to Castile. The Bragança castles and the vast ducal patrimony were confiscated and remained in royal hands for the rest of the reign.[49]

For the anti-centralist magnates, the failure of Bragança's conspiracy was a devastating defeat. Nevertheless, their resentment and opposition were by no means extinguished, and within a few months other nobles became enmeshed in a second plot. The new conspiracy again involved some of the most illustrious families in the country, including the Meneses, Coutinhos, Silveiras, Albuquerques and Ataides. A key instigator was Dom Garcia de Meneses, bishop of Évora. But the movement was headed by the king's cousin Dom Diogo, duke of Viseu, whose sister Leonor was João II's queen. Viseu was a young man of great ambition, but little sense. A passive sympathiser of the Bragança conspiracy, he had been duly cautioned; but the warning clearly fell on deaf ears. Viseu was nursing several personal grievances – such as the king's refusal to grant him the mastership of Santiago, which João had decided to reserve for his own son, Prince Afonso. The conspirators' plan was to assassinate both João II and Afonso, then elevate Viseu to the throne. Once he had become king, Viseu would recall the Bragança exiles, marry a Castilian princess and return to the pro-seigneurial policies of Afonso V.

The conspirators came close to striking on several occasions; but each time some circumstance prevented them from acting. Eventually João learned what was afoot and summoned Viseu to his private chambers in Setúbal. There on 28

[48] Sanceau E 1959, p 168; SHP vol 2, p 105.
[49] Resende G de 1973, pp 35–6; Moreno H B 1970, pp 49–51; SHP vol 2, pp 104–6; Moreno H B 1988, pp 9–11.

September 1484 he confronted him with the evidence and, in what has euphe-
mistically been called 'an act of private justice', promptly stabbed him to
death.[50] The other ringleaders were rounded up to be executed or imprisoned,
and the bishop of Évora was placed in a disused cistern in Palmela castle, where
he soon died. However, the king did not extend punishment beyond the immediate conspirators themselves. He also allowed Dom Manuel, Viseu's younger
brother, to inherit his patrimony and his second title of duke of Beja. At the
time Manuel was a frightened youth of fifteen; but he was also next in line to
the throne after Afonso, João's only legitimate son.

After the suppression of the Viseu conspiracy João II was able to dominate
the higher nobility to an extent impossible to previous kings. Unlike his father,
he kept the creation of new titles to a bare minimum. During his entire reign
only four individuals were granted peerages, one being his own much-loved
bastard son, Dom Jorge, and another the young Dom Manuel. Meanwhile the
prestige and power of the crown grew steadily – to the satisfaction of the
cortes, which in 1490 emphatically endorsed the trend. By then Fernando
and Isabel had agreed to the marriage of their oldest daughter to Prince Afonso,
to celebrate which a grand wedding festival was held at Évora. But just when
dynastic continuity, external security and internal stability all seemed to have
been secured, disaster struck. On 12 July 1491 Prince Afonso, João's only
legitimate son and therefore heir, was killed in a riding accident, so suddenly
confronting Portugal with a new succession crisis.

JOÃO II: THE LATER YEARS

After the death of Prince Afonso the heir presumptive to the crown of Portugal
was Manuel, duke of Beja. However, João II distrusted Manuel and at first
refused to endorse him, suspecting he would rehabilitate those who had been
disgraced after the Bragança and Viseu conspiracies. Instead, the king tried to
have his illegitimate son Dom Jorge recognised as his heir. He showered Jorge,
then ten years old, with honours and offices, made him master of the Orders of
Santiago and Avis and sought his legitimation from the papacy. But these
machinations were strongly resisted by Manuel's sister, Queen Leonor, whose
position had the support of Fernando and Isabel. With the Spaniard Alexander
VI occupying the papal throne, João's chances of legitimising Jorge were slight.
The king's own health was now deteriorating, and finally, under intense pressure from his Franciscan confessor, he accepted the inevitability of Manuel's
succession.[51]

---

[50] Sanceau E 1959, pp 184–200; SHP vol 2, p 107.
[51] Mendonça M 1991, pp 449–66.

Meanwhile, the ailing João II also found himself confronted by another crisis of a quite different order. In the late fifteenth century, resentment against Jews in neighbouring Castile, which had long been simmering, intensified. Fernando and Isabel decided that Judaism could no longer be tolerated, and all Jews were ordered to embrace Catholicism or leave the country, with a deadline set for 31 March 1492. Possibly as many as 120,000 Spanish Jews then tried to flee to Portugal, presenting the Portuguese with an urgent problem. João's response was to allow the refugees to stay temporarily, on payment of a substantial entry tax. But those who failed to pay, or to emigrate after eight months, were to be enslaved.[52] Many of the refugees' children were forcibly separated from their parents and Christianised, some being subsequently sent to colonise the island of São Tomé in the Gulf of Guinea. Only about 600 families with particular influence, wealth or skills were allowed to stay on in Portugal. Abraham Zacut, the celebrated astronomer, astrologer and physician, was among these favoured few. Overall the episode heightened anti-Semitism, with profound consequences for Portugal over the next two or three centuries. Meanwhile, João II had died in 1495 at the age of only forty, in his final months a rather sad and lonely figure. The cause of his death has been much debated; but the suggestion he was poisoned by Queen Leonor with arsenic is mere speculation.

LAW AND TAXES

In the century or so that elapsed between the acclamation of João I and the death of João II, Portugal began to move away from feudalism towards acquiring some of the key characteristics of a centralised modern state. However, the road was long and difficult – and the transition by the end of the fifteenth century was far from complete. The substantial autonomy still enjoyed by certain great churchmen and nobles, the corporate nature of society generally and the multiplicity of local and special jurisdictions all militated against change. Traditional rights and privileges were jealously guarded. A fundamental role of kingship was to uphold tradition in the name of balance and harmony – a solemn responsibility that João II, like all Portuguese monarchs, fully accepted. Sentiment in favour of doing things as they had always been done, or at least were believed to have been done, was deeply ingrained and had to be respected.[53]

What progress, then, was made under the early Avis kings towards the creation of a modern nation state? In the process of modern state formation

---

[52] Azevedo J L de 1922, pp 20–2; Saraiva A J 1969, pp 36–7.
[53] Cf Hespanha A M 1994, pp 523–8.

a fundamental role is usually played by the law and those who write and administer it, and this was certainly the case in early Avis Portugal. Portuguese jurists, trained in the tradition of the famous schools of Bologna, insisted that the king's law was supreme, universal and binding. In doing so they followed imperial Roman precedent, particularly as expressed in the code of Justinian, and provided the solid foundations of principle on which royal power could be posited.[54] The role in government of lawyers therefore expanded steadily, just as the quantity of royal legislation grew. By Avis times Portuguese law had become so voluminous and complex that codification was an urgent necessity, and work on this task, begun under João I, was finally completed during Pedro's regency. The result was the so-called *Ordenações Afonsinas* of 1446, which despite its name owed little to Afonso V. Promulgated before the use of the printing press, the *Ordenações Afonsinas* was diffused gradually; but it nevertheless became, and until well into the sixteenth century remained, the fundamental authority for Portuguese jurisprudence.[55]

Long before the reign of João II the basic institutions of the Portuguese judicial system had also been put in place. By the mid-fourteenth century the court of appeal for criminal cases (*Casa da Suplicação*) had been separated from the superior court, which dealt mostly with civil cases (*Casa do Cível*). There was also a third superior court that heard matters relating to the state finances, Jews and Muslims.[56] As proceedings became more standardised, more closely regulated and more conducive to the delivery of impartial justice, the reputation and authority of these various courts were strengthened. The kingdom was also divided up into six judicial circuits, each corresponding to a province (*comarca*) and presided over by a superior magistrate known as a *corregedor*. In addition, Lisbon and sometimes Santarém had their own *corregedores*. These magistrates exercised administrative and judicial authority in the king's name – though their right to enter and hold court in the seigneuries of the great lay and ecclesiastical magnates, and in the territories of the judicially privileged municipalities, was long resisted. Seigneurial immunities and protected local jurisdictions were especially strong under Afonso V, but the royal *corregedores* were much more assertive under João II.

By the final years of the fifteenth century the *corregedor* was a formidable figure. He progressed round his circuit accompanied by an entourage of assistants ranging from advocates to executioners, not to mention chained prisoners and innumerable dependents. All had to be accommodated in the towns where court was held. Often they remained for weeks, voraciously consuming

---

[54] HP vol 3, pp 363–4.
[55] SHP vol 2, pp 224–5; DIHP vol 1, p 22.
[56] NHP vol 4, pp 298–9.

supplies – a disruptive, expensive and perhaps fearful experience for the local populace. But the *corregedor*'s visit nonetheless demonstrated that the king's law extended ever more widely through the kingdom.[57] The impact of this by late in João II's reign may be sensed by comparing the *concelhos*' grievances voiced at the 1481 *cortes* with those expressed at the *cortes* of 1490. At the former there were many complaints about extortions and other abuses of power by the great magnates, plus demands that the royal *corregedores* exercise authority to override the judicial officers of seigneurial lords. But in 1490 such requests were replaced by protests against the increasing numbers, and excessive zeal, of crown officials. Apparently concern had shifted from the excesses of private power to the intrusiveness of an increasingly effective royal administration.[58] Meanwhile, at a more grass-root level the growing acceptance of, and familiarity with, the king's law can be seen in the work of public notaries (*tabeliães*), of whom there were perhaps as many as one for every 250 inhabitants by late in the period.[59] Since the appointments of all these officials required royal confirmation, their names can be traced in the Chancery records. For the first half of the sixteenth century they have now been systematically studied by João José Alves Dias.[60]

Another critical measure of the progress of centralisation was the crown's capacity to raise revenue on a continuing basis. In Medieval times, most regular revenues of the Portuguese crown came from the royal patrimony, and little distinction was made between the monarch's personal income and the receipts of the state. For special purposes, particularly military enterprises or royal weddings, kings resorted to loans; but to maintain credit worthiness and ultimately to repay what had been borrowed, they required additional revenues from their subjects: in other words, taxes. Traditionally, imposing a tax required the consent of the great men of the kingdom, and increasingly also the consent of the *concelhos*' representatives in the *cortes*. Taxes were imposed for specific purposes for limited periods only. However, by the late fifteenth century Portuguese rulers were striving to create a system of regular and permanent taxation – as were the kings of France and England.

The two main components of the Portuguese national taxation system as it developed in this era were *sisas* and customs duties. The *sisas* were payable by all subjects without exception and were imposed on any goods bought or sold, except gold, silver, horses, arms and bread. Originally *sisas* were municipal taxes; but they were granted to João I by the *cortes* of 1387 to fund the national

---

[57] HP vol 3, pp 518–20.
[58] Mendonça M 1991, pp 49, 208–21, 411–33.
[59] HP vol 3, p 519–20; Dias J J A 1996, pp 129–32.
[60] Dias J J A 1996, pp 129–47.

war effort and to provide for Queen Philippa's household. João I subsequently retained them as a permanent royal tax, and by the end of his reign they were providing some 75 per cent of the crown's revenue. Repeated protests by later assemblies of the *cortes* over this usurpation were of no avail. The *sisas* had become too important for the crown to relinquish, and João II made it clear in 1481 that their imposition would be permanent.[61]

Customs duties were collected at Portuguese ports at customs houses (*alfândegas*) and at frontier crossings through the so-called *portos secos*. Again, taxing goods in transit had formerly been a seigneurial and municipal privilege, but in the course of the fifteenth century it was transformed into a major source of revenue for the crown that eventually became even more important than the *sisas*. Customs revenue was greatly boosted as a consequence of the trade in exotic goods emanating from Portuguese overseas expansion in the fifteenth and subsequent centuries – with enormous long-term impact on the country's capitalist economy.

THE CHANGING ART OF WAR

Portuguese kings needed more revenue by the late fourteenth century especially because of their escalating military costs. These cost increases were mainly a consequence of developments in the technology of warfare. Chain mail, long worn by knights, was being steadily replaced by more expensive plate armour. Fortifications were being re-designed and strengthened to better withstand sieges. Perhaps most important of all, the introduction and escalating use of the crossbow amounted to a revolution in weaponry. Systematic recruitment and training of crossbowmen (*besteiros*) probably began in Portugal during the first half of the fourteenth century, but progressed slowly. The process required complex organisation on a national scale, but was an essential step towards the creation of a permanent royal army. Units of crossbowmen were raised on a quota basis by the Portuguese municipalities. The archers were recruited primarily from the sons of tradesmen, not members of the nobility or their retainers, and they were equipped with their weapons directly by the crown.[62]

Though in the struggle against Juan of Castile a substantial proportion of João I's army still consisted of feudal levies, the presence of the crossbowmen enabled Nuno Álvares Pereira to apply one of the most important lessons of the Hundred Years War – namely, that well-trained, disciplined bowmen drawn up in sound defensive positions could devastate slow-moving knights on horseback. So it had been at Crécy and Poitiers – and so it was at Aljubarrota. On

---

[61] DIHP vol 1, pp 256–7; NHP vol 4, p 305; HP vol 3, pp 521–3.
[62] NHP vol 4, pp 348–50.

that memorable field the Portuguese army, though smaller than that of Castile, was more coherent, better led and perhaps more advanced on the road to modernisation. While Portugal did not retain these advantages for long, they were nevertheless crucial in 1385, when the kingdom's need was greatest.[63]

Early in the fourteenth century the still more revolutionary powder weapons were introduced; but they were then too unreliable and therefore slow to gain acceptance. However, by the start of the fifteenth century cannon were proving their worth, especially in siege warfare. Under the early Avis kings they were gradually incorporated into the nation's arsenal. Firearms and gunpowder were kept strictly under crown control, with a central arsenal maintained in Lisbon.[64] Cannon were used to great effect by both Afonso V and later monarchs in Morocco. They were also mounted on warships.

All this meant that well before the end of the fifteenth century waging independent war was inexorably moving beyond the means of even the greatest of magnates – unless they could act in unison with powerful outside forces. Great nobles might still retain a capacity to put into the field significant forces, but were at a growing comparative disadvantage to the crown. This was graphically demonstrated by the downfall of the duke of Bragança in 1483. From the time João I became firmly established on his throne, no Portuguese noble dared to offer a direct challenge to the king militarily. The only exception was Pedro, the beleaguered ex-regent, who was easily overwhelmed at Alfarrobeira in 1449. Nobles who sought to get rid of a king were thereafter more inclined to try assassination. This helps to explain why from the time of Afonso V monarchs and their families were usually protected by a royal guard approximately 200 strong. In short, there is no doubt that by the Avis era advances in the art of war strengthened the king vis-à-vis the nobility and contributed significantly to Portugal's advance towards modern statehood.

More unusually, the Portuguese crown also developed one of the most effective fighting navies possessed by any contemporary European monarch in this period, its only serious rival being that of Castile. The origins of this Portuguese navy are obscure, though there are fleeting mentions of crown warships as early as the mid-twelfth century. In 1317 King Dinis, concerned to defend the coast and shipping from Muslim corsairs and to mount his own offensive operations, contracted with the Genoese Manuel Pessagno to establish a permanent galley fleet based in Lisbon.[65] This was a far-sighted, long-term investment, for navies even more than armies could not be created

[63] Elliott J H 1963, pp 123–4; HP vol 3, p 106.
[64] NHP vol 4, p 351.
[65] DIHP vol 1, pp 438–9; NHP vol 4, pp 358–64; DHDP vol 2, pp 687–8, 896–7; Albuquerque L de 1989, pp 40–8.

overnight. During the next few decades, the Portuguese crown accumulated the necessary resources and experience to sustain a permanent fleet and to begin to build up a great naval tradition. In the fourteenth century, the navy consisted mainly of galleys for which rowers were recruited from Portugal's coastal communities; but it must at times have also included various kinds of sailing ships.[66]

The high cost and technical proficiency needed to maintain galley squadrons meant they were a military arm which only the state could sustain. Already in 1369 King Fernando possessed thirty-two galleys. Later, galleys played a key role in the successful defence of Lisbon by João of Avis in 1384. Portugal also developed a capacity to move substantial military forces by sea using sailing ships. This capacity made serious campaigning in North Africa possible – and without it the famous Ceuta expedition of 1415 could not have been mounted. Moreover, it was Portuguese success in building and manning ocean-going sailing vessels that made possible the country's role in early Atlantic exploration.

[66] Godinho V M 1962, pp 33–4.

8

The Golden Age

The period from about the mid-1490s to the early 1540s is in many respects the most memorable in Portugal's history, an era which later generations came to view nostalgically as a Golden Age. During these years, Portugal attained a significance in world affairs it had never approached before and has never equalled since. Portuguese sailors rounded the Cape of Good Hope, and Portuguese pioneers founded settlements and trading posts from Brazil to the islands of southeast Asia. Meanwhile in Europe the kingdom itself overcame internal political tensions that had dogged it for centuries. Economic conditions were generally positive, some deterioration in the final decade or two notwithstanding. There were notable literary and artistic achievements, and the mood of the nation was decidedly optimistic.

The first phase of this Golden Age was presided over by King Manuel I (1495–1521). A grandson of King Duarte, he ascended the throne against all the odds – only after the fortuitous deaths of his cousin, Prince Afonso, and five older brothers of his own, and greatly against the will of João II. In the eyes of certain courtiers this marked Manuel out as a king by special divine grace, a last-born made first like the biblical King David. Manuel himself was deeply influenced by such perceptions and was encouraged, particularly by his secretary Duarte Galvão, to believe he was God's instrument for a sacred task. That task, he decided, was to lead a crusade against Islam, now identified as the great whore of Babylon whose imminent fall had been predicted by St John the Divine. The ultimate objectives were to capture Jerusalem, destroy Mecca and overthrow the Islamic powers. Then Manuel would be proclaimed emperor of the East, and a long peace under benevolent Christian rule would follow.[1]

Although not all Portuguese shared Manuel's crusading vision, he soon gained the reputation of being one of Portugal's most successful kings. As early as the mid-sixteenth century the humanist Damião de Góis called him 'most fortunate', and that description has continued to resonate ever since.[2] In his time the population of Portugal was rising steadily and its economy was growing. Dramatic overseas expansion was in progress, and Portugal quite suddenly became the principal commercial intermediary between Europe and Asia, a role it snatched from Venice. Though overseas expansion involved some significant economic and social costs, it certainly helped to alleviate fundamental internal tensions, particularly between crown and nobility. Manuel's reign also saw more progress towards the formation of a centralised bureaucratic state. The royal court became richer and more elaborate, and the figure of the king more remote. Progress was made in reforming the church, and major achievements occurred in nautical science. In short, this was a time when Portuguese accomplishments were greater than ever before, and Portuguese self-confidence and ambition attained new peaks. Manuel's international prestige exceeded that of any of his predecessors on the Portuguese throne – and, indeed, of his successors.

After Manuel's death the Golden Age seemed to continue through approximately the first two decades of João III's reign; but from about 1540 it began to show signs of fading. João himself, who was nineteen years old when he ascended the throne, proved a cautious monarch, inclined to consult carefully and weigh up options. The era of Portugal's most explosive expansion was now over, and the country was entering a period of imperial consolidation and rationalisation. João did not share Manuel's apocalyptic expectations, but he did develop a strong commitment to Christian proselytising overseas. His approach to expansion was pragmatic – and he soon reduced both the state's involvement in imperial administration and the crown's participation in overseas trade. João's government struggled to find the manpower and material resources it needed to maintain its commitments and was obliged to take careful stock. This process resulted in the abandonment of some territorial acquisitions and ambitions, particularly in Morocco – but the determined pursuit of others. João thereby came to terms in certain theatres with the challenging process of imperial withdrawal and decolonisation, whilst in others still vigorously pursuing expansion.

---

[1] Thomaz L F R 1990, pp 55, 78–86 and 1991, pp 99–101; Subrahmanyam S 1997, pp 54–6.
[2] Góis D de 1790 pt 1, ch 4.

THE GOLDEN AGE ECONOMY

The first-ever Portuguese census was conducted under Joao III in 1527–32 and revealed a total population of between about 1.25 and 1.5 million. This was slightly below the peak reached before the Black Death, when Portugal had an estimated 1.5 million inhabitants; but it did show a marked improvement since 1450, when numbers had slumped to less than a million. Moreover, the upward trend seemed firmly set and continued for the rest of the sixteenth century.[3] Most of the growth occurred in urban areas, and a steady influx of people from the countryside into the towns took place. Between the accession of King Manuel and the middle years of João III's reign seventeen new *vilas* were created in Portugal. Many existing towns expanded as well, with growth especially strong in Lisbon and the northwest. It was during this period that Porto rose to become the second city of the kingdom, with perhaps 15,000 inhabitants. Lisbon itself had a population of about 65,000 in 1527 and 100,000 by mid-century, by which time it was the largest city in the whole Iberian peninsula.[4] Demographic expansion was what underlay Portugal's prosperity during the Golden Age, made urban renewal necessary, stimulated the growth of bureaucracy, facilitated empire-building, drove emigration and even made the forced absorption or expulsion of Jews and Muslims more practicable.

An increasing population meant greater demands for food and other basic commodities, putting pressure on agriculture, pastoral production and land-use generally. Areas that had been abandoned as a consequence of the Black Death were now gradually re-occupied. Land that had never previously been put to the plough was cleared, forests were cut, marshes drained and river meadows extended through major hydraulic works.[5] However, Portugal did not have much vacant land suitable for agriculture, and it was not long before dubiously marginal tracts were being developed. Often such land gave quite good initial yields, but then became rapidly exhausted, sometimes to the point at which it had to be abandoned. Moreover, deforestation was steadily destroying woodlands traditionally used for communal foraging. Eventually Manuel became so alarmed at this trend that he introduced an extensive tree-planting program.

Wheat was the standard cereal crop in Portugal during the Golden Age with cultivation concentrated in the southern and central regions, especially Alentejo, Estremadura and the Tagus valley. With increasing demand wheat prices rose – slowly until the 1530s, then more rapidly. But there was little if any increase in production, and Portugal's problems as a grain-deficit country grew more acute.

---

[3] Marques A H de O and Dias J J A 1994, pp 178–9, 181, 186; NHP vol 5, pp 13, 21–2.
[4] Marques A H de O and Dias J J A 1994, pp 179, 187.
[5] NHP vol 5, pp 85, 167–8; HP vol 3, p 246.

A large wheat storage depot had to be constructed beside the Tagus in Lisbon to house the growing volume of cereal imports. Portuguese who could not afford wheat, or lived where conditions were unsuited to its growth, relied on rye, millet, barley or increasingly maize. Sixteenth-century Portugal would have faced far greater difficulty in feeding its population but for the introduction shortly before 1520 of maize from the New World. Maize was relatively easy for peasant farmers to grow, was highly nutritious to humans and could also provide fodder, fuel and even cushion fillings. Its cultivation therefore spread rapidly and enabled the land to support a denser population. Over time, especially in the crowded northwest, maize-growing transformed the rural landscape.[6]

Portuguese rural production during the Golden Age was becoming gradually more market oriented. There were growing urban outlets for staple crops like wheat; but most commercial farmers preferred to expand their plantings of vines and olive groves, which also had promising export potential. While these two commodities were practically ubiquitous, others were confined to particular areas, such as figs in the coastal Algarve where production surged during the sixteenth century.[7] Pasture was in high demand for commercial grazing of cattle and sheep. There was a trend towards leasing land out to entrepreneurs, who were willing to pay regular rents in advance to the ultimate owner while sub-letting to peasant farmers. In this way de facto control of agricultural production gradually passed from the seigneurial elite to enterprising capitalist intermediaries – who might be *fidalgos,* merchants or even richer peasants. Sub-letting also resulted in the traditional units of production – the *quintas* and *casais* – becoming more fragmented, especially in northern and central Portugal. Returns from rents and dues rose steadily, and competition for land placed common grazing rights under threat. The crown tried to regulate land transfers to ensure that holdings were used productively, and to protect the interests of local communities. In short, there seems little doubt that during this period demand for land in more and more of Portugal was exceeding supply.[8]

Notwithstanding all these developments, the changes that occurred in Portugal's rural economy during the Golden Age pale into insignificance compared with what was happening in the kingdom's external trade – especially that of Lisbon. In the century between the mid-1490s and mid-1590s the customs receipts at Lisbon grew a massive seventeen-fold.[9] Clearly seaborne trade was expanding phenomenally, in both absolute and relative terms. The trend was already apparent by the late fifteenth century when Portuguese

[6] MHP, p 272; NHP vol 5, pp 171–2, 243–5; HP vol 3, p 330.
[7] Magalhães J R 1993, pp 161–2; NHP vol 5, pp 173–4, 176.
[8] NHP vol 5, pp 85–6, 95–6, 100.
[9] DHP vol 2, p 257.

merchants regularly frequented Castile, England, France and the Low Countries, and Italian and northern European merchants settled in Lisbon. Portuguese salt, wine, olive oil, cork, dried fruits, wax and honey were exported; among the goods imported were cereals, textiles, ironware and firearms. This suggests a pattern of Portugal-based external trade that differed little structurally from that of the late Middle Ages. However, what was new – and indeed unprecedented – was the development of a spectacular Portuguese re-export trade in exotic products from outside Europe. This phenomenon was fundamental in creating the perception of the first half of the sixteenth century as a Golden Age.

Portugal was already re-exporting exotic overseas products well before Manuel's accession. This is most clearly demonstrated in the country's trading pattern with Flanders, a major external market as well as point of access to Germany and other parts of northern Europe. The Flanders *feitoria* was importing sugar from Portuguese Madeira by the mid-fifteenth century and soon afterwards began to take goods from the Portuguese West Africa trade – including malagueta pepper, ivory and above all gold. In 1499 the *feitoria* was shifted from Bruges to Antwerp where the Portuguese began selling pepper. Within five years Portugal had secured a near monopoly of pepper imports into Europe, mainly at the expense of Venice – and its dominance was not challenged till the mid-sixteenth century, and even then not very seriously.[10] The Antwerp *feitoria* also handled Portuguese re-exports of many other Asian goods, including Chinese porcelain, silk and an increasing range of spices such as cinnamon, ginger, nutmeg and cloves. Another exotic Portuguese re-export that grew rapidly in the sixteenth century was African slaves. They were eagerly bought in Spain, Italy, France, England and other parts of western Europe. But the Flanders trade had special significance, both because of its relatively high volume and because it gave the Portuguese access to central European silver and copper, which were essential for the India trade. During King Manuel's reign, much of this activity was state-controlled, and pepper itself was declared a crown monopoly in 1520.

Paucity of quantifiable data has made it difficult to measure the economic impact of these major commercial developments. However, Vitorino Magalhães Godinho, the leading economic historian of Portuguese expansion, considered that by the early sixteenth century external trade had become the Portuguese crown's most important source of revenue. In 1506, direct and indirect returns to the crown from overseas trade already accounted for 65 per cent of total receipts. In 1518–19, the proportion had risen to over 68 per

---

[10] Godinho V M 1981–83 vol 3, pp 81–94; DHDP vol 1, pp 75–7.

cent, with returns from Asian pepper and spices alone exceeding all internal Portuguese revenues. Clearly, it was the fruits of overseas expansion, rather than those of growth within Portugal itself, that accounted for most of the increased prosperity of the Golden Age.[11]

By the end of Manuel's reign Lisbon had new suburbs that spilled out beyond its walls towards the north and west and had far outgrown its old Medieval perimeter. The commercial district (*cidade baixa*) was particularly vibrant, with busy, crowded streets and houses up to four or five storeys high.[12] Besides traditional Portuguese and European commodities the shops here offered a rich variety of imports from Asia and Africa. As a contemporary verse boasted, anyone coming to Portugal could now find there an astonishing range of luxuries. They included gold, pearls and precious stones, spices, drugs and gums, porcelain and diamonds, and exotic wild beasts from elephants and lions to talking parrots.[13] This new-found opulence was accompanied by rising prices, Portugal being one of the first European countries to be affected by the Price Revolution. But for most of the first half of the sixteenth century increases were relatively gradual and therefore manageable.

These were also times when the Portuguese enjoyed remarkable monetary stability. From as early as 1457 access to West African gold had made possible the striking of the Portuguese gold *cruzado,* a coin that became renowned for exceptional purity and was much sought after throughout Europe. The *cruzado* was maintained at a fixed value of 390 *reais* to 1517 and then 400 *reais* until 1559. To celebrate Vasco da Gama's pioneer voyage to India, King Manuel also issued a massive ten-*cruzado* gold coin known as a *português*. This coin was almost pure gold, being assayed at 98.96 per cent.[14] It proved spectacularly successful, boosting Manuel's international prestige and creating a model which other rulers for years strove to emulate.

More prosaically, a Manueline commission reviewed and updated a multiplicity of municipal charters (*foraes*), with the aim of standardising taxation. The complex systems of customs and excise that had been inherited were simplified, and the government assumed direct responsibility for revenue collection rather than contracting it out to tax-farmers.[15] Government securities called *juros* were introduced in 1500, initially paying 7 per cent interest. *Juros* soon developed into a permanent feature of Portuguese state financing and were eventually consolidated into a national debt. In 1502 a floating debt offering

---

[11] Godinho V M in DHP vol 2, p 257.
[12] Marques A H de O and Dias J J A 1994, pp 178–9; Dias J J A 1996, p 112.
[13] Dias J S da S 1973, p 6.
[14] NHP vol 5, p 255; Gomes A J and Trigueiros A M 1992, p 108.
[15] NHP vol 5, pp 249–50, 395–6, 714.

much higher interest rates was also begun – and both debts grew rapidly. From time to time loans were raised from particular bodies or communities, including the municipalities, the clergy and the 'New Christians' (see below).[16] Though the *cortes* was summoned with decreasing frequency, when it did meet – in 1502, 1525 and 1544 – it voted subsidies. All this meant there was a substantial increase in state receipts: they almost doubled between 1500 and 1530, then rose by a further 50 per cent by the mid-1550s. Although expenditures rose even faster, the budget remained in surplus until the 1550s. The result was that the crown had the means to do much more than in the past, and there was a massive increase in fiscal activity.

However, it is important not to be too dazzled by these achievements. Beneath the glitter Portugal still remained a rather backward country, even by the modest standards of sixteenth-century Europe. Local communities were often stubbornly inward-looking, and a limited infrastructure restricted the circulation of both goods and people.[17] The internal economy was highly fragmented, and travellers in many parts of the kingdom faced formidable obstacles, particularly outside the major river routes. Roads were few and ill-maintained, and there were no coaches before the 1580s, so that people had to move by horse, mule, donkey or on foot. Goods were shifted by slow and cumbersome pack animals or ox carts, and bandits remained a serious hazard. Inns were few and primitive, and a religious house was often the traveller's only option for a night's rest.

THE COURT AND THE KING'S MAJESTY

In the late summer of 1502, King Manuel undertook a highly public pilgrimage in thanksgiving for the successful return of Vasco da Gama from India. He and his following travelled north to Coimbra where they visited the Santa Cruz monastery, cradle of Portugal's first royal dynasty. Finding the tomb of Afonso Henriques to be too modest, Manuel ordered its reconstruction. He then moved on, crossed the Spanish border and proceeded to the shrine of St James at Compostela. There he remained for three days of devotions and social engagements before returning to Lisbon. To commemorate his visit he gave the cathedral of St James a magnificent silver lamp fashioned in the shape of a castle – according to Damião de Gois, one of the richest objects ever presented to that major Christian shrine.[18]

Manuel's visits to Coimbra and Compostela reveal much about how he saw himself and his role. There was the desire to demonstrate publicly his

---

[16] Ibid, pp 252–3.
[17] Ibid, pp 195–203, 209–11.
[18] Gois D de 1790 pt 1, ch 64.

association with Afonso Henriques – symbolically significant not only because of the latter's prestige as founding father of the kingdom, but because of his close association with the Reconquest. For at the time Manuel was seeking to promote his own neo-Reconquest in Morocco and his great ambition to recover Jerusalem for Christendom. Then there was the self-evidently devotional element in the visit. To travel on pilgrimage to Compostela was to seek divine blessing in a manner that was quintessentially Catholic and Medieval. Of course, the event also provided a good opportunity for Manuel to display kingly opulence and so further enhance his growing reputation. Visiting Compostela underlined Manuel's Spanish connections, a point to which we shall return shortly. Moreover, the pilgrimage is a reminder that kings of that era travelled frequently. The royal court had no fixed location: it was simply where the king was. Manuel possessed castles and palaces in many places: they were to be found in almost every town of importance in the country, many of them having been captured or built during the Reconquest.[19] Both Manuel and João III, though less ambulatory than their predecessors, spent considerable periods at their various provincial residences – sometimes for reasons of state, often for reasons of health, but also just to spread the burden of supporting the court's presence. During 1506–7 when 'plague' was raging in Lisbon, the court resided successively in Almeirim, Abrantes, Setúbal, Évora and Tomar.

However, if only because a larger court meant greater transport and accommodation difficulties, the king's preferred and most common place of residence was in Lisbon. There Manuel at first lived in the old *alcaçova* – the bleak castle of São Jorge on its hill overlooking the city. His daughters Isabel and Beatriz were born in this castle in 1503 and 1504 respectively, and there the future João III was acclaimed heir.[20] But in 1505, the court moved to a more comfortable palace on the Tagus waterfront. Much extended and re-furbished over the next few decades, this became known as the River Palace (*Paço da Ribeira*). It was graced with many elegant Renaissance features, including galleries, staircases, numerous windows and eventually even a hanging garden projecting out over the Tagus. Within was also a great audience hall, a chapel royal and a library. As befitted the principal palace of a monarch whose fortunes were so closely associated with overseas trade, on the ground floor were the premises of various government departments, including the celebrated *Casa da Índia*.[21] Much altered and embellished over the years, the palace was destroyed in the great 1755 Lisbon earthquake.

---

[19] NHP vol 5, p 127.
[20] Goís D de 1790 pt 1, chs 75, 67, 82.
[21] NHP vol 5, pp 80, 348–9; Jordan A 1994, p 82.

Under Manuel the royal court grew ever larger and more magnificent, and around the person of the king was played out an increasingly elaborate ritual.[22] More attention was now paid to the niceties of distance. A symbolic royal space was maintained about the king's person, and his subjects were required to remain always at a level below him. The king's chair and the royal dining table were raised on a dais. On ceremonial occasions his magnificent robes, his heraldic devices and colours, his regalia and especially his sceptre all proclaimed the king's majesty. The tableau was completed by appropriate demeanour from all who came before him. One addressed the king's majesty on one's knees, with hat removed; one sat only on the monarch's express invitation, and always on a lower chair. When travelling the king rode on horseback sheltered by a canopy of rich brocade, his trumpeters and kettle drummers, his mace carrier, ministers, officials and courtiers preceding him. On great occasions subjects welcomed their king with dancers and mummers and by festooning the streets through which he passed. Under Manuel theatricality grew more pronounced, the participants more exotic. The first European monarch to possess large animals imported by sea from Asia and Africa, Manuel at one stage boasted five elephants, a rhinoceros, a Persian horse and a hunting lynx, which Goís tells us often took part in his cavalcades through Lisbon.[23] He was also the first Portuguese king to adopt the title 'Majesty'.

THE CASTILIAN CONNECTION AND THE JEWS

Under Manuel Portugal's dynastic links with Castile – which was now united with Aragon to form Spain – grew steadily closer. The new intimacy followed from the treaty of Alcaçovas, an agreement that brought peace between the two countries in 1479, but required as surety of good faith an exchange of royal children. As part of this exchange, Manuel had lived at the Castilian court between the ages of ten and thirteen – particularly impressionable years.[24] Not long after his accession he married Isabel, the Catholic kings' oldest daughter and widow of the late Prince Afonso. When the luckless Isabel died in childbirth in 1498, Manuel married her sister Maria. The latter patiently bore him nine children before she in turn died in 1517. Manuel then took as his third wife the much younger Leonor, Isabel and Maria's niece.

João III followed a very similar family strategy. In 1525 he married Catarina, Leonor's sister – and the close relationship between the two royal houses was further strengthened when the Emperor Carlos V, king of Spain (1516–56) and

---

[22] Alves A M 1984, pp 5–26.
[23] Goís D de 1790 pt 4, ch 84.
[24] Ibid pt 1 ch 5; NHP vol 5, p 712.

brother of Leonor and Catarina, married João's sister. Meanwhile opportunities to forge family links outside the peninsula were not entirely overlooked. There were efforts in the 1520s to arrange for João III's brother, Dom Luís, to marry a French princess or even Mary Tudor – though these ultimately came to nothing.[25] But the strongest dynastic links were always and deliberately with Spain.

The royal marriages of this period demonstrate just how completely the cautious dynastic policies of João I had been abandoned. A situation had again been created in which it was likely either a Portuguese or a Spanish prince would inherit both crowns, so uniting the peninsular kingdoms. For a brief period in 1498, when Manuel's pregnant wife Isabel was heir presumptive of the Catholic kings, it looked as though the prize might fall to the Avis. Isabel returned to Castile for her confinement amid much expectancy; but there she died giving birth to Manuel's first son, Miguel da Paz. The boy, now heir to the thrones of Castile, Aragon and Portugal, remained in Castile, presenting Manuel with the prospect that his successor would be a non-resident triple monarch. Arrangements were therefore hastily made for Portugal's governance in that eventuality, providing that the country be administered as a separate kingdom with all important offices held by Portuguese.[26] In the event Miguel da Paz died in infancy, making the arrangements for the time being unnecessary. Nevertheless, the provisions approximated those under which Portugal was joined to Spain some eighty years later. Clearly, even if the peninsula's unification had come through an Avis rather than a Habsburg prince, Portugal would still have been relegated to the periphery.

However, while a dual monarchy would doubtless have been a very mixed blessing for Portugal in these years, a close friendship with Spain offered many benefits. In particular it meant peace and security along the border, and by and large also peaceful co-existence overseas. The key to the latter was the Luso-Spanish treaty of Tordesilhas (1494), which, amplifying the overseas components of the earlier treaty of Alcaçovas, established an agreed theoretical boundary between the Portuguese and Spanish spheres of expansion. This recalls similar agreements during the later Reconquest. The Tordesilhas line was supposed to pass 370 leagues west of the Azores, the Portuguese sphere lying to its east. In 1529 the treaty of Zaragoça extended the agreement to the far side of the globe, contriving to assign the Moluccas to Portugal and the Philippines to Spain. The imperial interests of the two powers were thereafter increasingly treated as complementary, and they co-operated in various ways, such as protecting shipping routes.[27]

---

[25] Loades D 1989, pp 104, 123–6, 152, 201; NHP vol 5, p 735.
[26] NHP vol 5, pp 716–18.
[27] MedHP J vol 5, p 262.

Nevertheless, for some parts of Portuguese society close association with Spain proved disastrous. These were the large and important community of Portuguese Jews and the small remnant of Portuguese Muslims. Portuguese Jewry at the start of the Golden Age had been relatively free of serious molestation for many centuries – though Spanish Jews, who had fled to Portugal at the end of João II's reign, were accorded much less favourable treatment. Jews in Portugal were unpopular and provided obvious scapegoats in times of stress; but they were nonetheless fairly well protected by the crown and the great magnates – for they were essential to national well-being, comprising a vital component of the mercantile bourgeoisie. At the end of the fifteenth century, they owned perhaps a fifth of the moveable property in the country and probably ran most of its financial services. They played a more important role in Portugal than in any other European country.[28] Yet on 31 October 1497, Manuel ordered the expulsion, on pain of death, of all Jews and Muslims from his kingdom.

In Early Modern Portugal, as in Christian Europe generally, there was a widely held assumption that religious minorities were politically suspect and that conformity in matters of faith was essential in the national interest. Against this background, Manuel consulted widely before reaching his decision. His lawyers, the higher clergy and the town councils all favoured expulsion; some nobles, probably fearing a wave of Jewish exiles would help Portugal's enemies in North Africa, opposed it. But the real catalyst was less a hardening of anti-Semitic sentiment in Portugal than the insistence of Fernando and Isabel that Manuel 'cleanse' his kingdom of Jews before they would allow him to marry their daughter Isabel. That Manuel was prepared to comply underlines the great importance he attached to the Spanish connection. Of course, Manuel and his council were aware of the damage a Jewish exodus could inflict on the Portuguese economy and therefore made every effort to convert the Jews instead. All Jewish children under the age of fourteen were ordered to be forcibly baptised. Many reluctant adults were treated similarly, and the departure of the rest was so hindered that eventually all but a few were Christianised and therefore remained.[29]

Once all this had been done Manuel tried to re-assure what was by then a thoroughly traumatised community. Former Jews were guaranteed their property. They were to be officially known as New Christians (*cristãos novos*), and the use of insulting terms like *marrano* was prohibited. The government recognised it would take time for the new faith to take hold, so the New Christians were promised immunity from investigation into their beliefs and practices for

[28] Saraiva A J 1969, pp 18–20, 28–31.
[29] Ibid, pp 38–40.

twenty years.[30] Meanwhile social integration was encouraged. Former Jewish ghettoes were thrown open to outsiders and were gradually absorbed into the broader community. Synagogues disappeared, and houses abandoned by departing Jews were occupied by Christians. New Christians discarded such Jewish names as Jacob or Ruth and adopted instead Portuguese ones like Jorge or Maria.[31] But, despite everything, Manuel still remained suspicious of former Jews and their movements – and they were forbidden to travel overseas or to sell their property without special license.

The New Christians themselves remained tense and fearful. There was a steady trickle of emigrants to the Netherlands, other parts of northern Europe and North Africa. Despite government policies, the popular odium previously reserved for Jews was now transferred to New Christians, and soon there were renewed outbreaks of anti-Semitic violence. The worst occurred in Lisbon in April 1506 when a frenzied mob, egged on by Dominican friars, massacred several thousand terrified New Christians, throwing many of them onto a huge bonfire in Lisbon's central square, the Rossio.[32] Alarmed by such violence, Manuel tried to accelerate cultural integration by a combination of incentives and coercion. Restrictions on travel and sale of property were lifted, and New Christians were made eligible for honours and offices at all levels, including membership in the religious and military orders. At the same time, Jewish education and explicitly Jewish customs were prohibited. With a few exceptions such as medical texts, Hebrew books were banned and libraries confiscated. These Manueline policies were substantially continued by João III and were effective to the extent that New Christians were steadily entering the lower and middle ranks of the nobility by the 1530s, and even infiltrating the clergy.[33] The expulsion of unconverted Portuguese Muslims was meanwhile accomplished with less trauma. Unlike Jewish children, Muslim children were not forcibly baptised, Manuel desiring to avoid reprisals against Christians in North Africa. Converted former Muslims (*Cristãos novos mouros*) faded into the general population within a couple of generations.[34]

ELITE SOCIETY, GOVERNMENT AND BUREAUCRACY

The nobility were generally quiescent when Manuel ascended the throne, having been forcibly brought to heel by João II; but they required sensitive

---

[30] NHP vol 5, p 722.
[31] Tavares M J P F 1992, pp 173–6.
[32] Goís D de 1790 pt 1, ch 102.
[33] Tavares M J P F 1992, p 178.
[34] NHP vol 5, pp 723–4; Braga I M D 1998, p 52.

management. Important individuals among them, mostly linked to the house of Bragança, had been marginalised. For both personal and political reasons, Manuel offered them reconciliation, allowing those exiled to return from Castile and reinstating the Braganças. Supporters of João II who had earlier been granted portions of the confiscated Bragança inheritance were obliged to relinquish them – but were then compensated from the royal purse.[35] The duke of Bragança again became Portugal's premier *grande*, in both rank and wealth. However, Manuel created a counterbalance by simultaneously building up the house of Dom Jorge, João II's bastard, who was confirmed as duke of Coimbra and given substantial endowments. A kind of two-tier peerage was therefore created, with Bragança and Coimbra standing out, their incomes almost matching those of all other *grandes* combined. Manuel, and later João III, both created new peers; but they did so sparingly. There were thirteen *grandes* at Manuel's accession, and still only sixteen at João III's death. The great nobles were thereby mollified, and their relations with the crown stabilised. Meanwhile, royal wealth and power vis-à-vis the *grandes* steadily increased. When Manuel died in 1521 he was by far the greatest lord in the land. Even before the Orders of Santiago and Avis were absorbed by the crown in 1550, almost all major towns and nearly 40 per cent of the Portuguese population were in royal lordships.[36] It was a major turn-around compared with the situation at the death of Afonso V forty years before.

Overall, nobles of middle and lower rank had little reason for discontent during the Golden Age. The rural nobility by definition lived off their estates, which were now benefiting from improved agricultural prices. Their social prestige was high, and they were clearly an important conservative force – even though, with almost static numbers, their influence was waning. By contrast the service nobility was growing rapidly. Service noblemen were mainly recruited from *fidalgos* of modest means on the fringes of the court, including many younger sons. It was they who provided the military spearhead for expansion, and their exploits in North Africa, Atlantic Africa, Asia and Brazil filled the pages of the sixteenth-century chronicles just as they did the service records of the royal chancery.

The rapid expansion of the service nobility in the Golden Age put much increased demand on royal patronage. This in turn meant the old struggle between king and elite became less relevant while competition for royal grants (*mercês*) grew more intense. Access to the king or influential ministers was now more crucial than ever, and the court appeared a centre of clamorous lobbying as individuals pressed their hopes and claims. This shift in Portuguese elite

---

[35] Braga I M D 2000, p 24.
[36] Ibid, p 23; NHP vol 5, pp 102–5, 108–9, 318–20.

politics was possible only because of overseas expansion. As we shall see in later chapters, the Golden Age kings had far greater capacity to respond to patronage demands than their Medieval predecessors because of the opportunities generated by the neo-Reconquest in Morocco and the Portuguese presence in maritime Asia. Manuel's vigorous pro-expansion policies, and in particular his enthusiasm for the neo-Reconquest, were promoted at least in part to direct *fidalgos* into overseas service.[37] Restless, down-at-heel noblemen who might otherwise have fomented discontent in Portugal were thereby drawn into activity faraway, yet remained useful to the state. Some carefully controlled increase in the size of the second estate also became possible, allowing the crown to reward with ennoblement bureaucrats and others who distinguished themselves in royal service.

Thus Portugal's overseas possessions and commitments provided a means through which the aspirations of a significant number of service nobles could be satisfied. At the same time, most *fidalgos* came to value overseas offices less for their intrinsic worth than for the private income-generating opportunities that often accompanied them. Therefore, notwithstanding the traditional view that nobles and merchants comprised separate social categories with quite different functions, increasing numbers of Portuguese *fidalgos* became thoroughly involved in trade.[38] It was this development, already becoming apparent in the fifteenth century, that led Vitorino Magalhães Godinho to speak of the emergence in the wake of expansion of a new type of nobleman – the 'knight-merchant' (*cavaleiro-mercador*), who blended gentility with trade, and honour with making profit.[39]

The increased prosperity of the Golden Age also had profound consequences on how Portugal was governed. The *cortes,* which had seemed earlier to be developing into a more significant national institution and which represented the bourgeoisie as well as the nobility, gradually lost much of its importance. It retained certain reserve powers that could be crucial in rare, special circumstances – particularly selecting a regent in a minority or even choosing a king if there were no obvious heir.[40] But in this period it failed to extend or even maintain its role as part of the normal apparatus of state, instead receding into the background and meeting ever less frequently. Manuel summoned it four times during the first seven years of his reign, when his regime was in the process of establishing itself; but after 1502 he never called

[37] Humble S 2000, pp 28–9, 33–4.
[38] Bouchon G and Thomaz L F R 1988, pp 409–13; Thomaz L F R 1994, pp 28, 57, 204–6; NHP vol 5, pp 325–6, 328.
[39] Godinho V M 1962, pp 213–14.
[40] NHP vol 5, pp 389–90.

it again. João III summoned it three times only, always for the purpose of voting subsidies. The *cortes* therefore met during the two reigns on average barely once a decade. The reality was that the Golden Age kings seldom needed to consult the *cortes* because extra revenues from overseas sources had made the crown fiscally more or less independent. Of course, had state revenues depended on internal sources alone, the story would have been very different.

As royal government strengthened during the first half of the sixteenth century, it grew steadily more committed to systematic record-keeping and quantitative accounting – in effect, more bureaucratic.[41] At the same time the king himself became increasingly remote from the day-to-day operations of government. These trends were helped by the introduction of printing, which, having reached Portugal by the reign of João II, came into regular use for administrative purposes under Manuel.[42] Printing made possible the issuing of the *Ordenações Manuelinas,* a new, five-volume compendium of statute law compiled by a commission of legal experts. First published during 1512–14 with a revised edition appearing in 1521, it replaced the *Ordenações Afonsinas* of fifty years earlier. However, as a printed work it achieved much wider distribution: 1,000 copies of the first edition were printed, of which many were distributed to the town councils.[43] Also compiled in the Golden Age was the *Leitura Nova,* a vast collection of chancellery records dating from the thirteenth century onwards. The originals in many cases were now too confused and difficult to read; so they were laboriously transcribed by hand onto parchment during the Manueline and early Joanine periods. Sixty-two volumes resulted, each with a magnificently illuminated frontispiece symbolically lauding royal power. The *Leitura Nova* was of particular interest to the nobility because it documented past grants and privileges formally recognised by the crown. Though the *Ordenações Manuelinas* was produced in print and the *Leitura Nova* in manuscript form, both were symptomatic of the new emphasis on record-keeping – and both illustrate the importance of books as symbols of order, privilege and royal power.[44]

The gradual eclipse of the old *conselho del rei,* the king's advisory council since the thirteenth century, was another sign of the shifting balance of power in favour of the king and his officials. The council's decline, already apparent under João II, accelerated under Manuel who allowed membership to increase to some 500. This ensured that by the accession of João III the title of king's

[41] DHP vol 2, p 256.
[42] Dias J J A 2000, pp 296–300.
[43] SHP vol 3, pp 215–18; NHP vol 5, pp 465, 714–15.
[44] Alves A M 1985, pp 95–99, 103–7.

counsellor had become purely honorific.[45] In practice, the Golden Age kings relied for advice on a small, informal circle of intimates that consisted partly of royal princes and illustrious nobles, and partly of lawyers and bureaucrats. Under Manuel the count of Vimioso, the count of Vila Nova and Dom António de Noronha, who served as the king's personal secretary, were among the more influential members of this circle. Later, João III relied heavily on trusted members of his own family, especially his brothers, Luís and Henrique, and Queen Catarina.[46] Yet on occasions political pressure could still oblige a king to listen to advisers whose views he did not share. This happened in 1515–18 when Manuel was forced to accept policies advocated by the baron of Alvito that curtailed the royal monopolies in Asian trade.[47] Eventually in 1569, the king's de facto inner circle of advisers was institutionalised and became formally known as the council of state (*conselho de estado*).

Even before the Golden Age the king's secretary of state (*secretário de estado*) was also developing into a figure of major importance, effectively superseding the old *escrivão da puridade*. Successive secretaries of state provided a strong element of administrative continuity and were the real instigators behind much royal policy. For a century this office was dominated by the Alcaçova-Carneiro family, of minor noble origin. Their service began with Pêro de Alcaçova, secretary of state from the reign of Afonso V through that of João II. Then in 1509 Manuel appointed António Carneiro, Pêro de Alcaçova's son-in-law, who served throughout the reign and well into that of João III. When he died in 1545 the secretaryship was divided between his sons, Francisco Carneiro and Pêro de Alcaçova Carneiro, who became responsible for metropolitan and overseas affairs respectively. Pêro de Alcaçova Carneiro remained an influential figure for the rest of the Avis era and even into the reign of Filipe I (II of Spain), whose succession he strongly backed.[48]

As royal power and responsibilities increased, the ethical dimensions of government became more complex – or so it seemed to the troubled conscience of João III. This concern contributed to one of the most unusual institutional innovations of the period – the creation of the board of conscience and orders (*mesa da consciência e ordens*).[49] Comprising five canon lawyers, this body was instituted by João in 1532. It was concerned on the one hand with the moral and religious implications of decision-making, in which capacity it advised the king on such matters as the legitimacy of embarking on particular

[45] NHP vol 5, p 393.
[46] Ibid, pp 393–4.
[47] Thomaz L F R 1991, pp 103–5.
[48] SHP vol 3, p 210; NHP vol 5, p 391.
[49] HP vol 3, p 87; NHP vol 5, pp 401–4.

overseas conquests. On the other hand, the board also exercised various ecclesiastical responsibilities, including control of clerical appointments in Portugal and overseas, administration of Catholic missions and supervision of the military orders. It was therefore much more than just a policy watchdog, for it effectively functioned as an instrument of the royal supremacy.

CHURCH REFORM WITHOUT A REFORMATION

At the start of Manuel's reign the Portuguese church was chronically under-resourced and in a state of considerable moral degeneration. There were not enough priests to fulfil pastoral requirements, and the level of education attained by most of the lower clergy was minimal. At the same time among the higher clergy plurality and absenteeism were rife. Many religious houses were poorly administered, and the spiritual commitment of regular clergy was often questionable. Much church revenue had been diverted to non-ecclesiastical use, from providing *comendas* to funding wars against Muslims.

The church itself was only partly responsible for these various abuses; but it lacked the means, and perhaps the will, to remedy them. The consequence was that serious reform of religious institutions during the Golden Age depended on the intervention of the state – and the royal government inevitably sought to incorporate such reform into its broader centralising and rationalising strategy.

In 1501 Manuel secured an agreement with the papacy that effectively meant his nominations to Portuguese bishoprics would be automatically endorsed by Rome. By 1517 the arrangement had been extended to cover abbots, priors and most cathedral dignitaries.[50] Manuel and João III used this power to appoint and endow their hand-picked agents, particularly members of the royal family. At the tender age of seven Manuel's fifth son, Dom Afonso, was made bishop of Guarda; later he became successively abbot of Alcobaça, bishop of Viseu, bishop of Évora and archbishop of Lisbon. Finally in 1523 he received a cardinal's hat. Meanwhile Dom Henrique, Manuel's sixth son, after taking holy orders at fourteen immediately became prior of Santa Cruz. Later, he was archbishop of Braga; then, after Dom Afonso's death in 1540, he was translated to Lisbon and made a cardinal.[51] Through such blatant nepotism the crown achieved ultimate control over church patronage – and the contrast with even the recent past was glaring. Cardinal Alpedrinha, the long-lived predecessor of Dom Afonso, resided for years at the papal court before dying at ninety-two, or perhaps even 102, in 1508, and used his influence to acquire for himself

---

[50] NHP vol 5, pp 418–19.
[51] Góis D de 1790 pt 3, ch 27; Oliveira M de 1968, p 231; SHP vol 3, p 244; DIHP vol 2, pp 414–15; NHP vol 5, pp 418–19, 523.

and his clientele multiple Portuguese ecclesiastical offices and incomes. Now such opportunities had passed to the king and his sons.[52] Moreover Manuel, who had been granted the mastership of Christ by João II, kept it when he became king. Later, João III assumed the masterships of Santiago and Avis when they became vacant in 1550, and thereafter all three orders remained annexed to the crown. Given the huge resources these orders had accumulated during the Reconquest, the benefits gained were substantial. By the end of the Golden Age the crown controlled, directly or indirectly, all the most important ecclesiastical appointments and patronage in the country.

Clearly the regalism of the Golden Age perpetuated some classic abuses. This is most obvious in the careers of Manuel's clerical sons which involved plurality, absenteeism, bestowing office on minors and engrossing revenues for purposes other than those originally intended. Nevertheless, increased state control over church affairs did make the review and rationalisation of ecclesiastical institutions more practicable. Early in his reign Manuel began a reform of the monasteries, bringing the Benedictines and Cistercians under firmer control by insisting their abbots be elected for fixed terms rather than appointed for life. The administration of each monastic order was scrutinised with a view to tightening internal discipline. A process was also put in motion to consolidate the mendicant orders, the goal being to merge the rival Conventual and Observant branches into which both the Franciscans and Dominicans had split.[53] Manuel employed the Hieronymites, his favourite religious order, to oversee these measures. Nevertheless, it was a slow, grinding process which continued through the reign of João III and beyond.

Of course, the reforms introduced into the Portuguese church during the first four decades of the sixteenth century were quite modest compared with what was happening in some other European countries. The Protestant Reformation had only a negligible influence on Portugal, and its ideas caused barely a passing ripple. The reality was that many of the conditions that bred Protestantism elsewhere were either entirely absent or severely muted in Portugal. The Portuguese had no tradition of questioning the established teachings and practices of the church and maintained a horror of anything that smacked of heresy. Their religious polemics were preoccupied less with reform as such than with alleged Judaizing in the New Christian community. The Bible was not available in the vernacular and therefore could not provide a catalyst for reform as it did in some

[52] HP vol 3, pp 155–6; Mendonça M 1991a, pp 46–9. (Traditionally Alpedrinha is said to have died at 102. However, Manuela Mendonça argues he was probably born in 1416, not 1406 as generally supposed. If so, he would have been ninety-two when he died in 1508. Mendonça M 1991a, pp 7–34.)

[53] NHP vol 5, pp 423–9; Oliveira M de 1968, pp 230–45.

other countries; the first (unauthorised) Portuguese translation, issued in Amsterdam, did not appear until 1681, and a complete Bible was not published in Portuguese in Portugal until the late eighteenth century. Moreover, as a relatively centralised state, Golden Age Portugal was better placed than most to protect itself from religious nonconformity – and Manuel was able to dominate the Portuguese church to an extent that made any thought of a formal break with Rome quite superfluous. Nor did the kingdom ever produce any influential patrons of Protestantism under whose wings adherents might have found sanctuary. Finally, the emphatic commitment of neighbouring Spain to Catholicism made the possibility of Protestant ideas becoming established in Portugal still more remote.

Nevertheless, the Portuguese church during the Golden Age faced a new and unparalleled external challenge. This was brought on by Portugal's spectacular overseas expansion and vastly increased contacts with distant non-Christians. Under Manuel expansion was accompanied by a brief re-kindling of crusading fervour, though this later subsided under João III. Day-to-day interaction with Muslims occurred along a vastly extended frontier. Prisoners had to be ransomed in North Africa, and both there and in the Indian Ocean the growing problem of renegades – people converting to Islam or other exotic faiths, and sometimes later reverting again to Christianity – had to be confronted.[54] Above all, from the start of the Golden Age the Portuguese church found itself responsible for conducting overseas evangelisation on a scale and over distances for which there were no precedents.

Responding to all this required a major effort. It involved developing a mission strategy and creating a whole new ecclesiastical infrastructure remote from Europe to implement it. The kings of Portugal received the exclusive right to establish churches in their overseas conquests and spheres of influence, through a series of papal bulls issued between 1452 and 1514. They were also formally authorised to found dioceses, appoint clergy, propagate the faith and exercise spiritual jurisdiction (except in matters of doctrine) under what came to be known as the *padroado real* or royal patronage of the colonial church.[55] The institutional foundations for this ambitious enterprise were slowly laid. In 1514 a bishopric was created at Funchal in Madeira, initially with jurisdiction over all Portuguese Asia, Africa and Brazil. This diocese of impossible dimensions clearly could not last, and in 1534 new bishoprics were established for Angra (Açores), the Cape Verdes, São Tomé and Goa. More followed later in both the East and Brazil, with Goa raised to metropolitan status in 1551. The hierarchy of this colonial church functioned quite separately from that of

---

[54] Braga I M D 1998, p 83; Couto D S 2000, pp 183–7.
[55] Rego A da S 1940, pp 7–15; Boxer C R 1969, pp 228–32.

Portugal, and little interchange of senior personnel occurred between the two systems. A high proportion of the overseas bishops, and most missionary priests, were recruited from the religious orders.[56]

SOCIAL WELFARE AND THE *MISERICÓRDIA*

The provision of social welfare was regarded as a religious obligation in Portugal; but it was an obligation for which laymen shouldered much of the responsibility. Since at least the twelfth century there had existed within the kingdom a network of charitable institutions known as *albergarias* or *hospitais*, most of which were linked to associations of pious laymen (*confrarias*). Although *albergarias* and *hospitais* sometimes provided accommodation for travellers and the sick, respectively, the main role of both was to serve as almshouses for the indigent poor and the marginalised, and the two terms were often used interchangeably.[57] However, provision of relief through these bodies tended to be highly fragmented, and eventually in the late fifteenth century a process of institutional consolidation was commenced. In 1479, the crown received papal approval to amalgamate the *hospitais* of Lisbon, and in 1486 those of the provincial towns. By the end of the century this process had led to the creation of the Hospital of All Saints in Lisbon, and similar amalgamations had occurred in other cities.[58] Then, at just about the time these developments were occurring, a dynamic new brotherhood suddenly appeared known as the *Misericórdia* – and it was the *Misericórdia* that within a few years came to play the dominant role in the Portuguese welfare system.

The *Misericórdia* was founded in 1498 by a group of prominent Lisbon burgesses. Almost immediately it received enthusiastic support from King Manuel who resolved to use it to co-ordinate and supervise a range of charitable services. Manuel also encouraged the *Misericórdia* to spread throughout his dominions, and by 1525 there were already some sixty branches operating in Portugal, the Atlantic islands and Goa. A century later the number had doubled, and the brotherhood was flourishing in virtually every corner of the Portuguese world.[59] This remarkable progress may be attributed partly to royal support and partly to the enthusiasm with which the *Misericórdia* was embraced at all levels of society. Rapid growth was certainly facilitated by its special privileges, such as the almost exclusive right to collect alms in Lisbon. On the other hand, the privileges were offset by some highly onerous

---

[56] HP vol 3, pp 158–9, 163–4.
[57] Oliveira M de 1968, p 279; Vasconcelos e Sousa B 1990, p 32.
[58] Russell-Wood A J R 1968, pp 13–14; Vasconcelos e Sousa B 1990, pp 33–5.
[59] Russell-Wood A J R 1968, pp 14–17, 23; HP vol 3, pp 88, 150, 186; NHP vol 5, p 442.

responsibilities that included caring for prisoners and accompanying the condemned to the scaffold. Eventually, the *Misericórdia* took control of many existing hospitals and founded others of its own. Besides tending the sick, it buried the dead, handled deceased estates, reliably transmitted legacies to heirs across the seas and developed its own banking services. In many places, it founded chapels, and played a prominent role in liturgical processions.[60]

The *Misericórdia* was able to fund its multifarious activities mostly from donations and legacies. It was an independent lay organisation which assiduously maintained its autonomy and community character, each branch being administered by a board selected from its own members. Membership was coveted and numbers grew rapidly. The Lisbon and Goa *Misericórdias* were both eventually limited to a maximum of 600 brothers, regulations requiring half of them be nobles. Often their presidents were *grandes* or viceroys. All in all, the *Misericórdia* became one of the country's most widespread and important social institutions, and remained for centuries the cornerstone of organised charity.

THE PORTUGUESE LITERARY RENAISSANCE

By the start of the sixteenth century, support for learning in Portugal within influential circles was quite extensive. Patrons included wealthy nobles, various elite churchmen, certain members of the royal family and above all the king himself. In the previous century, the regent Dom Pedro, Afonso V and João II had all sought to attract learned men to their courts and to sponsor Letters. Leonor, João II's widow, did likewise, while Manuel, in whose reign increased national wealth made possible more generous patronage, enthusiastically espoused and expanded the same tradition. At least until the 1550s João III was also an important patron of learning, maintaining scholars and teachers, accumulating books and manuscripts, granting offices and pensions to deserving writers and personally corresponding with celebrated foreign scholars. In other words, the sixteenth-century Manueline and early Joanine courts each in turn nurtured the flowering of a Portuguese literary Renaissance.[61]

In roughly the same period Portugal also improved and significantly expanded its education system. Some of the groundwork for this was laid during the late fifteenth century, when several foreign or foreign-trained tutors were brought in to educate the elite. Among the most influential was Catuldus Siculus, a Sicilian-born Italian Classicist who came to Portugal in the 1480s,

---

[60] Russell-Wood A J R 1968, pp 18, 86, 96–9; Boxer C R 1969, pp 291–2; HP vol 3, pp 150–1, 191; Gracias F da S 2000, pp 57–78.
[61] Boxer C R 1981, pp 14, 17–18.

taught João II's bastard son, Dom Jorge, and remained in the country until his death some thirty years later. Meanwhile, Portuguese students were increasingly encouraged to go overseas for an education, mainly to Italy, France or Spain. Afonso V and his successors all allocated funds for this purpose, and by the 1520s João III was providing fifty scholarships for study in Paris at the Collège de Sainte Barbe.[62]

In Portugal itself some twenty new colleges were founded, offering instruction that ranged from university to sub-university level. The most famous was the College of the Arts or *Colégio Real,* modelled on the Collège Royale in France. This institution was established by João III at Coimbra in 1547 and staffed by a team of distinguished foreign and Portuguese masters. André de Gouveia, an Erasmian Humanist and former principal of colleges in Paris and Bordeaux, served as rector. Efforts were also made to reform the University of Lisbon, a deeply conservative institution still wedded to the scholastic traditions of the Medieval Schools. Manuel gave it new regulations and a new building; but it stubbornly resisted change, taking refuge in its ancient privileges and its church connections. Finally in 1537 a frustrated João III closed it and established a new university at Coimbra – with more staff and a rector no longer elected, but appointed by the crown. However, João's priority was to bring higher education under crown control and not to reform the traditional curriculum or teaching methods; so these latter remained much as before. Then in 1541 Portuguese students were forbidden to receive foreign degrees. This startling reversal of earlier policy was an ominous foretaste of things to come.[63]

At a more workaday level the number of schools imparting basic literacy skills grew steadily in Portugal during the early sixteenth century, and it became possible to make a reasonable living from teaching. By about 1550 in Lisbon alone there were some 8,000 children learning to read and write Portuguese. Latin was also widely taught, and even Greek and Hebrew in a few places.[64] Such educational progress was possible only because of the rapidly growing use of printed material, from the time of João II, who at one stage abolished customs duties on imported books. The first known printing press in Portugal, introduced during the same king's reign, was operating by 1487.[65] Initially Portuguese printing was confined to brief official documents; but soon more ambitious works were produced – religious and legal texts, then the Latin classics, commentaries, grammars, historical chronicles and Portuguese poetry and drama. About 60 per cent of works published in the sixteenth century were

[62] Mendonça M 1991, p 71; NHP vol 5, p 469.
[63] Boxer C R 1981, pp 15, 19–20; NHP vol 5, pp 471–6.
[64] NHP vol 5, pp 468–9.
[65] Boxer C R 1981, p 15; NHP vol 5, pp 491–2, 497; Dias J J A 2000, p 296.

in Portuguese, the remainder in Latin or Spanish. Printed editions were obviously much cheaper to mass-produce than handwritten manuscripts, and runs of 1,000 or so became quite common, making the written word accessible to a much expanded readership. By about 1550 Lisbon boasted at least twenty bookshops, suggesting a thriving local market.[66]

A consequence of these developments was that Classicism, with its veneration for Ancient texts and its rigorous grammar and philology, established a growing foothold in Portugal. At first Classicism in Portugal was largely confined to the church, which used it as a tool to improve clerical education; but in time it spread and took on a more Humanist tinge. Appearing in Portugal relatively late, Classical Humanism was derived mainly from foreign models. But it was nevertheless a fruitful seedbed from which a vigorous vernacular literature developed during the course of the Golden Age. A major early exponent was Garcia de Resende, a court poet, chronicler and compiler of a famous collection of *trovas* known as the *Cancioneiro Geral*, who died in 1536. Probably more talented, and ultimately more influential, were the playwright and satirist Gil Vicente, who was the founding father of Portuguese drama, and the poet Francisco Sá de Miranda. The latter's early residence in Italy followed by a period at court and then withdrawal to a rustic retreat in Minho suggest a quintessential Classicist-Humanist mentality.

But there was also another kind of Portuguese Humanism quite distinct from Classical Humanism and far more original. This was Empirical Humanism that in Portugal was largely a by-product of the voyages of discovery. Empirical Humanism was a tradition based on direct observation and not, like Classical Humanism, on written authorities from the Ancient past. Portuguese ocean voyaging of the fifteenth and sixteenth century involved extensive reconnaissance and information-gathering. The desire to describe what had been found, partly for reasons of practical utility and partly out of sheer intellectual curiosity, was strongly felt.[67] This imperative gave rise to a literature that was often technically less accomplished than writings by Portuguese Classical Humanists, but made a far more important and original contribution to European knowledge. Duarte Pacheco Pereira's *Esmeraldo de Situ Orbis* is an early example of Empirical Humanism. At core a set of sailing directions for ships voyaging along the coasts of western and eastern Africa written in a straightforward, down-to-earth prose, this work combined navigational data with reports on the physical geography, inhabitants, fauna and flora of nearby regions. Literature in the Empirical Humanist tradition reached its peak during the 1530s with the treatises of Dom João de Castro on how to sail a ship between Lisbon and Goa,

---

[66] NHP vol 5, pp 453–4, 464–7.
[67] Marques A H de O 2000, pp 39–41.

along the west coast of India, and through the Red Sea. These were arguably the most rigorous scientific writings on nautical astronomy, navigation and voyaging of the whole European Renaissance.[68]

Classical and Empirical Humanism seem so different in their assumptions, the one embedded in book-learning and the other in experience and field-work, that it is tempting to see them as mutually incomprehensible, even antagonistic modes of discourse.[69] However, their differences can easily be exaggerated, and in practice they intersected at many points. The historian and man-of-letters João de Barros, who combined a large literary output with formidable practical experience including a long bureaucratic career, at least one voyage to West Africa and involvement in colonising projects in Brazil, represents this kind of intersection, and his *Ásia,* written between the 1530s and 1550s, is one of the great literary treasures of Europe's expansion. Even Damião de Goís, Portugal's finest Erasmian scholar and a distinguished Classical Humanist, was so fascinated by the process of expansion that over three-quarters of the chapters in his chronicle of the reign of King Manuel concern Portuguese exploits in Asia, North Africa and other exotic regions. There is thus little doubt that overseas voyaging was one of the major inspirations of Portuguese Renaissance literature.

THE ARTS

His fascination with exotic worlds notwithstanding, Damião de Goís also took care to celebrate Portuguese achievements within the kingdom itself – and in the penultimate chapter of his chronicle he proudly reviewed the remarkable array of churches, monasteries, palaces, fortresses, bridges and other monuments built or embellished by King Manuel during the course of his reign.[70] While some of these structures had been commenced in earlier times and many were not completed until years after Manuel's death, the magnitude of the overall program was extraordinary for what had hitherto been just a small, rural kingdom. Nor is it only the number of monuments that impresses, but also their quality. The Jerónimos monastery, the tower at Belém, the restored convent of Christ at Tomar, the transformed unfinished chapels at Batalha and the Hall of Blazons in the royal palace at Sintra all belong to this period – and are numbered among Europe's architectural treasures. If the glories of a Golden Age are often associated with achievements in the Arts, then in regard to monumental architecture early-sixteenth-century Portugal was no exception.

---

[68] DHDP vol 1, pp 222–3.
[69] HP vol 3, p 377.
[70] Goís D de 1790 pt 4, ch 85.

The dominant architectural style of this period in Portugal is usually called *Manuelino*. There has been much debate over the influences that lay behind this style, which appears to have been highly composite. *Manuelino* certainly began as an expression of Late Gothic; but later it became influenced by Italian Renaissance ideas, though mostly filtered through Spain and France. Islamic motifs were also present, either derived directly from North Africa or, more probably, from Mudéjar models. In any event, the real distinctiveness of *Manuelino* lay in its sculptural forms and exuberant decoration rather than building design.[71]

Many architects of *Manuelino* were either foreigners or foreign-trained Portuguese. The latter included Diogo de Arruda, designer of the famous great west window at the convent-church at Tomar, and his brother Francisco, who was responsible for the Torre de Belém.[72] An even more central figure was the rather mysterious Frenchman Diogo Boitac, who favoured the north European tradition of *Hallenkirchen*. Boitac initially worked on the unfinished chapels at Batalha. Later, he drew up plans for the Jerónimos monastery at Belém, where he oversaw the building of much of the walls and part of the cloisters. João de Castilho, a Biscayan, succeeded Boitac as chief architect of this great project in 1517 and introduced elements of the Plateresque of Fernando and Isabel's Spain. The Jerónimos was destined to become the greatest architectural monument of Portugal's Golden Age – a building Damião de Góis proudly declared was second to none in Europe.[73] Góis added that Manuel built the Jerónimos for three reasons: to show his devotion to the Virgin Mary, to create a religious sanctuary for sailors and to provide a mausoleum for himself and his dynasty.[74] The last reason was doubtless the most important, but indicates a change of thinking, for Manuel had previously chosen Batalha for this purpose.

All the late Avis kings from Manuel onwards – apart from King Sebastião – were eventually buried at the Jerónimos. Nevertheless, in time the monastery came to be regarded not just as an Avis family mausoleum, but a national shrine to the great age of Portuguese voyaging. Such a symbolic role was not inappropriate, for there had previously stood on the site a small chapel built by João I's famous son, Prince Henrique, sponsor of the earlier fifteenth-century voyages – and, to acknowledge the association, Henrique's statue was incorporated into Castilho's great southern portal. Moreover Vasco da Gama had departed on his pioneer voyage to India from a point close to where the monastery was subsequently built. Much later, at the end of the nineteenth century, the supposed

---

[71] HP vol 3, pp 431–7; DIHP vol 1, p 426–7; NHP vol 5, pp 517–31.
[72] Smith R C 1968, pp 22–56.
[73] Góis D de 1790 pt 4, ch 85.
[74] Ibid pt 1, ch 53.

remains of both Gama and of the national poet Luís de Camões were transferred to the Jerónimos, though in neither case was their authenticity certain.[75]

Most Portuguese painting in the Manueline era was run-of-the-mill and did
not achieve the same distinction as the country's architecture. The greatest and
most celebrated of all Portuguese paintings – the magnificent polyptych redis-
covered in 1882 in the patriarchal palace of São Vicente de Fora and now in the
Lisbon Museum of Ancient Art – was produced half a century before Manuel's
accession. In a remarkable piece of detective work, Jorge Filipe de Almeida and
Maria Manuela Barroso de Albuquerque have recently demonstrated that this
painting was almost certainly the work of Nuno Gonçalves, whose discreetly
disguised monogrammatic signature appears to have been worked into the
boots of two of the figures portrayed.[76] Partly on the basis of dendrochronol-
ogy, the same authors also show that the polyptych was painted in 1445 –
towards the end of the regency of Prince Pedro – and not 1471–2 as previously
thought.[77] It was commissioned by the brotherhood of Santo António in honour of Prince Fernando, the 'holy prince' who had died in captivity in Fez in
1443 and was widely regarded as a martyr.[78] Fernando appears as the central
figure in each of the two principal panels. He is surrounded by his mourning
family and other clearly identifiable individuals, the group including King
Duarte (by then deceased), Queen Leonor, King Afonso V at the age of thirteen,
Prince Pedro as regent and – most renowned of all – Prince Henrique wearing a
dark Burgundian hat. Painted in the Flemish tradition, the work is a masterly
portrayal of fifty-eight persons, most of them known royal, noble or clerical
celebrities. All are drawn with extraordinary realism. There is no background
landscape, the focus being entirely on the human figures.[79]

While this celebrated polyptych of Nuno Gonçalves is clearly a stunning
achievement, it is also unique in Portugal, with no known parallels and no
successors. Gonçalves, who was court painter to King Afonso V, died
apparently without disciples, and the extraordinary originality that he represented was lost with him. Artists at the sixteenth-century Manueline and early
Joanine courts, as in most contemporary provincial centres, continued to paint
in the Flemish tradition, but mostly routine religious compositions. Many
altarpieces with multiple panels set in gilt wood were produced, either by
immigrants from Flanders or by Portuguese trained in the same tradition.

---

[75] Subrahmanyam S 1997, pp 11–16.
[76] Almeida J F de and Albuquerque M M B de 2003, pp 13, 22–7, 30–40.
[77] Ibid, pp 41–4.
[78] For Prince Fernando's death see ch 15.
[79] Almeida J F de and Albuquerque M M B de 2003, pp 77–94. See also Smith R C 1968, pp 195–
7; NHP vol 4, pp 450–1.

Today these works embellish churches and chapels from Minho to Madeira. Invariably they depict richly coloured but somewhat stylised figures with the folds and patterns of their clothing set out in meticulous detail against traditional landscape backgrounds.[80]

This style persisted in Portugal through the first half of the sixteenth century because it was both fashionable and relatively easy to produce and reproduce. Works in the tradition appealed to many contemporaries from King Manuel himself downwards. They could be purchased in Bruges, Antwerp and other Flemish cities where Portugal had commercial ties, and later directly from Portuguese workshops.[81] This is probably why Jorge Afonso, the most influential court artist of Manuel's reign and a great exponent of the Flemish style, has left so little clearly authenticated work. Yet most of the leading painters of the Golden Age, such as Gregório Lopes and Cristovão de Figueiredo, were either Afonso's pupils or at least associated with his workshop. Even the enigmatic Vasco Fernandes of Viseu, universally known as 'Grão Vasco', who was probably the most original artist of the era, eventually joined Jorge Afonso in Lisbon.[82]

The abandonment of the Nuno Gonçalves tradition, and the dominance achieved by increasingly rigid stylistic patterns from Flanders, meant that in the end Portugal contributed little to either Late Renaissance landscape painting or portraiture. This is particularly unfortunate given the rich subject opportunities that had become available to the Portuguese through their voyaging. While the Portuguese were the first Europeans to see much of the world outside Europe, they mostly viewed it through the eyes of navigators and merchants. No accomplished Portuguese artist came forward during the Golden Age to interpret and display on canvas that exotic world, its peoples and its creatures, despite Europe's eager thirst for images of the new.[83]

On the other hand, a more significant contribution to European art was made during the Golden Age and beyond by finely illuminated Portuguese maps and atlases. These works resulted from the convergence of nautical cartography – a science in which Portugal was then in the forefront – and the ancient art of illumination. The latter was fortuitously flourishing in Portugal early in the sixteenth century, when many magnificently illustrated choir books, books of hours, genealogies and chronicles were painstakingly produced.[84] Soon cartographers and illuminators combined to form a number of workshops

---

[80] SHP vol 3, pp 400–1.
[81] NHP vol 5, p 567.
[82] HA vol 2, pp 349–50.
[83] Godinho V M 1990, pp 87–8.
[84] NHP vol 5, pp 595–7.

specialising in the production of decorated maps, the best known being those of Pedro and Jorge Reinel, Lopo and Diogo Homem and, later in the century, the Indo-Portuguese Fernão Vaz Dourado. The surviving output of these workshops is now scattered round the great libraries and museums of the world, from New York to Istanbul. The 'Miller Atlas', presented by King Manuel to François I of France in 1519 and now in the Bibliothèque Nationale in Paris, is a particularly splendid example. It combines rigorous accuracy with magnificent decoration, including representations of cities, ships, human figures, animals, birds and banners. The atlas was a joint product of cartographers from the Reinel and Homem workshops and the illuminator Antonio de Holanda.[85] Such treasures demonstrate splendidly how Portuguese empirical geography triumphed over traditional Ptolemaic cosmography during the course of the Golden Age.

Finally, Portugal's involvement in the late European Renaissance did not mean that its people totally abandoned those of their cultural links that led back to al-Andalus. Such links were to some extent nurtured in this era by renewed contacts with North Africa. Despite the swift obliteration of most Muslim monuments after the Reconquest, Islamic traditions lingered on, particularly at the grass-roots level in Alentejo – in agricultural practices, in architectural forms such as horseshoe arches and Moorish windows, in the decorative arts, in certain behavioural conventions and through the incorporation of many Arabic terms into spoken Portuguese. Even King Manuel, despite his fervent espousal of a crusading ideology, was personally much attracted to Mudéjar culture for which he may have acquired a taste as a boy in Spain.[86]

The use of decorative tiles (*azulejos*) as ornamentation on both the interior and exterior walls of buildings was one of the strongest and most lasting manifestations of this Islamising trend. The revival of *azulejos* may have begun after Afonso V brought back a number of Muslim tile-workers from his expedition to Morocco in 1471.[87] In any event *azulejos* with Islamic geometric, heraldic and floral designs were popular during Manuel's reign and were often imported from traditional Mudéjar workshops in Seville. Later, Portuguese ceramic tiles became more Italianate; but their popularity persisted, and they are still today among the most characteristic and best-loved forms of Portuguese artistic expression.

Mudéjar music and dance were likewise popular in the Golden Age. Manuel loved them and maintained his own 'Moorish' musicians at court where they both sang and played traditional instruments. Of course, he also maintained a

[85] Godinho V M 1990, pp 208–9; Marques A P 1994, pp 55–8, 73–4, and 1994b, pp 53–7.
[86] Perez R M (coord) 1997, pp 95–6.
[87] NHP vol 5, p 607.

strong commitment to Christian sacred music. In the king's chapel, where practices were modelled on the Chapel Royal at Windsor, both Manuel and João III retained some of the best church musicians and choristers to be found anywhere in Europe, including a number recruited from overseas. Sacred music was likewise nurtured in various cathedrals and private chapels and was particularly promoted by João III's brother, Cardinal Henrique, who encouraged the systematic adoption of a polyphonic liturgy.[88]

[88] Goís D de 1790 pt 4, ch 84; NHP vol 5, pp 615–17; Perez R M (coord) 1997, pp 95–6.

9

The Tarnished Age

JOÃO III AND HIS FATED FAMILY

From about 1540 onwards the Portuguese Golden Age gradually lost its lustre. The change was apparent in many different spheres, including the economy, imperial expansion, individual rights, learning and the Arts. The royal house, accounted so fortunate in the time of King Manuel, was now struck by a succession of devastating family tragedies that eventually imperilled the survival of the nation itself. Portugal had entered what was becoming, compared with the recent past, a distinctly Tarnished Age.

The João III of the Tarnished Age has left to posterity a very different image from the João III of the Golden Age. A previously conscientious, relatively open-minded and quite intelligent monarch, who had generously patronised the Arts and education, by the 1540s had seemingly changed into a suspicious, indecisive and morbidly introspective recluse, increasingly captive to priestly influence. So negative was the later João's reputation that one of Portugal's most respected nineteenth-century historians dismissed him summarily as 'an incompetent and malignant fanatic'.[1] Part of the explanation for this transformation undoubtedly lies in the series of cruel misfortunes that overtook the royal family. When King Manuel died in 1521 he was survived by nine healthy legitimate children, varying in age from eighteen years to six months.[2] Such a progeny seemed to guarantee the dynasty's long-term survival. João III also sired nine legitimate children; but there the parallel ceased – for tragically all preceded him to the grave.

The high death rate in João III's family first began to rouse concern in the late 1530s. By that time João and Catarina had already lost three children, although

---

[1] Herculano A 1972, p 500.
[2] SHP vol 3, pp 421–3.

two sons called Manuel and Filipe and a daughter called Maria still survived. But Manuel and Filipe died in 1537 and 1539, respectively, each at the age of six. Then Maria, who married the future Felipe II of Spain in 1543, died in childbirth two years later. Catarina subsequently managed to produce two more sons – of whom only one survived – before her pregnancies finally ceased.[3] The surviving son was Prince João, a sickly boy who nevertheless somehow managed to live through childhood. Eventually in 1552, at the age of fifteen, this João married Joana, a daughter of the Emperor Carlos V. But ominously his wedding celebrations were interrupted by a deeply offensive act of sacrilege. During the nuptial Mass a visiting Englishman, apparently offended by what he saw as 'popish idolatry', snatched the consecrated host from the officiating priest and crushed it underfoot. He was swiftly seized, condemned by an episcopal court and released to the secular authorities for execution. The sacrilege had a profound impact on the king, who entered a period of extreme penitential depression during which he virtually abandoned his public responsibilities to Catarina.[4] Then in January 1554, barely a year after his marriage, Prince João died – and the extinction of an entire royal generation was complete.

Nevertheless, even at this tragic point not all was lost, for when Prince João died he left Joana in a state of advanced pregnancy. At the time João III also had one legitimate grandson in the person of nine-year-old Infante Don Carlos (1544–68), son and heir of Felipe of Spain and the deceased Maria. Had Carlos, who eventually developed into a singularly unpleasant and vicious young man, ascended the Portuguese throne it would have meant Iberian union under a king born and raised in Castile. Portugal therefore waited anxiously until on 20 January 1554, eighteen days after her husband's death, Joana gave birth to a son. There was then much rejoicing, for this was the *desejado* or longed-for one, on whom everything now depended. He was christened Sebastião in memory of the third-century soldier-martyr and patron of warriors on whose feast-day he was born. Sebastião managed to survive the dangerous years of infancy – and, when João III finally died in 1557, was duly proclaimed king at the tender age of three.

SEBASTIÃO AND HENRIQUE

Sebastião was one of the most extraordinary monarchs that Portugal ever produced. Ascending the throne in an atmosphere of great emotion, he was widely acclaimed as the answer to his subjects' prayers and a prince who would save his country's independence. Two decades later, he achieved precisely the

---

[3] Lima D P de 1993, p 235; Costa J P O 2002, p 89.
[4] Pereira I da R 1984, pp 597–605; NHP vol 5, p 740; Braga P D 2002, pp 103, 136–7.

opposite, dying heroically but unnecessarily on the distant North African battlefield of Al-Ksar al-Kabir on 4 August 1578, leaving no heir to succeed him. How did this debacle come about?

From 1557 until Sebastião attained his majority Portugal was governed by regents. The first was his grandmother – João III's widow, Catarina. Her principal ministers had all served in the previous reign, and her government was largely one of continuity. But, in a sign of growing Spanish influence, in foreign and dynastic affairs she followed policies openly aligned first with those of her brother Carlos V and then of his son Felipe II. In so doing she stirred widespread suspicions – particularly in the third estate, always fearful of excessive influence from Castile. Eventually tiring of office, Catarina resigned in 1562, allowing the *cortes* to replace her with Cardinal Henrique, Sebastião's great uncle. Henrique tried to steer a neutral course in foreign affairs, seeking friendship equally with Spain, France and England. Meanwhile, Sebastião was being raised in accordance with the standards and values of his time. His mother Joana, who had returned to Castile, was allowed no part in his upbringing. His principal teachers were Jesuits, most notably Fr Luís Gonçalves da Câmara, and there was a strong emphasis on Counter-Reformation theology in the instruction he received. Nevertheless, for a while Sebastião was also exposed to some Humanist influences and acquired a certain interest in the Sciences.[5] As late as 1572 he recalled to court the celebrated Jewish mathematician and cosmographer Pedro Nunes, who had earlier tutored his great uncles Luís and Henrique.

By the time he reached puberty Sebastião, like King Manuel nearly seventy-five years before, had firmly convinced himself he was God's chosen instrument to fulfil a sacred mission. But his anxious minders were more concerned about the question of his marriage – and even in 1559, when Sebastião was only five, were already searching for his bride. The favoured candidates then were Isabel of Bohemia, whose father was soon to be Holy Roman Emperor, and Margaret of Valois. Margaret was preferred by the *cortes;* but Felipe II of Spain, who considered he had a family right to intervene in such matters and did not want Sebastião to contract a French match, at first lobbied strongly for Isabel. Years of intrigue followed until in 1568 Felipe II's own wife died – and he then promptly changed his position. Felipe now wanted a trio of marriages: himself to Ana of Austria, Charles IX of France to Isabel and Sebastião to Margaret. In 1569 Sebastião's council finally agreed to this plan; but Sebastião himself, by then fifteen years old and having begun his personal rule the previous year, inconveniently refused to comply.[6]

---

[5] Segurado J 1984, pp 11–14; Alden D 1996, pp 81–3.
[6] PHP vol 5, pp 71–80.

After Sebastião had assumed power it soon became obvious that he had little interest in women. Instead he surrounded himself with impetuous young *fidalgos* – men like Dom Cristovão de Távora, who shared his enthusiasm for warrior prowess. Perhaps he was reacting against the rather stifling court and ageing minders of his boyhood. In any event, his martial interests combined with his obsessive sense of mission to produce an unshakeable resolve. He would lead in person a great expedition against Islam in North Africa, even though both the former regents, virtually all his more experienced counsellors and Felipe II of Spain unanimously advised against it. Such foolhardy stubbornness is usually attributed to Sebastião's alleged physical and mental abnormalities, which have long been the objects of fascinated speculation. His disinterest in young women, upon which many contemporaries commented, has inevitably raised questions about his sexuality. However, not all historians accept his traditionally misogynist image, and it has recently been suggested he suffered from acute urethritis possibly aggravated by inappropriate medical treatment.[7] The truth is nobody really knows what, if anything, was medically wrong with Sebastião. But there is no doubt about his restless physical energy. He was always on the move and constantly undergoing strenuous manly activity. Often irascible and easily confused, he apparently found it hard to concentrate, yet on occasions he could be remarkably quick-witted. He was in many ways conscientious about the duties of kingship, enacted much legislation and showed considerable compassion for the poor.[8]

As Sebastião moved from his teens into his twenties during the 1570s, the question of his marriage caused ever more concern to his council. A new succession of possible brides was considered; but the king's evasiveness was insurmountable. His grandmother Catarina, who favoured a Castilian marriage, also complicated matters by urging him to wait for Felipe II's daughter, Isabel Clara Eugenia, to reach marriageable age. Eventually in 1576 Sebastião and Felipe met at Guadelupe, and Sebastião himself raised the possibility of this match. However, it is likely his real purpose was less to secure the princess for his bed than Castilian military support for his Moroccan expedition. Felipe wisely delayed his answer, and, given that his daughter was then only ten, marrying her to Sebastião would not have immediately resolved the problem of Portuguese succession.[9] In the end, Sebastião embarked for Morocco in 1578 still a batchelor and still without an heir – and his sensational death at Al-Ksar al-Kabir, which is described in Chapter 15 – precipitated Portugal's greatest political and dynastic crisis since 1383–5.

---

[7] Boxer C R 1969, p 368; Loureiro F S 1989, p 103; SHP vol 3, pp 68–70; NHP vol 5, pp 746–7.

[8] Loureiro F S 1989, pp 96, 105; DIHP vol 2, p 218.

[9] PHP vol 5, pp 80, 99; NHP vol 5, pp 747–50.

Sebastião was the last living descendent of João III, and therefore it was necessary to go back two generations to find his successor. The next in line was clearly Manuel's surviving son, Cardinal Henrique. Despite some initial hesitation over whether a priest could reign, Henrique was duly proclaimed – so providing the unusual spectacle of a deceased king being succeeded by his great uncle. But Henrique was a frail sixty-six-year-old already suffering from tuberculosis who had to be brought out of retirement. As a priest he was also unmarried and childless. This meant that once again the most pressing issue of his brief two-year reign was to determine the heir. For some time it seemed Henrique might secure a papal dispensation to marry and try belatedly to beget his own successor. Several possible brides were contemplated, including Maria, thirteen-year-old daughter of the duke of Bragança. But the dispensation was blocked at Rome by Felipe II's agents so that Henrique was forced to abandon marriage as a practicable solution.[10] Of course, Felipe was far from a disinterested party, for he claimed to be Henrique's heir himself. However, before describing how the impending crisis of succession was eventually resolved, let us for the moment put aside dynastic questions and consider the state, during the Tarnished Age, of Portugal itself.

A FALTERING ECONOMY?

Slowly but steadily the population of Portugal grew during the Tarnished Age, particularly in the north and centre of the kingdom. The drift to coastal towns continued, even though the vast majority of Portuguese still lived off the land. Lisbon's pre-eminence was now unassailable, and by 1620 its population had reached about 165,000, despite a great 'plague' in 1569 that killed perhaps 50,000 of the city's inhabitants.[11] Meanwhile, a lasting tradition of emigration was setting in, with on average some 2,400 people leaving Portugal for Asia or Brazil each year of the sixteenth century – more than the contemporary emigration from Spain to the Spanish Indies.[12]

The 'Little Ice Age' that brought colder and wetter weather to many parts of Europe in this era had but a minor impact on Portugal. Of course, there were natural disasters and lean years: the mid-1550s, late 1560s and early 1570s were all characterised by drought and food shortages, and a devastatingly cold winter hit Alentejo in 1572–3.[13] But the overall pattern of rural life differed little from what it had been in earlier times, periodic droughts and famines

---

[10] Queirós Veloso J M de 1946, pp 128–9; NHP vol 5, pp 757–8.
[11] MHP, p 271; Roque M de C 1982, p 89.
[12] MHP, p 271; Engerman S L and Neves J C das 1997, pp 484–5.
[13] SHP vol 3, pp 288–94; NHP vol 5, p 163.

being depressingly recurrent realities. A number of significant initiatives in land management were introduced during the period, among them a crown-sponsored re-afforestation program involving extensive plantings of oak and pine. Efforts to control river flows were also intensified: in particular, a major scheme for diverting the Tagus above Santarém was begun in the 1540s, which was intended to halt contamination of river meadows by sand. This project at one stage involved up to 30,000 workmen.[14] Nevertheless, the general impression is of an economy that was experiencing mixed fortunes, but overall slowly deteriorating. Certainly by the mid-1550s João III's government was beginning to encounter difficulties in meeting its financial obligations. For years expenditure had been growing more rapidly than revenue and the crown had responded simply by issuing *juros*. By 1557 consolidated public debt and floating debt together totalled almost four million *cruzados,* and three years later the state was forced to suspend payments on its loans.[15] The suspension in itself was not critical: the government soon resumed issuing *juros* and raised the loans it needed with little difficulty. But the 1560 bankruptcy signalled a disturbing change for the worse in the financial standing of the Portuguese crown.

The economic well-being of Portugal in the Tarnished Age was closely linked to overseas expansion, and this meant that when in the late 1540s and early 1550s a significant 'structural break' occurred in the economic evolution of the empire it had far-reaching repercussions on the kingdom itself.[16] There were various elements involved in this 'structural break'. In North Africa João III's switch to a defensive policy confining the Portuguese to just three coastal fortresses meant access to the wheat-lands of southern Morocco was lost. French marauders and Barbary corsairs were now playing havoc with Portuguese Atlantic shipping, while the English and other European rivals competed with increasing effectiveness against the Portuguese in Guinea. In the western Indian Ocean Portuguese expansion was slowing, reducing crown revenue and profits. Portugal's share of European pepper imports fell, and by the 1540s marketing crown pepper through Flanders had become uneconomic. The *feitoria* at Antwerp was therefore closed, and Portuguese maritime trade to northern Europe declined.[17]

At the same time, the 'structural break' accelerated new growth in other areas. A crucial shift in the geographical focus of Portuguese expansion from the East to the West – from the Indian Ocean to Brazil and Angola – began to gather pace. In 1549 a royal colony was established in Brazil, which was

---

[14] SHP vol 3, p 299; NHP vol 5, pp 161–3; Dias J J A 1988, pp 153–76.
[15] NHP vol 5, pp 253–5.
[16] Godinho V M 1981–3 vol 4, pp 215–16; Subrahmanyam S 1993, pp 84–5.
[17] Godinho V M 1981–3 vol 4, pp 216–17.

followed by the rapid growth of a Brazilian plantation industry. This created demand for African slaves from Angola, stimulating a Portuguese Atlantic trade circuit. Beyond the Cape Portuguese commercial activity expanded strongly in East Asia, even as it slowed in the western Indian Ocean. The trend was evident especially in the founding of Macau in the mid-1550s and in the development of the Japan trade. While pepper became less important on the Cape route, trade in products like cotton piece goods, silks and porcelain increased. The crown monopolies, introduced on various commodities and routes in maritime Asia in King Manuel's time, were gradually abandoned in favour of private trade.[18]

The impact of these developments on the metropolitan economy was mixed. Some of the service nobility, certain merchants with particular interests in North Africa or Guinea and to an extent the crown itself were adversely affected. The Algarve ports also lost business owing to João III's pull-backs in Morocco. However, initially Portuguese private trade flourished well enough; as Oliveira Marques has pointed out, the mercantile bourgeoisie in the mid-sixteenth century enjoyed considerable prosperity.[19] Nevertheless, a generation later the picture seemed less positive, many late-sixteenth-century Portuguese merchants finding their trade increasingly hampered by restrictive regulations, by the commercial privileges granted to the nobility and by the growing influence of Lisbon-based foreign merchants. New Christian businessmen were often singled out for harassment because of their suspect faith. The Price Revolution was also having an adverse impact, making key commodities more expensive.[20] Wages failed to keep pace – and social tensions increased correspondingly.

Perhaps the most ominous of all the changes in Portugal's economic situation during the Tarnished Age was the gradual loss of national control over the country's own destiny. Portugal seemed to be drifting inexorably into the economic orbit of Castile. The main catalyst for this was Spanish American silver, which flowed into Portugal at a rapidly growing rate from approximately the middle of the sixteenth century. Portugal needed silver to pay for wheat imports and to maintain its trade with India. Silver was also essential for trade with China, which displayed a voracious appetite for the white metal.[21] Of course, the Portuguese eagerly searched for precious metals in their own overseas conquests – but, in this period, with negligible success. Portuguese merchants at Macau managed to obtain Japanese silver through Nagasaki. But the main source of supply was always Spanish America, where a reciprocal

---

[18] Ibid, pp 217–18.
[19] MHP, pp 292–3.
[20] Ibid, pp 279–80; NHP vol 5, pp 243–4.
[21] Flynn D 1991, p 334.

market developed in Peru and Mexico for Portuguese-procured African slaves. Even the Macau Portuguese accessed Mexican silver by linking indirectly into the trans-Pacific trade through Manila. Both in peninsular Spain, and in Spanish America, Portuguese Old and New Christians steadily infiltrated the local economies, while in North Africa the Portuguese fortresses became heavily dependent on Andalusia for their supplies. In short, the Portuguese and Spanish economic systems were becoming increasingly inter-dependent, with a logic probably neither government could have successfully resisted.[22]

The various economic challenges that confronted Portugal from about the mid-sixteenth century developed gradually and resulted from a complex of factors, many of which were beyond the crown's control. But in 1578 Portugal was faced with a sudden economic crisis that was entirely self-inflicted, for it resulted solely from King Sebastião's ill-fated expedition to North Africa. To pay for this enormously costly adventure the crown raised well over a million *cruzados* from a range of extraordinary sources including subsidies, loans, the sale of *juros* and the imposition of de facto war taxes.[23] Also many individual *fidalgos* borrowed heavily to finance their own participation. Much was allegedly expended on display rather than military equipment – the pyrotechnics of vanity, as Vitorino Magalhães Godinho called it.[24] In any event, as explained in Chapter 15, all was irretrievably lost in Morocco.

After the disaster in North Africa, an already heavily indebted crown and service nobility were saddled with the immense burden of meeting an unprecedented number of ransoms. King Henrique agreed to redeem an initial group of eighty *fidalgos* at 5,000 *cruzados* a head – a total of 400,000 *cruzados*.[25] The crown alone could not provide this amount, so much of it had to be raised by the captives' families. This was done slowly and with great difficulty, largely through the sale of personal jewellery and valuables. Ransoming continued well into the Habsburg era; but many of the 15,000 or more captives, particularly common soldiers without influence, were never freed. Instead they died in captivity or turned renegade. The loss of so many men and boys, many of whom had been recruited against their wills, caused significant labour shortages in some areas of Portugal.[26] Meanwhile Castile's economic influence increased. Sebastião not only destroyed the flower of Portuguese manhood in the deserts of North Africa; he also in one blow so crippled his country that it was soon delivered to Felipe II's 'silver bullets'.

---

[22] Godinho V M 1981–3 vol 4, p 218.
[23] SHP vol 3, p 76; NHP vol 3, p 750.
[24] Godinho V M 1980, p 243.
[25] Queirós Veloso J M de 1946, p 18.
[26] Ibid, p 55; SHP vol 3, p 76; Cook W F 1994, p 253.

THE COMING OF THE INQUISITION

By the start of the Tarnished Age royal government in Portugal was more firmly established than ever before, and in succeeding years it continued to consolidate and expand. The sheer quantity of legislation increased markedly, reaching an unprecedented peak in the reign of King Sebastião. The *cortes*, while it continued to have a role in times of crisis, was not much needed for everyday central government, and it now met rarely. However, João III did condescend to maintain contact with a permanent standing committee of the *cortes* – or at least its Lisbon members – since he believed it important to remain on good terms with the bourgeoisie.

For regular advice on affairs of state João III relied on an inner group of his councillors made up of prominent noblemen, churchmen, professional bureaucrats and members of his own family. With the creation of the *conselho de estado* in 1569 this situation was effectively formalised. A little later one of the councillors was singled out as a kind of chief minister, who was sometimes called a *valido*. The first *valido* was King Sebastião's Jesuit mentor, Martim Gonçalves da Câmara, who held the position until dismissed in 1575. This priest's pre-eminence is indicative of a new trend which saw court clergy, particularly royal confessors, exercising serious political influence – a development closely linked to the coming of the Jesuits.[27] Thus overall the Tarnished Age was an era of steady rather than spectacular growth in royal government, building upon trends set earlier in the century. However, there was one institution introduced in this period that deserves special attention because of its quite exceptional impact – namely, the Inquisition.

Portugal's great nineteenth-century liberal historian Alexandre Herculano (1810–77) was the first to examine on the basis of documentary evidence how the Portuguese Inquisition came into being. Herculano was uncompromising in his condemnation of this tribunal.[28] However, his views were vigorously contested at the time, while the Inquisition still had its defenders as late as the 1930s and 1940s, when the spectre of anti-Semitism was again stalking Europe. Alfredo Pimenta' s 1936 biography of João III contended that the Inquisition's ferocity had been grossly exaggerated, adding that the tribunal had as much right to defend itself from 'crimes and offences against the faith' as had a sporting club to prescribe its own rules and penalties.[29] João Ameal, another well-known historian of that era, argued that Jewish provocation had brought about the founding of the Inquisition and that its creation enabled the

[27] NHP vol 5, pp 390–5, 398–9.
[28] Herculano A 1972, p 499.
[29] Pimenta A 1936, pp 160, 187, 216–18, 221.

crown to safeguard the 'moral health' of the people, thereby securing society's peace and well-being 'at the cost of punishment to some'. Furthermore, the Inquisition employed force only proportionate to the 'hideous crimes' of offenders – and it enabled João III to break up 'the Jewish nucleus threatening the unity of the country'.[30] Such views eventually found a response in the powerful and well-grounded study of the Inquisition and the New Christians by José António Saraiva, published in 1969.

The Portuguese Inquisition did not have an easy birth. King Manuel had applied to the papacy in 1515 for leave to found it, but had not pursued the matter with much vigour. Subsequently João III was stirred to action by pressure from Castile, where an Inquisition had been active since 1480 – and by reports from informers, confirmed by a secret inquiry held in 1524, that Judaizing was rife within the New Christian community and integration had failed.[31] How true these claims were is unclear, though some historians argue there was little tradition of clandestine Judaism in Portugal and integration had been progressing steadily.[32] Be that as it may, a number of alleged incidents of anti-Christian sacrilege helped to intensify public hostility to Jews, and eventually João was persuaded to abandon his father's conciliatory line and seek to establish an Inquisition. Over ten years of painstaking negotiations with Rome were required before a Portuguese Inquisition, with restricted powers, received papal sanction in 1536, and another decade passed before a reluctant pope granted it roughly the same powers as the Inquisition of Castile.

The principal intended purpose of the Portuguese Inquisition was to detect and root out 'Lutherans' (that is, Protestant heretics) and Judaizers – the two groups perceived as most threatening to Catholic orthodoxy. In practice, since there were hardly any Protestants in Portugal, the overwhelming concern was with Judaizers. Before the forced conversions of 1496–7 there had been few *conversos* in Portugal and Jews, and Muslims, although not exactly loved, were reasonably well tolerated. However, as a result of these forced conversions Portugal acquired overnight a large population of former Jews, which quickly became the target of anti-Semitism, like its counterpart in Spain. The delay João III experienced in getting his Inquisition sanctioned by Rome resulted partly from lobbying by these New Christians, and partly from the fact that Rome itself now had serious reservations about such tribunals. Allegedly only after João III had made a thinly veiled threat to follow Henry VIII of England and deny the authority of Rome altogether did the papacy finally give in.[33]

[30] Ameal J 1962, pp 282–7.
[31] Tavares M J P F 1992, pp 182–8.
[32] Saraiva A J 1969, pp 41–6.
[33] Ibid, pp 70–1.

While the founding of the Portuguese Inquisition owed much to João III its consolidation can be attributed largely to his younger brother, Cardinal Henrique. In 1539, when already an archbishop at the barely canonical age of twenty-seven, Henrique was appointed the first Portuguese inquisitor-general. Six years later he became a cardinal and in 1552 an apostolic legate. In 1562–8 he was regent for the young King Sebastião and finally in 1578–80 king in his own right, all the while remaining inquisitor-general. In his long career Henrique was therefore able to combine to a greater degree than any other figure in Portuguese history the power and authority of both church and state. During his tenure as inquisitor-general the Inquisition developed institutional structures and meticulously detailed procedures that eventually made it the most powerful and feared tribunal in Portugal. In Saraiva's words, it was a state alongside the state, which on occasions presumed itself even above the state.[34] The inquisitor-general was always nominated by the king. However, once appointed, he was irremovable by king or pope. He himself appointed all other Inquisition officials and had the ex-officio powers of a papal legate. He therefore constituted a virtually independent authority over whom even the monarch had little control. The Inquisition's supreme governing body was the general council of the holy office which consisted of the inquisitor-general and three colleagues. Separate Inquisition tribunals were located in Lisbon, Évora, Coimbra and Goa, each with three inquisitors and several deputies, who were invariably canon lawyers or theologians. Most were Dominicans, often recruited from the university. Each tribunal possessed its hall, offices and dungeons, together with legal, clerical and security staff. These latter were backed up by a network of 'familiars' or volunteer auxiliaries, who were recruited from all classes.[35]

THE INQUISITION IN ACTION

All Christians in Portugal were subject to the Inquisition. On the first Sunday in Lent each year the people had to gather in the kingdom's churches to hear the Edict of Faith. This pronouncement formally outlined the errors to be exposed and extirpated and enjoined on all their duty to confess or denounce others on pain of excommunication. On receipt of written denunciations accused persons were arrested, their possessions seized and their houses sealed. These unfortunates remained incarcerated indefinitely while their cases proceeded – usually a slow-moving process, given the chronic shortage of qualified investigators and the inquisitors' heavy workload. Prisoners were not told details of the charges

[34] Ibid, p 237.
[35] Bethencourt F 2000, pp 45–6.

brought against them, nor the identities of their accusers, but were urged to confess and to implicate others involved.[36] If, after due opportunity had been given to reveal all, the inquisitors considered a confession to be incomplete or doubted the truth of what had been said, the prisoner could be tortured. This was performed on the hoist or rack while an accompanying inquisitor constantly urged the prisoner to make a full confession. Torture was used sparingly in the early years, but more frequently from the late sixteenth century.

Convicted prisoners were eventually either 'reconciled' (allowed re-admission to the church) or 'relaxed'. Penalties imposed on those reconciled varied according to the seriousness of the offence, but could be flogging, service in the galleys, further imprisonment, fining or performing various penances while wearing penitential garb.[37] Relaxation was reserved only for the most serious offenders – generally relapsed or incorrigible Judaizers and heretics or sodomites. It meant being handed over to the secular authorities for execution by burning at the stake. Sentences were pronounced at autos da fé, and the earliest of these great spectacles for which a clear description survives took place in Lisbon in 1544, when nineteen prisoners were burned alive.[38]

Autos da fé followed an elaborately orchestrated ritual. They were held in the less-crowded period of the liturgical year, between Pentecost and Advent, and were conducted in a festive atmosphere after weeks of preparation. The day began with a formal procession from Inquisition headquarters to a designated open space. In Lisbon this was usually the square adjoining the River Palace, fronting the Tagus. Large crowds gathered and were controlled by soldiery. The procession was led by a group of Dominicans holding aloft the Inquisition banner with its salutary motto, 'Justice and Mercy'. The prisoners followed, wearing *sanbenitos* (garments of penitential sackcloth) and conical hats – the *reconciliados* first, then the *relaxados* with their Jesuit counsellors. Next came the effigies of those to be burnt in absentia, then troops of Inquisition familiars on horseback. At the rear were the inquisitors themselves, escorted by members of the higher nobility. The square served as an amphitheatre, with an altar in the centre. If the king were present he played a spectator role only, viewing proceedings from a palace window. It was the inquisitor-general who presided, seated with his colleagues on one side of the square amid rich banners of red and gold and symbolic Christian crosses. The prisoners were ranged opposite where the trappings were dark, signifying the diabolical. To be most visible the *relaxados* were placed on the highest benches.[39]

[36] Saraiva A J 1969, pp 82, 85.
[37] Bethencourt F 2000, pp 247–8.
[38] Saraiva A J 1969, pp 146–8.
[39] Ibid, pp 149–63; Bethencourt F 2000, pp 219–63.

When all was in place proceedings began with prayers followed by a sermon, usually exalting the work of the Inquisition and denigrating Jews. A succession of priests then read out the offences and sentence of each prisoner as they knelt in turn at the altar. This procedure could last many hours, with the tension gradually rising. The *reconciliados* made their public recantations. The *relaxados* were delivered to the state authorities and, after brief formalities, their *sanbenitos* were removed and executions commenced. To the last possible moment, Jesuit counsellors strove to persuade the victims to die as Catholics. If they agreed they were strangled before being burned; if not, they were burned alive. On the Tagus waterfront, where the river breezes often prevented a swift death through smoke inhalation, the end could be agonisingly long.

Autos da fé were highly popular and attracted large crowds. They were both a manifestation of mass hysteria – a kind of ritual sacrifice of collective purification – and a form of religious theatre.[40] Everyone, from the king at his palace window to the barefoot urchin from the back-alleys, could share in self-righteous community solidarity against the hated outsiders – be they heretics or Jews masquerading as Christians. Autos da fé demonstrated the awesome authority of the inquisitors. They also kept before the public eye the dire threat that Judaizers were supposed to constitute to Portuguese Catholic society, and the constant vigilance it demanded. In such a context there could be no sympathy for the victims, for they had cast themselves out of the tribe by their own deliberate actions. To reinforce these lessons, after an auto da fé the sanbenito of each *relaxado,* with the individual's name and date of execution attached, was displayed in a prominent city church.[41]

Of course, there was resistance to the entrenchment of the Inquisition, and to the attitudes it encapsulated, both from New Christians and from some elements within the church itself, including a hesitant papacy. In the period up to 1580 the number of *relaxados* was small; the nineteen executed in 1544 and another ten in 1563 were the largest groups known to have been burned at single autos da fé. The New Christians were able to buy collective pardons for their community in 1547 and 1578, and it was not until the first half of the seventeenth century that Inquisition activity reached its peak. The most active year was probably 1629 when over 550 victims were sentenced. It has been tentatively estimated that in the first seventy years of its existence the Portuguese Inquisition processed in all about 10,000 cases.[42]

One of the most resented practices of the Inquisition was the confiscation of prisoners' houses and possessions. Because of strong lobbying at Rome by the

---

[40] Saraiva A J 1969, p 162; Bethencourt F 2000, p 227.
[41] Saraiva A J 1969, p 159.
[42] Torres J V 1978, p 59; NHP vol 5, p 438.

New Christians, Cardinal Henrique was not able to get papal approval for this practice until 1563; but thereafter the Inquisition routinely seized and administered the estates of prisoners for as long as they remained under investigation. Of course, all was meant to be returned to those acquitted (after deducting costs for their maintenance while incarcerated), though long delays could be expected. But the possessions of *relaxados,* and also of *reconciliados* under some circumstances, were retained or sold off as the Inquisition saw fit, leaving families destitute.[43] In theory the revenue from confiscations reverted to the crown; but in practice the Inquisition retained it to cover 'costs'. The Inquisition therefore had a strong vested interest in securing confiscations, becoming in effect an agency for pillaging the New Christian bourgeoisie. Moreover, goods in the possession of a suspect were liable to be seized even if held on credit from third parties. This meant the economic repercussions of an Inquisition arrest could extend well beyond the individual, and even outside the New Christian community. There was also a debilitating haemorrhage of New Christian capital and expertise out of Portugal, and commercial operations were inevitably hampered in an atmosphere so fraught with uncertainty. Foreign merchants became more wary of doing business. Ultimately all this contributed to the country's decline as a trading nation, though the full consequences did not become evident until well after the Tarnished Age had passed.[44]

How was it that an institution such as the Inquisition was able to become so powerful in Portugal and to remain so firmly established in national life for well over two centuries? Part of the answer is that it enjoyed almost universal support among Old Christians, a natural constituency it always carefully cultivated. Old Christians had little cause to feel threatened by the Inquisition because by definition they did not, and could not, themselves Judaize – and Judaizing was the Inquisition's principal preoccupation. Old Christians had been conditioned to see Judaizers as anathema and so applauded their exposure and removal from society. Thousands of Old Christians from all classes eagerly competed to enlist as Inquisition familiars, and it was because of these ubiquitous auxiliaries, informers and enforcers that the institution could penetrate society so thoroughly and maintain its grip so firmly.[45] The Inquisition enjoyed strong backing from the royal family, the higher clergy and the nobility and overwhelming support from the *cortes* and the lower clergy. There were a few concerned nobles and clergy who from time to time voiced reservations about the damage that overzealous persecutions could inflict on the country, and who

---

[43] Saraiva A J 1969, pp 252–5; Shaw L M E 1989, p 423.
[44] Shaw L M E 1989, pp 415–31.
[45] Saraiva A J 1969, p 243.

sometimes succeeded in securing short-term concessions for the New Christi-ans. But broad acceptance of the Inquisition's values and attitudes was rein-forced by heavy censorship for which the Inquisition itself was largely responsible. By the end of the Tarnished Age censorship was steadily convert-ing the Portuguese into one of the intellectually most deprived and least well-informed peoples of Western Europe.

PORTUGAL, THE COUNCIL OF TRENT AND THE JESUITS

In 1545 the Catholic church began a long drawn-out general council at the imperial city of Trent in northern Italy, the underlying purpose of which was to deal with Protestantism. At first many delegates hoped that a return to the Catholic fold at least of the German Lutherans might be possible. However, negotiations to this end proved fruitless; so the council concentrated instead on clarifying dogma, resolving liturgical differences and prescribing long overdue reforms in church discipline and practice. Given that the participants repre-sented several different traditions within Catholicism, and each state sent a national delegation bent on protecting its own interests, achieving consensus was a huge challenge. The council, which was also forced into two lengthy recesses, was as contentious as it was prolonged. Nevertheless, it was eventually able to agree upon a series of decrees that were formally confirmed by Pius IV in 1564. Broadly, they restated Catholic doctrine in terms of Thomist Scholasti-cism, clearly differentiating it from Protestantism and effectively closing the door to reconciliation.

The Portuguese participated fully and earnestly at every stage of the Council of Trent with their delegates taking a strongly pro-reform line, especially in matters of discipline.[46] When the bull ordering implementation of the decrees reached Portugal Cardinal Henrique, then both regent and papal legate, staged a solemn ceremony of acceptance in the presence of the boy-king Sebastião in Lisbon cathedral. The decrees were then published throughout the kingdom and the state authorities instructed to assist the church in carrying them out. Apart from Venice, Portugal was the only significant state to accept the Tri-dentine decrees in entirety and without reservation, and no other government made more strenuous efforts to implement them. Henrique initiated the proc-ess; but later Sebastião, who ardently declared his desire to serve the church, granted prelates the power to enforce the decrees even in matters normally falling within the crown's jurisdiction. This astonishing concession, which amounted to surrendering voluntarily a key sovereign prerogative, proved so

[46] Oliveira M de 1968, pp 262–3.

controversial that it subsequently had to be re-defined to allow royal judges power to rule on issues of jurisdictional conflict.[47]

Largely in response to the Tridentine decrees the Portuguese crown and bishops embarked on a program to upgrade the training of priests. A series of seminaries was founded eventually covering most dioceses from Braga to Goa. Residence requirements were enforced more strictly at all levels and bishops themselves required to perform their spiritual duties more conscientiously. Greater uniformity was introduced into church liturgy, and the missal and breviary were updated and standardised. Meanwhile certain cults, such as those of St. Roque, St. Sebastian and the Most Holy Sacrament, increased in popularity, and there was growing enthusiasm for ever more elaborate religious processions.[48]

Efforts to reinvigorate religious life during the Tarnished Age coincided with the appearance in Portugal of the Society of Jesus, the most dynamic religious order of the sixteenth century. The Society, founded by the Navarrese Ignatius Loyola and five companions at the University of Paris, received papal approval in September 1540. By that time Diogo de Gouveia, the Portuguese principal of the Collège de Sainte Barbe where Loyola studied, had already suggested to João III that the Jesuits might make excellent missionaries in India. João expressed keen interest and requested his ambassador in Rome to arrange for a few of them to come to Portugal. Accordingly, Simão Rodrigues and Francisco Xavier arrived in Lisbon in June 1540.[49]

At first the Jesuits tried to develop a popular urban ministry in Portugal, preaching, teaching, reconciling, caring for prisoners and the sick and moving indiscriminately between slum and palace. But because the king, the royal family and many of the elite were soon numbered among the Society's greatest admirers, such a down-to-earth focus became difficult to maintain. João III came to regard Rodrigues and Xavier as veritable apostles and requested a personal copy of Loyola's *Spiritual Exercises*.[50] João, Sebastião and Henrique each in turn engaged Jesuit confessors, as did other members of the royal family and numerous courtiers. João also asked Rodrigues and Xavier to hear the confessions of his court pages – no small undertaking, given they numbered over 100. So the Jesuits were rapidly drawn into the highest circles and gained great influence – but at the cost of burdensome responsibilities of a kind they never originally intended.[51] The enthusiastic support accorded the Jesuits in

[47] Caetano M 1965, pp 10–41, 51–2.
[48] Oliveira M de 1968, pp 272–3; NHP vol 5, pp 431, 445–6.
[49] Schurhammer G 1973–82 vol 1, pp 543–4; Alden D 1996, p 25.
[50] Schurhammer G 1973–82 vol 1, pp 604, 620.
[51] Ibid, p 605; Alden D 1996, pp 26–7; 60.

Portugal, notwithstanding the hostility of some bishops and heads of other orders, stemmed from their outstanding dedication and high reputation for spirituality, morality and educational rigour. All candidates for the Society were carefully screened, and those selected underwent a process of exceptionally thorough training. A novitiate twice as long as usual was followed by eight years of further study. Integrity, commitment, discipline and the highest possible intellectual excellence were all demanded.

In accordance with João III's wishes, in April 1541 Xavier set sail for distant Asia, so launching a career that would make him perhaps the most famous Christian missionary since St. Paul. There is no doubt that the greatest mark made by the Jesuits in a Portuguese context was not in Portugal itself, but in the vast territories claimed for the *padroado* in Asia, Africa and Brazil. Nevertheless, João III was determined that the Society would also continue its presence in the metropolis – and, on the king's insistence, Rodrigues reluctantly agreed not to accompany Xavier to India, but instead organise Jesuit work in Portugal. In 1546 Portugal became a separate Jesuit province with Rodrigues as its provincial. Later, the five overseas provinces of Goa, Brazil, Japan, China and Malabar were combined with the province of Portugal to form one of the four (eventually six) great Jesuit 'assistancies'.

Jesuit novitiates were quickly established in Lisbon, Coimbra and Évora, and membership of the society in the various Portuguese provinces had grown to over 300 by 1550. Nevertheless, there were always far too few Jesuits for the work to be done. The Society arrived in Portugal at a time when educational reform was much needed and high-quality instruction was difficult to secure, so that members were increasingly drawn off into the education arena. Much the same was happening elsewhere in Catholic Europe, so that Loyola was eventually obliged to commit the Society to teaching students beyond its own membership. From 1546 he allowed sons of the elite to attend Jesuit classes, and from the 1550s it was accepted that the Society had a responsibility to secondary and higher education in general.[52] The Jesuit curriculum contained a mixture of the Scholastic and conservative Humanist traditions; but the pedagogy was sophisticated and involved ingenious mnemonic devices. As a matter of principle tuition fees were not charged.

Several Jesuit colleges were founded in Portugal during this era, the first being Santo Antão, which opened in the former Muslim district of Lisbon in 1542, using a site granted to the Society by João III. In 1547, the Jesuits began another college at the University of Coimbra, and this institution subsequently absorbed João III's College of the Arts. A third college was founded in 1559

---

[52] Alden D 1996, pp 16–17, 36.

at Évora where Cardinal Henrique was seeking to establish a new Jesuit-administered university; smaller foundations also appeared at Porto, Braga, Bragança, Faro, Funchal, Goa and elsewhere.[53] The Jesuits were now the leading educators of Portugal's elite, either in their colleges or on an individual basis. Young Sebastião himself was taught by two successive Jesuit tutors and was said to have regarded the first of them, Luís Gonçalves da Câmara, as virtually a surrogate parent. Later, when Sebastião proved a stubborn fanatic, the Jesuits were accused of mis-educating him, and therefore of indirect responsibility for the disaster of Al-Ksar al-Kabir.[54]

As well as becoming pre-eminent educators the Jesuits were drawn into a range of community and social welfare roles. Soon they were dispensing medicines from their colleges, and they often acted as almoners aboard ships that took them to overseas missions. They regularly attended the sick and dying and in Goa were made responsible for the royal hospital. They showed particular interest in the plight of the incarcerated, and Cardinal Henrique soon asked them to act as confessors and spiritual instructors to prisoners of the Inquisition. Xavier and Rodrigues, who arrived in Portugal only three months before the first auto da fé in 1540, quickly began daily visits to that tribunal's prison in Lisbon.[55] From there they inevitably moved on to preaching regularly at autos da fé and serving as the victims' confessors. Then in 1550 João III invited the Society to take over the Lisbon Inquisition, and a little later that of Coimbra. Diogo Mirão, the Portuguese Jesuit provincial, was eager to accept, even though some of his colleagues were more wary.[56] But Loyola ordered the invitation be declined.

THE FATE OF LETTERS AND THE ARTS

In 1545 Damião de Goís returned to Portugal after an absence of over twenty years and was promptly invited by João III, whose patronage and friendship he had long enjoyed, to teach nine-year-old Prince João his letters. The king also asked the Jesuit superior, Simão Rodrigues, to instruct the prince in Christian doctrine. This could be seen as a judicious compromise – a distinguished Erasmian Humanist counter-balanced by a reliable conservative theologian. But not so to Rodrigues, who never wavered in matters of faith. In September 1546, he denounced Goís to the Évora Inquisition for alleged Protestantism, on

[53] DHP vol 2, p 590; Alden D 1996, pp 29–34; NHP vol 5, pp 428–9.
[54] Alden D 1996, pp 80, 82, 88.
[55] Schurhammer G 1973–82 vol 1, p 645.
[56] RHC vol 1, pp 693–7; Alden D 1996, pp 670–3.

the basis of comments made by the Humanist in Padua seven years earlier.[57] The Inquisition initially dismissed the case for lack of evidence. But the king nevertheless withdrew his patronage from Goís, who returned quietly to private life. Five years later Rodrigues renewed his denunciation. Again the case was suspended, this time apparently on the intervention of Cardinal Henrique. Finally almost twenty years afterwards in 1569, when Goís was nearly seventy, the charge was revived yet a third time. Now no patron came to Goís's protection, and he was duly arrested. Two years later he was formally convicted and sentenced to life imprisonment with confiscation of his property.

Against the background of Trent, the arrival of the Jesuits and the rapid consolidation of the Inquisition the Goís case suggests a progressive hardening of official attitudes. In 1545 Erasmianism still had some influence, although repressive forces were already closing in. Five years later Erasmian Humanists were clearly no longer acceptable, even if illustrious figures from an earlier era might still secure some protection. By the end of the 1560s, the remnant of these Humanists was in a hopeless position, with religious and intellectual reaction deeply entrenched. Erasmus himself had become the object of suspicion, and only a narrow orthodoxy was now tolerated. The errors of ageing Humanists committed forty years before could no longer go uninvestigated or unpunished.

Apart from the Inquisition, conservative orthodoxy in Portugal had two particularly effective weapons for imposing its views: the Jesuit education system and the censorship. Jesuit education had many strengths. It stressed personal discipline, proficiency in Latin, skill in Rhetoric and mastery of a carefully sanitised body of knowledge centred on Theology. For the Society's own ranks it produced an elite body of men (for there were, of course, no women members), with extraordinary devotion to their ideals and great determination to propagate them. As linguists and students of exotic cultures the Jesuits excelled – always with the prime objective of achieving conversions. Unlike Erasmian Humanists they pursued knowledge and understanding in the service of God and not for their own sakes. Jesuits sought to shield their students and converts from any contact with the contaminating influence of unorthodoxy, believing that on the hard core of Catholic truth there could be no compromise. Their education system was widely appreciated, and all their colleges and schools were over-enrolled.[58]

The struggle between the Jesuit and Erasmian approaches to education in Portugal reached its turning point in the 1550s at the College of the Arts in Coimbra. The founding rector of the college was an Erasmian, André de Gouveia, who gathered like-minded scholars around him. But Gouveia soon

---

[57] RHC vol 2, pp 23–5; Hirsch E F 1967, pp 96, 186, 189, 211–14.
[58] RHC vol 1, pp 435–6, 443.

died and was succeeded by a conservative – and bitter disputes between Erasmian and conservative faculty members followed. Finally in 1550 João III, perhaps acting under Jesuit influence, forcibly removed the leading Erasmians, several of whom, including the prolific Humanist writer Diogo de Teive and the Paris-educated Scot George Buchanan, were denounced to the Inquisition. They were tried and condemned to prison terms, though most were later freed on the intervention of Cardinal Henrique.[59] All were replaced on the faculty by conservatives, and in 1555 the college was handed over to the triumphant Jesuits.

While books, including works by Wyclif and Hus, had occasionally been banned in Portugal in the late Middle Ages, there was no tradition of systematic censorship. However, the Portuguese Inquisition, following the lead of its Italian and Spanish counterparts, introduced an index of prohibited books in 1547 which was revised, expanded and re-issued at regular intervals thereafter. The aim was to ban all works 'against our Holy Faith, and good customs'.[60] In 1551 the index already contained nearly 500 titles, and by 1581 many more had been added. The whole corpus of Erasmus's works was banned, while most major writings of the Portuguese Humanists, including Gil Vicente, Sá de Miranda, João de Barros and Damião de Góis, were either prohibited outright or subjected to deletions and alterations before publication. Enforcement of censorship was progressively strengthened. Regular inspections of libraries and bookshops commenced in the early 1550s, incoming ships were subjected to searches and printeries were inspected annually. All publications needed authorisation from the crown authorities, the local bishop and the Inquisition, so requiring three imprimaturs.[61]

Some historians have attempted to defend the censorship on the grounds it was intended only to protect the integrity of Catholicism, and that learning and the Arts did not suffer any damage from its imposition.[62] There is some truth in the first part of this contention, but virtually none in the second. Some major works of Portuguese literature were indeed produced in the late sixteenth or early seventeenth centuries. They include Luís de Camões's great epic poem *The Lusiads,* the most famous composition in the Portuguese language, which was first published in 1572 and which earned the poet a modest crown pension. Diogo do Couto also wrote in this period, his works including the continuation of Barros's *Ásia.* In the missions various Jesuits – some of them Portuguese, others foreigners – diligently studied such non-European languages as Konkani, Tamil, Mandarin, Japanese and Tupí-Guaraní, and compiled pioneering

[59] Hirsch E F 1967, pp 172–6.
[60] NHP vol 5, p 480.
[61] Ibid, pp 479–80; Bethencourt F 2000, pp 199–202.
[62] Pimenta A 1936, p 223.

dictionaries and grammars.[63] They and other missionaries also wrote invaluable descriptions and histories of exotic lands and peoples. Nevertheless, censorship deprived the public of almost anything that was controversial from a strictly Catholic standpoint. It discouraged writing and greatly limited publishing. Many important works, such as Gaspar Correia's *Lendas da Índia,* never got to press until at best centuries later. Presses were relatively rare in the Portuguese world, freedom to print being so circumscribed. When a press was eventually established in Goa it was soon taken over by the Jesuits. They used it primarily to produce material for their missions, and virtually everything it published was written by religious. A rare exception was Garcia da Orta's *Colloquies on the Simples and Drugs of India* (1563), the first modern European treatise on tropical Asian pharmacology and medicine. However, Orta himself was posthumously condemned for Judaizing, and his remains were exhumed and burned, on Inquisition orders.[64]

The change of mood during the Tarnished Age was also reflected in the Arts. Mannerist architecture, with its barrel-vaulted naves, compartmented façades and geometric decoration, had reached Portugal from Italy and Spain by the mid-sixteenth century. The new cathedrals of Portalegre and Leiria, along with numerous Jesuit churches in Portugal and the overseas territories, were built in this austere style.[65] In painting the Flemish tradition of Manueline times now gave way to Italian Rafaelesque with its formal religious scenes, anaemic figures and gentle colours. There was a flowering of portraiture, briefly impressive and too-often underrated. Cristovão Lopes, who succeeded his father Gregório Lopes as court artist in 1551, painted several fine portraits of João III and Catarina. Another acclaimed portraitist was the Fleming Antonis Mor who arrived at court in 1552. About this time Catarina founded a portrait gallery in the royal palace, probably the first in Portugal.[66] But gradually opportunities for artists diminished – a trend that would accelerate after the union of crowns in 1580, when there was no longer a permanently resident monarch to provide patronage.

THE CRISIS OF 1580 AND THE SUCCESSION OF FILIPE I

When King Henrique finally accepted in 1579 that he was not going to marry and beget his own heir there were four possible successors to the Portuguese throne. One was António, love-child of King Manuel's third son, Luís. He

[63] Boxer C R 1978, pp 42–3.
[64] Boxer C R 1963, p 11.
[65] Smith R C 1968, pp 84–6.
[66] Ibid, pp 201–2; Jordan A 1994, pp 81, 84.

enjoyed much popular support; but, as a bastard, he was automatically disqualified unless he could somehow prove his parents had been secretly married. A second candidate was Felipe II of Spain who was the son of Manuel's oldest daughter, Isabel. Felipe was by far the most powerful contender, but faced widespread hostility because of popular anti-Castilian xenophobia. A Spanish ambassador of the time facetiously remarked that the Portuguese would sooner turn Muslims than unite with Castile.[67] A third candidate was Manuel's granddaughter Catarina, wife of the duke of Bragança. She claimed precedence over Felipe because she was descended through a male line, being daughter of Manuel's youngest son, Duarte. Though Catarina was born and bred in Portugal, she was much less popular than António. She was also not helped by being a woman competing with men, nor by her husband's reputed indecisiveness and arrogance. Moreover, if Catarina's own legal arguments were accepted, there was another contender with a strictly better claim than hers. This was Ranuccio Farnese, nine-year-old son of Duarte's other daughter, Maria, who had been older than Catarina. But in the real world Ranuccio's claim had no hope: he had not been brought up in Portugal, and his father, Alejandro Farnese, being Felipe II's governor of the Netherlands, could not oppose his sovereign's interests.

In February 1579 King Henrique invited all the candidates to submit their claims for investigation by a special panel of jurists. António, who was intensely disliked by Henrique, was quickly eliminated when the panel confirmed his illegitimacy, leaving only Felipe and Catarina in formal contention. Henrique wished to preserve Portugal's independence, but was desperately anxious to spare his people a disputed succession and possible invasion from Castile. Gradually he came round to the view that Felipe was really the only viable option and so began negotiations with him, even though the panel was still deliberating. When Henrique died in January 1580, Felipe believed an agreement in principle already existed. Yet there had been no public pronouncement from the dying king, nor had he designated Felipe his heir in his will. Henrique himself had always insisted that the final decision rested with the *cortes* – and that body remained divided with most nobles and higher clergy favouring Felipe, but most of the towns' representatives opposing him.[68]

For years before 1580 Portugal had been moving steadily towards political Hispanisation. Despite popular Portuguese hostility to Castile, this had been long the likely final outcome of dynastic policy. Moreover, the dream of a united Hispania under a single monarch as in Visigothic times had a seductive appeal to some – and in the sixteenth century, with the recent union of crowns

[67] Bouza Álvarez F J 1998, p 110.
[68] Queirós Veloso J M de 1946, pp 395–401.

between Castile and Aragon, the emergence of a united France and the trend towards unity in the British Isles it seemed more achievable than ever. But political Hispanisation inevitably also meant long-term Castilianisation, a process already well under way. Castile, much larger and more populous than Portugal, was indisputably one of the great powers of Europe. It had a vast empire and immense resources of silver and was bound to be the controlling centre of any combined monarchy. Already the Portuguese economy was being drawn towards that of Castile and, as Portugal's own problems multiplied, there was a growing tendency to regard all things Castilian as somehow exemplary. Looking enviously across the border, people murmured that affairs ought to be handled in Portugal more as they were in the great Felipe II's dominions.[69]

There were similar trends regarding the Spanish language and the culture of the Castilian court, which both appealed strongly to the Portuguese elite. Successive Castilian queens in Portugal encouraged cultural Castilianisation, particularly Maria and Catarina. Most Portuguese writers of the era, including Camões himself, spoke fluent Castilian and frequently chose to write in that language. By the late sixteenth century the overseas interests of Portugal and Castile both had much to gain from a closer association. They were more complementary than competing and often faced the same external enemies. Each kingdom was striving to maintain possessions far from the metropolis, promote vast missionary enterprises and defend extended lines of seaborne communications. In the Atlantic, in particular, this task could be made easier by close co-operation.

Felipe II demanded Portugal – for he saw it as his rightful inheritance. But beyond that conviction, acquiring Portugal's Afro-Asian empire offered him the alluring prospect of becoming literally the first truly global monarch. There were also important strategic advantages to be gained: control of Portuguese naval resources and a much longer Atlantic coastline. Through Portugal Felipe could broaden his campaign against the rebel Dutch by cutting off their traditional supplies of salt and spices, and he would also be strengthened vis-à-vis the Turks.[70] Therefore, during the two years between the deaths of Sebastião and Henrique, Felipe waged a tireless campaign to secure the Portuguese succession. His principal agent was Cristovão de Moura, a Portuguese nobleman who had earlier arrived in Castile with Joana, Sebastião's Castilian mother. Moura entered Felipe's service and was appointed Spanish ambassador in Portugal on Sebastião's death. Highly trusted by his Spanish master, he handled all the crucial succession negotiations. Because Felipe wished to avoid using

[69] Thomaz L F R 1995, p 499.
[70] Bouza Álvarez F J 1992, pp 689–72.

force, Moura's brief was to negotiate and to persuade. He duly tried to win over as many of the Portuguese elite as possible, including individual churchmen and noblemen, senior bureaucrats, jurists, *câmaras* and interest groups within the *cortes*. He lobbied tirelessly – persuading here, re-assuring there, giving promises of future favours and making carefully targeted payments in silver. Henrique's government was constantly pressured for a favourable decision.[71]

When Henrique finally died in January 1580 he left a board of five governors to administer the kingdom until a successor was found. António was the first of the claimants to act, trying to enter Lisbon to win the throne by popular acclamation. However, he was promptly shut out by the governors. Catarina and her husband were more cautious, having resolved to await the finding of Henrique's panel of jurists. Felipe at first also waited, expecting the governors would quickly recognise his claim. Three of them wanted to do this; but they dared not make a move because of intense popular opposition. Many nobles were opting for Felipe, sensing greater patronage potential from a monarch already so powerful. The Jesuits are often held to have backed Felipe but never did so as a group.[72] The weeks passed and Felipe grew increasingly impatient. He did not want to enter Portugal as a conqueror; but he prudently made military preparations. The duke of Alba and the marquis of Santa Cruz were appointed to assemble land and naval expeditions respectively while Felipe himself moved close to the frontier. Meanwhile, tensions rose as the governors continued to prevaricate – until Felipe informed their envoys he would tolerate delay no longer. To their plea to await the decision of the panel he replied that his claim was manifest, and they had one month to recognise it.[73]

Felipe's deadline expired on 8 June 1580. Ten days later Alba's forces crossed into Portugal at Elvas where the fortress commander had been suborned to admit them. On receiving the news at Santarém, António immediately had himself proclaimed king, then entered Lisbon without opposition. The three governors who supported Felipe fled to the Castilians, taking what they could of the crown jewels with them. They were promptly required to declare Felipe the rightful king, transfer to him formal control of all Portuguese fortresses and denounce António as a rebel. Catarina and Bragança now submitted, leaving Alba free to concentrate on António. Alba's army of about 20,000 Spanish, Italian and German troops began advancing on Lisbon in late June. Resistance was only light, with towns and fortresses along the route submitting rapidly. Alba's behaviour was generally conciliatory; but when opposition was encountered, as in Setúbal, there was killing and looting.

[71] Queirós Veloso J M de 1940, pp 20–35; Bouza Álvarez F J 1998, pp 112–13.
[72] Alden D 1996, pp 89–91.
[73] PHP vol 5, p 215.

By late July both Alba by land and Santa Cruz by sea had closed in on Lisbon where António and his followers, with little money and few arms, hastily prepared their defences. António's *fidalgo* support was limited and dwindling, and he could rely on few experienced officers. His difficulties were increased by an influenza epidemic that killed perhaps 10 per cent of the city's population that summer. But popular opposition to a Castilian king remained strong, and an improvised force of some 8,000, its recruits ranging from freed African slaves to local friars, was eventually assembled.[74] The Lisbon *câmara* had no faith in this ragtag army's capacity to withstand Alba; but nevertheless, a defensive line was established downstream at the Alcântara creek. Alba attacked this line early on 25 August 1580. Initially there was spirited resistance; but it was soon broken. When the fighting ceased some 2,000 of António's 'rebels' lay dead, their bodies strewn along the Alcântara-Lisbon road down which they had fled. The city itself was then pillaged, and even the remaining crown jewels were stolen – though they were recovered later when the audacious thieves put them up for sale at Málaga.[75] Militarily a modest affair, 'the battle of Alcântara' was decisive politically, sealing Portugal's fate.

António fought bravely in defence of his capital and was himself wounded. After his defeat he fled north to Coimbra where many students, as well as canons from the monastery of Santa Cruz where he had studied, joined his cause. In September, as he struggled to re-group, news reached him that Felipe was seriously ill; but if António was encouraged by this intelligence, it was not for long. Felipe soon recovered, and Alba moved detachments north to hunt the 'rebels'. António survived as a fugitive in northern Portugal for several more months before moving in May 1581 first to England, then France. From these foreign lands he continued his forlorn struggle for almost fifteen years, eventually dying in Paris in 1595. To his sympathisers, and to some patriotic Portuguese historians, António was a king wrongfully deprived of his birthright; to others he was an unprincipled adventurer with little to recommend him. But whatever one thinks about his claims there is no doubt he was personally resolute and courageous, and that he was the people's preferred king.

Once Alba was firmly in control, Felipe II crossed into Portugal. Because of the epidemic in Lisbon he summoned the *cortes* to meet in Tomar, where in April 1581 he was formally acclaimed king as Filipe I of Portugal. Filipe (as we shall now call him) wished to appear magnanimous and to behave as a king by hereditary right. Those who had opposed him were pardoned – apart from about fifty individuals who were placed on a list of exceptions. The terms of his succession were clearly spelled out at Tomar and followed closely the principles

---

[74] Ibid, pp 223–6.
[75] SHP vol 3, p 90; Bouza Álvarez F J 1998, p 112.

laid down by King Manuel in 1499. Portugal would retain all its traditional liberties, customs and uses as recognised by previous monarchs. All offices under the Portuguese crown and trade and navigation with and within the Portuguese empire were to be reserved exclusively for Portuguese. The official language remained Portuguese, and the kingdom would keep its own coinage. When not in Portugal the king would be represented either by a viceroy selected from the royal family, or by governors of Portuguese nationality. A council of Portugal comprised exclusively of Portuguese would be created at court to advise on the kingdom's affairs.

The package of conditions sworn at Tomar was generous, giving Portugal almost total autonomy. There was to be a union of crowns creating a 'dual monarchy', not an incorporation of Portugal into Castile.[76] A whole range of material benefits was granted – including abolition of customs barriers on the Portuguese-Castilian frontier, provision of Castilian grain and a cash injection for various urgent purposes such as ransoms in North Africa. Many Portuguese now hoped Portugal would be better protected militarily and that Spanish silver would reanimate Portuguese trade. Much royal patronage was also expected. Of course, it remained to be seen whether all these promises and hopes would be realised.

[76] PHP vol 5, pp 239–40

10

Habsburg Portugal

FILIPE I IN LISBON

Many biographies of Felipe II of Spain have been written by Spaniards and by foreigners; in English alone, at least five have appeared since 1960. This is perhaps not surprising, for the king presided over the Spanish monarchy at the peak of its power and prestige. But, with a single recent exception, no one has ever written a life of Filipe I of Portugal – a stark reminder of the country's diminished standing after union.[1] For regardless of Filipe's confirmation of Portuguese rights sealed at Tomar in 1581, Portugal was now politically and constitutionally a mere peripheral part of a much greater Castilian-dominated whole. Autonomy within the union could never be complete and would arguably always be more apparent than real.[2] It was a situation that required of the Portuguese major psychological readjustments and raised important questions about national identity.

Nevertheless, by restoring the sovereign status quo as it had supposedly existed before the Muslim conquest of the eighth century, the union of crowns fulfilled an old dream. An idealised past, Roman and Visigothic, had finally triumphed. Hispania was reconstituted. At the same time, the union of crowns also represented the realisation of another, newer, more ambitious dream. Filipe had become the ruler of two great empires: the Castilian primarily in Europe and the Americas and the Portuguese scattered through maritime Asia, Africa and Brazil. As such, he presided over imperial possessions that were

---

[1] The five biographies of Felipe II in English were by Charles Petrie (1963), Edward Grierson (1974), Peter Pierson (1975), Geoffrey Parker (1978) and Henry Kamen (1997). There is now a biography of Filipe I, in Portuguese, by a distinguished Spanish historian. See F Bouza Álvarez, D. Filipe I, Círculo de Leitores, Lisbon, 2005.

[2] Oliveira A de 1990, p 10.

indisputably global, far exceeding in size what Rome had ruled. His were dominions on which the sun never set. Yet Filipe himself did not deliberately flaunt his greatness, preferring to project a more modest down-to-earth image.[3] Of course, the acquisition of the Portuguese crown meant more than just the realisation of dreams – it also promised attractive tangible benefits. When the king consulted his advisers about whether to pursue his claim he was given three main arguments for doing so: a dual monarchy would increase the security and prosperity of both kingdoms, it would benefit the church and it would strengthen the Catholic powers in their struggle against Protestantism.[4] Filipe accepted all three as compelling justifications for proceeding with the enterprise of Portugal. Yet eventually all proved flawed.

On 24 June 1581 Filipe I made his formal entry into Lisbon. It was the most triumphant and iconographically ostentatious such occasion of his reign, though the onlookers' response was subdued.[5] After receiving the keys of the city, Filipe rode to the cathedral along garlanded streets and through triumphal arches erected by the various guilds, extolling his greatness. For those who had worked for it all – and for his local adherents, who believed or half-believed the imperial imagery – it was a euphoric occasion; even for Filipe himself, it was perhaps the most satisfying moment of his reign. Nevertheless, whether or not the vast majority of Portuguese eventually accepted union would depend not on symbolic ceremonial but on practical outcomes. Like the king himself, the Portuguese expected solid benefits, and in the long run their attitude would be heavily influenced by whether or not those benefits were forthcoming. Moreover, there was widespread concern about how Portuguese institutions, customary rights and privileges would fare under the new regime. As we have seen, Filipe I was sensitive to this concern and had tried to reassure his Portuguese subjects by publicly swearing at Tomar to keep the two crowns distinct and separate, so preserving Portugal's autonomy. But in practice this was always going to be hard to achieve, and it seems that initially men of goodwill on both sides of the frontier underestimated the difficulties.

Filipe remained in Portugal from December 1580 to March 1583. It was a time when the focus of Spanish foreign policy was shifting decisively from the Mediterranean to the North Atlantic, coincidently enhancing the strategic importance of Lisbon. There were those among Filipe's advisers, most notably Cardinal Granvelle, who saw sense in the court moving permanently to the Portuguese capital. Filipe himself showed signs he envisaged a prolonged

[3] Elliott J H 1991, p 51; Parker G 1995, pp 253–4, 259; Kamen H 1997, p 230; Bouza Álvarez F 1998, pp 105–6.
[4] Parker G 1978, p 143.
[5] SHP vol 4, p 20; Parker G 1995, pp 253–4; Kamen H 1997, p 230.

stay, summoning his landscape gardeners and the architects Juan de Herrera and Filippo Terzi from Castile to make the River Palace more to his liking.[6] Certainly as long as the king resided in Lisbon the Portuguese had little to complain about. They remained as close to the centre of affairs as they had ever been in Avis times. For the court nobility, honours and offices under the crown of Portugal were as readily available as before, though opportunities within the Habsburg household itself were probably less accessible. Many individuals who had backed Filipe's cause were well rewarded. The king was scrupulous in observing his promises confirmed at Tomar and interfered little in strictly local affairs. But the death of his heir, Diego, finally persuaded Filipe to return to Madrid. He left in early 1583, after first calling the Portuguese *cortes* to pledge loyalty to his next son, another Felipe. He never came back to Portugal.

INSTITUTIONAL CHANGE, MARGINALISATION AND AMBIGUOUS AUTONOMY

After Filipe I's departure significant institutional changes gradually crept in; they came partly in response to local need, but also within the context of a broader reform agenda. Under the terms agreed at Tomar, in the king's absence he would be represented in Portugal either by a viceroy (who must be Portuguese, or a member of the royal family within a specified range of blood relationships to the king) or by a board of all-Portuguese governors. In 1583 Filipe decided to appoint a viceroy and selected his nephew, Cardinal Archduke Alberto of Austria, a great grandson of King Manuel. Alberto governed for about a decade (1583–93), easily the longest and most stable administration in Portugal of the Habsburg period. Like Cardinal Henrique before him he was appointed inquisitor-general and commissioned papal legate, so conveniently combining the authority of church and state. During his term much legislation was enacted, with a strong focus on institutional reform. He governed with a firm hand, but was not much loved.[7]

After Alberto's departure the alternative form of government was tried. Portugal was administered by a five-man board of governors comprising the archbishop of Lisbon, the count of Portalegre and three other nobles – all experienced men who had supported Filipe I in 1580.[8] When the new king, Filipe II of Portugal, succeeded in 1600 he again appointed a viceroy. His choice was the now ageing Cristovão de Moura, marquis of Castelo Rodrigo,

---

[6] Parker G 1995, p 250.

[7] SHP vol 4, pp 33–4.

[8] Ibid, p 41.

who twenty years before had done so much to secure a Habsburg succession. Viceroys presided for the rest of the reign, eight of them following in rather rapid succession down to Filipe II's death in 1621. Meanwhile, Filipe II himself paid a three-month visit to Lisbon in 1619, making his ceremonial entry into the city amid glittering Baroque magnificence. It was only the second occasion that a ruling Habsburg monarch had been to Portugal – and it would prove the last. During the reign of Filipe III (1621–40) Portugal was run first by a board of governors, then again by successive viceroys.

Over time the Portuguese came to realise that the absence of a resident monarch constituted a crucial change; whether the kingdom was administered by a viceroy or governors also made a significant difference. A viceroy exercised full powers in the name of the king, enjoyed quasi-regal dignity and could live in the River Palace. Governors had similar powers, but not the equivalent dignity.[9] However, only a king in person could summon or preside over the *cortes*. An attempt by Filipe III's *valido,* the count-duke of Olivares, to have the viceroy instead of the king convene the *cortes* in 1634 to raise taxes encountered insuperable constitutional difficulties and had to be abandoned. Since the king was absent for almost fifty-eight of the sixty years of Habsburg rule, meetings of the *cortes* became a rarity. Between 1580 and 1640 it convened precisely three times: in Tomar in 1581, briefly in 1583 to swear allegiance to the future Filipe II and in 1619 when Filipe II visited Lisbon. Even on these rare occasions the king showed little interest in attending to grievances.[10] One of the main lines of formal communication between subject and monarch had therefore become virtually inoperative.

Rule by viceroys and governors was not the only institutional innovation introduced into Portugal during the Habsburg era. Contemporary Spain had adopted a system of government through councils, and this too was gradually extended to Portugal. In 1582, shortly before Filipe I left for Madrid, a council of Portugal was created. Composed of six members, all Portuguese and mostly prominent nobles, it was to wait upon the king at court and advise him on Portuguese affairs – as the council of Castile already did on Castilian affairs. Meanwhile in Lisbon the old council of state was retained but was largely supplanted in the final Habsburg years by a smaller viceroy's council. In 1591 a treasury council (*conselho da fazenda*) was created to control fiscal affairs, and from 1604 to 1614 an India council (*conselho da Índia*) supervised administration of the empire.[11] In this way a conciliar system substantially modelled on that of Castile was developed for Portugal.

[9] Oliveira A de 1990, pp 11–12.
[10] SHP vol 4, pp 14–23, 88–9.
[11] Luz F P M da 1952, pp 81–2, 97–107; Oliveira A de 1990, pp 12–13; Elliott J H 1991, p 54.

Habsburg rule in Portugal certainly meant that administrative decisions took longer to reach because of the more complex institutional structures used to generate them and because the king's court was usually in Castile. Although the problem of distance should not be exaggerated, for despatches were sent weekly between Lisbon and wherever the king resided, a central administration in Castile with vast and varied dominions to manage could never act as swiftly as a ruler in Lisbon, focused solely on Portuguese affairs. Nor could Madrid be expected to behave with the same understanding of the particular interests of Portugal. There were crucial policy areas that affected Portugal profoundly, such as war and foreign relations, where all important decisions were made by the king personally or his Castilian favourites and advisers. Those decisions were supposedly taken in the interests of the monarchy as a whole – interests which might, or might not, be the same as those of Portugal. Then there was the question of access to the crown, so important particularly to the nobility. It was no longer enough to lobby at the River Palace in Lisbon; from 1583 Portuguese seeking high-level patronage had to either repair to court in Castile, at considerable expense, or act through intermediaries.

Portuguese autonomy was far more circumscribed in practice than in theory. It was also highly susceptible to corrupting influences from within. *Validos* in Madrid with their own agendas to pursue found the limitations on their actions imposed by Portuguese autonomy frustrating. Though not deliberately unmindful of Portuguese sensitivities, when the needs of Spain seemed to conflict with the undertakings given by Filipe I at Tomar, *validos* tended to look for ways to get round them or even change them. Under Filipe II the exclusively-Portuguese councils were partially by-passed by the creation of various ad hoc *juntas* which were more flexible and included Castilians as well as Portuguese.[12] The king became less scrupulous in making key appointments. In 1617 Filipe II made the count of Salinas viceroy even though he was a Castilian, simply giving him the fig leaf of a Portuguese title. In 1634, the widowed Princess Margarida of Savoy became viceroy; but as a cousin of the king, and not his daughter, sister or niece, she did not come within the stipulated range of blood relationships. She also introduced Castilians into her viceroy's council. By the mid-1630s, the subversion of Portuguese autonomy was such that it was beginning to erode local support for the union itself.

Portuguese autonomy was also undermined by an insidious process that evolved as a by-product of rule from a distance, in which the key player was the secretary of the council of Portugal. Unlike viceroys or governors, these secretaries held office in the king's pleasure. They controlled the records,

---

[12] Meléndez S de L 1992, pp 119–21.

operated the flow of communications between the king's court and Lisbon and knew more about the machinations of government than anyone else. An able, ambitious and manipulative secretary, enjoying the confidence of the king and *valido* in Madrid, could effectively run much of the administration. Such was Diogo Soares in the 1630s.[13] Another by-product of Habsburg government was the aggravation of social tensions between the nobility and the *povo*. The nobility, even if no longer under normal circumstances a serious threat to royal authority, still exercised lordship over about half the country's population. Filipe I and his successors, by guaranteeing privileges and refraining from intervening in local affairs, endorsed this state of affairs and so helped to consolidate elite power. This was particularly evident when Portugal was administered by governors – which the nobility preferred, for governors were invariably selected from their own number, with an occasional bishop added. But to townsmen such rule compromised justice, governors being seen as too closely identified with their own family networks and clienteles.[14] Most commoners therefore preferred a viceroy.

Habsburg rule, regardless of its form, was never welcomed by the *povo*. Nostalgia for a past when Portugal had its own independent monarch lingered and merged in the popular mind with hope and conviction that a patriot king would one day reappear. Though such ideas had many roots including selective reading of the Christian scriptures, contemporary Jewish Messianism and even Arthurian legend, they drew especially from the writings of a certain Gonçalo Anes nicknamed Bandarra (the vagrant), an obscure cobbler from Trancoso in Beira Alta. In the 1530s, Bandarra composed a series of mysterious *trovas* in which he seemed to predict a new age ruled over by a king called the hidden one (*encoberto*) who would liberate his people. By the late sixteenth century, the *encoberto* had become popularly identified with King Sebastião. Many Portuguese apparently convinced themselves Sebastião had not been killed in Morocco. Instead he was thought to be waiting in some secret hideout, either held captive or doing sorrowful penance, and at the right moment he would reappear to reclaim his kingdom. Sebastianism, a phenomenon that persisted in various forms down to the nineteenth century, was thus born.

Inevitably various opportunist imposters appeared during the course of the Habsburg era, posing as the much-mourned Sebastião come back to claim his kingdom. They included during Filipe I's reign the so-called 'king of Penamacor' who was actually an expelled Carmelite monk (1584), Mateus Álvares the 'king of Ericeira' (1585) and Gabriel Espinosa the 'pastry-cook of Madrigal' (1594). All three were quickly disposed of by the authorities. Slightly more of a

[13] Oliveira A de 1990, p 13.
[14] Ibid, pp 16–22, 27–38.

nuisance because he made his claims in Venice, forged a papal brief ordering his restoration to the throne and attracted some Portuguese émigré support was the Calabrian Marco Tulio Catizone. But Catizone, who did not speak Portuguese, was eventually handed over to the Spanish authorities and hanged in 1603. Though none of these imposters seriously threatened Habsburg rule, their repeated appearances demonstrate something of the depth of popular anti-Castilian sentiment.[15]

Habsburg government in Portugal, its various problems notwithstanding, was relatively efficient by contemporary standards, and it left one particularly positive legacy. By the late sixteenth century the volume of legislation since the *Ordenações Manuelinas* was such that a further codification had become overdue. Filipe ordered this formidable task be undertaken – and the result was the *Ordenações Filipinas* of 1603. Retained long after the Habsburgs had departed, this code served as the foundation of Portuguese statute law well into the nineteenth century.[16]

THE HABSBURG ECONOMY

At Tomar in 1581 Filipe I accepted a proposal from his Italian engineer, Giovanni Batista Antonelli, to make the River Tagus navigable as far as Toledo, so linking Lisbon by water to the heart of Spain. As Antonelli pointed out, such a project had become possible because the whole peninsula, for the first time since the days of King Rodrigo, was now united under one lord.[17] This proposal, which was at least partly implemented over the next few years, indicates just one of the exciting economic opportunities that the union of crowns seemed to promise. There is little doubt that initially the union was from an economic viewpoint a positive development.[18] There were winners and losers, of course; but overall, before about 1620, union delivered significant benefits. After that the costs began to mount rapidly, and by the end of Habsburg rule generally outweighed the gains. The origins of this ultimately negative outcome lay in circumstances that we shall review shortly; but they had little to do with Portugal's economic fundamentals, and even less with the ability of the Portuguese to respond to the opportunities union had to offer.

Demographic trends in Portugal during the Habsburg years remain difficult to establish because of confused and inadequate sources.[19] According to

[15] MedHP vol 7, pp 89–90; DIHP vol 2, p 217; O Sebastianismo 1978, pp 10–14.
[16] SHP vol 4, pp 257–8.
[17] Checa F 1992, p 270.
[18] MHP, pp 307–8.
[19] HP vol 4, p 49.

Veríssimo Serrão population increased between 1580 and 1640. However, José Vicente Serrão argues growth slowed after 1580 and then entered a phase of stagnation or actual decline lasting several decades from 1620. António de Oliveira, less tentative, endorses the widely-held contemporary view that population was already declining by the first decade of the seventeenth century. He points out there were pestilences in Portugal in the late sixteenth and early seventeenth centuries, food shortages in the early 1620s and 1630s and perhaps generally decreasing marriage and birth rates.[20] At the same time significant emigration was occurring, not only to the Portuguese empire, but to Spain and Spanish America at a rate probably averaging 5,000 to 6,000 a year.[21] The evidence therefore suggests that during the Habsburg period metropolitan Portugal was struggling to maintain its population.

A demographic slowdown is also reflected in declining consumption and rising wages. While there were frequent fluctuations and local variations in these trends, production of basic consumer commodities was generally down in the 1610s, rose for most of the 1620s and declined again during the late 1630s. Prices fluctuated, but by 1640 were roughly back to the levels of the early 1580s. Accordingly, landed incomes gained little during the Habsburg era.[22] Contemporaries were very concerned about agriculture and gave much consideration to improving it. Nevertheless, patterns of production remained unchanged with wheat, rye, maize, vines and olives the principal crops.[23] Maize growing was expanding, but not cultivation of the traditional cereals, despite Portugal's chronic grain shortage. The country now imported a third of its grain needs, and, according to the contemporary pamphleteer Duarte Gomes Solis, about a million *cruzados* in gold was expended every year for this purpose.[24] Not surprisingly, therefore, the major objective of agricultural reform was to increase cereal production.

It was widely believed in the early seventeenth century that there was too much uncultivated land in Portugal which could and should be planted in grain. But in practice much of this land was already used for activities like grazing, beekeeping and collecting firewood. Moreover, efforts to increase cereal production had a long history of failure in Portugal, mainly because overall climatic and soil conditions were only marginally suitable and wheat could be imported more cheaply from overseas. Most local producers preferred to invest in vines, olives, wool or fruit rather than wheat, which remained

---

[20] SHP vol 4, pp 267, 275; HP vol 4, pp 49–50; Oliveira A de 1990, pp 52–3, 55.
[21] Godinho V M 1978, p 9.
[22] Oliveira A de 1990, pp 56–65.
[23] HP vol 4, p 74.
[24] Oliveira A de 1990, p 82.

primarily a small-scale subsistence crop.[25] Nevertheless, in 1619 a survey was ordered to determine which land was most suited to cereal production. Local commissions were then to allot to individuals tracts where grain had to be grown compulsorily. Nobles were also to grow cereals on suitable land or let it out to tenants for that purpose. How seriously these measures were pursued in practice is unclear; but it seems they met stubborn resistance, and they certainly failed to solve the grain-deficit problem.[26] Despite a reform-minded Habsburg government agriculture continued largely as before.

The coming of Habsburg rule had a much greater impact on Portugal's international trade and financial operations. Through the union of crowns Portugal became part of the greatest economic bloc in the world, with a reach extending to every known continent. Spanish America was opened to Portuguese business enterprise while Brazil remained a Portuguese monopoly market. Portuguese businessmen gained easier access to Spanish American silver, which was produced in increasing quantities during the Habsburg period.[27] Meanwhile, the Portuguese continued to exercise exclusive control of seaborne trade between Europe and Asia via the Cape of Good Hope until the early seventeenth century. They also gained access to the Spanish trans-Pacific route between Manila and Acapulco. In the peninsula itself Filipe I abolished customs duties on the Luso-Castilian frontier even before he entered Portugal in 1580.[28] For many Portuguese, with Portugal now part of a much greater whole, cross-border opportunities beckoned. Businessmen, sailors, artisans and itinerant wage-seekers were soon pouring into Castile in unprecedented numbers, and perhaps 25 per cent of the population of Seville, Spain's largest city, came to consist of Portuguese during the union.[29]

Businessmen, particularly New Christians, were the most vital element among these emigrants. Before the union most Portuguese emigrants of Jewish descent went to Muslim North Africa or the Middle East; but after about 1580 their destination was often Spain. Many of them were practising Catholics or even religiously indifferent rather than Judaizers. They settled especially in the larger Spanish cities, the principal draw-cards being business opportunity and the fact that from about the mid-1580s the Castilian Inquisition was notoriously less oppressive than its Portuguese counterpart.[30] Certainly for some emigrants going to Spain proved remarkably profitable. A dynamic network

[25] HP vol 4, pp 81–2.
[26] Oliveira A de 1990, pp 83–5.
[27] Barrett W 1990, pp 238–44.
[28] SHP vol 4, pp 374–5.
[29] Godinho V M 1968 vol 2, p 265.
[30] SHP vol 4, pp 325–6; Israel J I 1985, pp 24–6, 58–9.

of wealthy New Christian families made a very significant contribution to Castile's capitalist economy and ultimately came to play a vital role in Castilian state finances. Most within this group were already established international merchants or financiers in Lisbon. There they controlled some two-thirds of private trade between Portugal and Asia and were often also involved with the Brazil and West Africa trades, especially in slaves.[31] These merchants required silver and welcomed access to Spanish American markets. They were eager to take advantage of the commercial opportunities that union offered.

Business penetration of Spain began well before 1580; but even under Filipe I considerable suspicion still prevailed against New Christians, who were only allowed to do business provided they posted bonds. Conditions eased under Filipe II and his corrupt but pragmatic *valido,* the duke of Lerma. In 1605, Portuguese New Christians were granted a formal pardon for past Judaizing and allowed freedom of movement in return for a 1,700,000 *cruzados* subsidy. Perhaps to avoid contributing to this payment, some New Christians then dispersed beyond the peninsula mainly into northern Europe; but others were drawn to Spain, despite continuing popular hostility and official discrimination against them. Rules concerning purity of blood (*limpeza de sangue*) excluded New Christians from honours and public offices, and in 1619 the government was pressured into re-imposing restrictions on their travel.[32] However, when Olivares assumed control in the 1620s he was determined to utilise New Christian capital and financial expertise. Judaizers were again pardoned, prisoners released from Inquisition custody and freedom of movement restored. New Christians were permitted to settle anywhere in Castile and to participate in official trade between Seville and America.[33] Their immigration into Spain consequently intensified, and by the end of the Habsburg period they had become a distinct Spanish community.[34]

The result of these developments was that during the Habsburg period an influential network of Portuguese New Christian merchants and financiers gradually became established in Spain. It included men like Manuel de Paz who possessed strong family and business connections in Antwerp, Amsterdam, Hamburg, the Atlantic slave trade, Brazil and all over maritime Asia. In 1626 Paz shifted to Madrid where he conducted business till his retirement in 1639. In Castile enterprising New Christians like Paz dealt in anything from spices to wool. They eventually controlled perhaps 20 per cent of the official trade between Seville and the New World and contracted to collect various

[31] Boyajian J C 1983, pp 8–9, 11.
[32] SHP vol 4, pp 55–6, 58–60, 322; Israel J I 1985, p 58.
[33] Boyajian J C 1983, pp 18, 24; Elliott J H 1986, p 303.
[34] Yerushalmi Y H 1971, p 9; Baroja J C 1974, pp 47–8.

taxes, including the customs. From 1626 they participated in the annual *asientos* or contracts to provide loans to the Habsburg crown.[35] At first they shared these contracts with the Genoese, who were the established lenders; but eventually New Christian financiers assumed control of the operations. By about the end of Habsburg rule in Portugal they had delivered some sixty-five million ducats in fulfilment of the *asientos*. Their role in enabling the Spanish government to implement its military and diplomatic agenda was clearly crucial. Indeed, as crown bankers they eventually dominated to such an extent that when the state declared bankruptcy in 1647, all but six of the thirty-three contractors affected were Portuguese New Christians.[36]

Of course, it does not follow from this that the Portuguese economy itself in the end gained much from union. The economic consequences of union were complex and are difficult to disentangle. However, as long as the monarchy was expanding, Portugal on balance probably benefited; but when the economy of the whole faltered, the monarchy began to have difficulty protecting its constituent parts, and the benefits quickly evaporated. Moreover men like Manuel de Paz operated on an international stage, shifting the focus of their business across borders as circumstances dictated. By moving from Lisbon to either Madrid or Seville they contributed to the gradual economic provincialisation of Portugal, just as surely as those nobles who moved to the Habsburg court contributed to the country's political and social provincialisation. Economically speaking, union may have brought access to wider markets – but it also meant the surrender of ultimate control, the promises made at Tomar notwithstanding. There was a salutary indication of what this might entail in 1602 when the crown diverted 500,000 *cruzados* from pepper sales in Lisbon to help finance its war effort in the Netherlands, so depriving the official Portugal-India trade of its investment capital.[37] Moreover Portuguese entry into Spanish and Spanish American markets soon faced increasingly bitter opposition from established vested interests. Above all, the Habsburg crown's imposition from 1585 of a series of embargoes on trade with the Dutch and English, Portugal's major overseas customers, demonstrated just how damaging policies directed from Madrid could be to Portuguese economic and imperial interests.[38]

Between 1580 and 1640 the pattern of Portugal's external commerce underwent major change. The crown's monopoly trade with Asia declined, in both absolute and relative terms. Annual pepper imports to Lisbon via the Cape fell from about 20,000 *quintals* in the early 1580s to 8,000 *quintals* in

[35] Boyajian J C 1983, pp 26–9, 43, 107.
[36] Ibid, pp 24, 42, 58, 175–6.
[37] Ibid, p 15.
[38] Israel J I 1990, pp 189–210.

the mid-1590s, then remained fairly constant through to 1640.[39] By contrast private trade on the route prospered, an outcome assisted by the union of crowns. As late as the 1620s Portuguese private merchants, especially New Christians, were allegedly investing more in seaborne trade between Europe and Asia than the English and Dutch East India companies combined. They were also profiting more than ever from the Asian inter-port trade, especially in East and Southeast Asia. The Portuguese Macau-Nagasaki trade reached its peak in the late Habsburg years, and Macau-based merchants took advantage of the union to develop business links with Manila. They financed their operations by reinvesting returns from the Asian inter-port trade and by importing Spanish American silver. When from the 1620s security on the Cape route deteriorated, they were able to redirect some cargoes via the Spanish Philippines and Acapulco.[40]

Even more important changes occurred in the Atlantic. Here, Brazil developed into Europe's prime source of sugar and tobacco, causing Portugal's imperial focus to shift more emphatically from East to West. This boosted certain Portuguese ports with links to Brazil, like Viana do Castelo. Meanwhile the slave trade grew and prospered, Portuguese slavers supplying African labour not only to the Brazilian plantations, but also to Spanish America. Immigrants from Portugal flowed into the Spanish Indies: by the late Habsburg era there were some 6,000 Portuguese in Peru alone, while Portuguese comprised perhaps 7 per cent of the population of Mexico and 30 per cent that of Buenos Aires.[41] Portuguese immigrants became an important economic force in the Spanish Indies, just as they did in Spain.

THE UNION OF CROWNS AND FOREIGN RELATIONS

Once Filipe I was king of Portugal there was an expectation he would provide strong protection against outside foes. In the early 1580s, the Habsburg monarchy was at its peak, and Spanish self-confidence was correspondingly high – so high that in 1583 Santa Cruz urged Filipe to conquer England. At the other side of the world Spanish and Portuguese schemes for the conquests of China, Japan and various parts of mainland Southeast Asia were likewise being earnestly proposed, if in most cases not endorsed by the crown itself.[42] Yet by the late 1580s the Habsburg image of invincibility was already receding, and the

[39] Godinho V M 1981–3 vol 3, pp 75–6; Boyajian J C 1983, pp 22, 27, 40; Ahmad A 1991, p 195.
[40] Boyajian J C 1983, pp 51–2, 241–2.
[41] Israel J I 1990, p 330.
[42] Parker G 1995, pp 247–8, 254–6.

assumption that association with Spain meant greater security for Portugal looked less sure.

Before the union Portugal had maintained generally friendly relations and traded extensively with the Dutch and English. But the Protestant Dutch had been at war with Spain since 1566 while Anglo-Spanish relations became heavily strained through the 1570s. The English, excluded from the Indies, preyed on Spanish shipping and aided the Dutch. Then in 1581 António, Filipe's ousted rival for the Portuguese crown, fled to England where he received backing for his cause. In 1585 Filipe responded by placing embargoes on all Dutch and English ships entering the ports of his dominions – and Dutch and English trade with Portugal was formally terminated. The embargo remained on English ships until the Anglo-Spanish treaty of 1604; it was lifted from Dutch vessels in 1590, but reimposed in 1598 until the start of the Twelve Years Truce in 1609; then it was imposed again from 1621 to 1647. Jonathan Israel has shown that these embargoes, despite some successful evasion, were quite effective. In particular the 1621–47 embargo reduced Dutch sailings to Iberian ports by 90 per cent.[43] Serious difficulties followed for Holland's herring industry, which relied on Portuguese salt. The Dutch were also cut off from direct supplies of bullion, spices, sugar and other commodities from the Spanish and Portuguese Indies. Adverse repercussions for Portugal were inevitable and were soon being felt.

Despite their occasional clashes with the Portuguese on the Guinea coast, the English had generally respected Portugal's neutrality before the union of crowns. However, after the union the Anglo-Spanish struggle intensified and the old rules changed. In 1582–3 the English aided António in two abortive expeditions to the Azores. Then in August 1585 Sir Francis Drake raided Portuguese settlements in the Cape Verde Islands, sacking various towns including Santiago.[44] Clearly the English now saw Portuguese shipping and possessions everywhere as legitimate targets.

Filipe I's response was to activate existing plans to invade England by despatching the 'invincible' Armada in 1588. The Armada was based on Lisbon and included twelve large warships and 5,000 men contributed by Portugal. All these ships and almost all the men were lost.[45] The disaster forced Filipe onto the defensive, and the Portuguese coast became vulnerable to English counter-attack. In 1589 Drake and Sir John Norris (or Norreys) accompanied by António landed an expeditionary force near Lisbon to restore the pretender to the Portuguese throne. But they received little local support and soon

[43] Israel J I 1990, pp 190–207.
[44] Keeler M F (ed) 1981, pp 26–8; Parker G 1995, p 253.
[45] MedHP vol 7, p 66.

withdrew. This was just as well, for António had promised his allies a one-off payment of five million gold ducats, subsequent payments of 200,000 gold ducats a year in perpetuity, permission for the English to sack Lisbon and garrison the Tagus forts at Portuguese expense and freedom to trade in Portuguese overseas possessions.[46] These outrageous conditions would have converted Portugal into an abject English dependency – and suggest the Portuguese were well advised not to rally to António's banner. A few years later, in July 1596, another English expedition attacked and sacked Faro.[47]

Meanwhile English privateers took a relentless toll of Portuguese shipping. The most disastrous incident involved the loss of two large and richly-laden Indiamen, the *Santa Cruz* and the *Madre de Deus,* near the Azores in 1592, the former driven ashore and burned and the latter captured. Despite such spectacular setbacks Portuguese communications with India were not seriously disrupted in this period. However, the English began to show an alarming interest in sailing to Asia themselves, first to plunder and then to trade.[48] In the 1580s and 1590s their ventures were tentative, then in 1600 the East India Company (EIC) was chartered, and English activity in the Indian Ocean became systematic. Though peace between Spain and England was signed in 1604 the Habsburg government refused to relinquish its monopoly claims in Asian seas. But the English could not be excluded from the India trade, and in 1622 English ships aided the shah of Iran to seize Portuguese Hurmuz. Eventually in 1635 a pragmatic Portuguese viceroy at Goa concluded a truce with local EIC officials, which proved lasting.

The first of a succession of Dutch trading voyages to the East occurred in 1595–6. At this stage the Dutch attitude to Portugal was ambiguous. The Dutch government recognised António rather than Filipe as Portugal's rightful king. They knew the Portuguese claimed a monopoly of the Cape route, but believed them to be unwilling subjects of a Spanish tyrant, like themselves. The earliest Dutch voyagers to the East were therefore cautiously hopeful of a friendly Portuguese reception. These hopes were dashed in 1601 when the Portuguese seized Dutch crewmen in Tidore and Macau and brutally executed many of them.[49] From that point on the Netherlanders treated the Portuguese as enemies, and a war of attrition ensued.

In 1602 the Dutch East India Company (*Vereenigde Oost-Indische Compagnie* or VOC) was founded. It moved aggressively into the Asian market, concentrating especially on island Southeast Asia. In 1605 VOC forces drove

---

[46] SHP vol 4, pp 34–5; MedHP vol 7, pp 66–8.
[47] MedHP vol 7, p 69.
[48] Godinho V M 1981–3 vol 3, pp 49–50.
[49] Blussé L and Winius G 1985, pp 74–6.

the Portuguese from Tidore and Ambon, in 1606 they besieged Melaka and in
1607 and 1608 they attacked Mozambique. The Portuguese could find no
answer to the inexorable growth of VOC power, and by 1640 the company
had decisively replaced the Portuguese *Estado da Índia* as the principal European force east of the Cape of Good Hope. Meanwhile, in the Atlantic Dutch
raids had been launched on the Portuguese islands of São Tomé and Principe in
1598–9 followed by repeated attacks on Portuguese shipping. In 1621 the
Dutch West India Company (*West-Indische Compagnie* or WIC) was formed
to trade, plunder and make settlements in the Americas. WIC forces captured
the Portuguese captaincy of Bahia, Brazil, in 1624. It was recovered the following year, but in 1630 the WIC responded by seizing Pernambuco, which
remained in Dutch hands for the rest of the Habsburg era. Sugar imports into
Portugal were disrupted, and ports like Viana do Castelo suffered severely.[50]

Would the English and Dutch have challenged the Portuguese outside Europe
had their traditional markets and sources of supply remained open? Geoffrey
Parker has argued it is unlikely: the two Protestant powers would hardly have
risked the heavy investment required for direct involvement in intercontinental
maritime trade and colonising activities but for Filipe I's embargoes.[51] Equally
clearly, if Portugal had not been brought into the Habsburg monarchy it would
not have closed its ports to the two northern powers. In the event, the damage
inflicted on Portuguese interests in both the Atlantic and east of the Cape was
enormous. The Portuguese empire in Asia was reduced to a shadow of its former
self, and Brazil, for almost a generation, was all but lost.

THE REFORM PROGRAM OF OLIVARES

In March 1621, Filipe II died and was succeeded by his son Filipe III (Felipe IV
of Spain), a youth of sixteen. The new king was anxious to do his duty; but his
inexperience and rather irresolute character placed him firmly in the hands of his
valido, the count (later count-duke) of Olivares. The count-duke was a man of
commanding presence, devoted to Spain and immensely hard working. For two
decades he virtually ran the Habsburg monarchy, with a directing hand far surer
than any other since the death of Filipe I.[52] Olivares had come to power at a time
when the monarchy was seriously ailing and in urgent need of reform. Its
principal revenue base was in Castile; but already in the dying days of the
preceding reign the council of Castile had reported that the fiscal burdens on
that kingdom had become intolerable and had to be alleviated. At the same time,

[50] Oliveira A de 1990, pp 72–3.
[51] Parker G 1995, p 265.
[52] Elliott J H 1986, pp 30, 135, 166, 169–71.

crown imports of American silver had passed their seventeenth-century peak and were beginning to decline. So Olivares desperately needed to find new sources of revenue, especially as the start of Filipe III's reign coincided with the formal resumption of war against the Dutch. The only possible solution seemed to lie in making the outlying kingdoms contribute more. But how could this be done without breaching the constitutional guarantees of these kingdoms, and seeming to override their cherished rights and liberties?[53]

After careful consideration Olivares drew up reform proposals which he presented to the king in 1624.[54] To transform the monarchy into a more centralised structure he recommended a process of gradual integration, with the laws and constitutions of the outlying kingdoms being gently coaxed into line with those of Castile. In return, the outlying kingdoms would receive more recognition and attention from the centre, and the support of their citizens would be courted by providing them with increased opportunities for office and access to patronage. Royal visits were to be more frequent and intermarriage between different nationalities encouraged. All this would help to make the monarchy less exclusively Castilian. The ultimate aim was to achieve an equitable distribution of responsibilities and benefits – and an increased flow of contributions from the periphery to the centre.

The plan had important implications for Portugal in two particular areas, one military and the other fiscal. Militarily the core idea was to establish what Olivares called a 'union of arms'. This meant creating a single army to serve the whole monarchy, to which all the kingdoms and provinces would contribute and which could be drawn on for deployment anywhere. A total of 140,000 men was envisaged, Portugal, Catalonia and Naples each providing 16,000.[55] The scheme was proclaimed in 1626, but immediately provoked a cool reception from the Portuguese. They insisted that under the terms agreed at Tomar they were exempted from serving outside Portuguese territory. So Olivares had to be content with only limited contributions from Portugal. Men and money were raised for particular enterprises identified with Portuguese interests, and some success was achieved in persuading Portuguese nobles to perform personal military services; otherwise, little was achieved.[56]

Olivares's fiscal reforms faced the same kinds of obstacles. New taxes could not be imposed in Portugal without the consent of the *cortes*, which could be convened only by the king in person. This meant Olivares was restricted to raising 'voluntary' subsidies (*socorros*) to help fund specific undertakings

[53] Elliott J H 1963, p 317.
[54] Ibid, pp 324–5.
[55] Ibid, pp 325–6.
[56] Oliveira A de 1990, p 48.

within Portugal and its empire. He had some success in doing this. In 1622 the Inquisition was persuaded to provide a *socorro* of 80,000 *cruzados* for the Portuguese war effort in the Indian Ocean, and in 1623 the clergy were required to pay 200,000 *cruzados* for the same purpose.[57] Three years later Olivares achieved an apparent major breakthrough with the recapture of Bahia from the Dutch by a combined Castilian-Portuguese armada. Both kingdoms, believing their national interests were at stake, strongly supported this expedition: the Castilians feared for the silver mines of Peru, while the Portuguese faced the potential loss of all Brazil.[58] A third of the ships in the expedition and almost a quarter of the men were Portuguese. Both crowns contributed substantially to the cost as did various Portuguese nobles and churchmen, the duke of Bragança and marquis of Vila Real leading the way with 20,000 *cruzados* each.[59] Such cooperative efforts were precisely what the count-duke had been seeking. But could they be repeated?

The military and financial pressures on both the Portuguese and Castilian crowns through the late 1620s and early 1630s increased relentlessly. In 1628 the Dutch captured an entire Spanish silver fleet. Spain was at war with England in 1625–30 and by 1635 had also drifted into full-scale war with France. In an unconnected development the Portuguese Atlantic fleet in 1627 was virtually destroyed by a huge storm; all but one of its galleons were lost, plus two returning India carracks and thousands of men. It was Portugal's greatest disaster since Al-Ksar al-Kabir.[60] Meanwhile, there were major challenges to be faced overseas, such as the loss of Hurmuz in the east and Pernambuco in the west. Olivares duly devised a plan to 'restore' the *Estado da Índia* and recapture Hurmuz, using exclusively Portuguese resources. Between 1630 and 1635 *socorros da Índia* totalling over 500,000 *cruzados* were with difficulty raised – but the plan of restoration nevertheless failed.[61]

To mount an expedition to recover Pernambuco Olivares also sought *socorros do Brasil* totalling a million *cruzados* a year.[62] Secretary Vasconcelos suggested half this could be found by rigorous collection of crown debts; the rest the regime first tried to raise through a royal monopoly on salt, which effectively doubled its price. Popular resistance was widespread, and the Lisbon *câmara* embargoed the decree imposing the monopoly because it lacked the *cortes's* approval. So in December 1631 Olivares ordered that 25 per cent of all

[57] Rooney P T 1994, p 559.
[58] Boxer C R 1957, pp 23–4.
[59] Guedes M J 1990–3 vol 2 pt 1A, pp 51–2, 54.
[60] Melo F M de 1977, pp 119–209; Blot J-Y and Lizé P (eds) 2000, p 7 and passim.
[61] Disney A R 1978, p 62.
[62] Elliott J H 1986, p 525; Elliott J H 1991, p 61.

emoluments paid by the crown other than salaries be suspended until the required 500,000 *cruzados* a year were forthcoming. This put urgent pressure on a large segment of the elite – people who received income from *comendas,* pensions, grants and other state sources. Either they would have to come up with a general impost to raise what was required, or bear the cost themselves. The governors in Lisbon reacted by proposing a subsidy to be apportioned between the various municipalities; but this meant the *povo* would have to pay, and their spokesmen naturally opposed the idea.[63] Finally in March 1635, ignoring constitutional objections, Olivares imposed his own solution. Money would be raised by increasing the *sisas* by 25 per cent and levying a special tax on wine and meat. Although the latter was not strictly new, having been collected earlier in Lisbon and elsewhere by the municipal councils, it was now to be extended to the whole country and levied by the crown. On top of this, in 1637 a new *donativo* to be levied on both capital and income was announced.[64]

The fiscal demands of the 1630s set the stage for an explosive confrontation. Contemporaries conceded that taxes were necessary, but expected them to be 'just' – in proportion to the subject's capacity to pay. Complaints suggest a widespread conviction that the demands now being made had gone beyond what was reasonable. A governor of the Algarve even claimed people were being forced to sell their own beds to pay the government. Moreover, taxes levied for the defence of Portugal's own borders were better tolerated than taxes imposed for campaigns overseas. People who derived little personal benefit from empire were inclined to think that overseas possessions which could not be defended at reasonable cost were not worth defending at all. Why did the king not rely more on his own resources? Some popular spokesmen suggested too much crown land had been alienated to the elite, especially Portugal's fifty-two titled noblemen, and that nobles should contribute more.[65] It seems one incidental consequence of tightening the fiscal screws was to exacerbate social tensions.

THE DEFECTION OF THE PORTUGUESE NOBILITY

From the early 1580s to the mid-1630s, the Habsburg kings controlled Portugal with, by and large, the cooperation of the Portuguese nobility. Under the first two Filipes, a key role in this was played by Cristovão de Moura, marquis of Castelo Rodrigo, who was twice viceroy (1600–3, 1608–12). His son Manuel, second marquis of Castelo Rodrigo, was later closely allied to Olivares during the

---

[63] Melo F M de 1967, p xlvi; Oliveira A de 1990, pp 134–5.

[64] Andrade e Silva J de (ed) 1855, pp 203–4, 220–5; Oliveira A de 1990, pp 132, 135, 161–2, 164–6; Rooney P T 1994, pp 560–1.

[65] Oliveira A de 1990, pp 105, 108, 127–8, 130.

valido's rise to power, and in the early 1620s this younger Moura and his associates acquired many of the offices within the royal household reserved for Portuguese.[66] But in 1626 Olivares and Moura fell out, and the count-duke forced his erstwhile ally from court. Moura was sent to Rome as ambassador and did not return until well after 1640.

Despite the break between Moura and Olivares the regime continued its strategy of governing Portugal with the collaboration of the Portuguese nobility, at least until the mid-1630s. Olivares cultivated the loyalty of key nobles assiduously, enticing them to court, granting them offices and *mercês* and encouraging them to merge with the Castilian elite through intermarriage. Though the count-duke's split with the Mouras had deprived him of a linkage into the Portuguese nobility of proven value to the Habsburg monarchy, he tried to make up for the loss by courting the Braganças, promoting marriage links between this great Portuguese house and his own clan, the Guzmáns.[67] In 1632, he encouraged the eighth duke of Bragança – later João IV – to marry Luísa de Guzmán, daughter of the duke of Medina-Sidonia. However, the political advantage gained by this move proved illusory – for the duke of Bragança maintained a studious aloofness from court, though his interests were well represented in the council of Portugal. Moreover, when the final crisis came João's Guzmán wife proved a steely proponent of Portuguese independence.

During the late Habsburg years those Portuguese nobles most actively involved in the administration of Portugal were loosely associated in a group known as the 'Portalegre faction' or sometimes simply 'the faction'. As well as the count of Portalegre himself its members included the counts of Basto, Castro Daire, Val de Reis and even Castelo Rodrigo. At first Olivares tried to work through this network. In 1633, he supported the appointment of Basto as viceroy and gave him responsibility for imposing the regime's fiscal and military reforms. But Portalegre and his associates opposed these measures, insisting they were invalid without approval from the *cortes*. This stance was strongly backed by most nobles as well as the towns, and Basto soon found himself bereft of support. So he resigned and rejoined the faction's mainstream.[68]

To push through his reform program Olivares now had little alternative but to by-pass the Portalegre faction. His next move therefore was to secure the appointment as viceroy of Margarida of Savoy, the king's cousin. Margarida was expected to act as a figurehead, leaving actual government in the hands of her Castilian advisers, particularly the marquis of Puebla, and an inner group of pro-regime Portuguese. Among the latter the key figures were Diogo Soares, the

[66] Elliott J H 1986, p 36; Bouza Álvarez F 2000, p 220.
[67] Bouza Álvarez F 2000, p 220–1.
[68] Oliveira A de 1990, pp 142–4.

secretary of the council of Portugal in Madrid, and his brother-in-law, Miguel de Vasconcelos, secretary of the council of state in Lisbon. Soares and Vasconcelos were both highly unpopular, and in Lisbon Vasconcelos required constant protection. Moreover, an intense power struggle soon developed at Margarida's court between Vasconcelos and Puebla.

These problems apart, Margarida's administration faced a formidable challenge. In 1634 the Portalegre faction was well entrenched in all branches and at all levels of government from the advisory councils to the judiciary, and Soares and Vasconcelos were obliged to wage a constant covert struggle against it.[69] Soares gradually built up his own body of collaborators, including several high-profile figures such as the archbishop of Braga and the bishop of Porto. In the council of Portugal before its abolition in 1639 he steadily wore down his noble opponents. Nevertheless, the whole strategy was perilous, for the nobility were the cornerstone on which continuing Habsburg control of Portugal had long rested – and Soares, Vasconcelos and their collaborators were hardly convincing alternatives. A growing number of noble dissidents were now bent on getting rid of Soares and the kind of administration he stood for. Indeed, as Bouza Álvarez points out, toppling Soares was an objective with which even nobles who ultimately stayed loyal to the Habsburgs readily sympathised.[70]

The situation in Portugal was now explosive, and popular disturbances finally erupted in August 1637 – in Évora, where the local *corregedor* was trying to arrange allocations for the new *donativo*.[71] Initially, Olivares was not unduly concerned, expecting the local nobles would quickly bring matters under control; but within weeks the trouble had spread throughout southern Portugal and was even beginning to extend north of the Tagus. This was more worrying, though the disturbances received little elite support and seemed not dissimilar to other tax protests occurring elsewhere in Europe at about the same time. Yet the local Portuguese nobility, including the duke of Bragança, showed noticeably little interest in forcefully suppressing the dissidents, instead simply endeavouring to calm matters. Several preachers actually encouraged the protests, although the church hierarchy firmly backed authority. The leaders of the Jesuits, Dominicans and Franciscans all supported the nobles in seeking to restore order by persuasion.[72] Olivares quickly mustered Castilian troops on the frontier, and these eventually intervened in both Algarve and Alentejo. By the summer of 1638 order was restored. Nevertheless, Madrid was left with heightened mistrust of the Portuguese nobility. It was a mistrust proved more

---

[69] Ibid, pp 145–6; Disney A R 2001, p 117.
[70] Bouza Álvarez F 2000, p 41.
[71] Melo F M de 1967, p xxxiv; Oliveira A de 1990, pp 165–6.
[72] Alden D 1996, p 97.

than justified some three years later by a very different kind of uprising, with momentous consequences.[73]

THE REVOLT OF 1640

After the disturbances of 1637–8 popular discontent in Portugal continued to simmer; but it lacked leadership and to some extent direction. There was considerable resentment against the Portuguese elites for evading their fair share of the tax burden. Dissatisfaction with government, perceived to be run by and for members of the nobility, was widespread. But the principal oppressor in the people's mind undoubtedly remained the Olivares regime. Popular acceptance of Habsburg rule had always been lukewarm and was now more grudging than ever. Disaffection within the Portuguese nobility was also hardening, particularly among lesser nobles. Moreover, after the Évora disturbances every potential noble conspirator knew that a determined move against Madrid would have little difficulty in attracting popular support.

Anti-Habsburg sentiment was certainly widespread among the lower clergy and even extended to some among the higher clergy. The bourgeoisie remained cautiously watchful: international merchants were aware that anti-Portuguese sentiment in Spain had been growing at all social levels and that in Mexico and Peru it had reached alarming proportions.[74] Moreover, the seemingly endless French and Dutch wars were seriously hampering business. The economic rationale for union was therefore waning, while mutual antipathy was growing at a people to people level. In the late 1630s, Olivares was continuing to demand greater fiscal and military contributions from the Portuguese. He complained bitterly about Portugal's stubborn particularism – and finally in 1638 he summoned to Madrid an extraordinary gathering of Portuguese notables, to consult them on possible constitutional change. Conveniently, the summons also brought to court, where they could be watched, various Portuguese considered unreliable. Nevertheless the gathering achieved little, apart from an agreement to abolish the council of Portugal in which pro- and anti-Soares members had been wrangling with increasing bitterness.[75]

Conspicuously absent from the 1638 gathering of notables was João, eighth duke of Bragança. João was grandson of Catarina, Filipe I's rival for the throne in 1580. Since inheriting the dukedom he had remained quietly at his palace in Vila Viçosa. However, Olivares was well aware of the potential threat to the Habsburgs such a figure presented. Sebastianism in recent years had become

[73] Melo F M de 1967, pp xli–xlii; Elliott J H 1986, pp 530–2; Oliveira A de 1990, p 199, 207.
[74] Elliott J H 1986, p 607; Bouza Álvarez F 2000, p 222.
[75] SHP vol 4, p 136.

increasingly associated with the Braganças, and prophecies had appeared identifying the duke with the *encoberto*. Eventually in 1639 João felt compelled to issue a formal statement stressing that Sebastião was dead.[76] Meanwhile, the French had become interested in using João to undermine their Spanish enemy and as early as 1634 had made secret contact with him.[77] Olivares's tactics were to humour the duke while simultaneously trying to lure him from Portugal – or at least to bring him into the regime's service. Bragança, who declined an invitation to govern Milan in 1634, was too wary to be drawn in by such blandishments. But when Olivares offered him command of the army in Portugal itself in 1638 the duke reluctantly accepted.[78]

Olivares's attention was now more focussed than ever on military problems. That autumn a Luso-Spanish fleet had sailed to recover Pernambuco from the WIC; but it was poorly handled, suffered a series of setbacks and in the end achieved nothing significant.[79] The failure was an ominous indication that the regime no longer had the capacity to protect Portugal's overseas interests. Moreover it was accompanied by other military reverses in the European theatre, such as the severing of 'the Spanish road' that linked Madrid to the Netherlands and the Spanish naval disaster at the battle of the Downs in 1639. In the eighteen months from July 1638 to January 1640 the monarchy lost some 100 warships and perhaps 20,000 seamen.[80] Meanwhile, the French had invaded Catalonia, and there were rumours they would soon attack Portugal. A desperate Olivares sought to wring just one more supreme effort from his master's overburdened subjects. His aim was to secure a better position from which to negotiate honourable terms for peace with both France and the Dutch.

Against this background, in 1640 Olivares requested that Portugal provide 8,000 men for deployment in Italy. Objections that the Portuguese had no obligation to fight outside the borders of their own kingdom and empire were simply ignored.[81] Portuguese nobles were to lead the levies that had been demanded as well as to take responsibility for raising them. But this had unintended consequences, for with Portugal's nobility officially gathering troops and Bragança in overall command, a Portuguese military network developed outside Madrid's control. Inadvertently, Olivares had provided opportunity and cover for the co-ordination of conspiratorial action.[82] Then in May 1640 Catalonia suddenly revolted – and the bubble burst.

[76] MedHP vol 7, p 90.
[77] Godinho V M 1968 vol 1, p 275.
[78] Silva L A R da 1971–2 vol 4, pp 39–40; Elliott J H 1986, pp 525–6, 532.
[79] Boxer C R 1957, pp 88–94.
[80] Elliott J H 1986, p 551.
[81] Ibid, pp 566–7.
[82] MedHP vol 7, p 97.

Within a month of the Catalan revolt, Bragança was sounded out by a small group of Portuguese *fidalgos* about his attitude to a possible uprising in Portugal. The precise beginnings of the conspiracy are obscure, though it was certainly linked with opposition to the regime's fiscal and military policies in the 1630s, general resentment against Olivares's 'innovations' and hatred of Soares and Vasconcelos. Bragança had known since at least 1635 that he would receive overwhelming popular support were he to claim the crown. But in June 1640 he was still too cautious to sanction a coup. Meanwhile, Olivares had decided Filipe III should convoke the Aragonese *cortes* to rally support against the Catalan rebels and that the Portuguese nobility must accompany the king to Aragon. It was this last demand that finally spurred the conspirators to action – and a group of some forty *fidalgos* now drew up plans for a coup against the viceroy. Several of them, like Miguel de Almeida, were experienced veterans, while some had links to great houses. But most were youths from the middle or lesser nobility, and the conspiracy was therefore a collective enterprise without any outstanding leader. In October Bragança finally agreed to accept the crown, and the uprising was set for 1 December. The duke himself remained on the sidelines until the coup had succeeded. This was not through indecisiveness, let alone pusillanimity, as sometimes alleged. It was rather appropriate caution in pursuing an enterprise where one false step could have brought disaster to himself, his numerous supporters and his country.[83]

On 24 November 1640 Olivares ordered that the Portuguese levies be armed and despatched, at Portugal's cost, to help suppress the Catalan revolt. The Portuguese nobility, on pain of forfeiting their possessions and being branded traitors, were also to go. Many Portuguese nobles then in Castile complied; but most of those in Portugal, including Bragança, did not.[84] A week later the conspirators struck as planned. They infiltrated the viceroy's palace in Lisbon, overpowered the guards and murdered Vasconcelos, flinging the hated secretary's body from a window. They then arrested the viceroy and sent her unharmed back to Spain. There was no serious resistance, and bloodshed was minimal with the few Castilian troops in the city quickly surrendering. Within hours the rebels controlled Lisbon – and the central organs of government were theirs.[85]

[83] SHP vol 5, pp 14–16; Torgal L R 1984, p 308.
[84] SHP vol 4, p 38 and vol 5, pp 17–19.
[85] Silva L A R da 1971–2 vol 4, pp 157–71.

I I

Restoration and Reconstruction

João duke of Bragança arrived in Lisbon from Vila Viçosa on 6 December 1640. Nine days later he was formally proclaimed King João IV of Portugal before a large gathering of nobles and dignitaries.[1] The new king then proceeded immediately to issue writs summoning the Portuguese *cortes*. This act in itself was highly significant for it involved exercising a power strictly exclusive to ruling monarchs.[2] In response to his summons nearly all the relevant *concelhos* dutifully selected their representatives and sent them to Lisbon while most of the eligible clergy and nobles also attended. On 28 January 1641, the *cortes* held its opening session at which João was duly sworn in as king.

In the months that followed copious pro-Bragança propaganda steadily flowed from the country's presses. This propaganda claimed that Filipe I had unlawfully seized the throne in 1580 from the forebears of João IV, who was now simply reclaiming what was legitimately his. It also argued that all the Habsburg 'usurpers' had ruled unjustly and failed to respect their solemn promises to uphold Portugal's traditional rights and privileges. In particular Filipe III, current occupant of the Habsburg throne, was a manifestly unjust tyrant – and the *cortes* therefore had the right and responsibility to depose him, which it had duly done. The *cortes* also had the authority to elect a new king when the throne was vacant, and it had given its resounding endorsement to João.[3]

The successful installation of the Bragança regime emphatically did not represent a revolution, but was rather the triumphant culmination of a coup

---

[1] HP vol 5, p 24.
[2] Cardim P 1998, p 110.
[3] Ibid, pp 105, 109–10.

d'état. This coup was organised and staged by a group of conservative nobles, determined to restore what they considered to be Portugal's traditional order. They had no intention of altering the constitution, still less of disturbing long-established social relationships based on privilege. Their principal aims were to sever the union, put a stop to Olivares's alleged innovations and restore 'customary' government under a resident Portuguese king.[4] The *cortes*, once it had been convened by the new king, likewise displayed little interest in anything that could reasonably be described as revolutionary or even nationalist. On the contrary, it spent its energies striving to safeguard and in some cases revive the immunities and privileges of special interest groups, seeking harmony between different jurisdictions and presenting endless petitions about local issues. In other words, it had the preoccupations of a deeply conservative, Old Regime society. Olivares had made the cardinal error of disturbing tradition; now, under a Bragança king, ancient relationships and customary government were to be happily restored.[5]

The nobles who took an active part in the events of December 1640 included few *grandes*. Most were service *fidalgos* of relatively youthful age, many being second sons.[6] Moreover, while there was widespread support for the Bragança cause within the ranks of the second estate, it was not universal. In Habsburg times a significant proportion of the Portuguese elite, including many of the greater nobility, had gravitated to the royal court in Castile. Some of these people were in Spain when the uprising occurred; others were serving with Habsburg armies in Flanders or Catalonia. Olivares, after he had learned of the coup, was therefore able to convene a credible meeting of prominent expatriate Portuguese in Madrid to discuss what should be done. About eighty persons, overwhelmingly nobles, attended this gathering, and most subsequently maintained their loyalty to Filipe III, despite all of João IV's efforts to attract them back to Portugal.[7]

As a group the higher clergy were deeply divided over the Restoration. The archbishop of Lisbon was staunchly for João IV, but both the archbishop of Braga and Inquisitor-General Francisco de Castro, while in public cautiously equivocal, were by conviction pro-Habsburg. Although none of the various religious orders played a very active part, the Jesuits – perhaps sensing advantage for their overseas missions – aligned themselves with the Braganças and soon became influential at João IV's court.[8] Overall the higher clergy and

[4] DHP vol 3, pp 609, 620; Torgal L R 1984, pp 318–19; Hespanha A M 1993, p 34.
[5] Hespanha A M 1993, pp 31, 34–5, 50.
[6] HP vol 5, p 18.
[7] Valladares R 1998, p 45.
[8] DHP vol 3, p 621; Alden D 1996, p 103.

leading religious institutions accommodated to the new regime as best they could, but often seemingly without much conviction. Of course, the lower clergy were strongly for the house of Bragança while João was also much helped by the fact that most magistrates and the state bureaucracy adhered to his cause. On the other hand, the attitude of the business community was more complex. No substantial merchants or financiers had participated directly in the conspiracy of December 1640; nevertheless many, especially those with links to Brazil and northern Europe, quickly adapted to the new order once it had been installed. There were also Portuguese businessmen of substance, mostly New Christians, who possessed important interests in Spain – extending in some instances to the Spanish court. The Bragança government was wary of such persons and moved against those whom it deemed too close to the enemy. It confiscated their property in Portugal and Brazil where it could. But there is no evidence of any organised, broadly-based capitalist support for a return to Habsburg rule.

While apparently no commoners played an active part in planning the Restoration of December 1640, certain trusted leaders of the *povo* in Lisbon were given advance notice of what was afoot and responded with their unreserved backing. Throughout the long years of struggle that followed, popular support for the Braganças in both towns and countryside never seriously wavered. This was of fundamental importance for it was the third estate that provided the military recruits and the tax revenue that made the national war effort possible.

Despite the widespread popularity of the new regime its situation in the early months after the coup was highly precarious. In August 1641 a noble conspiracy to assassinate João IV and return the Habsburgs to power was uncovered in Lisbon. Its instigators were probably in contact with other Portuguese nobles in Spain, although the extent of Madrid's direct involvement is uncertain.[9] The prime mover appears to have been the archbishop of Braga. However, some of the greatest nobles in Portugal were also involved, including the marquis of Vila Real and his son the duke of Caminha. Both these *grandes* were arrested, condemned and then publicly beheaded.[10] Another personage implicated was the New Christian merchant Pedro de Baeça, who had lent heavily to the Habsburgs. He too was arrested, tried and hanged.[11] The August 1641 conspiracy shows clearly that the elite, particularly the greater nobility and higher clergy, remained for some time quite divided over the Restoration. This led in due course to a redistribution of Portuguese titles and the rise to prominence of several new families. Some titles disappeared altogether – or became Castilianised and hence removed permanently from their former Portuguese

[9] Silva L A R da 1971–2 vol 4, pp 389–407; SHP vol 5, pp 28–9.
[10] Meneses L de 1945 vol 1, pp 510–11.
[11] DHP vol 3, p 624; Boyajian J C 1983, pp 128–9.

context. One way or another, all noble opposition to the Bragança monarchy was either crushed or excised.

Ecclesiastical disloyalty, which was mostly less overt but at least as insidious as noble opposition, proved in many respects more difficult to deal with. From the start João IV faced a highly obstructive Inquisition. He was anxious to co-opt New Christian businessmen to his cause, being much in need of their financial support – and he was prepared to grant them, in return, protection against persecution. New Christian interests did provide invaluable backing for the Restoration.[12] But the Inquisition, heavily reliant on the confiscated wealth of convicted Judaizers for its financial survival, vehemently opposed concessions to this despised community. João had no legal means of removing an uncooperative inquisitor-general from office, and the Inquisition's stance, which was generally popular, received support from most though not all Portuguese nobles.[13] Meanwhile the pope, who was under Spanish influence, refused to grant João recognition – which in turn caused a creeping ecclesiastical crisis because no new bishops could be installed. Portugal's sees fell vacant one by one until by 1649 the bishop of Elvas was the sole surviving incumbent. Only after peace had finally been concluded with Spain in 1668 did Pope Clement IX acknowledge Portugal as an independent kingdom and begin to confirm new bishops.[14]

João IV was a rather reluctant central figure in all this unfolding drama. When he became king in 1640 at the age of thirty-six he was precipitated into an unfamiliar and dangerous world. His background was that of a country gentleman who before his elevation to the throne had never left Portugal. Indeed, he had seldom ventured from the ducal seat at Vila Viçosa. A decent and pious man, he had a fondness for music, was always cautious in his movements and remained firmly traditional in his values. Of course, these attributes did not endear him much to anti-monarchist and anti-clerical propagandists of the late nineteenth century – but subsequent historiography has tended to view him rather more kindly. It cannot be denied that João presided over a singularly bloodless and unvengeful Restoration, in which the only stern justice meted out was to Miguel de Vasconcelos and his associates and to the counter-conspirators of 1641. João subsequently proved a wary ruler who relied much on the advice of his councils and – particularly in his final years – on the input of individual advisers, such as his secretary António Pais Viegas and the charismatic Jesuit António Vieira.[15] A realist and a pragmatist, he played the rather weak hand fate had dealt him with considerable tenacity.

---

[12] Azevedo J L de 1922, p 265.
[13] DHP vol 3, p 622; Hanson C A 1981, p 78; Shaw L M E 1989, pp 421–3.
[14] Oliveira M de 1968, pp 290–4.
[15] DHP vol 3, pp 620, 626.

JOÃO IV, WAR AND DIPLOMACY

One of the most urgent tasks that awaited João IV after the 1640 coup was to contact the Portuguese overseas settlements and secure their adherence. Special couriers were therefore hurriedly despatched to all corners of the empire, the sensational news reaching Bahia in February 1641, Goa that September and distant Macau in May 1642. The Restoration was acclaimed with enthusiasm virtually everywhere, and the smooth transition of loyalties was much facilitated by strong support from the Jesuits and the absence of Spanish troops. Only in Tangier and Ceuta – possessions geographically close to Spain, heavily dependent on Spanish supplies and exposed to Habsburg retaliation – was the issue seriously in doubt. But in the end Ceuta alone stayed with Filipe. In 1643, having won the loyalty of Portugal's overseas possessions, João went on to create a new council – the *conselho ultramarino* – to take responsibility for administering them. This important new body was deliberately based on a Habsburg model, an indication that João's regime, despite its traditionalist orientation, was quite prepared to innovate where it saw the need.[16]

The successful installation of the Braganças, and their widespread acceptance throughout the Portuguese world, did not alter the fact that the country was woefully equipped in 1641 to conduct the war of independence that was now inevitable. Military organisation was rudimentary, there were desperate shortages of equipment and horses, border fortresses had long been neglected and many of the kingdom's most experienced soldiers were absent, serving the Habsburgs in Catalonia or the Netherlands. Yet Castile too was hardly in better shape, with its armies tied down against the French, the Dutch and the Catalan rebels, its revenue and manpower extremely over-stretched and its nobility racked with discontent. In 1641, under the leadership of the duke of Medina Sidonia (João IV's brother-in-law), Andalusia revolted. An ill-prepared Portuguese David faced a Spanish Goliath, tormented and all but exhausted. Nevertheless, Portugal's struggle to regain its position in the community of nations was inevitably long and tortuous. The kingdom could not simply resume the independent status it had enjoyed in 1580; it had to beat off Castilian attempts at reoccupation – and it had to prove to a sceptical world that it merited recognition.

Military action by both Portuguese and Spaniards was at first small scale. Villages were raided, crops and olive groves were destroyed and cattle seized on either side of the border in a manner that recalled the Reconquest. Portugal gradually expanded its forces and improved its fortifications; but the emphasis remained heavily on defence, with only minor offensive operations being

[16] Luz F P M da 1952, pp 193–4.

conducted as opportunity offered. In 1644, a small army under Matias de Albuquerque crossed the Spanish border and won a cheering victory at Montijo. Nevertheless, the struggle dragged on with neither side gaining a decisive advantage and gradually developed into a war of attrition Portugal could ill afford. Ominously, by the late 1640s Spain was beginning to wind up its crippling commitments elsewhere. In 1648 it conceded Dutch independence and then four years later finally brought the Catalan revolt under control. Spain was still at war with France when João IV died in 1656 – but Filipe III was moving steadily towards a position from which he could at last concentrate his forces against the Braganças.

João IV was confronted not only with a daunting military challenge, but with formidable diplomatic obstacles. Spain vigorously opposed recognition of the Braganças in every European court. Portugal, which had possessed no functioning foreign service for over half a century, began the struggle with just one experienced diplomat – the urbane and indefatigable Francisco de Sousa Coutinho.[17] Yet envoys were required urgently not only to seek recognition, but also to secure desperately-needed foreign assistance. João was particularly hopeful of succour from the French, for France was Spain's long-standing rival. In the years immediately preceding the coup French agents had visited Portugal, encouraged revolt and promised backing. France's subsequent recognition of the Bragança regime – and its support for the Catalan rebels, which helped tie down Castilian forces away from Portugal's border – were of great assistance.[18] However, when João proposed a formal Franco-Portuguese alliance, the French, unwilling to be too committed against Spain, equivocated, and a somewhat ambiguous relationship between the two kingdoms persisted for years. João made a desperate bid to secure a French alliance shortly before his death in 1656. He offered the hand of his daughter Catarina, along with a dowry of one million *cruzados* plus either Tangier or Mazagão, to the young Louis XIV. But the offer was not accepted.

The only other country from which Portugal might realistically hope for significant help in its struggle against Spain was England, and in January 1642 Portuguese representatives successfully negotiated a treaty with King Charles I. This treaty was to have important long-term commercial consequences; but any expectations the Portuguese may have had of immediate diplomatic and military benefits soon evaporated because of civil war in England. Seven years later Charles I was tried and executed – and in 1650 João found himself briefly at war with the Republican Commonwealth. This was a situation fraught with potential disaster for Portugal.[19]

---

[17] Prestage E 1928, p xiv.
[18] Prestage E 1935, p 133.
[19] Shaw L M E 1989, pp 44–8; Valladares R 1998, pp 118–19.

Although the new English regime of Oliver Cromwell was thoroughly repug-
nant to João, he had little alternative but to negotiate with it. This he soon
proceeded to do – encouraged by an English naval blockade of the Tagus
imposed because Portugal had briefly given shelter to Prince Rupert's Royalist
fleet. The negotiations were difficult, but eventually resulted in a new Anglo-
Portuguese treaty. Although drawn up in 1654, this treaty was not ratified until
two years later, mainly because of Inquisition objections to granting English
Protestants the free exercise of their religion in private.[20] Setting aside for the
moment commercial terms, which from a Portuguese viewpoint were extremely
onerous, it can be said that the 1654 treaty guaranteed Portugal English protection and opened Lisbon to the Cromwellian navy for repairs and replenish-
ment. There is no doubt that for the Bragança it was a vital breakthrough,
without which the Restoration could scarcely have been sustained. Cromwell
might easily have decided instead to sign a treaty with Spain – a course of action
he seriously considered. The Anglo-Portuguese accord, for all it faults, would
also prove an invaluable long-term investment, for English power was growing
rapidly and England was soon to enter on a prolonged era of naval supremacy.
Alignment with England would therefore go a long way towards ensuring
Portugal's maritime communications. Meanwhile in 1655 war broke out between
England and Spain, and Spanish ports were blockaded. In 1656 and 1657, the
English seized Spain's silver fleets, so easing the pressure on the Bragança.

Portugal's troubles during João IV's reign were not restricted to Europe. In
the late Habsburg years various parts of the Portuguese empire were attacked
and seized by the Dutch, and, when the Restoration occurred, Luso-Dutch
hostilities were still continuing. But the war had begun as a consequence of
Holland's struggle to break away from Spain, and a now independent Portugal
had no reason to continue it. However, though peace with the Portuguese
suited Holland well enough in Europe, this was not the case elsewhere. In
maritime Asia the VOC, and in the South Atlantic the WIC, both preferred
to prolong hostilities in order to maximise their gains. So when a ten-year Luso-
Dutch truce was signed in 1641 and came into force in Europe immediately, it
was not proclaimed in Brazil until mid-1642. This allowed the WIC time to
seize various additional Portuguese possessions, including Maranhão. In Asia
the truce took effect only in 1644 and even then was soon broken.[21]

Under these circumstances, and given the struggle against Spain in Europe, it
is hardly surprising that many Portuguese, including João IV himself, believed
Portugal had little hope of forcing the Dutch out of Brazil – and still less
of expelling them from conquered Portuguese possessions in maritime Asia.

[20] Shaw L M E 1989, pp 57–64; Valladares R 1998 120–31.
[21] Boxer C R 1957, pp 103–4, 108; Boxer C R 1965, pp 86–7.

Fr António Vieira, who became the king's personal adviser on Brazilian affairs, thought the most João could realistically attempt was to buy off the Dutch. If that failed he would simply have to accept the loss of Pernambuco as the price of peace.[22] But then in 1645 the inhabitants of Dutch-occupied Pernambuco suddenly rose up against WIC rule, giving the Portuguese renewed hope. João IV's government at first reacted cautiously, but when the rebels took control of most of Pernambuco it began to support them actively. By the end of 1654 the WIC had been forced out of its conquests, and all colonial Brazil was back in Portuguese hands. However, in maritime Asia the VOC continued to make gains at Portugal's expense for another decade.

AFONSO VI AND NATIONAL SURVIVAL

When João IV died in 1656 the future of the house of Bragança was still far from assured. João's promising eldest son, Dom Teodósio, had died three years before; so the late king was succeeded by his far less suitable second son, Afonso VI. Afonso was both physically and mentally handicapped, probably as a consequence of meningitis contracted in infancy, which seems to have left him a hemiplegiac.[23] At the time of his accession he was only thirteen years old – and in accordance with his father's wishes Luísa de Guzmán, the queen mother, was made regent. She maintained the key functionaries and policies of the previous administration and held firm to the ongoing struggle for Portuguese independence, her own Spanish origins notwithstanding.

In January 1659, when Portugal won the battle of the lines of Elvas at which some 5,000 of Filipe III's troops were taken prisoner, it was the first major Portuguese victory of the war.[24] However, that September Spain finally made peace with France at the treaty of the Pyrenees. This peace was sealed by Louis XIV agreeing to marry Filipe III's daughter, Maria Teresa. Filipe believed the deal would facilitate his re-subjugation of Portugal, and so the Portuguese were excluded from the negotiations.[25] It also suited France for Portugal's status to remain for the time being unresolved, with the Bragança regime a lingering thorn in Spain's side. Therefore, the treaty of the Pyrenees was an alarming development for Lisbon, where it increased fears of renewed and more formidable Castilian invasions.

One consequence of the treaty of the Pyrenees was to force Luísa's administration to rely more on its other ally, England. In 1660, Portuguese agents

---

[22] Boxer C R 1957a, pp 9–10, 13–14.
[23] SHP vol 5, pp 46, 196.
[24] Ibid, pp 43–5.
[25] Lynch J 1964–9 vol 2, p 123.

gained authorisation from the Cromwellian Protectorate to buy arms and horses and recruit up to 12,000 men in England. Shortly afterwards Charles II was restored, England was again a monarchy and its relations with Portugal grew warmer. In 1662 a new Anglo-Portuguese treaty was negotiated and then sealed by the marriage of Charles II to King Afonso's sister, Catarina. Known in England as Catherine of Braganza, this was the princess whom Louis XIV had earlier rejected. The deal with Charles II was an important breakthrough for it re-affirmed the Anglo-Portuguese alliance, brought Portugal explicit promises of English protection against Spain and Holland and signalled international acceptance of the Braganças' royal credentials. But the price was high: confirmation of all the concessions granted to England in 1654 plus a dowry for Catarina comprising Bombay, Tangier and two million *cruzados* in cash. The cash component long remained a burden on the Portuguese people – and in the end was never fully paid.[26]

Meanwhile, Afonso VI, who had reached the age of eighteen and could not despite all his limitations have been kept in tutelage much longer, was persuaded in June 1662 by a group of younger court nobles to terminate his mother's regency. Their leader, Luís de Vasconcelos e Sousa, third count of Castelo Melhor, was promptly appointed Afonso's confidential secretary (*escrivão da puridade*). Using that key office to full advantage, Castelo Melhor swiftly gained commanding influence over the impressionable Afonso and for the next five years, with the aid of a few loyal collaborators, effectively ran the Portuguese government.[27] During this period Castelo Melhor displayed no less determination than had João IV and Luísa in defending the Restoration. However, he was well aware that the longer hostilities continued the more exhausted Portugal would become – and the greater the risk independence might not in the end be sustainable. He therefore intensified efforts to achieve a negotiated peace, at the same time prosecuting the war with such vigour as could be mustered. To increase pressure on the Spaniards he sought closer diplomatic relations with France – but the French, happy enough to see Luso-Castilian hostilities continue, did not agree to a formal alliance until March 1667.[28]

If France's attitude for long seemed distinctly ambivalent, England in the wake of Catarina's marriage to Charles II soon began to urge Spain to come to terms with Portugal. However, Filipe III remained deeply reluctant to drop his Portuguese claims, negotiations progressed painfully slowly and the war dragged on. Meanwhile, during the early 1660s Portugal had begun to engage the services of various foreign military experts to try to improve its performance

---

[26] Ibid, pp 154–6, 168.
[27] DHP vol 1, pp 46–7; SHP vol 5, pp 46–8.
[28] HP vol 5, pp 56–7, 66, 196–7; DUP vol 2, p 934.

in the field. Among them was Count Schomberg, a German officer contracted to the Braganças through the good offices of the French, who was asked to take charge of the Portuguese army. Notwithstanding prickly relationships with certain of his Portuguese colleagues, and the tight constraints imposed on him by limited manpower and material resources, Schomberg was able to achieve some significant improvements in military organisation, training and tactics.[29] When the Spaniards subsequently embarked on a series of offensives they were convincingly repulsed, Portugal winning a succession of victories from Ameixial (1663) to Montes Claros (1665). At the latter battle, which was fought near the Braganças' ducal seat of Vila Viçosa, the marquis of Marialva routed the invaders.

Habsburg hopes of regaining Portugal rapidly faded after Montes Claros – and the death of Filipe III not long afterwards removed a major obstacle to reconciliation. With England mediating and France now agreeing that the time to end hostilities had arrived, the details of a comprehensive treaty were at last thrashed out. This was signed at Madrid in January 1668, Spain recognising Portugal's independence and the two old antagonists affirming mutual respect and friendship.[30] For both kingdoms the treaty marked an important watershed, ending as it did decades of debilitating war and beginning a long period of internal peace for the whole peninsula.

In the prolonged and often tortuous process that eventually brought an end to Luso-Spanish hostilities and general recognition of the Bragança regime, growing foreign interest in the Portuguese empire played an important role. Access to trade with Portugal's overseas possessions was the principal attraction drawing English support to the Braganças – and without that lure London would probably not have bestirred itself on Lisbon's behalf. At the same time, from a Portuguese viewpoint, alignment with a country now rapidly becoming Europe's principal maritime power made compelling sense if reasonably secure communications with Brazil, Africa and Asia were to be maintained. A long-term Anglo-Portuguese alliance therefore had much to offer the Braganças. Meanwhile Portugal's other war, its exhausting, seemingly endless struggle with the Dutch, was fought almost entirely beyond Europe. Pernambuco was recovered from the WIC in 1654, but it was not until 1661 that the Netherlanders agreed to give up all their Brazilian claims – in return for a massive Portuguese indemnity of four million *cruzados*. There followed much difficult haggling before a Luso-Dutch treaty applying to all war theatres was signed in 1663. Even then disagreements over implementation dragged on until 1669, and the Dutch insisted on retaining Portuguese Cochin and Cannanore,

---

[29] White L 2003, pp 86, 89.
[30] Elliott J H 1963, pp 352–4; DHP vol 3, pp 103–4, 626, 803; SHP vol 5, pp 53–6.

possessions they had seized from the *Estado da Índia* after the 1663 agreement had been signed.[31]

The next most pressing challenge for Castelo Melhor, as Afonso VI's *valido* or chief minister, was to secure the Portuguese succession. To achieve this it was necessary to find the king a bride and therefore the opportunity to beget an heir. Like King Sebastião's advisers a century before, Castelo Melhor treated this quest as a top priority; but the issue was complicated by Afonso's physical disabilities. Nevertheless, after various earlier proposals had come to nothing the minister eventually secured the consent of Louis XIV for Afonso to marry a minor Bourbon princess – Marie-Françoise Isabelle, daughter of the duke of Nemours. Marie-Françoise, an ambitious and strong-willed woman, duly arrived in Lisbon in August 1666.[32]

Had Afonso's marriage to Marie-Françoise been a success it is almost certain Castelo Melhor would have remained firmly entrenched in power. But the marriage, through no fault of the minister, proved a comprehensive failure. During 1666–7, as it became increasingly clear that Afonso VI was uninterested in his wife and probably incapable of consummating his marriage, mounting intrigue and controversy consumed the Portuguese court. Moreover behind the marriage crisis another, more profound issue was stirring. This was the conflict between reformists and conservatives – or those who stood for a more centralised, authoritarian state, and those who were deeply suspicious of 'innovations' and believed in a traditional style of government in harmony with the 'natural' order. Overtones of this conflict had already been present in the crisis that faced Olivares in the 1630s. During the Restoration period it had been partly allayed, and partly overshadowed by other more immediate issues; but now it re-emerged to torment Castelo Melhor.[33] In both the 1630s and the 1660s, central government was perceived as becoming more autocratic, and less consultative. To compound the problem for Castelo Melhor, his opponents also held him responsible for insidiously reversing the traditionalist revival of the reign of João IV. Thus, whereas under João the *cortes* had met four times, it was never convened during Castelo Melhor's ascendancy – not even for Afonso's formal acclamation.[34] Portuguese who had struggled to free themselves from Olivares would not easily tolerate yet another centralising minister.

During 1667, a group of prominent traditionalist nobles opposed to Castelo Melhor, which included the duke of Cadaval and the marquis of Marialva, began

---

[31] DHP vol 3, pp 635–6.
[32] Ibid vol 2, pp 933–4; SHP vol 5, pp 196–7.
[33] HP vol 4, p 136; Cardim P 1998, pp 31, 128.
[34] Cardim P 1998, pp 128–9.

to prepare for a palace coup. Probably from the start these nobles sought out and secured the support of Afonso's younger brother, Prince Pedro. They could certainly also rely on the backing of Marie-Françoise and her circle, for the queen despised her unfortunate husband and may have already begun an amatory relationship with Pedro. In November 1667, this increasingly confident opposition prised the hapless Afonso from Castelo Melhor's influence and procured the minister's dismissal.[35] Cadaval and his collaborators then intensified pressure for a more comprehensive solution to Portugal's constitutional and dynastic crisis, seeking the replacement of Afonso VI by Prince Pedro. Such a possibility had been foreseen by Queen Luísa, the two men's mother, who understood Afonso's limitations. As regent she had therefore taken care to nurture Pedro's development, removing him from court in 1662 when he was fourteen and giving him a separate household. Pedro had subsequently become the hope and figurehead of Castelo Melhor's opponents and the obvious alternative to the inadequate Afonso VI.

PEDRO II AND THE STABILISING OF THE BRAGANÇA MONARCHY

By the time Castelo Melhor had departed Afonso's position was already all but untenable. Not only a powerful element among the nobility, but the queen, Prince Pedro, the Lisbon *câmara* and most leaders of the *povo* were determined that in the national interest he too must go. The appropriate constitutional course was to call the *cortes,* and the hapless Afonso was finally prevailed upon to issue the necessary writs in November 1667. Marie-Françoise brought matters to a head by publicly declaring her marriage had never been consummated, demanding it be dissolved, fleeing to a convent and threatening to return to France. The council of state then requested Afonso VI to hand power over to Pedro, who duly began signing decrees on 24 November 1667.[36]

Pedro II ruled Portugal first in Afonso's name from 1667 to 1683, then as king in his own right from 1683 to 1706 – for a total of thirty-nine years, longer than any other Portuguese leader since the fifteenth century. On coming to power his political priorities were to consolidate his regime and secure the succession. The *cortes* met in January 1668 and quickly confirmed the legitimacy of his takeover: indeed, the third estate urged him to accept the kingship, believing this would strengthen his authority and make any attempt to reverse the coup constitutionally impossible. But Pedro baulked at this, partly for reasons of conscience and also because he needed to maintain proper legal procedure. Accordingly he chose the title 'Prince Regent' and continued to rule in the name of Afonso as long as the latter lived.

[35] Livermore H V 1966, pp 193–4; DHP vol 2, p 934; SHP vol 5, pp 199–200.
[36] SHP vol 5, pp 201–4.

Pedro also moved swiftly to overcome the problem of succession. The marriage of Marie-Françoise to Afonso was annulled in March 1668, both parties having formally acknowledged that it had not been consummated. Shortly afterwards, on receipt of a bull of dispensation from Rome, the queen and Pedro were married. The haste with which these developments occurred gave rise to rumours that the couple had already been lovers. Combined with Afonso's swift removal into exile, this endowed the marriage with a certain Hamlet-like quality – and it has ever since carried an aura of scandal. However, as Veríssimo Serrão points out, there were compelling reasons of state why it had to happen. Marie-Françoise could not have been left in limbo, while sending her back to France would have strained relations with a major ally and required the refunding of her dowry. Moreover, the marriage took place on the insistence of both the council of state and the *cortes,* which were acutely aware of the urgent need for an heir.[37] In any event, those who backed the marriage felt well vindicated when in 1668 the queen gave birth to a daughter, Isabel Luísa Josefa. This young princess was sworn in as heir presumptive in 1674 – but only after a conspiracy to kill Pedro and Marie-Françoise and restore Afonso VI had been crushed the previous year.[38] After this incident Afonso was brought back from exile in the Azores and confined in the palace at Sintra until his death.

From the late 1670s through the 1680s Pedro's position, and with it the future of the Bragança dynasty, became steadily more secure. At first much attention was focused on Isabel Luísa Josefa, and unsuccessful negotiations were conducted for her possible marriage either to the dauphin of France or the son of the duke of Savoy. When Afonso died in 1683 Pedro became king in his own right. But for some time he was troubled by an uneasy conscience, and his depressed state of mind was made worse by the death of Marie-Françoise later the same year. For a while he contemplated abdicating in favour of his daughter and retiring to Brazil: but he was apparently dissuaded from this course by his Jesuit confessor.[39] By 1687 he had recovered sufficiently to want to remarry. Sensibly avoiding entanglements with any of the great European courts, he selected as his new queen a relatively minor German princess – Maria Sophie of Neuberg, daughter of the Elector Palatine.

Pedro's marriage to Maria Sophie placed the final seal on his kingship and brought Bragança Portugal the solid political stability it had long sought. Like Philippa of Lancaster, that other queen imported from northern Europe some 300 years before, Maria Sophie was gracious, discrete, eminently fruitful and widely respected. She bore Pedro five sons and two daughters, including

[37] Hanson C A 1981, pp 13–14, SHP vol 5, pp 207–8.
[38] SHP vol 5, p 210.
[39] Ibid, pp 215–17; NHP vol 7, p 195.

the future João V who was born in 1689, Francisco, António, Manuel and Maria.[40] This felicitous turn of events placed the continuity of the house of Bragança beyond reasonable doubt – and was in stark contrast to the bleak situation in neighbouring Castile, where the once mighty Habsburgs were now represented by only the childless and feeble Carlos II. Meanwhile Pedro's oldest daughter, Isabel Luísa Josefa, died in 1690; but given the king's large new family her passing had little political impact.

The last two decades of Pedro's reign were untroubled by any major political crises. In its external relations Portugal continued to maintain a policy of studied neutrality, carefully avoiding involvement in international disputes. It was only with the much-anticipated death of Carlos II in 1700 and consequent demise of the Spanish Habsburgs that neutrality was briefly abandoned.[41] The rivals for the Spanish succession were the duke of Anjou supported by France and Spain and an Austrian archduke favoured by England, Austria and Holland. Known respectively as Felipe V and Carlos III, they struggled for the vacant throne, backed by their respective sponsors and allies in what became known as the War of the Spanish Succession (1702–13). Under English pressure, but also with the hope of territorial gains at Castile's expense, Pedro agreed in 1703 to join the alliance in support of Carlos.

Pedro's promised contribution to the War of the Spanish Succession was 15,000 troops plus the use of Portugal as a base for allied operations.[42] In the course of the ensuing struggle allied forces, including Portuguese troops, twice briefly occupied Madrid. Meanwhile in northern Europe, allied armies led by the duke of Marlborough and Prince Eugene of Savoy won a series of smashing victories that broke the hegemony of Louis XIV. But then the sudden death of the Emperor Joseph I of Austria in 1711 transformed the political context. Joseph's successor to the Austrian throne was Carlos, the allies' candidate for the throne of Spain. England was unwilling to accept a union of Austria and Spain and so now offered to recognise Felipe V, provided he renounced any future claims to the throne of France. This was formally agreed at the treaty of Utrecht (1713), which ended the war and determined the political map of Europe until the collapse of the Old Regime late in the eighteenth century.[43] England emerged from the War of the Spanish Succession with its influence much enhanced, and Portugal was drawn further into the English orbit. Meanwhile Pedro himself had died in 1706, at the reasonably advanced age of fifty-eight.

---

[40] SHP vol 5, pp 219, 446; NHP vol 7, p 196.
[41] Elliott J H 1963, pp 367–73.
[42] SHP vol 5, p 224.
[43] Kamen H 1969, pp 9–24.

It is easy to dismiss the period of Pedro's rule as a relatively uneventful interlude, particularly in comparison with the more spectacular periods that preceded and followed it. Moreover, its most interesting episode, the constitutional crisis with which it began, can easily be interpreted in a way hostile to Pedro – a king of dubious moral legitimacy, who usurped his throne from a helpless brother.[44] But such a picture is at best incomplete and misleading. It pays scant heed to the genuine fears of contemporaries for the kingdom's future in 1667 and underestimates the enormous political pressures brought to bear on Pedro at that time – as well, of course, as ignoring his subsequent achievements. Pedro II was an intelligent and generally responsible ruler whose administrative style was cautious, consultative and thorough. A physically impressive man, he rode and fenced well and led a quite frugal lifestyle. He seems to have been genuinely fond of first Marie-Françoise and later Maria Sophie – although this never deterred him from having a very active sex life outside marriage, involving numerous pretty young women. He suffered from time to time from bouts of depression, during which he was liable to behave erratically; but he struggled on and fought his way out from these dark periods. There have been many worse kings.[45]

THE INTERNAL BALANCE OF POWER

Tension between traditional particularisms and royal centralism had been endemic in Portugal since at least the late twelfth century, from time to time giving rise to serious conflict. Though less violently confrontational than in the past, this dichotomy was still a basic reality of Portuguese life in the post-Habsburg period. Ground-breaking work by António Manuel Hespanha has revealed something of the extent to which seventeenth-century Portugal was still a country of multiple jurisdictions and local autonomies. Portuguese society was theoretically composed of a series of corporate entities each jealously mindful of its rights and privileges. The modern notion of a community of individual citizens, all equal under the law, had no currency. Indeed, there was as yet no uniform legal system that could have supported such a notion, even though some progress had been made in earlier centuries towards creating one. The role of government had grown more complex, and some of the state's central institutions had become more sophisticated. But the seventeenth-century Bragança monarchs still presided over a hybrid system, a polity at the same time both monarchical and pluralist. At his accession the king swore to uphold this dual system, this supposed 'natural' order of things, with all the

---

[44] Hanson C A 1981, p 12; NHP vol 7, pp 192–3.
[45] Hanson C A 1981, pp 15–17; SHP vol 5, p 233.

rights, customs and uses associated with it. He was pledged to cherish not only the unity of the whole, but also the autonomy of its parts.[46]

The corporate entity enjoying the widest range of privileges and immunities in seventeenth-century Portugal was the church. The clergy, apart from those in minor orders, normally came within the jurisdiction of their own ecclesiastical courts, and not those of the king. Virtually the only exceptions were cases of treason or counterfeiting or where the crown's own rights were directly involved.[47] Clergy also had extensive tax privileges. In most circumstances, they did not pay *sisas,* customs or tolls, and they were exempted from contributing to general tributes unless explicit papal authorisation to the contrary had been secured. In addition, the more important ecclesiastical bodies enjoyed sweeping jurisdictional immunities. Thus, the court of the archbishop of Braga had virtually complete autonomy, while cathedrals and the greater monasteries such as Alcobaça and Tarouca remained largely exempt from intervention by the crown's *corregedores.* The church continued to control quite significant lands, seigneuries and vassals though on a much smaller scale than the nobility. If what was held by the military orders is excluded, ecclesiastical institutions possessed about 4 per cent of the land in Portugal, some 16 per cent of seigneuries and seven to 8 per cent of vassals.[48]

The church was also a highly pervasive presence within lay society generally. It orchestrated all explicitly religious behaviour such as attendance at mass, confessions, alms-giving, observing of saints' days and so on. It likewise supervised many aspects of life far less obviously religious, particularly matters relating to sexual behaviour and certain elements of commercial practice, including the taking of interest and the sealing of contracts under oath. Church authorities had jurisdiction over testamentary matters and a wide range of criminal offences like sacrilege, perjury, blasphemy, witchcraft, adultery, incest, sodomy, simony and keeping gaming houses. Each bishopric maintained its own court to enforce canon law. These courts imposed spiritual penalties that ranged from public penance to excommunication – and they could require the secular authorities to enforce their decisions. Of course, the Inquisition had its own tribunals that disposed of terrifying powers. At a more informal level the church exercised a pervasive influence through its network of parishes, priests providing their flocks with counselling and often arbitrating disputes. Finally, by tradition Christian fugitives from the secular courts could claim sanctuary on entering any one of a whole range of religious edifices – churches,

---

[46] Hespanha A M 1994, pp 523–8 and passim; NHP vol 7, pp 24–5, 68, 71, 278–9; Cardim P 1998, p 14.

[47] Hespanha A M 1994, pp 324, 326–33.

[48] Ibid, pp 429–30.

sacristies, cloisters, cells, hermitages, universities and even the pallium that sheltered the eucharist. There, as long as they remained, they could not be arrested, although Jews, Muslims, heretics, notorious bandits and offenders against the church itself were excluded from this privilege.[49]

Overall, the nobility enjoyed fewer exemptions and immunities than the church. However, royal *corregedores* were effectively excluded from the seigneuries of certain illustrious *grandes,* including the dukes of Bragança and Aveiro, the marquis of Vila Real, the baron of Alvito and several counts. Within these privileged jurisdictions it was the seigneur himself, or more likely his *ouvidor,* who performed the *corregedor*'s functions. Moreover in many secular lordships the seigneur had the right to appoint or confirm local municipal office-holders.[50] Also not only high-ranking nobles but also many persons only on the fringes of nobility enjoyed special judicial rights, often by virtue of their particular profession or occupation. Judges, lawyers, professors and even students at the universities of Coimbra and Évora, who had their own elected conservators, came into this category. Similarly, military personnel enjoyed legal privilege under their regimental judicial officers (*auditores*).[51]

However, the power and prestige of the nobility – and especially of the *grandes* – was underpinned less by judicial privileges than by vast lands and lordships. In 1640 some 40 per cent of the land in Portugal, 42 per cent of seigneuries and 41 per cent of vassals were controlled by nobles.[52] This was greater than the 36 per cent of the land, 30 per cent of seigneuries and 42 per cent of vassals held by the crown in its own right.[53] Furthermore, nobles enjoyed considerable security of possession, the principle of family heredity was broadly recognised and in most cases holdings passed on from generation to generation without difficulty. The *Lei Mental* – the law which regulated the succession process – did impose various conditions. Male primogeniture was required, all grants had to be confirmed and nobles' lands could not be alienated or divided up without the crown's consent. However, in practice the necessary confirmations and licenses seem to have been obtainable with little difficulty.[54]

All this may suggest that the seventeenth-century Portuguese nobility remained a formidable force. However, the second estate was not as powerful or influential as might at first appear, and its position relative to the crown was clearly declining. One reason for this was that almost every significant town in

[49] Ibid, pp 329, 333–5, 338, 342.
[50] Ibid, pp 396–7, 422, 430, 436–7.
[51] Ibid, pp 249–51.
[52] Ibid, p 431.
[53] Ibid, pp 422–7.
[54] Ibid, pp 407, 412–14, 436–7.

Portugal was in a crown lordship, and towns constituted the kingdom's most dynamic economic sector. Another reason was that the crown now possessed the vast holdings of the military Orders of Christ, Santiago and Avis. This meant the king controlled in addition to the royal patrimony a further 20 per cent of Portugal's land, 12 per cent of its lordships and 10 per cent of vassals.[55] In addition, at the Restoration the holdings of the dukes of Bragança, easily the greatest of Portugal's *grandes,* had reverted to crown possession and were promptly set aside for the heir to the throne. Then in 1654 another great patrimony, the *Casa do Infantado,* was put together to provide for the king's second son, its endowments incorporating the confiscated lands of the marquis of Vila Real and the duke of Caminha. The patrimonies of these two great houses, as well as that of another established for the queens of Portugal, comprised some 15 per cent of the nation's territory.[56]

If comparing the relative strengths of crown, church and nobility provides one indicator of the internal balance of power, then establishing how and by whom the country was actually administered on a day-to-day basis constitutes another. In this regard Hespanha's study is again revealing. He calculates that in about 1640 of some 11,700 persons who throughout Portugal held administrative office only about 10 per cent were actually in crown service. This was certainly insufficient to give the crown much control at the local level.[57] Even superior officials like *corregedores,* who had broad oversight of royal justice in their respective districts, were in practice quite limited in what they could do, and they had no jurisdiction at all in several key spheres, including military affairs and revenue collecting.[58] In practice, the vast majority of office-holders in Portugal worked for *concelhos* or municipalities, and it was these persons who performed most on-the-spot judicial, police and general administrative functions. Such officials, thoroughly embedded in their local power structures and often remote from court, could not be controlled from Lisbon. Moreover, their remuneration came from community-generated emoluments, not state salaries.

The effects of all this are perhaps most clearly visible in the exercise of local justice. In seventeenth-century Portugal most disputes were never brought before the formal courts, but were processed through a quasi-judicial system operated at *concelho* level. This system was derived from ancient custom and practice and was particularly firmly entrenched in the north. It was administered by local magistrates called *juizes ordinários,* who typically had little or no legal training, were in some cases even illiterate, but nevertheless possessed appropriate local

[55] Ibid, pp 339, 427–8, 436.
[56] NHP vol 7, pp 41, 83–6; DIHP vol 1, p 342.
[57] Hespanha A M 1994, p 259.
[58] Ibid, pp 268–9.

knowledge and prestige. Their decisions could be appealed to the crown courts, meaning that the system was linked if rather loosely to the king's justice.[59] But the appeal procedures were too daunting for most people, and the great advantage of a *juiz ordinário*'s court was that it provided accessible, oral, on-the-spot justice with an emphasis on mediation. Naturally, it did not carry the same authority as a royal court, but it was less intimidating and much less costly. This semi-informal justice system certainly had problems. It was vulnerable to pressure from locally powerful individuals and could sometimes operate as an instrument of oppression.[60] Nevertheless, for many, particularly the unlettered, it was their only legal resort, action through the formal courts being largely confined to the approximately 15 per cent of the population who were literate.[61] The *juiz ordinário*'s court is easily overlooked, and the importance of its role underestimated, because it generated so few written records.

In short, royal power in seventeenth-century Portugal was still far from absolute. However, the crown was continuing to extend and strengthen its control over the kingdom. The ultimate supremacy of the king's law through appeals to royal courts was now firmly established, as was the crown's authority to decide disputes between rival jurisdictions. All subjects had the right to petition the king as their supreme protector: that is, they could present to him their individual or community grievances, regardless of whether they lived in royal or non-royal lordships.[62] The crown exercised strong influence over the church hierarchy through its control of episcopal appointments. Rome's ability to assert itself in Portuguese territory was limited because papal orders required crown approval before they could be promulgated. The principal was now accepted that all landholdings and lordships, both ecclesiastical and lay, were ultimately delegated from the crown and that they required periodic confirmation.[63] The crown could use its legal powers to dispossess and destroy recalcitrant nobles – as happened with the marquis of Vila Real and duke of Caminha after their abortive conspiracy against João IV. Late-seventeenth-century Portugal may have been a patchwork of jurisdictional plurality and privilege, but the system was inexorably evolving, and the long-term trend was firmly towards strengthening the crown. Leviathan, Hespanha's personified image of the centralised state, may not yet have achieved dominance – but was nevertheless fast emerging from the shadows.[64]

---

[59] Ibid 1994, pp 440–4; NHP vol 7, p 73.
[60] Hespanha A M 1994, pp 448, 455.
[61] NHP vol 7, p 71.
[62] Hespanha A M 1994, pp 336–7, 397, 436, 438; NHP vol 7, p 68.
[63] Hespanha A M 1994, pp 384, 409, 437.
[64] Ibid, p 528.

THE SEVENTEENTH-CENTURY *CORTES*

The corporate nature of traditional Portuguese society, but also the way in which that society's institutions were steadily eroded during the seventeenth century, are exemplified in the story of the Portuguese *cortes* or parliament of the three estates. This body had evolved out of the old royal *cúria,* the advisory council of Portugal's Medieval kings, its first recorded meeting having occurred as early as 1254.[65] Because the *cortes* convened only when summoned by the monarch in person, its sessions were irregular and often occurred far apart. Throughout the Habsburg era successive monarchs ignored it almost completely so that it met only three times in sixty years. However, under João IV it experienced something of a revival, meeting successively in 1641, 1642, 1645 and 1653. But it did not sit during the reign of Afonso VI until Prince Pedro became regent, when it met in 1667, 1673 and 1679. After that, as Pedro's rule became more secure, he too dispensed with it. The *cortes* was called in its traditional form just once more, in 1698. Then it never met again until resurrected in the nineteenth century.[66]

The seventeenth-century Portuguese *cortes* was composed of some 400 members from the three estates of the clergy, nobles and *povo.* Except at opening sessions, which were joint sittings, each estate met separately in its own chamber. Archbishops, bishops, the inquisitor-general, representatives of the cathedral chapters and rectors of the universities had the right to sit as members of the first estate, though in practice many of them appointed substitutes. The second estate comprised the titled nobility, *alcaides-mores, donatários,* important officials of the royal household, senior judges, various military figures and certain leading members of the Lisbon *câmara.* Of all these an inner group of about thirty regularly attended the sittings, while the rest played only a limited part. As for the third estate, almost 100 *concelhos* from across Portugal each chose two representatives who were called *procuradores.* A few cities in the Portuguese overseas possessions including Angra, Goa, Salvador and São Luís do Maranhão were also entitled to send *procuradores.* This brought the total membership for the third estate up to about two hundred.[67]

The *procuradores* of the people were not elected; they were simply chosen in accordance with tradition in each *concelho,* usually by a small group of local leaders or oligarchs. *Procuradores* received travel expenses plus an allowance when the *cortes* was in session. So some poorer *concelhos* tried to reduce their costs by selecting to represent them persons who already lived in Lisbon.

[65] DIHP vol 1, pp 163–4; Cardim P 1998, pp 95, 115–17.
[66] Cardim P 1998, p 22.
[67] Ibid, pp 38–2, 44, 47.

Procuradores chosen in this way did not necessarily have strong personal ties with the communities they spoke for, and it was not unknown for the same person to represent more than one *concelho*. At the other end of the scale, major cities like Lisbon and Porto were regularly represented by prominent nobles, influential royal officials or superior judges.[68] When the *cortes* was in session strict rules of precedence applied, with the *procuradores* of the more prestigious *concelhos* always occupying the first three rows of seats.

The *cortes* was normally summoned for one or more of three purposes: to acclaim and swear in a new king or heir to the throne, to approve the raising of subsidies and to pass or amend legislation.[69] As far as law-making was concerned, the *cortes* acted as no more than a co-legislator. It enacted 'laws of the *cortes*', but the king also had the power to issue 'decree laws' on his own authority, and frequently did so. However, the king was not supposed to repeal or alter 'laws of the *cortes*' without that assembly's consent. In addition to its three official functions, the *cortes* also served as an important channel for airing grievances. Many communities, each of the estates individually and sometimes all three estates collectively submitted petitions to the crown through the *cortes*. Petitions were an old tradition, and Portuguese kings spent much time considering and responding to them. During the Habsburg years when the king was an absentee and the *cortes* seldom met, it had often been difficult for petitioners to get their grievances heard. But with the revival of the *cortes* after 1640 there was a marked increase in the flow of petitioner activity. Each of the three estates provided a box in the chamber where it met where petitions could be deposited.[70]

Hundreds of such petitions, particularly those submitted through the *cortes* in 1641 and 1645, have now been examined and analysed so that it is possible to determine broadly the pattern of people's concerns. Those submissions coming from individual *concelhos* show an overwhelming preoccupation with local matters such as safe-guarding privileges, resolving boundary disputes, tackling problems regarding food supplies, seeking to regulate the use of vacant lands, complaining about military recruitment methods and requesting the provision of arms and the repairing of fortifications for protection against Castilian invasion.[71] Petitions submitted by the estates collectively usually concerned broader issues. These included preserving traditional liberties, resolving jurisdictional conflicts, complaining about tributes, deploring 'innovations' and requesting measures to secure adequate supplies of grain and precious metals. There were also complaints, particularly from the third estate,

---

[68] Ibid, pp 46–8.
[69] Ibid, p 96.
[70] Ibid, pp 133–5, 137, 139.
[71] Ibid, pp 151–3; Hespanha A M 1993, pp 40–2, 46–7, 50.

about the wealth and privileges of the clergy and the alleged increase in influence of New Christians.[72]

Tradition demanded that all petitions be expressed in formal language, and they were therefore often drawn up by expert intermediaries. The king was expected to reply while the *cortes* was still in session, but the sheer quantity of requests received meant this expectation could not always be met. The crown's usual procedure was to create several ad hoc committees composed of trusted advisers and then give each of these bodies responsibility for drafting replies to petitions in a particular category. The replies were then approved and signed by the king personally, for it was important to convey the impression that each petitioner had received individual royal attention.[73] In reality the king's power to intervene effectively was often limited, particularly given the rudimentary nature of the kingdom's administrative infrastructure. From time to time kings imposed tributes, recruited soldiers, granted out offices and distributed rewards for loyal services; but otherwise they had little direct impact on the *concelhos*. Finally, as the sense of renewal stimulated by the Restoration slowly faded and supplicants discovered that the costs of petitioning often outweighed the benefits, the number of petitions diminished.[74]

The Restoration *cortes* stood squarely for conservatism, tradition and preserving the ways of the past. It was a bulwark against 'innovations' of the type Olivares and Castelo-Melhor had come to symbolise, and it saw itself as the guardian of a system of power-sharing that was 'natural' and God-given, and that even kings had no right to change.[75] But as the seventeenth century wore on this conservative ideal grew more and more divorced from reality. The crown was inclined to view the *cortes* as too often an impediment to efficient government and as having a useful role, if at all, only in exceptional times. It was cumbersome, slow moving and too unpredictable in its behaviour, it was costly to convene for both the crown and the *concelhos* – and when it did sit it usually achieved frustratingly little. Therefore, as royal power grew, the *cortes* found itself more and more marginalised with its laws revoked or altered as the crown saw fit. From about 1700 the influx of Brazilian gold so boosted the royal revenues that the government's need for voted subsidies largely disappeared – and the king became steadily more absolutist. Pedro II's successor, João V (1706–50), did not even bother to summon the *cortes* for his acclamation, instead inviting just the higher clergy and the lay aristocracy. There was little complaint.[76]

[72] Hespanha A M 1993, pp 34–8; Cardim P 1998, pp 159, 161.
[73] Cardim P 1998, pp 143, 145, 149, 161–3.
[74] Ibid, pp 167–9, 186.
[75] Ibid, p 118.
[76] Ibid, pp 169, 173.

RESTORATION PORTUGAL IN THE INTERNATIONAL ECONOMY

Portugal played a more significant role in international trade in the seventeenth century than its modest size and relatively backward domestic economy might suggest. The kingdom's strategic location, and a steady demand especially in northern Europe for some of its products, help to explain this situation. Portugal possessed a long coastline athwart the main Atlantic shipping route from the North Sea to the Mediterranean and was therefore conveniently accessible to the seafaring nations of western Europe. Its fruit, olives, wine and salt could be readily exchanged for the woollens and other manufactures of more industrialised countries. Portugal could also supply its trading partners with rare and exotic products from its overseas empire, while that empire itself was beginning to be recognised as a worthwhile market for European exports.[77]

Political separation from the Habsburg monarchy in 1640 meant that Portugal lost its formal status as part of the Spanish economic bloc, but regained its capacity to develop an independent trade policy. Of course, many ties with Castile remained. In particular, Portugal continued, though with more difficulty than before, to enjoy reasonable access to Spanish American silver. However, after the Restoration the Bragança regime inevitably looked to expand commercial relations with European countries outside the peninsula.[78] At the same time, the pattern of Portugal's trade with its own empire had been changing, as the focus shifted more and more from maritime Asia to Brazil and Atlantic Africa. Exports and re-exports of sugar, brazilwood and tobacco from the Brazilian settlements, and of slaves from Africa, were increasing rapidly. There was also growing demand in Brazil for Portuguese wine and olive oil, and for cereals, woollens and manufactures from other European countries.[79] As a consequence, Portugal's pressing need between 1640 and the late 1660s to align itself with European powers outside the peninsula harmonised quite well with the general flow of its international commerce. Treaties were sought, and eventually signed, with England, France and Holland – and while, from a Portuguese viewpoint, they were entered into primarily for diplomatic and military reasons they also all had important trade dimensions and were secured only at heavy commercial cost. Indeed, they were seen by the other parties involved – particularly the English – as principally commercial agreements.[80]

English merchants trading with Portugal had enjoyed various privileges since at least the fifteenth century, including the right to their own judge

[77] NHP vol 7, p 213.
[78] Hanson C A 1981, p 115.
[79] HP vol 4, pp 97–100.
[80] L M E Shaw 1998, p 5.

conservator. Now a series of new Anglo-Portuguese agreements, signed in 1642, 1654 and 1662, respectively, confirmed and significantly amplified these privileges. The 1642 treaty had little immediate impact, mainly because of the overthrow of Charles I soon afterwards; but it did create an important precedent by formally acknowledging the right of the English to trade directly with parts of West Africa.[81] The 1654 treaty struck between João IV and Oliver Cromwell was far more consequential, effectively establishing the long-term framework for Anglo-Portuguese relations. This treaty imposed some very unwelcome commercial conditions on Portugal and was accepted by João only with the greatest reluctance and out of dire political and military necessity. It gave English merchants the right to trade in Portuguese colonial ports – an obvious and potentially massive breach of one of the cardinal principles of Lisbon's imperial doctrine.[82] In the Brazil trade Englishmen could now deal in their own right in any commodity (other than olive oil, wine and cod, which were the Portuguese Brazil Company's monopolies). Extensive commercial, judicial and religious privileges were confirmed to the English community in Portugal, duties on English imports were limited to 23 per cent and it was agreed that if the Brazil Company required foreign vessels it would freight them from the English.[83]

For years after the signing of the 1654 treaty the English in Portugal complained that the Portuguese had failed to fulfil its terms and were instead following a policy of delay and evasion. The Portuguese do appear to have deliberately manipulated their translation of the treaty to create an impression of ambiguity – a manoeuvre made more effective by the English mislaying their own text.[84] During subsequent negotiations in 1662 for a new treaty, which was to be sealed by Charles II's marriage to Catarina of Bragança, Portugal tried hard to get the concessions of 1654 watered down. But the English essentially would not budge, though they did agree to limit the number of their merchant families permitted in each of the designated Brazilian ports of Salvador, Recife and Rio de Janeiro to a maximum of four. So the 1662 treaty essentially clarified and re-confirmed the commercial concessions that had been agreed to earlier.

Portugal also signed commercial agreements with France and Holland, giving these two countries privileges similar to those granted to England. Portugal's trading relationships were therefore quite diverse during the late seventeenth century, and the decisive English predominance of later times was yet to come. In the years from the Restoration down to the mid-1680s just over a third of

---

[81] Prestage E 1935, p 136.
[82] Prestage E 1928, pp 143–7.
[83] Azevedo J L de 1947, pp 389, 390, 392; Mauro F 1960, p 460.
[84] Boxer C R 1981, p 1; Shaw L M E 1998, pp 13, 17.

foreign ships entering the port of Lisbon were English.[85] But Anglo-Portuguese trade nevertheless grew steadily, with the balance tilting more and more in England's favour. Already by 1670 English exports to Portugal, primarily in the form of textiles, were worth more than twice Portuguese exports to England. An ominous trend was setting in.[86]

During the 1670s, Portugal's international trade imbalance began to reach alarming proportions. European demand for Portuguese colonial products was then declining, as England, France and Holland turned increasingly to their own West Indian possessions for sugar, tobacco and other tropical products they had previously acquired through Portugal from Brazil.[87] At the same time, traditional exports from continental Portugal were losing market share to France and Spain. Faced with a looming crisis, Portuguese policy-makers turned to contemporary economic theory and to foreign models for possible solutions. In France the minister of finance, Jean-Baptiste Colbert, had been demonstrating that much could be done for a country's balance of payments by pursuing policies of state-sponsored industrialisation. Portuguese who had witnessed the impact of Colbertian reforms in France – including Dr Duarte Ribeiro de Macedo (1618–80), former ambassador to the French court – now urged a similar strategy for Portugal. Support for the idea won backing from various pro-French nobles and from the third estate in the *cortes* and spread rapidly. But it was only after Dom Luís de Meneses, third count of Ericeira, had been appointed *vedor da fazenda* in 1675 that appropriate action was taken.[88]

Between 1675 and 1690, under Ericeira's able direction, Portugal pursued a policy of developing its own selected manufacturing industries. The aim was to overcome the country's adverse balance of trade by reversing its growing reliance on imports. Laws were introduced banning or restricting the use of specified foreign goods, including beaver hats, various types of glass and porcelain and a wide range of textiles. Domestic production was stepped up as rapidly as possible to provide substitutes for these imports. By imposing sumptuary legislation Ericeira avoided technically contravening Portugal's commercial treaties – for his restrictions applied only to Portuguese subjects using particular imported products and not to foreign merchants importing them.[89] This was the first time a Portuguese government had attempted to introduce systematic import substitution. Ericeira's strategy involved encouraging, facilitating and generally

[85] HP vol 4, p 101.
[86] Mauro F 1960, p 460.
[87] HP vol 4, p 102; NHP vol 7, p 283.
[88] Hanson C A 1981, pp 116, 122–7, 161, 169, 266; Macedo J B de 1982, p 27; DIHP vol 2, pp 408–9.
[89] Macedo J B de 1982a, pp 25–6; HP vol 4, p 90; NHP vol 7, pp 283–5.

developing existing Portuguese industrial enterprise rather than trying to create something totally new.[90] The initial focus was on textiles, particularly woollens and to a lesser extent silks, and Ericeira hoped the Portuguese would eventually be in a position to clothe themselves from their own resources. The kingdom already produced significant quantities of raw wool and could obtain further supplies from Spain, if necessary. It had a small existing woollens industry that could be built upon, though it was highly dispersed and had been much neglected during the Habsburg years.[91]

Of course, promoting a domestic woollens industry required sensitive management of international relations, for any measures that impacted negatively on cloth imports were bound to upset foreign merchants, especially the English. Moreover to modernise the industry it was necessary to import equipment and skilled foreign workers from England, France and elsewhere overseas – which had to be done discreetly. Ericeira sensibly decided to concentrate first on producing plainer woollens such as serges and baizes, utilising already established centres of production. The old wool town of Covilhã was singled out together with nearby Manteigas in the Serra da Estrela. There a New Christian–dominated syndicate was granted monopoly rights. English workers and looms were brought in, the industry in the region was re-dynamised, employment grew and production was significantly lifted. By the 1680s, encouraging savings were already being achieved on textile imports.[92]

Ericeira also paid attention to silk production, another old Portuguese industry probably first established in the days of Gharb al-Andalus. But output was limited and by the late seventeenth century had been further reduced as a result of imports from Asia. The main silk-producing centre in Portugal was Torre de Moncorvo in Trás-os-Montes – and there, with Pedro II's support, Ericeira tried to rebuild the industry. He introduced expert advisers from France and looms from England. He also established a new factory at Tomar and encouraged the planting of many more mulberry trees. Another industry Ericeira promoted was the manufacture of beaver hats. This presented an especially difficult challenge because the Portuguese hat industry had to be started from scratch – and not only the skilled workers, but all the raw materials had to be imported. Finally, efforts were made with French help to increase output of saltpetre and develop the production of key industrial metals such as iron, tin and lead. A more sophisticated and productive metals industry obviously had military importance – a fact not lost on Ericeira, who was a former artillery officer.[93]

[90] Macedo J B de 1982a, p 31–2.
[91] NHP vol 7, p 286.
[92] Hanson C A 1981, pp 168–76; Shaw L M E 1998, pp 17–18.
[93] Hanson C A 1981, pp 166–8, 176–9; NHP vol 7, p 286.

The impact of these various industrial schemes was mixed. Probably the least successful was the beaver hat project, which never really got off the ground and had to be abandoned after a few years. On the other hand, the far more important textiles industries did enjoy some real success, despite the fact that the sumptuary laws were not very well observed and smuggling was rife. Attracting investment capital was another problem: funding manufacturing industries in Portugal was always going to be difficult, for few Portuguese were willing to risk their money in such new and untried schemes. Eventually, Ericeira became so desperate he even sought for investment from the Inquisition.[94] Nevertheless, by the end of the century Portuguese imports of English woollens had allegedly declined in value by about 100,000 pounds per annum, a figure that suggests some gratifying progress in the struggle for import substitution. Portuguese international trade was becoming more balanced and more viable.[95] However, all this naturally alarmed the English and other foreign merchants, who did their best to undermine the program.

In the end, notwithstanding its promising beginnings, Portugal's program to increase domestic manufacturing through government intervention could not be maintained. During the 1680s, for a variety of reasons the strategy gradually attracted more and more opposition. Portuguese-manufactured goods struggled to achieve the same quality as foreign imports. Intensely unpopular, the sumptuary laws were widely ignored – and even the crown came to view them as having serious drawbacks, for they reduced customs revenue. Wool shortages and the extensive loss of mulberry trees in droughts during the early 1690s hampered production. There was also growing popular resentment against New Christian industrial entrepreneurs and 'heretic' immigrant workers, while interference from the Inquisition, which insisted on arresting suspect employers and their foreign workers, took its toll.[96] Discouraged and deeply depressed, Ericeira himself eventually committed suicide in 1690 – and the program, in this tragic fashion, lost its greatest champion.

Meanwhile, new economic developments were changing the program's context. By the final years of the seventeenth century Brazilian exports were beginning to show promising signs of recovery, while Portuguese wines succeeded in capturing the lion's share of the English market. Then suddenly, on the eve of the new century, gold was discovered in significant quantities in Brazil. All this meant Portugal's ability to buy its way out of economic trouble was much enhanced, pressure to replace imports with domestic manufactures

---

[94] Hanson C A 1981, pp 183–4; Macedo J B de 1982a, p 30.
[95] Azevedo J L de 1947, p 393; Sideri S 1970, p 27; Hanson C A 1981, p 182.
[96] Hanson C A 1981, pp 16, 267–9; NHP vol 7, pp 289–90.

declined – and the new industrial enterprises were allowed to fade quietly away.[97]

At the start of the eighteenth century, Portugal's ties with England were formally reconfirmed by the celebrated Methuen treaties of May and December 1703. The first of these sealed the Anglo-Portuguese political-military alliance while the second was a trade agreement, pure and simple. It was composed of just three articles: Portugal was to admit English woollens on the same basis as before the recent sumptuary laws, England was to admit Portuguese wines at a rate of tax no more than one-third of that applied to wines imported from France and the agreement itself was to be ratified within two months.[98] Building on and clarifying earlier agreements, the Methuen treaty of December 1703 locked a still largely agrarian Portugal into the economic embrace of an England on the verge of modern industrialisation. During the decades that followed, Portugal found itself more and more in a position of dependency vis-à-vis its powerful partner and protector – a dependency destined to cast a deep shadow over the Portuguese kingdom for the rest of its history.

[97] Hanson C A 1981, p 269; HP vol 4, pp 91, 102–3.
[98] Text reproduced in Shaw L M E 1998, p 212.

The Age of Gold and Baroque Splendour

SETTING THE SCENE

The first half of the eighteenth century was a relatively settled and comfortable period for Old Regime Portugal. There was peace and political stability, royal government was more firmly entrenched than ever before and the same advisers and ministers remained in place for many years. Portugal's economic fortunes had improved substantially and Portuguese society appeared tranquil. In artistic expression, this was the time of the Baroque – an era of ostentatious façades, gorgeous gilt interiors, lavish ceremonial, theatrical music and sonorous writings in prose and verse. Many of the kingdom's small elite enjoyed a certain affluence, while Portuguese in general felt more secure and confident than they had for generations.

Nevertheless, there were some aspects of Portuguese life in the early eighteenth century that were not so positive. In contemporary Western Europe, this was the era of the Enlightenment; but Portugal, notwithstanding its quite vigorous revival, was influenced late, selectively and only rather marginally by Enlightenment currents. Certainly there were some Portuguese – and their numbers were growing – who were genuinely enthused by new ideas and ways of thinking. Often they were individuals who had visited foreign countries or at least had secured access to intellectual currents from outside the kingdom – and were therefore referred to, with a touch of suspicion, as 'foreignised' (*estrangeirados*). However, the *estrangeirados* were a small minority, and, within mainstream Portugal, traditional values and patterns of thought strongly predominated at all social levels. Public debate and dissemination of new knowledge were still hampered by the triple censorship system – and carefully monitored by the watchful eye of the Inquisition. Moreover, despite its improving economic circumstances, Baroque Portugal remained at base a rather poor and technologically backward country.

Presiding over this classic Old Regime polity for nearly half a century was King João V (1706–50). One of the most favoured by fortune of all Portugal's kings, João nevertheless remains something of an enigma to historians.[1] He was only seventeen years old when he ascended the throne, but had already decided where his priorities lay, at least in principle. He was an absolutist by conviction and believed secular power and authority emanated by right solely from the king, to whom all other persons and jurisdictions were completely subordinate. He also considered that his overseas possessions, especially Brazil, were essential for Portugal's well-being and that he should therefore exercise strict control over their government, trade and communications.[2] In Europe, João V's favoured models were the great absolutist monarchies of late-seventeenth and early-eighteenth-century Austria, Spain and France. Accordingly, some two years after his accession he married Maria Ana, daughter of the Emperor Leopold I, so linking the Braganças to the Austrian Habsburgs. This marriage was initially slow to bear fruit, rousing fears that the new queen might be barren. There was therefore widespread relief in late 1711 when Princess Maria Bárbara was born – to be followed in subsequent years by five more royal children.[3]

Although João V has sometimes been dismissed as a mere self-indulgent pleasure-seeker, he was a much more substantial and complex individual than that label suggests. Of course, there is no doubt he did disport himself with a succession of mistresses from every social rank and that he was an incorrigible *freirático* who particularly enjoyed affairs with ladies of the veil. Among his paramours was Paula Teresa da Silva, a Cistercian nun widely known as 'Madre Paula'. João was addicted to luxury, and his court became renowned for its sheer extravagance, though it sometimes drew sneers from outsiders for its alleged provincialism. Most historians accept that João was also a thoroughly sanctimonious monarch who thought kingship was enhanced by sumptuous displays of religious grandeur. But he was nonetheless a genuinely enthusiastic patron of Baroque art, architecture and music. He presided over a number of major civil engineering projects, formed libraries, supported learned academies and above all built grandiose religious monuments.[4] He was quite proficient in French, Italian and mathematics and had a collector's enthusiasm for books. On the other hand, there is nothing to suggest this king regarded contemporary political philosophy with anything but suspicion. He showed no inclination at all to stray beyond the traditional bounds of Portuguese Catholicism.

[1] NHP vol 7, p 200.
[2] Ibid, pp 202, 206–7.
[3] SHP vol 5, p 447.
[4] GE vol 14, pp 260–1.

In personal terms, the reign of João V can be divided into two unequal phases, the first lasting from the king's accession in late 1706 to 1742 and the second from 1742 until his death in 1750. For most of the first phase, João remained physically robust. He was eager to observe and learn, and early in his reign he apparently felt quite frustrated that his responsibilities prevented him from travelling to see the world. But he soon settled down and conscientiously applied himself to his kingly duties for some three and a half decades.[5] This long phase eventually came to an end in May 1742 when João suffered what appears to have been a stroke, which left him partly paralysed.[6] Though his condition subsequently improved, recovery was never complete. His capacity to make decisions was so seriously reduced that at times the central government seemed rudderless.[7] The problem was compounded by the death in 1747 of Cardinal da Mota, the long-serving chief minister, and by João's unwillingness to replace other secretaries of state who were now ageing and struggling to do their jobs. It was then that the king's secretary, the able Brazilian-born Alexandre de Gusmão, came to play an increasingly influential role in government, especially in the formulation of foreign policy.

João V finally died on 31 July 1750 and was succeeded by his oldest surviving son, King José I (1750–77). José was thirty-six when he ascended the throne, had long been married to Mariana Vitória, daughter of Felipe V of Spain, and already had four children. But he had virtually no experience in affairs of state since João had always excluded him from any meaningful political role. Nevertheless, on his accession José acted swiftly to reanimate the government, sweeping aside the by then dithering ministry of his father and appointing a team of his own. Soon one member of this team – the hitherto little-known Sebastião José de Carvalho e Melo – emerged as its dominant personality. Carvalho e Melo, a minor nobleman who had previously seen service as a diplomat, was already fifty-one years of age when José appointed him secretary of state for foreign affairs and war. We shall hear a lot more of this formidable minister in the next chapter.

The usual image of King José himself is that of a nonentity who displayed almost no interest in or capacity for administration. He has been called an 'idle voluptuary', a monarch who did little more than 'sign the papers presented to him' and a leader who preferred the opera or hunting to governing.[8] However, Joaquim Veríssimo Serrão has questioned these dismissive judgements, arguing that José did indeed display some talent, was well educated and took a genuine

---

[5] Boxer C R 1962, p 145.
[6] GE, p 262; SHP vol 5, pp 264–5.
[7] NHP vol 7, p 201.
[8] Maxwell K 1995, p 4; Cheke M 1938, p 38; Livermore H V 1966, p 215.

interest in government.[9] Always overshadowed in the historiography by his chief minister, it may be he has been ignored and disparaged too readily – and that what has been written about him has too often been based on the unreliable gossip of malignant contemporaries. Certainly, José's early decisions as king did much to revive a central government that had lost direction.

The splendour of the eighteenth-century Portuguese court in the years down to 1755, the long stability of the regime and the fact power was concentrated in the crown to a greater extent than ever before may be attributed to several factors. These included the firm entrenchment of a dynasty that through these years had no serious problems of succession, avoidance of involvement in any major European hostilities and the seemingly inexorable march towards Enlightened Despotism in continental Europe more generally. In addition, both João V and King José were temperamentally well suited to fulfilling the symbolic role required of them. Of course, there were other European monarchies of the period that displayed very similar characteristics. However, there was one respect in which the Portuguese case stood out as exceptional. This was the sudden inflow into the kingdom of wealth from the newly-discovered gold and diamond mines of Brazil. It was especially this fortuitous development that made the first half of the eighteenth century for Portugal an Age of gold and Baroque splendour.

GOLD, DIAMONDS AND JOÃO V

During the course of their worldwide expansion the Portuguese often dreamed of enriching themselves through the discovery and exploitation of precious metals: but, until the beginning of the eighteenth century, their success had been rather limited. Certainly the gold of São Jorge da Mina had made an impact on Portugal during the half century 1470–1520. But even at its peak the inflow of Mina gold had amounted to only about 1,500 to 1,800 marks per year – in round figures no more than about 400 kilograms.[10]

The earliest recorded intimation that Portugal might be entering a new age of gold dates from 1697, when the French ambassador reported that the equivalent of about 115 kilograms of the metal had arrived in Lisbon from Brazil.[11] By 1711 the annual amount of Brazilian gold legally shipped to Portugal had risen to almost 15,000 kilograms. In other words, imports had grown more than a hundred-fold in just fourteen years. Suddenly Portugal was receiving from its prize overseas possession far more gold than any other European

---

[9] SHP vol 6, pp 15–16.
[10] For Mina gold see ch 17.
[11] Pinto V N 1979, p 228.

imperial power had ever before extracted from a colony.[12] Legal gold imports into Lisbon eventually peaked at 30,112 kilograms in 1720. A gradual decline then set in; but annual consignments still averaged 18,000 to 20,000 kilograms over the next three decades, before a steeper fall commenced.[13] Of course, these figures are minimums only. They are gleaned from fragmentary sources, they take no account of smuggling and they certainly understate the quantities actually shipped – probably by substantial margins.[14] All guesstimates are just that; but according to João Lúcio de Azevedo, during the course of the entire eighteenth century gold worth approximately 100 million pounds sterling was transferred from Brazil to Portugal.[15]

This huge influx of gold provided a major boost to the Portuguese crown's revenue flow. Traditionally the crown was entitled to its royal fifth or *quinto* – a 20 per cent share of all precious metals production. It was for this reason that incoming Brazil fleets were sometimes referred to as 'ships of the fifths' or *naus dos quintos.*[16] The proportion of crown gold each fleet carried in the form of *quintos* varied considerably from year to year, from literally nothing to as much as 60 to 70 per cent.[17] However, the crown also benefited from private gold shipments, for these stimulated the importation of consumer goods, which in turn increased customs revenue.[18] In this way, during the first half of the eighteenth century, despite smuggling and other forms of evasion, direct and indirect revenue from gold came to account for a major share of crown receipts.

Brazilian gold, as well as serving to increase quite substantially the volume of Portugal's international trade, did much to change its pattern. The value of Portuguese exports and re-exports to Brazil increased fivefold in this era while trade with Europe grew even more and British dominance of the Portuguese market intensified.[19] The Anglo-Portuguese commercial treaties, the substantial degree of reciprocity between Portuguese and British trade commodities and Portugal's new ability to cover its balance of trade deficit with gold all helped to reinforce the closeness of Britain's embrace.

In the eighteenth century the tendency for gold to flow from Portugal into British hands was seemingly irresistible. This was partly because Britain, more than any other European power, maintained an exchange rate highly favourable to gold while Portugal, being relatively short of silver, did the opposite.

[12] Godinho V M 1968 vol 2, p 310.
[13] Ibid; Pinto V N 1979, pp 234–5; 248–53.
[14] Boxer C R 1969b, p 470; Pinto V N 1979, p 245.
[15] Azevedo J L de 1947, p 364.
[16] Ibid, p 339.
[17] Pinto V N 1979, p 248–53.
[18] Azevedo J L de 1947, p 370; HP vol 4, p 104.
[19] HP vol 4, p 104; Arruda J J de A 1991, p 389.

In 1734 and again in 1747 Lisbon revalued silver upwards in terms of gold.[20] Although exporting gold from Portugal was formally forbidden – and had been since at least the early fourteenth century – large quantities of the yellow metal in practice poured out. Most was carried off, with the connivance of Portuguese officials, either by British naval vessels or by the regular packet boats that sailed between Lisbon and Falmouth and that were exempt from customs inspection.[21] Probably between a half and three-quarters of all Brazilian gold reaching Portugal between 1700 and 1750 flowed on to England in this way.[22] Of course, Portugal also exported other products to Britain in these years, particularly wine. But there is no doubt that for the English gold was always the main attraction. It was Brazilian gold that enabled Portugal to pay for its rapidly growing imports of textiles, wheat, cod and other consumer goods. In the first decade of the eighteenth century alone, Portuguese imports from Britain increased by some 120 per cent – and the trade deficit widened by 238 per cent. The quantities imported were such that the Portuguese prices of some foreign consumer items actually fell.[23] Meanwhile, the import substitution policies introduced by Ericeira in the late seventeenth century having been abandoned, Portugal gradually slid towards chronic economic underdevelopment and dependency.

The mines of Brazil enabled Portuguese mints during the first half of the eighteenth century to produce an exceptionally pure and stable gold coinage – just as they had during the era of Mina gold some two hundred years before. This was a notable turnaround from the monetary disorganisation that prevailed in Portugal for much of the seventeenth century.[24] Eighteenth-century Portuguese gold coins like the *moeda* and *dobra* justifiably enjoyed great international prestige and were still being used in many foreign countries as late as the early nineteenth century.[25] Meanwhile, the strength of Portuguese state finances made it possible for João V to embark upon an ostentatious building program.

As the gold boom neared its peak at the end of the 1720s news began to reach Lisbon of the sensational discovery in Brazil of rich diamond deposits. At the time Europe's main source of diamonds was in southern India where Madras, controlled by the English EIC, had now superseded Goa as the principal point of outlet for the gems. The Madras diamond trade was handled by a small

[20] Pinto V N 1979, pp 309–10.
[21] Boxer C R 1969b, pp 458–9, 465–9; NHP vol 7, p 357; Shaw L M E 1998, p 102.
[22] Boxer C R 1969b, p 470; Sideri S 1970, p 50; Fisher H E S 1971, pp 92–4.
[23] Godinho V M 1968 vol 2, pp 306, 311–12; Sideri S 1970, p 44.
[24] NHP vol 7, pp 356, 359–60, 362–3.
[25] Boxer C R 1969b, p 471.

group of specialist gem merchants – until the sudden appearance of Brazilian diamonds shattered their hitherto secure and comfortable near-monopoly.[26] Neither the volume nor value of diamonds reaching Europe from Brazil in the first half of the eighteenth century can be established with any certainty. However, John Gore, a well-placed English diamond-dealer who came to play a key role in the Brazilian diamond trade as the Portuguese crown's expert adviser, claimed some 300,000 carats worth five million *cruzados* were imported into Lisbon in each of 1732 and 1733. This amounted to four times the value of diamonds imported to Europe at the time from India.[27] Clearly, the Brazilian diamond trade provided another significant new income flow to the Portuguese crown, though a lesser one than that generated by gold. In the course of the eighteenth century the crown's income from diamonds amounted to probably about 10 per cent of what it gained from gold.[28]

Though the sudden influx of diamonds into Lisbon was a welcome development to João V's government, it also created its own problems. The crown's usual marketing procedure was to sell the stones to international buyers after first selecting various choice specimens for itself. But it was difficult to sell into so sensitive a market without driving down prices – and preventing or at least minimising contraband was another big problem. As soon as Brazilian diamonds began to be traded, oversupply became apparent – and the crown responded by trying to impose controls on output. In 1734 mining for diamonds was strictly prohibited in Brazil, except for in a specially-designated 'diamond district'. Between 1740 and 1771 the right to mine in this district was let out exclusively to monopolist contractors.[29] These measures helped to establish a degree of stability, and the downward trend in prices slowed. Meanwhile, diamond consumption was successfully increased by encouraging sales not just to princes and the higher nobility – the traditional customer base – but to Europe's prosperous bourgeoisie.

Brazilian diamonds were sold on the European market through English and Dutch gem-dealers, who alone had the required knowledge and expertise. For long the standard procedure was to release the stones for sale to the dealers in lots, at carefully determined intervals. But from 1753 it was decided instead to sell through monopolist contractors, the first being the English firm of Bristow Ward.[30] Nevertheless, smuggling could not be eradicated despite the best efforts of the authorities, and perhaps as much as half of Brazil's production

---

[26] Furber H 1976, pp 260–1; Yogev G 1978, pp 91–102.
[27] Boxer C R 1962, p 224; Pinto V N 1979, p 214.
[28] Azevedo J L de 1947, p 364; NHP vol 7, p 271.
[29] Boxer C R 1962, pp 207–14; Pinto V N 1972, pp 216–17.
[30] Pinto V N 1972, pp 213, 219.

reached Europe by clandestine means. It is likely most of these illicit gems eventually found their way to London.[31]

As the era of gold and diamonds unfolded, so João V's reputation for wealth and generosity grew, spreading far and wide throughout Europe. He was said to be the richest monarch in Christendom. He was also frequently portrayed, both in his own time and later, as scandalously extravagant and wasteful. However, as Lúcio de Azevedo pointed out, both his opulence and his alleged irresponsible prodigality are often exaggerated. Although João did become quite wealthy, he was never fabulously so. The frequently cited claim that he dispensed gifts worth up to 200 million *cruzados* to various persons in Rome alone appears unfounded.[32] Certainly, he spent heavily on building churches and other economically unproductive monuments, on elaborate displays of pomp and on grants to clerics and courtiers. But he also used part of his increased revenues to reduce state debt.[33] Overall, the eighteenth-century Joanine regime practised fairly sound financial administration. It may not have been a model of brilliant economic management – but to dismiss it as incompetent or merely frivolous is nevertheless grossly misleading.[34]

POPULATION AND AGRICULTURE

At the Restoration of 1640 Portugal's population totalled between 1.5 and 2 million people. It probably rose slightly during the rest of the seventeenth century, then fell by about 5 per cent through the first three decades of João V's reign. The reasons for the fall are difficult to pinpoint but probably included increased emigration to Brazil stimulated by the gold discoveries, devastation in border areas during the War of the Spanish Succession and perhaps a succession of unusually cold years. In any event, from the early 1730s the trend went into reverse, and for the rest of the century Portugal's population steadily expanded.[35]

The most densely peopled regions of Portugal in the first half of the eighteenth century were Minho, the Beiras and Estremadura. Minho alone contained some 25 per cent of the country's inhabitants – on a bare 8 per cent of its land surface. By contrast, Alentejo remained sparsely peopled, its share of the total population declining even further during this period. Put another way, in 1706 some 80 per cent of Portugal's population lived north of the Tagus and

[31] Ibid, pp 218, 221; Yogev G 1978, p 122.
[32] Azevedo J L de 1947, pp 365–71.
[33] Ibid, pp 374–5.
[34] NHP vol 7, p 370.
[35] Ibid, pp 385–7, 395–7; HP vol 4, pp 52–6.

only 20 per cent in the south, while everywhere the coast tended to be more heavily peopled than the interior. The vast majority of Portuguese still lived in the countryside: only some 10 per cent lived in towns of 10,000 inhabitants or more – a slightly higher proportion than in France but less than in Holland. Lisbon was still easily Portugal's largest city; but its population actually declined in the first few decades of the eighteenth century, then rose again in line with overall trends. By 1756 it stood at about 135,000.[36]

Throughout this era Portugal was an overwhelmingly agricultural country, the vast majority of its people being peasants subsisting on smallholdings. They grew basic cereals – usually wheat, maize or rye – and tended vegetable patches, fruit trees, vines and increasingly olive groves. The traditional livestock, particularly sheep, goats, pigs and chickens, were reared almost everywhere. Crops and cultivation patterns varied from region to region: wheat predominated in the centre and south, but maize was now the staple in the northwest, where it was often grown under irrigation. Maize cultivation was also steadily spreading southwards, especially into Estremadura. Indeed, what some historians and geographers have referred to as the 'Maize Revolution' belongs especially to this period.[37] At the same time, the cultivation of olive trees was expanding northwards while viticulture, mainly to produce wine for local consumption, was intensifying throughout the country.

Differences in climate, terrain, population density and local tradition were responsible for contrasting sizes of typical agricultural units in the north and south, and variations in field types and rotation systems. In the humid, fertile northwestern corner, and along much of the north and central coasts, enclosed plots surrounded by trees or vines predominated. During the growing season these plots were intensively cultivated, often with the aid of irrigation. They were then turned over to pasture through the winters. In the drier central and southern regions open fields were the norm. Everywhere trees were highly valued, especially oak and chestnut in the north, cork and holm-oak in Alentejo. Apple and pear trees were ubiquitous, almonds, figs and carobs flourished in the Algarve and stone-fruits were grown mainly in Estremadura.[38] Overall, subsistence agriculture in Portugal gradually intensified in this period, especially in heavily peopled areas like Minho. But there were no sudden or dramatic changes.

Commercial agriculture in eighteenth-century Portugal presents a somewhat different picture. In the first place, its development continued to be hindered by institutional structures inherited from the past. Much land was tied up in entailed estates and some in the hands of the church. Moreover, most properties

---

[36] HP vol 4, pp 54–6, 63–4.
[37] Ibid, pp 74–5, 77–8.
[38] Ibid, p 77.

were not directly worked by their owners. Instead, whether they were *concelhos,* noble seigneurs, ecclesiastical institutions, members of the royal family or the crown itself, owners farmed their lands out to tenants, usually under leasehold or emphyteusis. Tenants paid their landlords in kind or in a combination of kind and money. Often this involved handing over a set proportion of the harvest or perhaps just a fixed amount. In some cases landlords prescribed what was to be grown, although contractual arrangements of this kind were increasingly seen as too restrictive. Although land was generally held to be a desirable investment, it was also frequently acquired for reasons of social prestige. Also many properties were not only let, but sublet. In short, a rentier mentality prevailed – which meant there was relatively little interest from owners in improving land management or fostering innovative development.[39]

Nevertheless, the first half of the eighteenth century was a period of quite strong growth in Portugal's commercial agriculture sector. But it was uneven growth and in some respects disturbingly distorting in its impact. Wheat continued to be grown, but mainly as a subsistence rather than a commercial crop. Most commercial farmers found it more profitable to cultivate crops other than cereals, or to graze sheep and cattle. Investment in vines was said to return up to four times more than the same investment in wheat.[40] Wheat could often be imported into the coastal cities more cheaply than it could be supplied by domestic producers.[41] Therefore, despite the growing demand for flour and much concern about shortages, commercial production fell by some 25 per cent in the half century from 1730. In the same period wheat imports rose by 85 per cent, and by the late eighteenth century three-quarters of Lisbon's wheat supply came from overseas.[42]

However, although Portugal's domestic wheat industry was seriously ailing, other areas of commercial agriculture were faring much better. Olives and olive oil, cork and cork objects, traditional orchard fruits and dried fruits were all quite buoyant. One relatively new commodity starting to make an impact was the sweet orange (*citrus sinensis*) from China, now widely grown in the Algarve. While Seville oranges had been produced in southern Portugal for centuries, sweet oranges were introduced much later, most probably in the 1630s. But the new variety spread rapidly and in the eighteenth century was regularly exported to northern Europe, mainly from orchards around Faro and Monchique.[43] Of course, such an industry could not remotely compare,

[39] Ibid, pp 85–8.
[40] Schneider S 1971, p 38.
[41] Hanson C A 1981a, p 20.
[42] HP vol 4, pp 81–2.
[43] Ibid, p 78; SHP vol 5, pp 382–3; Magalhães J R 1993, pp 173–4; NHP vol 7, pp 258–9.

in magnitude of production or geographical spread, with Portuguese agriculture's clear front-runner: grape-growing for the burgeoning eighteenth-century wine industry.

THE WINE INDUSTRY AND THE PATTERNS OF OVERSEAS TRADE

Portuguese wine production grew approximately fivefold between 1670 and 1710 – an increase so spectacular that it seems reasonable to speak of a 'Revolution of the Vine'.[44] This revolution was made possible by simultaneous growth of demand in the domestic Portuguese market, the Brazilian market and the British market. The Portuguese market expanded steadily in almost all parts of the kingdom. This seems to have been partly because of increasing population but also reflected higher consumption per head. Demand was especially heavy in Lisbon and Porto, where sales were apparently boosted by a ban on importing the previously quite fashionable French wines. According to some accounts, the ban was contrived by the duke of Cadaval and the marquis of Alegrete – influential figures during the final years of Pedro II, who both had substantial interests in the Portuguese wine industry.[45] The strength of the Brazil market may be attributed to the colony's surging population growth and especially to the stimulus of gold. But it was in the British market that Portuguese wine exports registered their most spectacular growth.

Englishmen in the seventeenth century had consumed comparatively little Portuguese wine, being supplied mostly from France. As late as the 1680s the market for Portuguese wines in Britain was still quite modest, and imports averaged only about 120 tuns per year. But in 1689, when Britain was about to go to war with France, the British government banned the importation of French wines, so opening up a major opportunity for Portugal. Then in 1697 British import duties on Portuguese wines were lowered, creating a substantial tariff advantage. This advantage was subsequently entrenched by the Methuen commercial treaty of 1703. By then Portuguese wine exports to Britain had surged to 6,600 tuns a year, an enormous increase of some 5,500 per cent in just two decades.[46] Through the early eighteenth century the trade continued to grow. It received another hefty boost when war broke out between Britain and Spain in 1739 – and London promptly terminated Spanish wine imports. The consequence of all this was that Portugal achieved overwhelming dominance

[44] Sideri S 1970, p 46; NHP vol 7, pp 246–8.
[45] Godinho V M 1968 vol 2, p 306; NHP vol 7, p 254.
[46] Fisher H E S 1971, pp 26–7, 146; Shaw L M E 1998, pp 141–2.

in the British wine market. Portuguese wine shipments to Britain eventually peaked in the early 1740s at 13,100 tuns per year.[47]

It is against this background that the extraordinary growth in viticulture in eighteenth-century Portugal becomes more understandable. At the time it was often assumed, and much deplored, that in many areas of Portugal the vine was driving out wheat. This scenario was also until quite recent times widely accepted by agrarian historians. However, it is now realised that vineyards were extended for the most part into territory that had not previously been cultivated – or at least had not been under wheat. Where wheat was displaced, it was more likely to be by maize or the grazing of livestock than by vines.[48] New areas developed specifically to supply the British wine market were hardly ever converted wheat-lands. Also, while the expansion of viticulture was widespread and occurred almost everywhere in Portugal, it was particularly heavily concentrated in the Upper Douro Valley in the hinterland of Porto. This was a region not previously much noted for its wines, although vineyards had existed there since at least the twelfth century.[49]

Until the final years of the seventeenth century, the British tended to buy their Portuguese wines mostly from Ribatejo or from the more fertile regions of the north. So-called 'Red Portugal', a wine resembling Burgundy that was made from grapes grown in Minho, was particularly appreciated. It was normally exported through Viana do Castelo.[50] At this time the English import-export merchants in Porto comprised what was still quite a small community. This community had been dealing mostly in Brazilian sugar and tobacco, which were exchanged for textiles, cereals, cod and hardware. However, by the 1670s the English had established their own plantation colonies in the Caribbean and no longer required much sugar or tobacco from Brazil. So the factory in Porto, casting around for an alternative Portuguese export to exploit, began to look seriously at the Upper Douro region as a potential source of quality wine.[51]

The Upper Douro begins some sixty to seventy kilometres inland from Porto. At this stage of its course the river flows through mountains and is flanked by high gorges of granite and schist. The walls of the valley are often steep, the brown soils crumbling and stony and the whole area subject to hot dry summers and cold wet winters. To make the valley productive much laborious terracing was required. Before the English merchants began to show an interest in the

[47] Fisher H E S 1971, pp 28, 146; Schneider S 1971, p 32; HP vol 4, pp 102–3; NHP vol 7, p 255.
[48] HP vol 4, pp 82–3.
[49] Ibid, pp 76–7; NHP vol 7, p 248.
[50] Macaulay R 1946, pp 230–1.
[51] Schneider S 1971, p 25.

region, the Upper Douro had never produced much wine for export; but it was the nearest wine-producing country to Porto, and it was linked to that city by water. English merchants from the Porto factory, having recognised the area's strategic value, began to buy up its vintages and to encourage more vine plantings. Growers responded enthusiastically, and an infrastructure for transporting, processing and marketing the wine was established by the factory. Soon the merchants began fortifying the wine with brandy, producing a rich product with a high alcohol content that rapidly found favour with British customers – though it was seldom drunk by the Portuguese. Moreover, this fortified wine could be transported by sea without deteriorating in quality. So by 1715 the pattern of the Anglo-Portuguese wine trade had radically changed. Two-thirds of Portuguese wine exported to Britain now flowed out through Porto, and by the 1720s this had further increased to about three-quarters. Almost overnight, port wine – the wine of the Upper Douro, exported through Porto – had gained the lion's share of the British market.[52]

Portuguese wine production continued to expand and to enjoy prosperity through the first three-and-a-half decades of the eighteenth century. However, in the mid-1740s demand began to falter, and in the 1750s it spiralled in precipitate decline. The Portuguese domestic market had become saturated, and the Brazilian market proved unable to sustain growth when gold production fell. During the same years sales to Britain dropped by about 20 per cent and the price per tun declined sharply.[53] The Upper Douro was particularly hard hit by the downturn – and its difficulties intensified when British buyers began to look for cheaper grapes from other parts of northern Portugal. Many growers now faced ruin while hundreds of vineyard workers were thrown into poverty.[54] As we shall see in the next chapter, the Portuguese government eventually responded in the 1750s with a complete re-structuring of the industry.

While wine was easily metropolitan Portugal's most important export in the first half of the eighteenth century, it was only one element in a broader pattern of external trade. The pattern was made up of two main streams that consisted of trade with Portugal's own overseas possessions and trade with other European countries. As regards the first stream, in 1700 Portugal's colonial trade was conducted overwhelmingly with Brazil. Apart from wine, the Brazilian colonists imported Portuguese olive oil and a wide range of products supplied indirectly by the British and other foreigners. These products included dried cod, wheat and various manufactured goods such as textiles and hardware. In general, the Brazil export trade was lucrative, with many commodities being sold in Portuguese

---

[52] Ibid, pp 14, 19–33.
[53] Ibid, pp 33–4, 39; Fisher H E S 1971, p 78; HP vol 3, pp 80–8.
[54] Schneider S 1971, pp 39–40; NHP vol 7, pp 256–7.

America for double or more their European prices. Portugal received in return from Brazil chiefly sugar, tobacco and hides, plus Spanish American silver acquired through Buenos Aires. The value of these imports substantially exceeded that of Portuguese exports to Brazil. However, since most colonial products were subsequently re-exported the imbalance was not a matter for great concern.[55]

In the course of the first half of the eighteenth century, gold and diamonds had a major impact on the Luso-Brazilian trade relationship, virtually doubling the value of the colony's exports to the metropolis. Meanwhile, growing Portuguese emigration to Brazil and the extension of settlement into its interior progressively increased the size of the Brazilian market. Over fifty years, Brazil came to take as much as 80 to 90 per cent of Portugal's colonial trade.[56] However, much of this business was indirectly controlled by British merchants, who provided most of the manufactured goods and employed Portuguese – the so-called *comissários volantes* – as their commercial agents. The British dominated the Brazil trade as an extension of their trade with Portugal and throughout the period were easily the Portuguese world's principal commercial partner. As we have seen, the reasons were partly political, being related to the Anglo-Portuguese alliance. However, it is also true that the British and Luso-Brazilian economies were in many respects reciprocal, each producing goods complementary to the other. There was less reciprocity between the Luso-Brazilian economy and the economies of the two European powers that exerted the next most influence upon Portugal – France and Spain.[57]

Not only was Portugal too closely tied to one European trading partner during the first half of the eighteenth century, but it was also excessively dependent on just one metropolitan export commodity, making it particularly vulnerable to market fluctuations. For almost the whole half century wine comprised 80 per cent or more of Portugal's exports to Britain. British exports to Portugal were somewhat more varied; but textiles nevertheless usually made up about 70 per cent of the total.[58] The balance of trade, always strongly in Britain's favour, was still inexorably widening. In the first decade of the eighteenth century British exports to Portugal rose by 120 per cent while Portuguese exports to Britain rose by only 40 per cent. The difference, of course, was made up in Brazilian gold.[59] In short, the pattern established in Portugal's external trade – the failure to diversify beyond a few basic agricultural products, over-concentration on a single European market and a growing trade

---

[55] NHEP vol 7, pp 66–7; HP vol 4, p 100.
[56] Fisher H E S 1971, p 31; HP vol 4, p 104.
[57] Fisher H E S 1971, pp 35–6; HP vol 4, pp 105–6.
[58] Fisher H E S 1971, pp 15–19, 28; HP vol 4, pp 101, 103, 107.
[59] Sideri S 1970, pp 41, 44.

deficit – could be tolerated only as long as the flow of gold was maintained. When from the late 1750s that flow trended sharply downwards, the situation became unsustainable and made painful change inevitable.

Although Portugal grew increasingly dependent on British industrial imports during the first half of the eighteenth century the kingdom was not totally bereft of manufacturing. Ericeira's import substitution program may have been abandoned; but enough nonetheless happened in the sector for some historians, most notably Jorge Borges de Macedo, to discern a minor revival in the 1720s and 1730s. This revival embraced the silk, leather, glassware, iron, paper, wool and shipbuilding industries.[60] Some of these enterprises were survivors from the Ericeira years – particularly the textile works at Covilhã, to which João V granted a contract for the provision of military uniforms.[61] Another industrial enterprise that received government backing was the so-called royal silk factory (*real fábrica das sedas*) established in Lisbon in the 1730s. This entity was founded on the initiative of some French entrepreneurs working in association with several Portuguese collaborators. Having received a generous monopoly, they constructed quite an elaborate plant in which priority was given to using Portuguese raw silk – and to training and employing a Portuguese work-force. Nevertheless, the enterprise always struggled and by 1750 was effectively bankrupt.[62]

Manufacturing in Portugal was perennially hampered in this period by a chronic lack of competent entrepreneurship and by the suspicious reluctance of would-be investors to risk money in the sector. However, a wide range of cottage industries did continue to operate successfully in many parts of the kingdom. These industries were sometimes associated with particular regions or communities and were usually heavily dependent on female labour. For instance, in parts of the Algarve esparto grass and palm leaves were used to make a range of useful articles, including brooms, baskets and fishing-gear. Though such items were produced mainly for domestic use, some were exported to Spain and even to northern Europe.[63] Finally, under João V the crown promoted and helped to finance a series of major building projects. These undertakings often involved large work-forces and sometimes required advanced engineering and technical skills. A huge aqueduct was constructed to bring fresh water to Lisbon, and the royal arsenal, gunpowder factory and mint were all substantially rebuilt. Other projects included the deepening of the

---

[60] Macedo J B de 1982, p 72.
[61] Sousa A C de 1946–55 vol 8, p 143.
[62] Macedo J B 1982, pp 70–1; 255–61; Maxwell K 1973, p 51; HP vol 4, pp 89, 91; NHP vol 7, pp 298–9.
[63] Magalhães J R 1993, pp 216–18.

River Tagus, a significant road-construction program and the building or enlargement of several palaces.[64]

EIGHTEENTH-CENTURY JOANINE ABSOLUTISM

The revival of Portuguese colonial trade, plus the massive inflow of gold and diamonds from Brazil, meant João V was far better off financially than any of his Bragança predecessors. This circumstance – which was not replicated in other contemporary European monarchies – bestowed on the Portuguese crown the crucial advantage of fiscal autonomy, enabling João to by-pass traditional consultative procedures. In effect, it provided him with the material means to maintain a royal autocracy. But how far he actually moved in that direction is a different matter.

When João V became king Portugal's central government still maintained its formal conciliar structure, as in Habsburg and early Bragança times. There were four consultative councils: the council of state (*conselho de estado*), the council of war (*conselho de guerra*), the overseas council (*conselho ultramarino*) and the treasury council (*conselho da fazenda*). These were slow-moving bodies with rather formalised decision-making procedures. Almost all their members were recruited from the higher nobility and clergy, many of whom simultaneously held important offices in the palace. During the early years of João V's reign the most prestigious of the councils, the council of state, numbered among its members the long-lived Dom Nuno Álvares Pereira de Melo, first duke of Cadaval (1638–1727), and several marquises and counts.[65] Like all the Portuguese councils it was heavily factionalised.

However, as João V gained in experience he began to rely less on his councils and more on bureaucrats and small ad hoc committees. He turned especially to the office-holder through whose hands most central government business now passed – the secretary of the council of state, who soon came to be referred to simply as 'secretary of state' (*secretário de estado*). In this way João's style of government became less broadly consultative, more focused on executive efficiency and more ministerial. The royal councils, meeting with decreasing frequency, gradually became marginalised – and the influence of great nobles declined or at least grew less obvious. Significantly, Secretary of State Diogo de Mendonça Corte Real, who was at João's elbow for the first three decades of the reign, was not a *grande*. He was a minor nobleman from the provinces, a trained lawyer and an experienced diplomat.[66]

---

[64] Sousa A C de vol 8 1946–55, pp 136–45.
[65] NHP vol 7, pp 42–5.
[66] Ibid, pp 44–7.

The death of Corte Real in 1736 appears to have been the trigger for another significant re-structuring of central government. Three secretaries of state were now appointed, each tied to what amounted to a specific portfolio: foreign affairs and war (*negócios estrangeiros e guerra*), naval and colonial affairs (*marinha e ultramar*) and internal affairs (*negócios do reino*). Strictly speaking these secretaries of state did not wield executive powers, but to all intents and purposes they controlled matters within their respective spheres, as trusted royal advisers. The man behind the reform was an erudite Jesuit-trained theologian, João da Mota e Silva (1691–1747), whom the pope had appointed a cardinal in 1726 at João's request.[67] Cardinal da Mota soon became effectively João V's chief minister, while his brother, Pedro da Mota e Silva, was appointed secretary of state for internal affairs. The other two secretaryships went to experienced professionals: Marco António Azevedo Coutinho (foreign affairs and war) and António Guedes Pereira (naval and colonial affairs). The quasi-ministerial system set up in 1736 weakened further the old consultative tradition, laying the foundations for the rule of Pombal in the late eighteenth century.[68] It also brought more stability, for João tended to treat his key appointments as permanent.

European absolutist regimes often focused heavily on strengthening their military and security apparatuses. They were also inclined to see state-building and army-building as complementary – and to regard conflict with others as normal, perhaps even sometimes beneficial.[69] However, eighteenth-century Joanine Portugal did not conform to this model. João V pursued a generally peaceful foreign policy, designed to preserve Portuguese neutrality within Europe. The only real exception occurred during the War of the Spanish Succession(1701–13), which João entered briefly, with considerable reluctance and under heavy British pressure. He also sent naval forces to the eastern Mediterranean in 1715 and 1717 to support multi-national Christian operations against the Ottoman Turks. But these decisions were little more than demonstrations of his desire to impress Rome, of his personal religious convictions and of his instinct for the theatrical. A threat of renewed hostilities with Spain some twenty years later (1734–5) caused the mobilisation of troops on the Castilian border, but diplomacy averted any actual hostilities.[70] In this period, there was therefore no significant Portuguese military activity in Europe.

However, João V's government did pay some attention during the early years of his reign to military re-organisation. The now antiquated *terço* was

---

[67] DIHP vol 2, p 10.
[68] HP vol 4, pp 176–80; NHP vol 7, pp 48–9.
[69] Christensen S T (ed) 1990, pp 11, 18, 27, 40, 43.
[70] NHP vol 7, pp 134–5.

replaced as the basic military unit by specialist infantry and cavalry regiments. On paper it was decided Portugal should have an army of 30,000 men – although the number of actual effectives fell well short of this. More crucially, such reforms as were carried out did little in practice to enhance the power of the monarchy, either internally or externally.[71] As in the past, senior military commands were filled by prominent nobles – and there is no indication that much was done in Joanine Portugal to bring about officer professionalisation.[72] In short, João V does not look like a monarch seriously dedicated to military absolutism.

In assessing any system of government it is prudent to take informal networks and relationships into account as well as formal structures. Recent studies of a number of European monarchies in the early eighteenth century have shown just how important personal ties could often be. In particular, in this era patron-client bonds frequently underlay and sometimes undermined more formal arrangements and hierarchies.[73] So it was that at João V's court rival networks and factions strove to entrench themselves, their noble leaders contesting for position behind the scenes. Intrigue was endemic, and seemingly innocuous palace offices were among the most highly-valued and jealously-guarded prizes to which a great nobleman could aspire. When João V ascended the throne, the marquises of Marialva and Alegrete both held palace offices which entitled them to 'golden keys' to the royal bedchamber. These prized keys had been given to them by Pedro II; but when the two noblemen offered them back to João V he graciously refused to accept them, saying he desired both *grandes* to continue to have access to him. Likewise the duke of Cadaval in his capacity as *mordomo-môr* held a special key which allowed him entry into the chambers of both the king and the queen. A palace intimate throughout Pedro II's reign, Cadaval was also allowed by João V to keep his ceremonial offices and his key.[74]

The palace privileges enjoyed by *grandes* like Cadaval, Marialva and Alegrete were far more than just ornamentalist. On the contrary, through daily proximity to the king in person they bestowed active membership of the innermost circle of power, brought access to confidential information and provided many vital opportunities to exert influence.[75] Intimate palace officials, who were almost invariably great nobles, could support petitions, speak up for their friends and allies, advise and lobby. The extent of their influence vis-à-vis

[71] Ibid, pp 145–6.
[72] SHP vol 5, pp 262, 263.
[73] Henshall N 1992, pp 46–7.
[74] Sousa A C de 1946–55 vol 8, p 9; SHP vol 5, p 136.
[75] NHP vol 7, p 37.

formal state office-holders is difficult to measure; but in Joanine Portugal it was certainly real, and probably considerable. Of course, certain important *grandes* held multiple or serial offices in both the government and the palace. When Cadaval eventually died in 1725 at the age of eighty-seven he had served as *mordomo-môr* to two queens, long sat on the council of state, presided over the *desembargo do paço* and acted as military chief-of-staff.[76] Some palace intimates, male and female, were also linked into international networks of influence. This especially applied in the households of successive queens, for Pedro II, João V and José I had all married foreign brides.[77] What is quite clear is that every Portuguese monarch of this era had to distribute palace offices with great care, with an eye to maintaining balance and stability.[78] Even in the first half of the eighteenth century, it was still prudent to humour great noblemen and mighty clerics – and never take them for granted.

João V's absolutism appears to have been at its most unambiguous in relation to the church. He repeatedly pressured the papacy into granting him concessions to enhance his royal prestige, securing a major triumph in 1710 when Clement XI agreed to create the patriarchate of Lisbon. To accommodate this move the archdiocese of Lisbon was divided into two, and the new patriarch was made archbishop of the western division. Thirty years later the two divisions were reunited under a single archbishop, who thenceforth always carried the title of cardinal-patriarch.[79] João was also firmly insistent that papal legates accredited to Lisbon must be raised to the cardinalate, as were those sent to France, Austria and Spain. When the Vatican demurred, Portugal severed diplomatic relations (1728–31), forcing Rome to back down.[80]

João was undoubtedly a pious Catholic king in the Portuguese tradition; but he was also an uncompromising regalist, highly sensitive to any encroachments on his prerogatives. On several occasions he refused to allow the Portuguese clergy exemptions to which they strongly considered they were entitled. In particular, he insisted that they contribute to the special tax imposed to finance the Lisbon aqueduct. When the cardinal-patriarch threatened to retaliate by imposing an interdict, João ended the argument by simply declaring he would use his kingly powers 'granted by God' to lift it.[81] Nevertheless, provided the church paid due deference to the crown and did not stray outside what the king considered to be its proper sphere, it could normally count on strong royal

---

[76] Ibid, pp 38–40; SHP vol 5, pp 136–7.
[77] NHP vol 7, pp 41–2.
[78] Ibid, pp 37–8.
[79] Oliveira M de 1968, pp 309–11.
[80] Miller S J 1978, pp 35–6.
[81] NHP vol 7, p 92.

support. Great ecclesiastical institutions continued to operate as they had for generations. The Inquisition in particular, although its influence had waned since its seventeenth-century heyday, remained a formidable force – and hundreds of persons continued to be processed through its courts. Between 1734 and 1743 fifty-one victims were relaxed and burned.[82] At the same time individual churchmen were numbered among João's closest advisers. Cardinal da Mota was effectively his chief minister from 1736 to 1746, and the Franciscan canon lawyer Frei Gaspar de Encarnação (1685–1752) later filled the same role.

João V tends to be seen as an archetypal eighteenth-century absolutist monarch, more or less on the model of Louis XIV of France (1643–1715).[83] Indeed, just as Louis was called 'Le Roi Soleil', so João V was sometimes referred to as Portugal's 'Rei Sol'. Yet neither monarch actually wielded anything like unlimited power. Louis XIV's kingship was heavily circumscribed by hallowed notions of natural justice and by his subjects' traditional rights and liberties – and these could not be simply swept aside.[84] Similarly, although João V's Portugal displayed many characteristics of an absolutist state, and João himself was a relatively powerful Portuguese monarch, he was not particularly autocratic. The style of government that prevailed in eighteenth-century Joanine Portugal retained much that was traditional – and there was as yet little hint of the Pombaline upheavals that were to come. João V possessed many of the trappings, and some of the substance, of absolute government. But he was never an unmitigated despot.

BAROQUE CULTURE AND THE ROYAL COURT

The absolutist monarchies of Old Regime Europe had a fondness for ostentatious ceremonial that sometimes verged on the operatic. Louis XIV's Versailles set the standard for this kind of thing with its splendid masques, glittering processions and veritable obsession with elaborate etiquette – all enacted on a vast Baroque stage.[85] João V, an ardent admirer of Louis XIV, likewise espoused ceremonial and well understood how invaluable appearances could be for projecting a royal image.[86] At the Portuguese court, when the king dressed, went to Mass, took his meals, held audience, went out hunting, attended a bullfight or performed any one of numerous other public acts,

[82] Torres J V 1978, pp 57–60; NHP vol 7, pp 92, 108–9. Cf. MHP, pp 401–2.
[83] SHP vol 5, p 193; NHP vol 7, p 12. For examples of similar comments by English-speaking historians see Beloff M 1954, p 200; Livermore H V 1966, p 205.
[84] Henshall N 1992, pp 1–2, 176–7.
[85] Ibid 1992, p 38.
[86] NHP vol 7, pp 31–2.

ritualised procedures were followed. Everything was deliberately theatricised.[87] Joanine pomp and display was especially extravagant at formal embassies and receptions and when commemorating anniversaries and rites of passage within the royal family. Particularly lavish were the celebrations marking the king's marriage to Maria Ana of Austria in 1708, which were preceded by a splendid embassy to Vienna earlier in the year.[88]

The Arts, of which João V was a generous patron, were likewise directed to the regime's service. Music, portraits, medals, historical literature, even sermons – all were utilised to promote an image of royal grandeur. But perhaps João's most impressive gesture in this direction was his founding in 1720 of a Royal Academy of History (*Academia Real de História*). The principal objectives of this body were to research and record the history of Portugal and its empire and demonstrate the dynasty's achievements.[89] The academy, which had fifty members nearly all of whom were nobles and clerics, held regular meetings, sponsored scholarly writings and sought out, identified and preserved historical documents.[90] One of its greatest achievements was to publish in 1741 António Caetano de Sousa's multi-volume and highly informative *História Genealógica da Casa Real Portuguesa*. While this compilation was in one sense an elaborate panegyric to João V and the house of Bragança, it was also a very substantial work of scholarship – and is still consulted by historians today.[91]

In Portuguese Baroque culture the monarchy itself was the principal object of attention and the king the supreme patron.[92] Lesser luminaries such as *grandes* and princes of the church were also part of the scene, but they played only supporting roles. Baroque displays mirrored the traditional social order and helped to reinforce privilege – and Joanine court nobles tended to be among the culture's keenest supporters.[93] Nevertheless, it was royal might and grandeur that took centre stage, being triumphantly proclaimed in monumental buildings, works of art and eulogistic writings. In this regard no other Portuguese monarch projected so resplendent an image as João V.[94] It is still possible to catch a glimpse of this splendour in the gorgeous *talha dourada* – the carved and gilt wood – that was one of its particular glories. *Talha dourada* had been used in Portugal since at least the late fifteenth century, mainly to

[87] Ibid, p 545.
[88] Sousa A C de 1946–55 vol 8, pp 24–6, 28–34; NHP vol 7, p 36.
[89] SHP vol 5, p 426.
[90] Sousa A C de 1946–55 vol 8, pp 134–8.
[91] SHP vol 5, pp 426–8. João V's praises are particularly extolled in Sousa A C de 1946–55 vol 8, pp 136–80.
[92] On representational culture see Blanning T C W 2002, pp 6–7.
[93] NHP vol 7, p 33.
[94] Delaforce A 2002, pp 1–2.

beautify church interiors. At first applied with relative restraint, it gradually became more lavish, culminating in the magnificent 'golden churches' of the late seventeenth and early eighteenth centuries. Altar pieces, screens, choir stalls, pulpits, sometimes entire walls and ceilings were decorated or redecorated with such splendour that even today, when first seen, they often take the onlooker's breath away.[95]

Monumental architecture was a Joanine specialty, and the two greatest projects of the age were the conversion of the chapel-royal into a patriarchal cathedral and the construction of a vast church-monastery-palace complex at the small village of Mafra, some forty kilometres northwest of Lisbon. The patriarchal cathedral – begun in 1717, completed in 1746 and then destroyed in the great Lisbon earthquake nine years later – was planned on a massive scale and received lavish amounts of attention and money.[96] Mafra, which was also initiated in 1717, began ostensibly as a votive offering for the birth of Joao's first heir, Princess Maria Bárbara. But it also fulfilled the royal desire for a majestic country residence set in tranquil surroundings. João V took an impassioned personal interest in both these projects, frequently visiting the sites and reviewing their progress. Mafra was originally conceived on a relatively modest scale, but when eventually completed in 1730 had become the greatest single building project of the Portuguese eighteenth century.[97] It was the work of the Italian-trained German architect Johann Friedrich Ludwig (1670–1752), known in Portugal as Ludovice. He was backed by a team of Italian builders and a huge local work force that may at one stage have reached 50,000. The outcome was a massive square structure like the great Baroque abbeys of Germany and Austria. It comprised basilica, monastery and two vast wings of palace, so constructed as to represent the monarchy enveloping and protecting the church. Within its rather austere walls lay rich interiors, lavishly embellished with marble and a splendid array of sculptures and religious paintings.[98] Always more symbolic than functional, Mafra illustrated – in the words of Vítor Serrão – a 'theory of state'.[99]

João V's next major project was a highly practical one – the construction of an aqueduct to bring fresh water to the city of Lisbon. Built in 1731–9, this aqueduct solved a long-standing supply problem and was of great public utility. The project was bold and ambitious – and its scale and grace remain impressive

---

[95] Smith R C 1968, pp 127–31; NHP vol 7, pp 596–8.
[96] Delaforce A 2002, pp 180–203.
[97] Ibid, p 203.
[98] Delaforce A 2002, pp 203–15; Smith R C 1968, pp 101–3; SHP vol 5, pp 259–62; NHP vol 7, pp 587–92.
[99] NHP vol 7, p 591.

to this day. The principal channel was almost twenty kilometres long, but the aqueduct's greatest glory was its spectacular bridging of the Alcântara valley. Huge Gothic arches – the tallest almost sixty-five metres high – carried the pipeline into Lisbon, simultaneously supporting a public walkway. Primarily the work of the architect-engineers Manuel da Maia (1677–1766) and Custódio Vieira (1690–1744), the Lisbon aqueduct was a spectacular achievement for its age.[100]

Of the many other construction projects of João V's reign those that stand out most are the refurbishing of the River Palace, the building of the royal library at the University of Coimbra and installation of the chapel of São João Baptista in the church of São Roque. All three projects were largely exercises in interior design and decoration. The refurbishment of the palace, to which João gave his highest priority during the early stages of his reign, was comprehensive; but the building was later completely destroyed in the 1755 earthquake.[101] The library at Coimbra was a relatively simple single-storey building with three grandiose chambers. Lavishly decorated with *talha dourada* and pink and blue marble, it was probably designed by the Frenchman Claude Joseph Laprade (1682–1738), but was nevertheless quintessentially Portuguese Baroque. The São João Baptista chapel, with its sumptuous marble, ormolu and semi-precious stones, was built in Rome to João V's order. Blessed by the pope, it was transported to Lisbon in sections and re-assembled at São Roque. As Saramago has remarked, it is hard to imagine anyone talking to God about poverty in this magnificent jewel of the Joanine era.[102]

João V was not only a keen builder, but an avid collector of artworks. He spent lavishly on paintings, sculptures, tapestries, furniture, jewellery and scale models of buildings. In 1726, he purchased a particularly outstanding collection of paintings, mainly by Flemish and Dutch masters. This collection, originally accumulated by Dom Luís da Cunha (1662–1749), an urbane and highly-experienced Portuguese diplomat, included works by Rembrandt, Raphael, Titian, Rubens, Anthony van Dyck and Jan Breughel. João also acquired scores of paintings through his regular buyers and agents in France, Italy and elsewhere in Europe. Unfortunately many of these paintings, as well as other artworks, were destined to be lost in the 1755 earthquake.[103] However, those housed at Mafra survived – among them numerous marble reliefs and statues that João had ordered from Rome.[104]

---

[100] Ibid, pp 594–5; Smith R C 1968, pp 102–3; SHP vol 5, pp 258–9.
[101] Delaforce A 2002, pp 33–5.
[102] Smith R C 1968, pp 102–3; NHP vol 7, pp 602–3; Saramago J 2002, p 344.
[103] Sousa A C de 1946–55 vol 8, p 150; DA vol 25, pp 635–6.
[104] Smith R C 1968, pp 165–6; DA vol 25, p 301.

Like many of the Braganças, João V was extremely fond of music. He also delighted in most forms of drama. The king's passion for music, and his willingness to spend lavishly on it, meant Lisbon became for a while one of the finest musical centres in Europe.[105] The transformation of the chapel-royal into a patriarchal church created a first-class venue for sacred music. Profane music was much enhanced by the introduction of grand opera in 1731. Instrumentalists and singers, including *castrati,* were imported from Rome, and numerous operas, most by the Italian composer and librettist Pietro Metastasio (1698–1782), were performed.[106] Eventually, João built a court opera house, although it did not open its doors until 1753. Today the opera house has disappeared – another casualty of earthquake. But it is still possible to glimpse something of the theatricality of Joanine court life by visiting the national museum of coaches in Belém. This museum contains the three splendid vehicles used by João V's ambassador to Rome, the marquis of Abrantes, for his state entry into that city in 1716. Carved and gilded like rich Baroque interiors, the coaches represented 'Conquest', 'Navigation' and 'Commerce', respectively – that is, they symbolised and celebrated the achievements of João's forebears in the great Age of Expansion.[107]

Although various elements of Joanine court culture stemmed from Portuguese national tradition, others were clearly derived from the outside, mostly from Italy or France. This was possible because Joanine Portugal commanded the means to acquire cultural assets and expertise on the international market, just as it had the capacity to import foodstuffs and manufactures. There was therefore not only growing economic dependency on Britain, but significant cultural dependency on the Italians and French, particularly at the elite level. This cultural dependency was apparent in the visual and performing arts and in various aspects of everyday life. Elite Portuguese imported from France many of their material needs: personal attire, wigs, jewellery, gold watches, cosmetics and toiletries. French bookshops steadily multiplied in Lisbon, while fashionable preachers imitated the French style of public-speaking. Even traditional Portuguese ceramics were discarded in favour of foreign imports.[108] These tendencies helped to draw Portugal into the European mainstream; but they also tended to stifle rather than nurture Portuguese creativity.

However, one undeniable Portuguese characteristic of the culture of João's court was its ostentatious religiosity. João V was an adamant regalist; but he did not share the increasingly secular values of some other European rulers.

---

[105] Boxer C R 1969, p 359.
[106] NHP vol 7, pp 513–14.
[107] Delaforce A 2002, pp 135–43.
[108] DA vol 25, p 310; NHP vol 7, pp 503, 545, 550.

On the contrary, he always maintained a firm commitment to the Catholic faith and to maintaining its traditions as he understood them. He had a strong personal preference for ceremonial with ecclesiastical overtones, and during his reign a court etiquette was developed closely associated with the church calendar. He enjoyed nothing more than visiting a holy shrine or place of pilgrimage, and it is probably fair to say that he was addicted to religious festivals.[109] João regularly attended divine services, frequently entered convents to observe their liturgy and music, observed autos da fé and generously patronised sundry religious occasions. He also supported an extensive program of church-building, created the Lisbon patriarchate and finally accepted from a grateful pope in 1748 the splendid-sounding title of Most Faithful (*Fidelíssimo*). Some historians have dismissed João's religiosity as thoroughly anachronous for an eighteenth-century monarch, and his brand of Catholicism has been labelled 'almost cretinous'.[110] But such judgements seem to both misunderstand his motives and underrate his intelligence.

João V focused more on the form of Catholicism than its substance; he loved the beauty of holiness. As his contemporary Caetano de Sousa noted, he displayed his piety through such undertakings as the creation of Mafra.[111] But while João clearly appreciated the value of religious display for reinforcing royal power, he seems to have lacked the more profound religious sensitivity of some of his Avis and even his Habsburg predecessors. In 1715, he learned that a thief had broken into the sanctuary of the Jesuit church at Setúbal and stolen the sacred vessel containing the host. He responded by leading the court and chapter in a procession of mourning, but otherwise continued as normal.[112] By contrast João III, when confronted back in 1552 by a sacrilegious outrage, had sunk into profound depression and was unable for a long period to conduct affairs of state.[113] It was the kind of internalising response of which João V was probably quite incapable.

Despite these traits, João V may reasonably be described as an Enlightened monarch of the Age of Reason. He was well educated and had developed a genuine interest in rational knowledge, being fascinated particularly by mathematics, geography and astronomy.[114] He established an astronomical observatory at the River Palace on the Tagus, at which an eclipse was carefully observed on 1 November 1724.[115] Technological processes of all kinds

---

[109] NHP vol 7, pp 33, 36; Sousa A C de 1946–55 vol 8, pp 60–1, 117, 130–1.
[110] Boxer C R 1969, p 357.
[111] Sousa A C de 1946–55 vol 8, p 136.
[112] Ibid, pp 138–9.
[113] See ch 9.
[114] Sousa A C de 1946–55 vol 8, pp 148–9.
[115] NHP vol 7, pp 561–2.

intrigued him, and he enjoyed observing such activities as coining and printing. Not only did he preside over a series of major engineering and construction projects, but he also welcomed scientists and inventors to his court. Among them were the celebrated 'flying padre' – the Brazilian-born Jesuit Bartolomeu Lourenço Gusmão, who in 1709 demonstrated a flying machine that actually ascended from the floor of the palace ballroom.[116]

Under João, practical programs of fieldwork in mineralogy, botany and cartography all received generous royal support. A museum of natural history was established at the River Palace, and it was during his reign that systematic efforts were commenced to survey and map the whole of Brazil.[117] Angela Delaforce's assertions that João V seemed a Maecenas of science in his own day, but that his patronage of research and experimentation has not been adequately recognised since, are surely justified.[118] João was also an avid collector-bibliophile who accumulated manuscripts, books, musical scores, drawings and prints, constantly purchasing such items through his diplomats and agents abroad. He built up a series of outstanding royal libraries in his various palaces. Finally, he appreciated the value of history, encouraged the formation and care of Portuguese depositories and arranged for various documents to be copied from the papal or other overseas archives.[119]

Despite all these activities and interests, João V and his circle displayed little sympathy for, and certainly minimal knowledge of, progressive political philosophy associated with the Enlightenment. Debating and exchanging ideas about society and government openly and freely, or conducting politics by public discussion, were largely alien to Portugal in the first half of the eighteenth century – as they were to most European countries other than Britain, Holland and to a lesser extent France. There are therefore clear limitations to João V's Enlightenment credentials. The impact of rational thought on Portuguese society in general, as opposed to the king and court in particular, was even more problematic.

THE ENLIGHTENMENT AND THE PORTUGUESE PUBLIC

Although literacy rates in Old Regime Portugal are difficult to determine, and the concept of literacy itself lacks precision, there is no doubt that knowledge of reading and writing was spreading quite rapidly in João V's time, particularly in urban areas. Most of the clergy, nobility and upper bourgeoisie were

[116] Ibid, pp 463, 558–9; DIHP vol 1, pp 305–6.
[117] Boxer C R 1962, pp 297–8.
[118] Delaforce A 2002, p 83.
[119] Ibid, pp 91–3, 98–9; NHP vol 7, p 534.

reasonably literate, although probably many nobles did not use their writing skills too frequently.

Literate Portuguese of this period could, if they chose, read books, newspapers, periodicals, pamphlets and calendars. The most widely circulating newspaper was the *Gazeta de Lisboa*, first published in 1715. This publication came out twice weekly and was maintained for four decades. Meanwhile, the number of books published locally during roughly the same period – fewer than 100 titles most years – was still quite modest. Comparable with contemporary Russia, it was far less than in a country like England: there, by the first decade of the century, over 2,000 titles were appearing annually. The Portuguese, like the Russians, were offered a fare heavily slanted towards devotional works. Some 60 per cent of books published in Portugal between 1715 and 1750 were on religious themes, while only 4 per cent were on scientific subjects.[120] Of course, a significant proportion of the books available in Portugal were imported from abroad – mainly from France, Spain, Italy, Holland and the Swiss states.[121]

There is little to suggest the press in Joanine Portugal catered for anything more than a strictly limited public. Nevertheless, the consumption of reading matter was increasing, and there was now enough demand to justify producing cheap pamphlet literature. Most of this material was of a religious nature, usually sermons by well-known preachers. Called *literatura de cordel*, it was clearly designed for less sophisticated readers. Meanwhile, the overall proportion of works published in Portuguese was also growing and by the late 1760s had reached about 54 per cent. Most of the remaining 46 per cent were in Latin or Spanish.[122] Although religious publications always predominated, there was a robust market for poetry and history, followed by philosophy, ethics and works of self-instruction and self-improvement. Curiosity about the natural sciences was rather more limited. However, it was sufficient for the Oratorian Teodoro de Almeida to be able to publish in 1751 his *Recreação Filosófica*, a massive ten-volume work designed to disseminate scientific knowledge.[123]

The growing number of literate women in Portugal in João V's reign seems to have scandalised some men, who duly cast their barbed aspersions on female intellectual capacity. The usually progressive Francisco Xavier de Oliveira, better known as the *cavaleiro* de Oliveira (1702–83) – who lived for many years in England where he was converted to Anglicanism – was thoroughly reactionary on this issue. An avowed universalist who considered women, Hottentots and Turks were all part of one human family, he nevertheless

[120] NHP vol 7, pp 492–3, 495, 508; Blanning T C W 2002, pp 137, 140–1.
[121] NHP vol 7, pp 504–5.
[122] Ibid, p 475.
[123] Ibid, pp 563–4.

compared a learned woman to a circus horse. On the other hand, the celebrated theologian and educational theorist Luís António Verney (1713–92) considered it irrational to suppose women were intellectually inferior to men. He thought that educating women would benefit the whole of society – particularly children.[124] Significantly, a substantial proportion of the small but active group of well-lettered women in João V's Portugal were nuns. Some 134 Portuguese literary works by female religious are known to have been published between 1701 and 1750.[125]

The availability of published material in eighteenth-century Joanine Portugal was rigorously controlled by the triple licensing system – at least in theory. No printed work could legally be issued without the formal sanction of the local bishop, the Inquisition and the crown censor. Imported books had to be declared on arrival and were admitted only after inquisitorial approval. The holy office maintained an index of banned heretical and indecent works; but it had not been updated since 1624.[126] Although determined readers could usually find ways of accessing what they wanted, there is little doubt that censorship seriously hindered the spread of progressive ideas – and therefore the development of an informed public.

An outdated and inadequate education system reinforced this negative situation. Formal schooling was left almost entirely to the church, and, as it had done for some 200 years, the Society of Jesus dominated the system at all levels. The universities at Coimbra and Évora, the only ones Portugal possessed, were both Jesuit institutions, and both in the first half of the eighteenth century remained profoundly influenced by Counter-Reformation doctrines. Although some Jesuits were genuinely learned, and the Society was by no means as unresponsive to rationalist thinking as is sometimes alleged, its standard pedagogy was too narrow and cautiously conservative.[127] Over the centuries little in Jesuit education seemed to have changed. The basic textbook used in the Society's primary schools during João V's reign was still Marcos Jorge's *Doutrina Christam,* a work originally published in 1561. Almost as antiquated, the standard Latin grammar for secondary schools dated from 1572.[128]

The Oratorians, who arrived in Portugal in the late seventeenth century, offered the only serious educational competition to the Jesuits. From 1725 the Oratorians were allowed to matriculate students for university entry, thereby breaching a long-held Jesuit monopoly. Generally more progressive than the

[124] Ibid, pp 531–2; HP vol 4, p 32.
[125] NHP vol 7, p 557.
[126] Ibid, pp 507, 548–9.
[127] Cf Maxwell K 1995, pp 12–13.
[128] NHP vol 7, pp 519, 524.

Jesuits, the Oratorians were inclined to teach knowledge associated with the Moderate Enlightenment, including Newtonian physics. However, the two Jesuit-run Portuguese universities were notoriously suspicious of such ideas and ever fearful of heresy. Évora, a struggling institution with barely more than 300 students, taught only arts and theology. At Coimbra the curriculum was somewhat broader, embracing arts, theology, canon law, civil law and medicine. But in 1746 the rector of the College of Arts at Coimbra explicitly rejected the theories of Descartes and Newton, declaring that neither thinker – nor any other that did not conform to strict Catholic orthodoxy and well-tried Aristotelianism – could be taught at that institution. The overwhelming majority of students at Coimbra studied canon law or theology, and most graduates went on to become lawyers and administrators in the service of either the crown or the church.[129]

Other institutions that possessed some capacity to nurture informed opinion in this period included learned associations and academies. However, most of these organisations were too short lived and involved too restricted and privileged a clientele to have much impact. Moreover, though generally committed to rational discourse they tended to focus particularly on poetry and other forms of literature, even if they sometimes ventured into areas such as mathematics and medical science. Thoroughly aristocratic, the academies had little relevance to the broader public. The more prestigious among them, such as the *Academia Real de História*, were kept well under crown control.[130] Recipients of royal patronage and generous princely largesse, they were seldom seriously controversial.[131]

No genuine public lending libraries or reading societies existed in Portugal during the first half of the eighteenth century – unlike in northern Europe, where such institutions did much to spread and popularise knowledge.[132] But a few religious institutions, including the Dominican convent in the *Rossio*, allowed serious outside readers access to their shelves, as did certain benevolent nobles, most notably the fourth count of Ericeira.[133] There were no public museums or displays of specimens and artefacts in Joanine Portugal through which scientific knowledge might have been more widely spread. The earliest public museums in the kingdom were only formed after the dissolution of the monasteries in 1834. However, despite these limitations, within the eighteenth-century Portuguese elite was a small but quite impassioned intelligentsia,

---

[129] Ibid, pp 524–6, 530; SHP vol 5, p 421.
[130] SHP, pp 428–31; HP vol 4, p 444; NHP vol 7, pp 465–6, 536–9.
[131] Blanning T C W 2002, pp 46–8.
[132] Ibid, p 144; Cavallo G and Chartier R (eds) 1999, pp 21, 306–9.
[133] Kendrick T D 1956, p 33; Delaforce A 2002, p 72.

committed to new ways of thinking, mostly within the tradition of the Moderate Enlightenment. At the same time the Portuguese language was being honed into a more precise and flexible medium of communication, providing the basic instrument required for clear and rigorous reasoning. The French-born Theatine monk Rafael Bluteau, whose ten-volume *Vocabulario Portuguez e Latino* (1712–27) set the rules for standard written Portuguese, played a key role in this process.[134] Portuguese linguistic studies were also pursued in some of the Joanine academies.

Notwithstanding censorship, the existence of several fine private libraries in João V's Portugal meant that at least some individuals had access to written knowledge. However, almost all these libraries were in the hands of religious bodies or of cultured aristocrats – the two groups from which most of the Portuguese intelligentsia was drawn. The fourth and fifth counts of Ericeira were particularly prominent and erudite bibliophiles.[135] But even within the intelligentsia, there was little explicit debate on political philosophy. The works of sceptical thinkers such as Voltaire and David Hume were usually kept well off the agenda – at least publicly.

The most lively debate about reform in Joanine Portugal concerned education. Quite a number of thoughtful Portuguese, convinced the country's backwardness was fundamentally a consequence of its unprogressive national education system, were stirred by this issue. The most insistent critics were *estrangeirados*, among them Luís António Verney. After living for ten years in Rome, Verney published in 1746 his celebrated *Verdadeiro Método de Estudar* in which he recommended the secularisation of the entire education system. Verney was hopeful that once secularisation had been accomplished other desirable changes, such as the introduction of more science and mathematics teaching, would follow. Underlying his vision was the ardent belief that all people were born free and equally noble.[136]

Verney was by no means the only Portuguese to identify educational reform as essential if Portugal was to overcome its backwardness. Another contemporary who argued along similar lines was the venereologist and encyclopaedist Dr António Nunes Ribeiro Sanches (1699–1783). Of New Christian origin, Ribeiro Sanches lived most of his adult life in England, Holland, Russia and France. He too wanted control of education transferred from the church to the state.[137] However, little was ever done under the complacent and cautious João V to tackle this controversial issue.

---

[134] DIHP vol 1, pp 71–2; NHP vol 7, p 462.
[135] CRB OM vol 3, p 174; Delaforce A 2002, pp 72–4.
[136] DIHP vol 2, p 323; NHP vol 7, p 551.
[137] CRB OM vol 3, pp 203–14; DIHP vol 2, pp 173–4; HP vol 4, pp 430–3.

Given the lack of educational reform, and the strength of traditionalism, it is not surprising that progressive ideas had relatively little impact on the Portuguese general public in Joanine times and during the first few years of José I's reign. Enlightened thinking, even in the somewhat sanitised form in which it penetrated Portugal, could not and did not spread much beyond a limited circle of progressive nobles, churchmen and professionals. Serious change in this area was delayed until the time of Pombal. But when it came, it did so with a vengeance.

13

The Age of Pombal

POMBAL AND POMBALISM

Sebastião José de Carvalho e Melo (1699–1782), first marquis of Pombal, is by convention almost always referred to simply as Pombal, although he was not raised to the marquisate until quite late in his career in 1769. Pombal came from a minor noble family, was just twenty-one when his father died, lacked a powerful patron and possessed no great prospects. But he was quick to seize such opportunities as came his way. In 1723, he married a niece of the count of Arcos, despite her family's opposition. This improved his social standing, although he still had little influence at court – until in 1738 his cousin, Marco António de Azevedo Coutinho, became secretary of state for foreign affairs and war. It was Azevedo Coutinho who in 1739 secured for Pombal the important political appointment of Portuguese ambassador to Britain.

Pombal lived in London from 1739 to 1743. Although he apparently never learned much English, he was exposed there to a wide range of stimulating ideas, read voraciously and was able to establish friendly contacts with members of the prestigious Royal Society. In London Pombal tried to find out why England was so advanced technologically and prosperous commercially, how it had acquired such influence over the Portuguese economy and what could be done to make the Anglo-Portuguese relationship more equal.[1] Recalled to Lisbon in 1743, Pombal had little time to readjust before being appointed ambassador to Vienna, a position he held from 1745 to 1749. In Austria he was able to observe how a major continental power ran its affairs under a classic Enlightened despot, the Empress Maria Theresa. At the time Vienna

[1] SHP vol 6, pp 20–2; Maxwell K 1995, pp 5–8.

was in the process of curtailing both the role of the Jesuits and the influence of the papacy – precedents that would not be lost on Pombal. Meanwhile, his first wife having died, Pombal determined to remarry, once again selecting his bride with an eye to personal advantage. His choice was an illustrious Austrian noblewoman, the Countess Maria Leonor Ernestina Daun, lady-in-waiting to the empress. From a domestic viewpoint the marriage was highly successful, producing a fond relationship and five children; politically it gave Pombal access to the most privileged circles in Austria. It also brought much greater influence at the Portuguese court because Countess Daun had close links to Maria Ana, João V's Austrian queen. Through Maria Ana, Pombal eventually secured his recall to Lisbon in late 1749.[2]

After more than a decade abroad, Pombal was able to re-enter Portuguese politics at mid-century well informed about current thinking and with an intimate knowledge of contemporary European affairs. He had learned much not only about diplomacy, but about the manoeuvrings of central governments and the management of national economies. Overseas experience had also made him bitterly aware of his own country's weakness and backwardness – and determined to push for reform. His energy, powerful personality and uncompromising sense of purpose meant that any reform program in which he had a say was likely to be fearless and sweeping.[3] As fate decreed, his opportunity was not long delayed, for in August 1750 King José, who had just ascended the throne and was looking for ministers with new ideas, appointed Pombal secretary of state for foreign affairs and war.

For the next twenty-five years the towering figure of Pombal came to so dominate Portugal, and his presence has so haunted the historiography ever since, that the period itself has come to be known as Pombaline. During this remarkable era, unprecedented change occurred in the political, economic and social landscapes of Portugal, transforming some of its most deeply entrenched institutions almost beyond recognition. No other Portuguese statesman has ever cut a more commanding figure than Pombal, nor roused such hostility – nor has any subsequently stimulated such passionate debate and controversy.[4] The almost obsessive pre-occupation with Pombal by so many historians eventually led Jorge Borges de Macedo, in a memorable classic first published in 1951, to question the apparently ingrained assumption that attributes almost everything of note that occurred in the third quarter of the eighteenth century to this one individual. Macedo urged his fellow historians to desist from endless

---

[2] Cheke M 1938, pp 18–19, 42–3; Maxwell K 1973, pp 1–3, and 1995, pp 2–4, 8–9; DIHP vol 2, p 117.
[3] DIHP vol 2, pp 116–17.
[4] Antunes M 1983, p 9.

debates about the deeds and personality of Pombal and instead investigate more the economic and cultural context of the times.[5]

Part of the legacy of Macedo is that scholars now speak of Pombalism and not just of Pombal. Pombalism was a contemporary reform movement that sought to modernise Portugal in accordance with rational Enlightenment principles. It required a substantial shift of power from traditional elites, the church and in some respects even the king to the state, and a major upgrade of the institutional apparatus of secular government. Pombalism also sought to address the growing economic and fiscal problems confronting Portugal, through systematic state intervention. Firmer administrative control and increased economic development of the colonies were given top priority while a strategy was evolved to curb British dominance of Portuguese overseas trade. Where social, cultural or religious impediments stood in the way of these policies they were directly confronted and, if necessary, removed or neutralised.[6]

The principal intellectual precursors of Pombalism were the great classic thinkers whose ideas underlay the European reform movements of the eighteenth century more generally, such as Locke, Newton and Descartes. But also influential were Portuguese writers and reformers, including Verney and Ribeiro Sanches. The Portuguese reform program that unfolded over the period 1750–77 was clearly the work not just of Pombal, but of an extensive team of like-minded people. Within the team were members of Pombal's own family, particularly his two brothers and eventually his oldest son, Paulo de Carvalho Mendonça. There were also lawyers such as José de Seabra da Silva (1732–1813), churchmen including Cardinal Dom João Cosme da Cunha (1715–83) and Frei Manuel do Cenáculo Vilas Boas (1732–1814) and a cluster of collaborating merchants.[7] Pombalism was manifestly a collective phenomenon, and the reform ideas associated with it were by no means exclusively Pombal's.

The concept of Pombalism has certainly brought an added, more detached dimension to historians' understanding of the reign of King José. However, it has not reduced much the traditional and seemingly inexhaustible interest in Pombal as an individual – and his figure remains, and seems likely to continue to remain, the starting-point for almost all historical discussion about the period.[8] Pombal was certainly the principal arbiter of policy throughout most of the reign, and it was he who orchestrated its transforming changes. Yet it took five years for him to achieve the unassailable political ascendancy at court

[5] Macedo J B de 1982, pp 27–31.
[6] DIHP vol 2, pp 118–19. See also Maxwell K 1995 especially ch 1.
[7] DIHP vol 2, pp 117–18, 215.
[8] Cf. Macedo J B de 1982 chs 2–5 and 1982a, pp 187–231; Maxwell K 1995 passim.

that became his hallmark, and for which the catalyst was the great Lisbon earthquake of 1755.

THE 1755 EARTHQUAKE

Shortly before 9.45 A.M. on 1 November 1755 Lisbon was struck by a massive earthquake thought to have measured 8.5 to 9 on the Richter scale. The tremor, which was felt all across Portugal but particularly in the southwest, was followed by two major aftershocks. The list of towns that suffered serious damage, from Estremadura to the Algarve, is soberingly long: Leiria, Peniche, Alcobaça, Ourém, Santarém, Benavente, Setúbal, Sines, Tavira, Faro, Portimão, Silves and many others. In Silves the cathedral, castle and senate house were all destroyed and many people killed, injured or rendered homeless. There was also much destruction in neighbouring Morocco and Spain, while associated tsunami effects were felt as far away as Ireland and even the West Indies.[9] But it was in Lisbon, the major European city nearest to the earthquake's epicentre, that the impact was greatest.

Perhaps because it was All Saints' Day and many candles had been lit in the churches, the earthquake was swiftly followed by fire. It raged uncontrollably for almost a week, destroying much of what the shock itself had spared. Meanwhile, about an hour after the first tremor three successive tsunami waves had roared up the Tagus estuary and broken with tremendous impact on the docks along the square in front of the palace – the *Terreiro do Paço*. Many more deaths by fire and drowning resulted, and there was much additional destruction of property. When it was all finally over, some 10,000 to 15,000 of Lisbon's inhabitants had lost their lives and the city lay in ruins.[10] The greatest destruction had occurred in the lower part of the city (*cidade baixa*) and its immediate vicinity – the heart of Lisbon. The great River Palace had been reduced to rubble. The customs house, the arsenal, the high court building and the quays along the river bank had all been razed. The patriarchal church so beloved of João V was gone, as was the palace of the Inquisition. All but five of Lisbon's parish churches and many of its monasteries and convents had either been levelled to the ground or heavily damaged. The cathedral was gutted by fire, the castle of São Jorge had incurred significant damage, the new opera house had collapsed and many mansions of the nobility were in ruins. In all probably 80 to 90 percent of the houses in Lisbon were either completely demolished or rendered uninhabitable. Destruction of commercial buildings and plant was also widespread, and there was a heavy toll on trade stock.[11]

[9] Kendrick T D 1956, p 25; SHP vol 6, pp 31–2; Maxwell K 2002, p 25.
[10] Boxer C R 1956, p 237; Maxwell K 2002, p 25.
[11] Kendrick T D 1956, pp 30–3; Boxer C R 1955, pp 227–8 and 1956, p 238; SHP vol 6, p 28; Maxwell K 1995, p 24; Delaforce A 2002, p 287.

The cultural losses inflicted by the earthquake were quite simply incalculable. A magnificent collection of paintings, sculptures, furnishings and historic artefacts, many acquired by João V but some dating back to the time of King Manuel, had been housed in the River Palace. Virtually all were destroyed. Also gone was the palace library, believed to have been one of the greatest in eighteenth-century Europe, perhaps rivalling even that of the Vatican.[12] Much was lost from great noble and episcopal residences and the more opulent religious houses. The Annunciada Palace – the Lisbon home of the counts of Ericeira – contained more than 200 paintings, apparently including works by Titian, Correggio, Rubens, Hondius and Quillard. The third, fourth and fifth counts of Ericeira all collected books avidly so that by 1755 the palace also contained a library of over 18,000 volumes, along with the family archives, priceless maps, globes, navigational charts and mathematical instruments. All this, plus tapestries, antiquities, curiosities and much fine furniture, was destroyed or at least irretrievably damaged by the earthquake and fire.[13] However, the greatest regret of all – at least for future generations of historians – was the loss of so many irreplaceable records of Portugal's maritime and colonising past in the destruction of the *Casa da Índia*.

Fortunately for José and the royal family, they were not in the River Palace when the earthquake struck. They were in Belém on the city's western outskirts, where the impact was less severe. Around the badly shaken monarch ministers and counsellors forgathered as quickly as they could. 'Bury the dead and care for the living', Pombal is supposed to have said when asked by the king what should be done, though this utterance has also been attributed to the marquis of Alorna.[14] Nevertheless, it was Pombal who took command in the crisis, with the king's grateful support. His priorities were to re-establish order, dispose of the bodies and provide food and shelter to survivors. Troops were deployed, with orders to summarily execute looters, and a labour force assembled to tackle recovery and relief work. With the cardinal-patriarch's consent, corpses were collected and dumped at sea. Pombal also froze food prices at pre-earthquake levels and organised temporary shelter at designated sites. His ceaseless energy and frenetic round-the-clock activity set a towering example.[15]

The disaster that struck Lisbon in November 1755, terrible as it was, also created an unprecedented opportunity. As Pombal quickly realised, it would now be possible to reconstruct the Portuguese capital as a modern city, designed and planned in accordance with rational eighteenth-century principles. The chance to

[12] Delaforce A 2002, p 69.
[13] Ibid, pp 72–4, 230–2.
[14] Boxer C R 1962, p 363; SHP vol 6, p 28.
[15] Boxer C R 1955, pp 228–9; SHP vol 6, pp 28–9; Maxwell K 2002, p 28.

accomplish something exceptional was further enhanced when it became clear that José I, scared by his narrow escape, had developed a pathological fear of living in solid buildings and therefore had no interest in restoring the River Palace. For many years afterwards he lived in either temporary wooden pavilions or under canvas.[16] This enabled Pombal to rebuild the heart of Lisbon as a centre of commerce, administration and practical living rather than a monument to monarchical grandeur.

For the rebuilding of Lisbon Pombal thought it best to draw on the expertise of military engineers. The now aged Manuel da Maia, who had helped design and build João V's great aqueduct, was entrusted with preparing a master plan. Two younger men, Eugénio dos Santos and the Hungarian-born Károly Mardell, were engaged to work on the details. As the new city's centrepiece, the devastated *Terreiro do Paço* was now to be called the *Praça do Comércio* – in other words, what had been Palace Square became the Square of Commerce, a re-labelling of considerable symbolic significance. Extending inland approximately at right angles to this square were to be four parallel streets terminating at their northern end in two smaller squares – the *Rossio* and the *Praça da Figueira*. The four major streets were crossed by other smaller ones, so creating a huge grid. Within the area of the grid all buildings had to be constructed to mandatory guidelines, conforming in both size and appearance to a set pattern. Under Pombal's safety and sanitary regulations each house was to be built round an earthquake-resistant inner frame and provided with a cistern.

The *Praça do Comércio* itself was flanked by matching buildings on its three landward sides and fringed with street-level arcades. The buildings here were to house government departments and the commercial exchange. When completed they seemed to echo in appearance the Mannerist tradition of the Portuguese sixteenth century, but they also showed the influence of English Palladianism and especially Inigo Jones's Covent Garden. To improve national design standards more generally, in 1756 Pombal created a school of architecture that was directed successively by Santos and Mardell. Meanwhile, the volume of work generated by earthquake reconstruction gave such a boost to the building industry that standardised, prefabricated house components began to be manufactured. Even the repair and replacement of religious structures was made subject to Pombal's master plan, though church façades were permitted more elaborate decoration than other buildings. The final outcome was one of the finest examples of planned urban renewal in eighteenth-century Europe.[17]

---

[16] Maxwell K 2002, p 30.
[17] Smith R C 1968, pp 105–6; DIHP vol 1, pp 418–19; Maxwell K 2002, pp 29–35; Delaforce A 2002, pp 287–9.

POMBAL AND PORTUGUESE TRADE

Of the many problems besetting Portugal when Pombal came to power one of the most urgent was the country's rapidly deteriorating balance of trade. Throughout the first half of the eighteenth century Portugal had always had a negative balance of trade with Britain, its major international trading partner – but had readily made up the difference with Brazilian gold. However, in the 1750s gold imports began to fall off sharply, and the trend was maintained for the rest of the century. Also in the 1750s sales of Portuguese wine to Britain declined by about 20 per cent, just when imports of manufactured goods were rising sharply, stimulated by re-stocking in the aftermath of the earthquake. The trade deficit reached an all time high in 1756 when Portugal's exports were worth only about 11 per cent of its imports. Obviously this situation was unsustainable.[18]

Pombal came to power convinced that if Portugal were to overcome its weak position in international trade it would have to loosen the economic stranglehold of Great Britain. He was determined to assert Portuguese control over the trade of both the metropolis and the colonies and re-direct a greater share of the profits to Portuguese merchant houses. However, he had to be careful not to jeopardise Portugal's political and military alliance with Britain, which was considered essential for national security. He also realised Portugal needed British manufactures, and he had no intention of obstructing Anglo-Portuguese trade as such.[19] The solution Pombal decided to apply to these problems was to establish a series of monopoly companies. By this means he hoped to encourage a range of industries, in both Portugal and its colonies, with international market potential. The idea was not new in principle, for Portuguese monopoly companies had been tried before with varying degrees of success. But the Pombaline plan was more ambitious, extensive and carefully targeted than most of its predecessors. In the event, Pombal founded five major monopoly companies in the 1750s – a so-called India company (1753), the Grão Pará and Maranhão Company (1755), a whaling company (1756), the Upper Douro Wine Company (1756) and the Pernambuco and Paraíba Company (1759).[20] He probably planned others too; but if so, they never materialised.

The India company, which seems in practice to have amounted to little more than a series of voyage concessions, was short lived and achieved little. But the Grão Pará and Maranhão Company received a twenty-year monopoly on trade

---

[18] Fisher H E S 1971, pp 142–3; Pinto V N 1979, pp 246–7; HP vol 4, pp 105–6.
[19] Schneider S 1971, pp 176–7; Maxwell K 1973, pp 3–5 and 1995, pp 66–7; HP vol 4, pp 107–8.
[20] Macedo J B de 1982, p 47.

and navigation with the Amazon region and was a far more substantial enterprise. To help this company Pombal also banned from its monopoly area all itinerant Portuguese traders and commission agents – the so-called *comissários volantes* – many of whom had been acting for British merchants based in Portugal. There was little protest at the time, probably because British trade to Amazonia was so limited. The result was that during the next twenty years the Grão Pará and Maranhão Company virtually controlled trade to and from the Portuguese Amazon. While this situation caused periodic complaints from local settlers, who were confronted with shortages of some import commodities, plus higher prices, the company successfully stimulated the cacao, rice and cotton industries and provided much-needed African slaves.[21] A sister monopoly company – the Pernambuco and Paraíba Company – played a similar role in the northeast of Brazil, where it encouraged the production of sugar, tobacco, hides, cotton and cacao.[22]

In Portugal itself the most important of Pombal's new companies was the Upper Douro Wine Company. This venture was the administration's answer to a crisis in the wine industry that had developed very rapidly during the 1750s. The underlying cause of the crisis, which was felt particularly deeply in the Upper Douro region, was over-production stemming from uncontrolled vineyard expansion. Eventually in 1755 a group of larger Upper Douro producers, concerned about the number of smaller growers from outside the region entering the market, petitioned the government for protection. Pombal's response was to create the Upper Douro Wine Company. This company, which was founded in 1756, received monopolies for the export of wine and brandy from Porto to Brazil, and for all wine sales to retail outlets in the city of Porto and its surrounding district. The company was also authorised to establish an exclusive demarcated zone for port wine production – almost a century before such zones were similarly instituted for designated wines in France. Port wine, which by definition meant wine exported through the city of Porto, was now restricted to an area of the Upper Douro Valley with precisely defined boundaries.

These measures were taken by Pombal partly in an effort to stabilise wine output and prices, and partly to improve quality. However, they were also designed to favour established large producers over their smaller competitors, for almost all of the latter were excluded from the demarcated zone. Although Pombal's own estates were nowhere near the Upper Douro, but much further south along the Tagus, they were included as a special enclave.[23] The Upper Douro Wine Company survived in one form or another until 1865 and was

---

[21] Maxwell K 1973, pp 18–19, 41 and 1995, pp 55, 58–60, 154; SHP vol 6, pp 176–8.
[22] Maxwell K 1973, pp 41–2 and 1995, pp 88–90; SHP vol 6, pp 179–80.
[23] Schneider S 1971, pp 40–3, 69–76; Maxwell K 1995, pp 61–3.

easily the most enduring of Pombal's trading companies. This was despite a long struggle to raise sufficient capital and repeated failure to declare dividends. In the end, the company's greatest achievement was probably its transformation of port from a mundane working-man's drink into a fine wine fit for gentlemen. This was accomplished by creating the demarcated zone and through rigorous quality control. But the economic benefits were confined to the elite port producers of the Upper Douro and their associates in Porto. The company did nothing for the rest of the wine industry or for the economy of the north more generally. It simply privileged one small area at the expense of everywhere else.[24]

Just as Pombal's trading companies of the 1750s were getting under way the Seven Years War (1756–63) between England and France broke out, changing the international context. At first Pombal was able to stay neutral – but this eventually proved impossible. In 1762, after Portugal had refused to yield to French and Spanish demands to close its ports to the British, it was invaded by Spanish troops. Pombal was ill-prepared to fight and was obliged to seek British military assistance. However, the following year the war ended, with British maritime power much enhanced. By this time the British factories in Lisbon and Porto were more aware of the threat posed by Pombal's economic policies to important sectors of their trade and had begun to protest.[25] Moreover, British exports to Portugal, so buoyant in the aftermath of the earthquake, now declined sharply, although the export of Portuguese wine and other primary products to Britain remained steady. This situation was exacerbated by the slump in Brazilian gold shipments, which meant Portugal could no longer afford to buy foreign manufactures to the same extent as previously.

Pombaline economic policy in the 1760s tried to combat this new situation by promoting the production of any colonial commodities, old or new, which seemed to have export potential. In north and northeast Brazil this was done mainly through the Grão Pará and Maranhão Company and the Pernambuco and Paraíba Company, respectively. But it was no longer practicable, particularly given British attitudes, to extend the same monopoly system to the rest of Brazil. So instead colonial governors in the more southerly Brazilian captaincies, as well as elsewhere in the empire, were simply instructed to take every opportunity to promote economic development and increase exports. One governor who paid good heed to these orders was Luís de Almeida, marquis of Lavradio, who was governor of Bahia (1768–9), then viceroy of Brazil (1769–79). Lavradio encouraged expansion of tobacco cultivation and fostered the production of coffee, indigo, cochineal, rice and hemp.[26] Meanwhile, Pombal took steps to control

---

[24] Macedo J B de 1982, pp 48, 51; Schneider S 1971, pp 257, 266–9, 274, 280.
[25] Maxwell K 1973, pp 19–21 and 1995, pp 112–14.
[26] Alden D 1968, pp 360–80; Maxwell K 1995, pp 117–18, 124–5, 131–4.

and regulate more closely trade in the major colonial commodities, especially sugar and tobacco. Certain commercial collaborators of the regime, many of them linked to the tobacco industry, now received generous government backing – and grew notably prosperous. Later in the century European demand for Portuguese colonial exports increased, considerably improving Portugal's trade situation, although this process did not get into full swing until after Pombal's demise.[27]

Pombal also sought to encourage commerce by bestowing on it greater social prestige. In 1770, trade was officially declared 'noble, necessary and profitable'. Then in 1773 the pernicious distinction between Old and New Christians, which for so long had be-devilled business activity, was abolished. Meanwhile, a number of prominent merchants were granted ennoblement.[28] Eventually, government encouragement and support for the upper commercial bourgeoisie in both Lisbon and Porto helped create a group of elite businessmen that was dominant locally and competitive internationally. Within the group were some of the minister's closest collaborators, including members of the Cruz, Bandeira, Braancamp, Machado and Quintella families. Most of these people were associated either with the Pombaline monopoly companies or with the Brazilian tobacco industry. Some of them became so entrenched that even after Pombal's fall in 1777 they continued to play an important role in Portugal's economy.[29]

POMBALINE INDUSTRIAL AND AGRARIAN REFORM

When Pombal came to power in 1750 Portugal was not without manufacturing capability: it possessed an extensive network of pre-industrial workshops scattered around the country, producing a wide range of goods for local and regional consumption. The system was heavily decentralised, if only because the poor state of transport and communications precluded anything else. A handful of larger enterprises, particularly those for the manufacture of woollens, cordage and tobacco products, some of which were survivals from the count of Ericeira's earlier industrialisation program, did not essentially alter this picture.[30] In short, Portugal's manufacturing sector was not geared to economies of scale, was organised mostly along very traditional lines and remained technologically backward.

In the course of Pombal's stewardship much was done to remedy this situation. At first, during the surging balance of payments crisis of the 1750s, government action was only sporadic. Then, through the 1760s, the pace of

[27] Macedo J B de 1982, p 87.
[28] MHP, pp 396–7, 402–4; Maxwell K 1995, pp 84, 164.
[29] Maxwell K 1973, pp 48–9, 57–8 and 1995, pp 38, 140.
[30] Macedo J B de 1982, pp 107–8, 113–20.

action quickened, and finally in the 1770s there was widespread and coordinated state intervention.[31] By the late Pombaline period foreign commercial
interest in both the metropolitan and colonial Portuguese markets was, for
reasons mostly outside Portugal's control, quite subdued. It was this relative
external disinterest, together with Portugal's reduced capacity to purchase
imports, that provided national manufacturers in some industries with sufficient market opportunity to develop sustainable production.[32]

During the first phase of Pombaline administration through the 1750s
state backing was extended to various manufacturing enterprises on a case-
by-case basis. In 1751, an English entrepreneur called Henry Smith was
allowed to establish a sugar refinery in Lisbon, provided he used only Brazilian raw sugar and trained Portuguese apprentices in the art of refining. At
about the same time, the royal silk factory – one of the few industrial enterprises started in João V's reign, but which had subsequently sunk into bankruptcy – was given a new lease of life with state assistance. Then in 1759 a
state-sponsored hat factory was set up at the town of Pombal in northern
Estremadura. To assist this concern a ban was placed on the export of rabbit
skins, and, later, foreign competition was blocked by simply prohibiting hat
imports. In the same year, in response to appeals from the Covilhã *câmara*,
Pombal took steps to rejuvenate that town's woollen manufacturing industry.
He provided it with seeding finance, exempted imported raw wool from
duties and renewed state orders for military uniforms.[33] In 1756, the regime
went on to establish a board of trade (*junta do comércio*), a semi-official
body created to co-ordinate and up to a point manage economic development.
This board promoted many new manufacturing enterprises during the succeeding years, regularly furnishing them with subsidies, technical assistance,
tariff protection, tax exemptions, monopolies and other privileges. In 1767,
the board took over the royal silk factory and transformed it into a far more
effective, decentralised institution.[34]

Through the 1770s, when 80 per cent of manufacturing enterprises set up
under Pombal were initiated, a much more intensive campaign of industrial
protectionism was waged. State assistance for many manufacturers was
financed from the proceeds of a 4 per cent duty on imports. In effect, this meant
foreign goods were being taxed to subsidise domestic industry.[35] The royal
glass factory, originally founded in 1748, was now reconstituted and became

[31] Ibid, pp 125, 127.
[32] Ibid, pp 85, 87; Maxwell K 1973, p 51; HP vol 4, p 93.
[33] Macedo J B de 1982, pp 122, 126; SHP vol 6, pp 194, 200.
[34] HP vol 4, p 92; Maxwell K 1995, pp 69–70, 75, 136.
[35] HP vol 4, p 92.

one of the most successful of the Pombaline manufacturing companies. It was taken over by another Englishman, William Stephens, with Pombal's strong support. Aided by state subsidies, Stephens built up the business until it became the principal supplier of window panes for the houses of Lisbon and Porto and a source of extremely fine crystal-ware.[36] However, it was the establishment of a cotton textiles industry that ultimately proved the most important of all the Pombaline manufacturing initiatives. This industry was much aided by the availability of raw cotton from Brazil. Importantly, the domestic production of cottons could be openly protected in Portugal without violating the terms of the Methuen Treaty – because that agreement referred only to woollens. More co-opted foreigners played an important role in this enterprise, prominent among them being Jacome Ratton, a talented naturalised Frenchman who became a keen advocate of steam-power.[37]

Overall, some 200 manufacturing businesses were created in Portugal during the 1770s. A few were run directly by the crown, but most were privately owned though often in receipt of state aid. More than half were located in Lisbon and about a quarter in Porto – they were concentrated in areas with the best access to imported raw materials, to the main national markets and to colonial export markets. By the time Pombal left office Portugal was producing quite an impressive range of manufactured goods. This included old perennials such as woollens and silks, but also glass, leather, hats, cottons, refined sugar, tobacco products, cordage, paper, ceramics, soap, military and naval supplies and a myriad of minor items ranging from buttons to combs. Many of these products were made from raw materials produced in the colonies, which also comprised for Portugal a crucial protected market.[38] Nevertheless, most manufacturing in Pombaline Portugal still remained fragmented into small, local units, as it always had been. The largest single entity was the glass factory, which employed some 550 workers.[39] By and large it was not until after Pombal's departure that his industrial policy began to yield substantial dividends, aided by increasingly favourable external conditions. Among these were new export opportunities opened up as a consequence of the War of the American Revolution (1776–83).[40]

Pombaline agrarian policy is a rather different story. In Portugal itself, unlike in the colonies, Pombal's administration did little to reform agriculture – except, of course, for a privileged segment of the wine industry. The old problem of inadequate wheat production persisted and even intensified during

---

[36] SHP vol 6, pp 195–6.
[37] Maxwell K 1995, p 136; DIHP vol 2, p 139.
[38] Macedo J B de 1982, pp 155–60; HP vol 4, pp 92–3.
[39] HP vol 4, pp 95–6.
[40] Ibid, pp 109–11.

these years, requiring grain imports to be increased. There was uncultivated land, particularly in Alentejo, that might have been used to expand wheat output; but the prospect was not commercially attractive. Transport problems constituted another disincentive: there were too few tracks suitable for horse-drawn carts, and it was prohibitively expensive to convey wheat in bulk by mule. The Pombal administration belatedly showed some interest in these problems in its final years, but even then constructed few new roads.[41]

But Pombal's regime did make a serious effort to modernise fiscal admin-istration – and, to a lesser extent, the tax system. In 1761, it created a national treasury (*erário régio*) through which all state revenue and expenditure had to be channelled. The *erário régio* was staffed by competent professionals and followed modern accounting procedures, such as double-entry book-keeping, daily balances and regular financial statements.[42] In its practical orientation and scrupulous attention to detail, the *erário régio* was an institution typical of the era of Enlightened Despotism. Its responsibilities and staff steadily expanded, it carried out efficiently one of the most fundamental functions of a modern state and it lasted well into the nineteenth century.

After the earthquake the administration had introduced a 4 per cent tax on imports, subsequently used to fund state-assisted industrial enterprises. Another initiative was the so-called literary tax, a duty on wine and brandy imposed to fund educational reform. Also during the difficult 1760s certain existing imposts were increased, especially the *décima militar* or property tax. This had been introduced over a century before to help pay for the war of independence against Spain. Pombal likewise made the collection of customs more efficient – and finally, in a change that had social as well as fiscal impli-cations, he swept away many traditional exemptions, making taxes apply to everyone without distinction, including even nobles.[43] But tax reform, however sobering it might seem, was certainly not Pombal's strongest message for the nobility. He had some far more immediate challenges for them to think about.

THE COWING OF THE HIGHER NOBILITY

In 1750, the Portuguese higher nobility formed a small, tightly knit, extraordi-narily exclusive group of families that had barely changed since the Bragança Restoration over a century before. Some fifty elite houses had successfully maintained themselves by consistently placing their collective family interests above those of individual members. All *grandes*, as well many nobles of lesser

---

[41] Macedo J B de 1982, pp 102, 105–6; Schneider S 1971, pp 286, 288–9, 294–5.
[42] SHP vol 6, p 96; HP vol 4, pp 173–4, 236; Maxwell K 1995, p 90; DIHP vol 1, p 215.
[43] Macedo J B de 1982, pp 96–7; Maxwell K 1995, pp 65, 78, 97.

status, maintained *morgados* as perpetual and indivisible inheritances for their firstborn or oldest surviving sons. These sons invariably married, usually selecting their brides from the same pool of illustrious noble families. Indeed, the *puritanos*, a still more exclusive inner group, would not marry even a girl of *grande* status from outside the group, for fear of becoming 'tainted' with Jewish or Moorish blood. If the heir to one of these great houses was a woman, she was expected to marry an uncle or other male relative in order to perpetuate the family name as well as the line itself. Repetitive in-breeding was therefore quite common.[44]

Such a family strategy also required that younger sons normally remain unmarried and that they seek to carve out a career either in the church or in royal service. In the same way many daughters were denied marriage and were consigned to convents. Daughters who did marry received dowries. However, other daughters, like younger sons, got no share of the family inheritance though they could expect some form of maintenance along with other minor relatives, *criados* and sundry hangers-on. In this way great houses could sometimes find themselves supporting up to 100 dependents.[45] To help sustain this burden, younger sons who acquired bishoprics or any other lucrative office were expected to use their emoluments to subsidise the house from which they sprang. The reinforcement and perpetuation of great houses in this way had been encouraged by the crown itself since at least the sixteenth century. Kings facilitated the formation or extension of *morgados,* often transferring to great noblemen for this purpose lands belonging to the crown or the military orders, granting exemptions from the *Lei Mental* where necessary.[46] All this meant that when Pombal came to power in 1750 Portugal possessed one of the most closed and exclusive higher nobilities in Europe. All its major houses had survived intact for at least the previous 125 years.

During the course of the early 1750s hostility towards Pombal's supremacy among elements of this higher nobility brewed and festered. Up to a point this was a predictable manifestation of resentment by figures associated with the previous administration, who were now out of favour; but it also reflected the age-old tension between a centralising crown and an aristocracy clinging to traditional rights and privileges and seeing itself by-passed in a manner contrary to custom. The hostility was certainly exacerbated by personal dislike of Pombal, whom many *grandes* looked down upon as an arrogant and self-promoting upstart. They resented his influence over the king and felt slighted, excluded or even threatened by his overbearing manner. Among

---

[44] HP vol 4, p 365; Monteiro N G 2003, pp 4–7, 10.
[45] NHP vol 9, p 181; Monteiro N G 2003, pp 9–11.
[46] Monteiro N G 2003, p 10.

the more prominent members of this opposition – which tended to gravitate, for want of a better focus, round the unimposing figure of the king's younger brother, Prince Pedro – was José de Mascarenhas, eighth duke of Aveiro.[47]

By the mid-1750s, Aveiro and the other noble malcontents found themselves faced by a minister they resented and despised, but who was rapidly becoming entrenched, his personal standing much enhanced in the aftermath of the earthquake. At the time that catastrophe struck he was formally just secretary of state for foreign affairs and war, while the key office of secretary of state for internal affairs continued to be occupied by Pedro da Mota e Silva, an elderly leftover from the previous reign. But as soon as Mota e Silva died in 1756 Pombal moved to take his place. At about the same time he also persuaded the king to dismiss Diogo de Mendonça Corte Real, the secretary of state for naval and colonial affairs, and replace him with a compliant nonentity. These moves so alarmed Pombal's aristocratic opponents that during the course of 1756 a conspiracy began to take shape against him. The details of this conspiracy are rather hazy, but it seems those involved included several prominent *grandes,* among them Aveiro and the duke of Lafões. A petition detailing complaints against Pombal and demanding his dismissal was delivered to King José. But that monarch emphatically rejected it, reaffirmed his confidence in his minister and ordered some of the leading complainants arrested.[48] Pombal emerged from the affair more powerful than ever, and it seemed that his rivals' only legal resort was closed off.

Through the late 1750s it must have been obvious to any Portuguese aristocrat with the slightest political awareness that Pombal and his collaborators constituted an administration of unusual strength, energy and sense of purpose. To those born to the old ways the changes he seemed bent on introducing probably seemed puzzling – and certainly disturbing. Nevertheless, just how far Portugal would be driven down the road to modernisation during the second half of the eighteenth century, first under Pombal and then under his successors, few could have foreseen. Meanwhile, continuing underlying tensions between disgruntled members of the higher nobility and the Pombaline administration came to a sudden and dramatic head in the autumn of 1758.

On the night of 3 September 1758, King José was returning to the Ajuda Palace by chaise after visiting his mistress when he was waylaid by gunmen in a narrow alley. Shot twice, he was slightly wounded in an arm and a thigh; but the coach managed to speed away to the nearby house of his surgeon, where the royal wounds were swiftly treated. At first little was publicly divulged about the incident, while Pombal's agents feverishly gathered evidence. However, the

---

[47] Azevedo J L de 1922a, p 125.
[48] SHP vol 6, pp 34–8.

mistress with whom King José had been liaising on the night concerned was Teresa de Távora, wife of the first son of the old marquis of Távora, one of the country's most illustrious *grandes*. Suspicion therefore inevitably fell upon the Távoras. Eventually, on 9 December 1758, Pombal was ready to move. He announced the immediate formation of a special investigatory tribunal, its members to include himself and the other secretaries of state. A series of arrests swiftly followed, and among those taken into custody were the duke of Aveiro, his sixteen-year-old son the marquis of Gouveia, the marquis and marchioness of Távora, their two sons, Teresa de Távora the king's mistress, the marquis of Alorna and the counts of Atougeia, Óbidos, Vila Nova and Ribeira Grande.[49] All these members of the inner circle of great nobles were closely linked by bonds of blood and marriage. Also arrested were about a dozen Jesuits, one of them being Fr Gabriel Malagrida, confessor to the marchioness of Távora. Finally, the tribunal ordered the detention of several commoners, most of whom were attendants or servants of the accused *grandes*.

Over the next few weeks the prisoners were interrogated, with fairly frequent resort to the rack. They received but the barest opportunity to defend themselves before verdicts were pronounced on 12 January 1759, some sixty individuals being convicted. Most of these, including the marquis of Alorna, the counts of Ribeira Grande, Óbidos and Gouveia, four brothers of the marquis of Távora and nine Jesuits, were sentenced to indefinite imprisonment. But six *grandes* and five commoners were sentenced to death, the executions to be carried out the following day. Watched by a huge crowd, the duke of Aveiro and marquis of Távora were broken alive on the wheel – tied down and their ribs and all the bones in their arms and legs broken with heavy hammers, then left to die in agony. Two sons of the marquis of Távora, the count of Atougeia and several of the condemned commoners were similarly broken, but after first being strangled. The marchioness of Távora was beheaded, while the retainer of the duke found to have actually fired at the king was burned alive. These barbaric proceedings filled most of the day. When all was over, the huge wooden scaffold specially constructed for the occasion was set alight and consumed in a massive conflagration, along with all its bloody contents. The ashes were disposed of in the Tagus.[50]

There is much about the Távora conspiracy that remains obscure. Was the king deliberately shot at on that fatal 3 September? Were those held accountable in reality guilty – and, if so, what were their motives? In the days immediately after the ambush a persistent rumour was current, reported by several ambassadors, that the shots had never been intended for José, but for the lackey

[49] Ibid, p 40; Dutra F A 1998, pp 221–2.
[50] Ibid, pp 42–3; Cheke M 1938, pp 120–8; MedHP vol 7, p 295; Maxwell K 1995, p 79.

who accompanied him on his nocturnal sallies. Francis Dutra inclines to this view, yet there is no compelling reason to doubt that an attempt on the king's life was indeed made.[51] Anecdotal evidence suggests up to 250 people may have been aware beforehand that a plot was afoot.[52] At the time thinly veiled anti-Pombaline sentiment within the aristocracy was widespread – and it is possible the failed attempt to persuade King José to dismiss Pombal in 1756 had convinced malcontents there was no other way.

As for the Távoras, the family did have personal reasons to feel aggrieved on a matter of honour – the king's seduction of Teresa de Távora. But this amorous affair had already been going on for several years, apparently without arousing much objection.[53] Moreover behaviour of this kind was not uncommon. Again, at a personal level the Távoras certainly disliked Pombal, and the old marquis of Távora was said to have been deeply offended when he failed to receive a dukedom after completing his term as viceroy at Goa in 1754. The resentment felt by the marchioness at this perceived slight was allegedly even stronger – and her influence behind the scenes may have been considerable. Yet the grievances attributed to the Távoras hardly seem to have constituted sufficient reason, either singly or in combination, to attempt regicide.

The duke of Aveiro's case was rather different. Generally regarded as the central figure in the conspiracy, Aveiro at first had protested his innocence. But he later confessed to his interrogators that he had paid three of his men to fire the shots. His motives included the crown's decision to cut off his income from certain *comendas* and to stop his son's proposed marriage to a daughter of the duke of Cadaval. He apparently thought he would get his way on these matters if José were replaced as king by his brother Prince Pedro.[54] Aveiro's role was confirmed by various other prisoners. Of course, much of the evidence against him was extracted under torture and was therefore hardly untainted. However, a judicial review of the Távora case conducted twenty-three years later, after Pombal had departed the political scene, confirmed guilty verdicts only on Aveiro and three of his servants.[55]

The brutal form of execution visited upon the Távoras roused strong emotions in Portugal at the time, of which there are still echoes even today. In the outside world, particularly among the European intelligentsia, the revulsion was considerable. Attempts to explain the brutality usually stress the political

[51] Smith J 1843 vol 1, p 210; Azevedo J L de 1922a, p 176; SHP vol 6, pp 40–1, 44; Dutra F A 1998, pp 223–9.

[52] Smith J 1843 vol 1, p 207.

[53] Azevedo J L de 1922a, p 175.

[54] Azevedo P de 1921, pp 157–9.

[55] Cheke M 1938, pp 149–50, 290–3; DIHP vol 2, pp 268–9.

need for a salutary example. They also point out that in the eighteenth century harsh punishments, particularly for attacks on the person of a monarch, were standard practice.[56] But it was clearly not the European tradition to execute persons of high rank by breaking them on the wheel. This procedure was also a clear departure from previous Portuguese practice. Great nobles condemned in the past for treason, such as the duke of Bragança in 1483 and marquis of Vila Real and duke of Caminha in 1641, had always been beheaded.[57] Moreover, if the primary aim was to cow those *grandes* who were hostile to the Pombaline regime, this could have been achieved without resorting to sadistic barbarities. Finally, while there is little doubt Pombal himself wanted the *grandes* taught a salutary lesson, he cannot be held solely responsible for what was done. King José and Queen Mariana Vitória were both determined the attackers should be punished with the greatest possible severity – and in matters of this nature it was the royal will that usually prevailed.[58]

Nevertheless, Pombal's unyielding commitment to the absolutist monarchic state and his ideas about how power should be distributed within it probably made the Távora case or something like it inevitable. In any event, his attitude had an important long-term impact on the higher nobility, its behaviour patterns and ultimately its role in the social and political life of the kingdom. In the first half of the eighteenth century, great nobles still formed a small but coherent political elite. They retained a near-monopoly of palace offices and high military commands and filled the leading positions on the central judicial and administrative tribunals. From generation to generation, such nobles expected, and received, copious crown patronage in the form of grants and pensions and enjoyed an overwhelming share of *comendas*. By the eighteenth century only about one-fifth of the income drawn by these personages came from their own properties. Almost all *grandes* eventually abandoned their country seats and came to live in Lisbon – to be near the court. By Pombal's time few were visiting their rural lands and lordships on a regular basis, and their seigneurial ties withered accordingly. Now they built or acquired mansions in Lisbon, where they maintained their dependent relatives and large servant retinues and lived the lives of rentiers. After 1755 many struggled to recover from earthquake losses.[59]

Of course, there was never any intention on the part of the Pombaline regime to assail, still less destroy, the aristocracy as an institution. Pombal believed strongly in an hierarchical society, a world in which *grandes* had an essential place. In some respects he sought to make elite social differentiation more

---

[56] Cf. Smith J 1843 vol 1, pp 199–202; SHP vol 6, p 131; Maxwell K 1995, p 80.
[57] See chs 7 and 11.
[58] SHP vol 6, pp 45–6; Leite A 1983, p 29; MedHP vol 7, pp 296–7.
[59] HP vol 4, pp 340, 370–2; NHP vol 9, p 181.

pronounced: for instance, by introducing strict controls on the right to form *morgados*.[60] When aristocratic titles became extinct in King José's reign they were replaced by new ones, so that the total number remained stable. Pombal himself became one of the new title-holders, receiving the designations of first count of Oeiras, then marquis of Pombal, and the personal status of *grande* was certainly something he prized. But this did not deter him from rigorously excluding most traditional *grandes* from central decision-making – and simultaneously nurturing the new nobility, which was mostly recruited from successful merchants and bureaucrats and more like an elite of merit.[61] Pombal allowed the *grandes* no substantive political privileges, either formal or informal, by virtue of their being *grandes;* certainly no privileges that could in any way be interpreted as infringing upon the prerogatives of the crown.

It was during the Pombaline era that social attitudes among the higher nobility at last began to show some signs of change. This was in part a product of official coercion and manipulation – such as Pombal's termination in 1768 of the restrictive marriage practices of the *puritanos*. However, regardless of government intervention, the pressures for modernisation were inexorably growing, forcing the *grandes* to make adjustments. A significant decline in the practice of consigning daughters and younger sons to the church was one significant outcome. This trend was already noticeable among the nobility in Lisbon by the 1760s, although not among provincial nobles until somewhat later. At about the same time a decrease in the use of entails suggests long-established strategies for perpetuating great noble houses were losing their attraction.[62] Be that as it may, Pombal was always careful to preserve the exclusiveness of the higher nobility – which, in the course of his administration, was never allowed to expand beyond its traditional numbers.

POMBALINE REGALISM AND THE EXPULSION OF THE JESUITS

Aristocratic opposition to Pombal had been effectively silenced by the end of the 1750s; but powerful forces that did not fit comfortably with his ideas remained active within the church. Prominent among them was the Society of Jesus, which in the sixteenth and seventeenth centuries had been one of the most respected and successful religious institutions in Portugal. The Society had traditionally attracted high-quality recruits, often from elite families. The Jesuits controlled all university and most secondary education, were renowned for the skill and power of their preaching and were the acknowledged leaders in

---

[60] Monteiro N G 2003, pp 7, 12.
[61] MHP, p 397; HP vol 4, p 365; Maxwell K 1995, pp 78.
[62] Maxwell K 1995, p 138; Monteiro N G 2003, pp 13–14.

missionary enterprise overseas. Because the prestige of the Society of Jesus was so great, individual Jesuits often acted as spiritual advisers and confessors to Portuguese kings and *grandes* – and acquired commensurate political influence.

However, during the first half of the eighteenth century, the Jesuits in Portugal began to show signs of losing their influence. They continued to attract recruits; but fewer were coming from the kingdom's elite.[63] The Society's teaching practices were increasingly questioned, and the Oratorians emerged as rival educators with different pedagogical ideas. By mid-century a so-called 'contentious war over learning' (*porfiada guerra literária*) had broken out between these two orders, its origins apparently in a dispute over how to teach Latin.[64] Meanwhile, fewer members of the Portuguese elite were engaging Jesuit confessors and tutors or electing to be buried in Jesuit churches. Benefactions decreased, and the Society's income in Portugal fell.[65] The changing attitude of João V himself was as good an indicator as any of the Jesuits' gradual deterioration. He had been Jesuit-educated and at first employed Jesuit confessors; but later he tended to choose Oratorians. A respected Italian Jesuit, Giovanni Bautista Carbone, eventually became one of the king's trusted confidants; but no member of the Society ever served him as a minister of state. Ominously, twice during João V's reign the Jesuits found themselves accused of trespassing on the royal prerogative. Finally, by the mid-eighteenth century the Portuguese Jesuits' contribution to learning and high culture in general was clearly on the wane. They produced few writings of note and played virtually no role in the major architectural and artistic undertakings of the era.[66] The general impression is of an institution that was being progressively left behind.

Yet, despite these problems and setbacks, at the beginning of King José's reign the Society of Jesus remained a considerable force, in both metropolitan Portugal and the Portuguese empire. The watering down of its near-monopoly by Oratorian competition notwithstanding, it still dominated the education system. Moreover, the Jesuits' formidable preaching ensured they maintained considerable influence in the shaping of religious opinion – and even, to some extent, of political opinion.[67] Their capacity to interfere in affairs of state was less than in the past, but had not disappeared, and in 1750 the Society continued to enjoy the crown's confidence and protection. At this stage it seems Pombal himself was not especially hostile to the Jesuits. Although he was wary of their influence and had concerns about their pedagogical conservatism, he

---

[63] Boxer C R 1978, p 120.
[64] Miller S J 1978, pp 165–8.
[65] Maxwell K 1995, pp 13–14; Alden D 1996, pp 604–5; NHP vol 7, pp 100–1.
[66] Alden D 1996, pp 605–11.
[67] HP vol 4, p 295.

was certainly not bent on getting rid of them. Nor were the Jesuits too concerned when Pombal entered the government; indeed, they appear to have supported his rise and to have considered him an ally.[68]

Why then, by the mid-1750s, had Pombal's attitude to the Society of Jesus become one of such unremitting hostility? The explanation probably lies, in the first instance, in contemporary developments in faraway Brazil. In January 1750, six months prior to Pombal's becoming secretary of state for foreign affairs and war, Portugal and Spain signed the treaty of Madrid in an attempt to establish agreed-upon borders between their respective empires in South America.[69] The treaty included a provision that two Jesuit mission clusters that had been established under Spanish patronage now be transferred to Portuguese control. One of these areas – in western Amazonia east of the Guaporé River – had already been abandoned and so presented little problem. But the other – the so-called Seven Missions, lying east of the River Uruguay – contained a string of painstakingly-constructed Jesuit churches, well-populated villages and flourishing agricultural and pastoral estates. All were to be relinquished, without compensation, to the Portuguese authorities, and their almost 30,000 inhabitants were to re-settle in Spanish territory.[70]

The Amerindians of the Uruguay missions were understandably devastated on learning that they were to be sacrificed to political expediency. Their unhappy Jesuit leaders told them they had no alternative but to move; but they chose defiance, forcibly preventing a joint Luso-Spanish boundary commission from carrying out its work. Even after the Jesuit leadership formally relinquished control to the Portuguese, the grass-roots defiance continued – with how much if any complicity from the local missionaries is unclear. In any event, during 1754–6 a series of full-scale Luso-Spanish military operations had to be mounted to enforce the evacuation, accomplished at the cost of considerable bloodshed.[71] Meanwhile, the Jesuits in the Portuguese Amazon – where the Society had long been the dominant missionary organisation – found themselves confronted by similarly unpalatable demands. Pombal had determined as a matter of principle that Amerindians were to be fully integrated into the colonising process, which effectively meant they could no longer be kept in protective isolation on missions. He instructed his brother, Francisco Xavier de Mendonça Furtado, who had been appointed governor of Grão-Pará e Maranhão in 1751, to implement this policy. However, this could not be done without undermining the missionary enterprise – and by as early as 1754 Mendonça Furtado and the Amazon Jesuits

---

[68] Antunes M 1983, pp 126–7; Maxwell K 2001, p 173.
[69] Boxer C R 1962, pp 244–5; Davidson D M 1973, pp 94–102.
[70] Hemming J 1978, pp 452, 462–3.
[71] Ibid, pp 469–74.

found themselves on a collision course. Virulent reports from the governor, excoriating the missionaries for obstructionism and accusing them of abusing in all kinds of ways the Amerindians placed in their charge, were soon streaming back to Pombal in Lisbon.[72]

By 1755 Pombal had become convinced that the continued presence of Jesuit missionaries in Brazil was incompatible with the exercise of Portuguese sovereignty. Accordingly he persuaded the king to issue a series of decrees declaring the Amerindians to be full and free subjects of the crown. The mission villages were to be removed forthwith from Jesuit control and converted into regular towns run by their own inhabitants. For the time being, missionaries could remain – but only to serve as local priests devoted solely to parish duties. That same year the Grão Pará and Maranhão Company was created and granted a trade monopoly for the region. Taken together, these moves clearly spelled the end for any credible Jesuit enterprise in Amazonia, and the Society and its allies immediately mounted a desperate campaign of appeals and protests in Lisbon. Such opposition Pombal would not tolerate, and he swiftly suppressed it.[73]

By this time Pombal's hostility towards the Society had been greatly intensified by the behaviour of certain Jesuits in Portugal. He was incensed by a series of sermons preached after the November 1755 earthquake, exhorting the populace to give religious acts of attrition priority over the practical work of reconstruction. The most prominent preacher involved was an elderly Italian Jesuit, Fr Gabriel Malagrida. A former missionary with a long and distinguished record of service in Brazil, Malagrida was a fiery speaker. He had exercised quite some influence at court in the last days of João V, to whom he had ministered on that monarch's deathbed. Later, Malagrida had accepted the patronage of King José's brother Prince Pedro and of the Távora family, before returning to Brazil. But by 1754 he was back in Portugal, perhaps recalled by the Society to campaign against Pombal's anti-Jesuit policies.[74] It was then that Malagrida had infuriated Pombal by his preaching, and subsequent publishing, of a highly emotional interpretation of the Lisbon earthquake as divine punishment. Accordingly he was exiled from the city in November 1756.

Barely three months after Malagrida's exile the Society of Jesus suffered yet another setback, when Pombal apparently convinced himself that it was involved in an outbreak of violence in Porto against the Upper Douro Wine Company. Although the supposed subversive connection was never proved, in September 1757 to prevent the Society from exercising any further influence at palace level Pombal had King José's Jesuit confessor removed and replaced by

[72] Ibid, pp 454–61; Maxwell K 2001, pp 173–5.
[73] SHP vol 6, pp 48–9; Hemming J 1978, pp 475–7; Maxwell K 1995, pp 69–70.
[74] Kendrick T D 1956, p 88; Leite A 1983, p 50.

priests he could trust.[75] Probably by this time Pombal had decided that the Jesuits were a fundamental threat to his reform program and therefore had to go. In any event, he now embarked on a relentless campaign to destroy the embattled Society. In May 1758, the cardinal-patriarch was persuaded to suspend all its members from preaching or hearing confessions, and it was about this time that they were also forbidden to engage in commerce.[76] Finally on 3 September 1759, the Jesuits were declared in rebellion against the crown and orders issued for their mass deportation. It took about two years to implement these orders – but eventually nearly a thousand Jesuits were forced out, including some 600 from Brazil and 282 from Asia.[77]

Meanwhile, the fate of Malagrida had finally been decided. Despite his arrest for alleged complicity in the Távora plot, no convincing evidence was produced against him – or, for that matter, against any of seven other Jesuits similarly detained – at the subsequent investigation and trial. Nevertheless, Malagrida was then denounced to the Inquisition for heresy, blasphemy and false prophecy and promptly imprisoned by that tribunal. Soon afterwards, perhaps as a result of harsh conditions in custody, he became mentally unbalanced and started hallucinating. His ravings now provided the 'evidence' his accusers wanted, and he was duly tried and convicted. On 20 September 1761, this elderly Jesuit was strangled and burned at the stake.[78]

Most other Jesuits suffered more prosaic fates. Many simply left the Society and became secular priests. Some took up entirely new occupations, while the less fortunate underwent varying terms of imprisonment. The largest group, numbering several hundred, was shipped off to Rome. Jesuit property was made forfeit to the crown, but most of the productive assets quickly found their way into private hands. The government used its modest windfall to help cover its military and other short-term costs.[79] Pombal went on to orchestrate an intensive propaganda campaign against the Society throughout Europe – and soon the rulers of France, Spain and Naples decided to follow his example and expel their Jesuits. In July 1773 Pope Clement XIV, buckling under strong international pressure, agreed to suppress the Society throughout the Catholic world. Pombal's triumph over the so-called black robes could hardly have been more complete.

The expulsion of the Society of Jesus from Portugal amounted to a radical change of direction – for in no other European country had this once formidable

[75] Schneider S 1971, p 117.

[76] Oliveira M de 1968, p 303; Hemming J 1978, p 478; Miller S J 1978, p 62.

[77] Hemming J 1978, p 479; Alden D 2000, pp 362, 370.

[78] Azevedo P de 1921, p 20; Cheke M 1938, pp 94–6, 152–7; Kendrick T D 1956, pp 89–91; Oliveira M de 1968, pp 302, 304; Maxwell K 1995, pp 82–3.

[79] Alden D 1984, pp 159–60; Borges C J 1994, p 133; Maxwell K 1995, p 129.

order been more entrenched, more influential and more powerful. Its downfall was followed by a period of strained relations between Portugal and Rome, with a long break in diplomatic ties from 1760 to 1769. However, despite the slightly hysterical papal fears at this time that Portugal might be about to go down the Anglican road, the creation of a Portuguese church separated from Rome was never on Pombal's agenda. While strongly regalist, his ecclesiastical policy was modelled on the Gallican and not the Anglican precedent. He envisaged a church loyal to the pope in spiritual matters but otherwise free from Vatican bureaucratic controls.[80] There is no doubt that neither Pombal, nor King José, ever had the slightest intention of moving away from the Catholic faith as such.

Pombal was able to muster in support of his ecclesiastical policy much weighty and learned opinion from within the Portuguese church, beginning with that of the cardinal-patriarch. In this he was doubtless helped by the fact that the Jesuits were viewed with considerable resentment and suspicion by many of their rivals in the other religious orders. Moreover, there were many progressive clerics touched by Enlightenment thinking who saw the need for reform and believed Pombal was on more or less the right track. He was therefore able to co-opt to his cause a number of churchmen of high repute and intellectual stature. Among the most impressive of them was the Oratorian Latinist and musician António Pereira de Figueiredo (1725–97). Pereira de Figueiredo wrote a series of learned treatises in the 1760s and 1770s, strongly endorsing regalism. His work was eagerly embraced by Pombal, and he eventually became an important propagandist for the regime. But Pereira de Figueiredo himself long survived his patron and was still writing well into the reign of Maria I. He was never a mere puppet of Pombal, but a genuine scholar in his own right whose most remarkable work was his translation of the entire Vulgate into Portuguese. This, the first ever Portuguese version of the whole Bible, was published progressively between 1772 and 1790.[81]

Steps were also taken during Pombal's supremacy to bring under state control that other formidable religious institution from the reign of João III – the Portuguese Inquisition. It is not surprising, given his strong commitment to regalist principles, that Pombal should have wanted to reform the Inquisition, a body that had wielded semi-autonomous power for so long. He was doubtless aware that throughout Western Europe inquisitions were now a symbol of backwardness and bigotry, giving Portugal the kind of image he was anxious to dispel. Nevertheless, within the kingdom itself the Inquisition remained a powerful, prestigious and much-feared force, still active enough in the 1750s to

---

[80] Miller S J 1978, pp 161, 163, 169, 188, 197, 199; Maxwell K 1995, pp 90–1.
[81] Silva I F de 1858–23 vol 1, pp 223–30; GE vol 4, p 643 and vol 21, pp 214–16; Miller S J 1978, pp 147–8, 163–5, 167–70; DIHP vol 2, p 103.

burn another eighteen victims.[82] Moreover, many prominent Portuguese were familiars of the Inquisition, including Pombal himself.

In extending state control over the Inquisition Pombal did not need to mount – or perhaps felt it best not to attempt – the kind of head-on confrontation he had launched against the Jesuits. Instead, he adopted a policy of change through administrative manipulation, the ultimate objective being to reduce the Inquisition to the status of just another government tribunal. In 1760, Pombal's brother and ally, Paulo de Carvalho e Mendonça, was appointed to the key office of inquisitor general, and under his direction the religious rigour of the tribunal slackened, the number of autos da fé declined and burnings ceased entirely. In 1768 the Inquisition lost its police and censorship powers, and in 1773 its jurisdiction over Judaizing lapsed, for the distinction between Old and New Christians was formally abolished and all discrimination against the latter became illegal. These changes removed much of the raison d'être of the holy office. In any case, by this time the New Christians had become more or less integrated into Portuguese society.[83] In 1774, the Inquisition was finally secularised – becoming, in Samuel Miller's words, 'Pombal's docile instrument'.[84]

Pombaline regalism also required a compliant and submissive national episcopacy, bishops confining themselves to pronouncing on strictly spiritual matters only.[85] Most bishops seem to have accepted this situation and behaved accordingly. Francisco de Saldanha, the cardinal-patriarch of Lisbon, was a friend and protege of Pombal. His cooperation with the regime was such that a papal nuncio once called him Pombal's complete slave.[86] João Cosme da Cunha, bishop of Leiria and later archbishop of Évora, collaborated particularly closely with the administration, eagerly embracing such draconian policies as the campaign to destroy the Jesuits. Pombal moved his own supporters into key ecclesiastical positions as opportunity offered. Any prelate who presumed to entertain ideas of acting independently was swiftly brought down, a salutary example being that of Bishop Miguel da Anunciação of Coimbra. In 1768, Bishop Anunciação issued a pastoral letter prohibiting a number of books in his diocese, on his own authority. They included works by such 'atheist' authors as Voltaire, Montesquieu and Rousseau, but also certain regalist writings approved by the regime. The bishop's action was immediately interpreted

[82] MHP, p 402.
[83] Oliveira M de 1968, p 307; SHP vol 6, pp 130–3; Leite A 1983, p 39; Maxwell K 1995, p 91; Bethencourt F 2000, pp 283–4.
[84] Miller S J 1978, p 228.
[85] Maxwell K 1995, p 94.
[86] Miller S J 1978, pp 51, 109.

by Pombal as a breach of the royal prerogative. Anunciação was promptly charged with *lèse-majesté* and imprisoned for the rest of the reign.[87]

Pombal faced opposition from many quarters during the course of his rule, including titled nobles, certain elements within the church, segments of the upper bourgeoisie excluded from the benefits of his economic reforms, traders and vineyard owners squeezed out of privileged markets and even some segments of the proletariat. But the opposition was never sufficiently widespread or coordinated to threaten the regime seriously. As long as Pombal retained the favour of the king and control of such instruments of central government as the military, the police and the state propaganda machine, he remained irremovable.

DEFENCE AND EDUCATION

Portugal managed to stay relatively free of military threats in the Pombaline era, despite a brief invasion by Spanish forces in 1762–3 during the final phase of the Seven Years War. Nevertheless, Pombal was acutely aware of Portuguese vulnerability in what was again becoming an increasingly dangerous world for small powers – and he often worried about the aggressive intentions, real or imaginary, of potential enemies. The invasion of 1762–3 exposed major deficiencies in Portugal's defence capability, obliging Pombal to ask Britain for military aid. London responded by sending an expeditionary force commanded by Count Wilhelm von Schaumburg-Lippe, an experienced officer of German extraction. After the peace of 1763, Lippe stayed on to re-organise the Portuguese army. He modernised the ranking system, strengthened discipline and introduced a new emphasis on skills, particularly stressing the need for officers to receive professional training. He also systematically repaired and strengthened Portugal's border fortresses. Meanwhile, Pombal moved to expand and modernise the Portuguese navy.[88] But once the immediate crisis was over and Lippe had departed, it seems interest in improving the armed forces gradually waned.

On the other hand, Pombal presided over an educational reform program that was bold, far-reaching and lasting. During his period in London and Vienna, Pombal had become acutely aware of just how backward Portugal's education system then was, particularly when viewed from the outside. At the time, he was developing his lasting interest in the Moderate Enlightenment, with its emphasis on empiricism and experimental science. This stream of Enlightenment thought, emanating from the work of men like Robert Boyle (1627–91), John Locke (1632–1704) and Isaac Newton (1642–1727), was

---

[87] Oliveira M de 1968, pp 304–6; SHP vol 6, pp 117–18; Maxwell K 1995, pp 82, 95; NHP vol 6, p 117.

[88] Smith J 1843 vol 1, pp 333–5; SHP vol 6, pp 58, 60–3; DIHP vol 1, pp 228, 389.

closely associated with England's Royal Society to which Pombal himself had been admitted. In the 1730s and 1740s Moderate Enlightenment ideas were also having a major impact in Italy, and Italian thinkers, such as the strongly anti-scholastic Antonio Genovesi (1712–69), exerted much influence on contemporary Portuguese intellectuals like Verney and Ribeiro Sanches.[89] Almost all these Enlightenment figures regarded educational reform as crucial.

Apparently for almost a decade after his rise to power Pombal did not have the time or opportunity to do much about educational reform, and it was only in early 1759 that he took his first significant step down this road by founding a school of commerce (*aula do comércio*). Created on the new board of trade's recommendation, this innovative institution was designed to teach such practical skills as cost analysis, double-entry book-keeping and management of differential weights, measures and currencies. Students were accepted at the age of fourteen with priority given to sons and grandsons of businessmen. Up to fifty boys could be enrolled at any one time, and the course lasted three years. The founding of this institution was thoroughly consistent with Pombal's long and deeply-held conviction that Portuguese business, if it were to be competitive internationally, must adopt more professional practices. Establishing the school proved a particularly worthwhile investment, for it helped to lay the first foundations of a Portuguese technical education system.[90] The *aula do comércio* might well have served as a model too for broader educational reform – but this was not to be. Instead, Pombal plunged the kingdom into a process of sudden forced change – confusing to many, intensely painful to some, but probably inevitable after the decision in June 1759 to close down the Jesuits.

When Pombal expelled the Society of Jesus there were some 20,000 students enrolled in thirty-four Jesuit secondary schools (*colégios*) scattered throughout Portugal. By contrast only 3,000–4,000 students attended Oratorian *colégios*. Therefore the expulsion meant that 80–90 per cent of Portuguese secondary students were deprived overnight of their schooling, and about the same proportion of secondary-level teachers was dismissed.[91] Pombal fully understood the seriousness of this situation and moved swiftly to remedy it. He established a directorate general of studies (*directoria geral dos estudos*) or de facto department of education, which was ordered to organise, as quickly as possible, a state-controlled, secularised education system. It was also to draw up curricula, recruit teachers and select textbooks, paying particular regard to the educational ideas of Verney and Genovesi.[92]

---

[89] Gomes J F 1983, p 236; Maxwell K 1995, p 12; Israel J 2001, p 115.
[90] SHP vol 6, pp 248–50.
[91] Leite A 1983a, pp 171–2.
[92] Ibid, p 174; Carvalho R de 1983, p 215; Maxwell K 1995, pp 96–7.

As a first step the directorate general of studies tried to appoint at least one *professor régio* – an approved and duly licensed teacher, salaried by the state – to teach Latin in every town and in every suburb of Lisbon and Porto. Also sought was a smaller number of instructors in Greek and rhetoric. As far as curricula were concerned, the directorate was able to fall back on the Oratorian system. The 1752 *Novo Método da Grámatica Latina* by the Oratorian António Pereira de Figueiredo, a close collaborator of Pombal, was endorsed as the new standard Latin textbook, replacing long-established Jesuit grammars. Nevertheless, it seems that much teaching at this level differed little from past practice.[93] A more difficult problem was the acute shortage of appropriately qualified candidates for the new teaching positions. This, plus lack of money, made it impossible to recruit anything like the number of *professores régios* needed, particularly outside the major cities, and by 1770 only thirty-nine had been licensed. Meanwhile, to secure for their sons instruction in basic literacy and numeracy parents were encouraged to resort to private schoolmasters. But this meant paying fees, whereas Jesuit instruction had been free. One result was that the schoolmasters tended to be paid late or never, forcing some to abandon their work altogether.[94]

With the secondary education system seriously handicapped by all these difficulties, in 1771 the Pombaline regime determined on a further shake-up. Responsibility for the system was transferred from the directorate general of studies to the royal censorship board (*real mesa censória*) and given more financial backing by means of the new literary tax. This made it possible to appoint additional *professores régios* and then gradually extend state control to primary education. Under Pombal the man most associated with this new wave of reform was Frei Manuel do Cenáculo Vilas Boas (1724–1814), president of the royal censorship board and later bishop of Beja. Cenáculo shared both Pombal's anti-scholastic, anti-Jesuit leanings and his enthusiasm for the Moderate Enlightenment. He became effectively minister for education.[95]

Meanwhile, another experiment in secondary education was introduced in the form of the royal college for nobles, now installed in an abandoned Jesuit novitiate in Lisbon. This was an elite school for sons of the nobility between seven and thirteen years of age and was designed to prepare them for crown service in the armed forces, the diplomatic corps and the colonial administration, or at court. The college was not a new concept, for similar institutions already functioned in France and elsewhere. However, it was very much in line with Pombal's vision of creating a more enlightened and useful Portuguese

[93] SHP vol 6, p 253; Leite A 1983a, pp 174, 176; Maxwell K 1995, p 97.
[94] SHP vol 6, p 257; Leite A 1983a, p 175.
[95] Maxwell K 1995, pp 97–100.

nobility. Students at the college were to learn not just the traditional Latin, Greek and rhetoric, but also mathematics, the natural and physical sciences, military and civil engineering, French, Italian and English. In addition, they would receive instruction in riding, fencing and dancing.[96]

But the college never really lived up to its creator's expectations. Originally intended to cater for 100 students, it opened in 1766 with just twenty-four. As might have been expected, great difficulty was experienced in finding the specialist staff needed to teach its ambitious curriculum, and professors had to be sought overseas. Mathematics and science instructors were hired in Italy, and a modern physics laboratory was built and equipped with state-of-the-art instruments imported from England. Yet the college never made much impact on Portugal's great noble houses or on the behaviour and career patterns of individual nobles. As Nuno Gonçalo Monteiro has pointed out, the spread of modern ideas among Portuguese elite families remained extremely limited for most of the eighteenth century, a few notable exceptions notwithstanding.[97]

The royal college for nobles functioned in its original form for only six years. During this time, it matriculated a mere forty-seven students, only seven of whom actually attended the mathematics and science classes. In 1772 these subjects were therefore discontinued, and the laboratory, with all its equipment plus the surviving Italian physics professor, was transferred to the university at Coimbra.[98] Even Pombal acknowledged the founding of the college had been over-ambitious. The curriculum was too demanding for boys so young; nor could they cope with non-native instructors teaching in Latin and Italian. Eventually, in the reign of Maria I, a separate academy was established to train military engineers. The royal college for nobles lingered on – as a more traditional institution – until dissolved in 1837.[99]

The removal of the mathematics and science program from the royal college for nobles was closely linked to Pombal's reform of the University of Coimbra. In 1770 he had established a special board for educational affairs (*junta de providência literária*) to conduct a thorough review of the university. This board, which included both Pombal himself and Cenáculo, handed down its report to King José in August 1771 – and, on the basis of its recommendations, the university received a comprehensive new set of statutes and a major overhaul was commenced of buildings, equipment, faculties, staff and curricula.[100]

---

[96] SHP vol 6, pp 250–1; Leite A 1983a, p 177; Carvalho R de 1983, pp 215–16; Maxwell K 1995, p 106.

[97] Monteiro N G 2003, pp 13–14.

[98] SHP vol 6, pp 250–2; Leite A 1983a, pp 177–8; Carvalho R de 1983, pp 215–19.

[99] SHP vol 6, p 252; DIHP vol 1, p 135.

[100] Gomes J F 1983, pp 236–9.

The objective was to modernise Portugal's only university – Évora had been closed when the Jesuits were expelled in 1759 – and rid it of its alleged moribund Scholasticism. To this end the Faculties of Theology, Canon Law and Civil Law were all updated and the Faculty of Medicine was comprehensively reformed, being required to introduce the study of anatomy and hygiene. New faculties were created for mathematics and philosophy, the latter incorporating physics and chemistry. Numerous existing instructors were compulsorily retired, including all thirteen members of the Faculty of Medicine. Additional professors were appointed, of whom many were foreigners. There was also a massive upgrade of material infrastructure and new or re-cycled buildings were allocated to the Faculties of Medicine, Mathematics and Philosophy. A hospital, anatomy theatre, dispensary, laboratories, museum of natural history, botanic gardens and university press were likewise provided.[101]

In the wake of these reforms, every effort was made to encourage students, particularly young nobles, to study mathematics and science. Mathematics was therefore made a prerequisite not only for medicine and philosophy, but for law and even theology. Mathematics students were also accorded preference for commissions in the army and navy, and for teaching appointments – and an attempt was made to create a new and prestigious social category of 'mathematician'.[102] But there was passive resistance from traditionalists, and the new unfamiliar subjects were greeted with much suspicion and failed to attract students.[103] Eventually, when Pombal had left office, the rector of the university revealed that during the first two years after the reforms the Faculty of Philosophy remained well under-subscribed and only ten students had enrolled in advanced mathematics. After that there were no enrolments in advanced mathematics for the next three years – while the two law faculties continued to draw students by the hundreds. The reality was that career opportunities for mathematics and science graduates in a country as underdeveloped as eighteenth-century Portugal were too limited, and the traditional prestige subjects remained by comparison far more attractive.[104] Nevertheless, a new direction had been set for higher education, and in the longer term this would help to bring change.

Pombal launched into radical educational reform in 1759 because he had no alternative, after deciding to destroy the Jesuits. Earlier, he had seemed to want cautious educational change, adapting and adding to the existing system rather than mounting a direct assault on it. The creation of the *aula do comércio* was

[101] Ibid, pp 242–9; Carvalho R de 1983, pp 220, 228–9; Maxwell K 1995, p 102.
[102] Carvalho R de 1983, pp 224–5, 227.
[103] Ibid, p 225.
[104] Ibid, p 232; Gomes J F 1983, pp 249–50.

in line with this earlier strategy, which, had it been maintained, might have avoided much of the profound upheaval that from 1759 engulfed the system. Without doubt Pombal was strongly committed to educational reform, which he saw as essential to Portugal's modernisation. Yet the way he went about it illustrates once again that his regime was not only reformist, but incorrigibly despotic.

14

The Late Eighteenth Century: Finale of the Old Regime

MARIA I AND THE *VIRADEIRA*

Pombal was spectacularly successful in vanquishing his enemies; but there was nevertheless still one nagging political uncertainty over which even he exerted little influence. Who would succeed to the throne when José I died? As the king grew older this became a matter of real concern – for if José I were followed by a monarch unsympathetic to Pombal, then the latter's power would quickly evaporate. His reforms would most likely be undone and perhaps even his life made forfeit. Pombal was manifestly aware of these threats and did his best to guard against them. But there were no easy answers.

José I had no male heir. However, he did have four legitimate daughters each of whom, piously if somewhat confusingly, was called Maria. The oldest, Maria Francisca Isabel, was already sixteen when her father became king, and it was soon proposed that she marry her paternal uncle, Prince Pedro. At first Pombal opposed this match because he feared it might give rise to a rival court where his enemies could find refuge. So nothing happened – until overtures arrived from Madrid proposing the princess marry instead Prince Luís, son of Carlos III of Spain. This was even more unacceptable to Pombal for it raised the old spectre of a Spanish succession to the Portuguese throne. But by this time Pombal had subdued both his noble and his clerical enemies, and it had become apparent that neither Maria Francisca Isabel nor the lightweight Prince Pedro was capable of leading an effective opposition. So Pombal withdrew his objections to their marriage, which was duly solemnised in June 1760.[1]

---

[1] Azevedo J L de 1922a, pp 119, 224.

The marriage between niece and uncle produced in rapid succession six children, three of whom survived into adulthood. The oldest was the alert, intelligent Prince José (1761–88), whom Pombal quickly recognised as a potential ruler of real promise. He accordingly appointed his close collaborator, Frei Cenáculo Vilas Boas, to supervise the boy's education. Eventually, when Prince José had attained the age of sixteen in 1777, he was married off to Princess Maria Francisca Benedita, his mother's youngest sister. This princess was by far the most intelligent of the old king's four daughters and supported Pombaline policies. Possibly in overseeing the formation and marriage of Prince José, Pombal was hoping Maria Francisca Isabel could be by-passed and the prince brought forward to succeed his grandfather directly. However, if this was so, the strategy failed, and Maria Francisca Isabel, succeeding her father in 1777, was duly proclaimed Maria I. The first regnant queen in Portuguese history, she was already a mature forty-two years old at the time of her accession. She had received a good educational grounding in music, painting and languages, was exceedingly pious, but had no experience in affairs of state. Her inconsequential uncle-husband was granted the courtesy title of Pedro III.[2]

On Maria I's accession the numerous enemies of Pombal, who had lain low for so long, naturally hoped and pressed for a *viradeira* – a comprehensive about-turn in the policies pursued for the past twenty-seven years. There were those who sought a reversion to the ways of the past and others who wanted justice for the victims of Pombalism. But in the end the new regime brought only limited change – indeed, it opted for a considerable degree of continuity. Pombal himself was swiftly forced from office. Then some 800 prisoners of the Pombaline administration were released from their jails, as the dying King José had requested. Among them was a cluster of gaunt survivors from the Távora trial, incarcerated indefinitely since 1759. Various other individuals who had been driven into exile under Pombal were also now permitted to return. They included the duke of Lafões and the lawyer José de Seabra da Silva. A number of noblewomen forcibly confined to nunneries, such as the progressive and highly literate marchioness of Alorna, were freed.[3] But there was nevertheless no widespread campaign of reprisals against those associated with the outgoing administration. Pombal himself retired quietly to his country house in the town of Pombal, northern Estremadura.

Early in Maria's reign a conciliatory gesture was made to the *grandes* by distributing to them a raft of favours, including nine new titles for first sons.[4] However, as a group the *grandes* were not permitted to resume their previous

---

[2] SHP vol 6, p 295; DIHP vol 1, pp 362–3, 437; Maxwell K 1995, pp 98,100, 150–1.
[3] SHP vol 6, pp 295–6.
[4] Ibid, p 298; DIHP vol 1, p 435.

prominent role in central decision-making.[5] Moreover, their ranks were gradually expanded and therefore diluted. Particularly from the 1790s the number of titled aristocratic houses, which for so long had remained almost constant, increased substantially. By 1820 they had almost doubled, rising from 54 to 103 – and the remaining judicial functions, seigneurial rights and tax exemptions of the *grandes* virtually disappeared.[6] Meanwhile, the traditional *fidalguia* – in effect, the middle or provincial nobility of hereditary lineages – had also become a much reduced political force. However, the lower nobility (*nobreza simples*) continued to expand, until it eventually embraced almost everyone else above the status of manual worker. In this way nobility came to signify little more than genteel social pretensions – and by the end of the Old Regime the principle of equal citizenship was, for most practical purposes, generally accepted in Portugal.[7]

It was almost three years into Maria's reign before Pombal's administration was finally subjected to judicial investigation. There were two inquiries, of which the first, lasting from December 1779 to August 1782, examined Pombal's conduct during his time in office. Despite being over eighty years of age and increasingly sick and frail, Pombal defended himself with skill and vigour. In the end the judges failed to reach a united decision; so the queen simply declared him deserving of punishment, then pardoned him. For her, this ambiguous decision had the advantage of avoiding any implied criticism of her father, but it disappointed the former chief minister's many enemies and victims. Not long afterwards, on 8 May 1782, Pombal died. The second inquiry – a review of the Távora trial – had meanwhile brought down its report in May 1781. It endorsed the guilty verdict on the duke of Aveiro, but exonerated the Távoras themselves, concluding they had all been condemned unjustly. The Távoras' name and rights were restored – but not their titles and property, which had passed into the hands of others.[8]

The Jesuits, also hoping to benefit from Pombal's demise, pressed for their expulsion to be revoked. They submitted a closely-argued appeal backed by the king-consort, a former patron. Maria was not unsympathetic; but the new political landscape meant the chances of success were always slight. The Society had now been formally suppressed by Rome in 1773, and in both Portugal and the empire Jesuit property had long since passed into the hands of others. The Jesuits themselves were widely viewed with suspicion and had many influential enemies. Meanwhile, the Spanish government – with which the Portuguese

[5] HP vol 4, pp 340, 373.
[6] Ibid, pp 364–5; Monteiro N G 2003, pp 4–5.
[7] NHP vol 8, pp 179, 181.
[8] Azevedo J L de 1922a, pp 388–9; SHP vol 6, pp 297, 300–2; Maxwell K 1995, pp 157–8; DIHP vol 2, pp 268–9.

were anxious to maintain friendly relations – had made it clear that any attempt to restore the Society would be most unwelcome. Given all these circumstances, it is not surprising that the Jesuits' petition was firmly rejected.[9]

Nevertheless, the Marian government not only chose largely unvengeful compromise in its handling of legacies from the past, but also tried to steer a middle course between continuity and change in respect of the future. This attempted balance was already evident in Maria's first ministry. Two of the ministers – Martinho de Melo e Castro (secretary of state for naval and colonial affairs) and Aires de Sá (secretary of state for foreign affairs and war) – had previously held office alongside Pombal. At the same time two other key figures in the ministry – the viscount of Vila Nova de Cerqueira (secretary of state for internal affairs) and the elderly marquis of Angeja (state treasurer) – had been moderate oppositionists.[10] Despite a few inevitable changes of personnel, this leadership balance remained more or less stable throughout the fifteen years of Maria I's active rule (1777–92). The policies adopted could reasonably be described as neo-Pombaline.[11]

THE MARIAN ECONOMY AND THE MARIAN ENLIGHTENMENT

Although the government of Maria I maintained broadly similar economic settings to those of Pombal in his later years, it partially phased out reliance on monopolistic trading companies. When the charters of the Grão Pará and Maranhão Company and the Pernambuco and Paraiba Company came up for renewal, in 1778 and 1780, respectively, they were allowed to lapse.[12] By then these companies had achieved much of their original purpose, having stimulated new colonial export industries, such as cotton, rice and coffee, and re-invigorated older ones like sugar, tobacco and hides. They had also helped a number of merchant collaborators of Pombal to grow in strength and confidence and compete successfully against foreign rivals.

Economic conditions through the first three decades of Maria I's reign were generally positive for Portugal. Exports grew faster than imports – until in 1790, for the first time in the eighteenth century, the kingdom's balance of trade with Britain turned positive.[13] This was achieved mainly through a massive increase in colonial re-exports. In the final decade before 1807, 64 per cent of Portugal's exports originated in Brazil, and colonial trade roughly quadrupled. During this

---

[9] Azevedo J L de 1922a, pp 383–5.
[10] Maxwell K 1973, pp 71, 74; SHP vol 6, pp 297–8; HP vol 4, p 179.
[11] SHP vol 6, pp 308, 310; HP vol 4, pp 179–80.
[12] Maxwell K 1973, pp 72–4.
[13] Macedo 1982a, pp 235–6; HP vol 4, p 106; Shaw L M E 1998, p 42.

period Portugal was consistently selling more to its main European trading partners – Britain, France, Spain, Italy and the German states – than it imported.[14] This was a major economic achievement – an objective for which Pombal had long planned and striven. Under the stimulus of Europe's rapidly growing demand for industrial raw materials, Portugal had once again become a significant commercial intermediary, as in the sixteenth century. Re-exports of Brazilian cotton, first to Britain, then after 1801 more to France, accounted for most of the surge.[15] Meanwhile, although Anglo-Portuguese trade continued to be controlled largely by the British factories in Lisbon and Porto, Britain's share of Portuguese foreign trade overall was declining and by the end of the period had slipped to below 40 per cent. Portugal, her commercial relationships diversifying rapidly, was no longer simply an economic dependency of Britain.[16]

The industrial component of Portugal's exports grew significantly in the late eighteenth century, and by the 1790s textiles (mainly cottons), ironware and other manufactures comprised the greater part of what the mother country sent to Brazil.[17] Portugal was therefore no longer just a producer and re-exporter of primary products, but a country on the road to proto-industrialisation. The turnaround in the balance of payments was dramatic. In 1792 Sir John Hort, the British consul-general in Lisbon, was moved to comment, with only slight exaggeration, that 'all nations in Europe are Portugal's debtors'.[18] In many cases, the same merchant-capitalists who led the late eighteenth-century revival in Portuguese trade also orchestrated Portugal's upsurge in manufacturing. Colonial cotton, hides and other raw materials were now increasingly imported to provide Portugal's own factories, and not just to be sold on to Britain, the German states, Italy and France. European minerals such as iron, copper and lead were similarly imported. In the Marian era several crown industrial enterprises, such as the woollen factories at Covilhã and Portalegre, became privatised, while hundreds of new industrial workshops sprang up.[19] However, in the final years of the Old Regime, it is clear Portugal's economic prosperity was fundamentally dependent on privileged access to Brazilian raw materials on the one hand, and to the Brazilian market for manufactures on the other.[20]

Nevertheless, while economic policy continued to be an important concern, it was the threat of ideological subversion from overseas plus the deteriorating international military situation that most pre-occupied the

---

[14] Alexandre V 1993, pp 25, 32–3.
[15] Maxwell K 1973, pp 59–60; HP vol 4, p 111; Alexandre V 1993, pp 33, 35, 127.
[16] Alexandre V 1993, pp 36, 69–70, 162.
[17] Maxwell K 1973, pp 56–9, 72–3; Pereira M H 1986, p 286; HP vol 4, pp 109–10.
[18] Cited in Shaw L M E 1998, p 42.
[19] Maxwell K 1973, p 75; Macedo J B de 1982a, p 230; HP vol 4, p 111.
[20] Alexandre V 1993, pp 798–9; Arruda J J de A 2000, pp 869, 873–4.

Portuguese government during these years. In France, revolution was stirring while in Europe overall tensions were intensifying – and small powers like Portugal had to tread particularly carefully. As Anglo-French hostility grew, and Europe divided into two opposing camps, Portugal sought to maintain its neutrality, but in such a way as not to prejudice its alliance with Britain, the ultimate guarantor of its seaborne communications.

In the early Marian years the emphasis was on cultivating better relations with France and Spain. The treaties of San Ildefonso (1777) and El Pardo (1778) were negotiated with Spain, easing though not completely resolving a number of territorial disputes regarding their respective empires, outstanding since the treaty of Madrid in 1750. 'Permanent' peace between the Iberian neighbours was proclaimed, the rapprochement subsequently reinforced by reciprocal royal marriages in 1785 – the future João VI of Portugal to the Spanish princess Carlota Joaquina, and João's sister Mariana to the Spanish prince Gabriel de Bourbon.[21] Portugal also contrived to remain neutral during the Anglo-French hostilities of 1778–83 and in the concurrent struggle between Britain and its North American colonies. Lisbon recognised the independence of the United States six months before Britain formally did so.[22] Nevertheless, the Portuguese crown had serious misgivings, for United States independence had disturbing implications for Brazil. The first of a series of Brazilian conspiracies against Lisbon's rule occurred in 1789 and was partly inspired by the North American example.[23]

Meanwhile, inside Portugal – apart from among a small and restricted circle of intellectuals – attitudes and values remained overwhelmingly traditional. Even among elite Portuguese families modern ideas had spread little, despite a few notable exceptions.[24] Public displays of often exaggerated religiosity were common, especially in the north and centre of the country and despite the best efforts of a few Enlightened churchmen, who decried superstition. The Virgin Mary, along with other popular cult figures such as Santo António, continued to be widely venerated. Pilgrimages and religious processions remained an integral part of life, the queen herself setting a pious example. William Beckford, a rich English visitor with a witty, satirical pen, told many tales of this Portuguese religiosity. On the eve of Santo António's day in 1787 he observed that popular saint's image displayed, decked in flowers and candles, at the door of almost every house and hovel as he passed through Lisbon.[25] It was also Beckford who

[21] SHP vol 6, pp 299, 304, 462; DIHP vol 1, p 435; Alexandre V 1993, pp 96–7.
[22] Magalhães J C de 1977, pp 10–11.
[23] Maxwell K 1973, pp 126–7, 130, 135–6.
[24] Monteiro N G 2003, pp 13–14. Cf also Higgs D 1979, pp 62–3.
[25] Beckford W 1834 vol 2, p 58.

remarked, with some amusement, that while the flame of 'devout enthusiasm' had all but disappeared in Europe, yet it still glowed in Lisbon.[26]

A much commended feature of Portuguese court culture in the Marian era was its passion for fine music. Beckford, who was well travelled and not easily satisfied, heaped particular praise on this element of Portuguese life. He pronounced the music of the queen's chapel, both instrumental and vocal, to be the finest in Europe surpassing anything that even the papacy could offer.[27] A related characteristic of the period was keen interest in the building and reconstruction of churches. The great basilica at Estrela with its splendid cupola and Rococo exterior, perhaps the most striking architectural creation of Maria I's reign, dated from precisely these years (1779–90).[28]

Religious houses remained pervasive in Marian Portugal despite Pombal's expulsion of the Jesuits, there being still some 538 of them scattered throughout the country.[29] A few of the larger ones, such as Alcobaça, maintained considerable grandeur. Beckford claimed he was greeted on arriving at Alcobaça in 1794 by the abbot and no fewer than 400 monks and retainers. He was then taken to the abbey's sumptuous kitchen which he described as 'the most distinguished temple of gluttony in all Europe'.[30] Nevertheless, most Portuguese religious houses were now struggling institutions, often heavily burdened with debt. No more new religious orders were admitted to Portugal after 1782, and on the recommendation of a board of inquiry recruitment to existing religious houses was suspended from 1791.[31] The numbers and prestige of monks, friars and nuns were by then in steady decline. While the church still remained a pervasive presence for most Portuguese in early Marian times, there was certainly less identification with the religious orders – especially among the elite.

Although mainstream culture in Marian times continued to be firmly traditional, the fall of Pombal, the Marian *viradeira,* the release of political prisoners and the return of exiles from abroad all served to reinvigorate the minority of more progressive spirits among the Portuguese intelligentsia. A proliferation of academies, libraries, societies, intellectual circles and educational enterprises of varying kinds sprang up in the kingdom during these years. One of the key figures in this mini-Renaissance was João Carlos de Bragança, second duke of Lafões (1719–1806). A grandson of Pedro II, Lafões had been living abroad for over twenty years when Pombal fell from power. Most of the time he had spent in England where he was

[26] Ibid, p 253.
[27] Ibid, pp 123–4, 253–4.
[28] Smith R C 1968, p 106; SHP vol 6, pp 458–9.
[29] Oliveira M de 1968, pp 316–17.
[30] Beckford W 1972, pp 35, 37.
[31] MHP vol 1, p 398; Oliveira M de 1968, p 318; Higgs D 1979, p 56.

admitted to membership of the Royal Society. He also travelled widely in western and northern Europe and the Middle East, visiting France, Austria, Switzerland, Italy, Prussia, Poland, Scandinavia, Greece, Turkey and Egypt.[32] Lafões, one of the most intelligent of his generation of Portuguese *grandes*, was well acquainted with Enlightened philosophical and scientific thinking.

On his return to Portugal Lafões became an important local champion of the Arts and Sciences. He pressed for the establishment in Lisbon of a national institution to promote scientific knowledge and scholarly research, modelled on the royal academies of France and England. Largely as a result of his persistent lobbying the queen eventually founded the Portuguese Royal Academy for the Sciences (*Academia real das ciências*) in 1779. The most famous and lasting of all the eighteenth-century Portuguese academies, this prestigious body was initially divided into three 'classes', catering respectively to natural science, mathematics and letters. From the outset the academy was strongly influenced by Physiocratic ideas and adopted a highly practical orientation. It was equipped with a science museum and a library and undertook an impressive program of scholarly research, writing and discussion. Still active today, but now known as the *Academia das ciências de Lisboa,* it boasts a long and distinguished publications record.[33]

Nearly all this early Marian intellectual activity remained embedded in the Moderate Enlightenment with its emphasis on politically uncontroversial 'useful' knowledge. This is apparent in such enterprises as the *Jornal Encyclopédico,* a review founded in 1779 that focused on spreading awareness of innovative technology, economic issues and world affairs.[34] However, there was some interest – often secretive, but slowly growing – in the politically more risky Radical Enlightenment. A few Portuguese of this era were attracted by such notions as Liberty, Equality and Fraternity and by the Rights of Man. These ideas, and others later identified as 'liberal', reached Portugal sometimes from sources in Britain, but mostly from France. After 1783 the independent United States of America was another source. But those who toyed with radical political thinking in the Portugal of Maria I were generally viewed by the authorities in both church and state – and probably by the overwhelming majority of the populace – with scandalised horror. A contemporary archbishop of Lisbon dismissed them as nothing but a bunch of 'smooth-tongued, Frenchified, Italian Voltaireists and encyclopedians', who had 'poisoned all sound doctrine'.[35]

---

[32] GE vol 14, pp 544–5; DIHP vol 1, pp 369–70.
[33] MHP, pp 409, 411; SHP vol 6, pp 440–2; DIHP vol 1, pp 15–16.
[34] Nevins L 1971, pp 1–12.
[35] Beckford W 1834 vol 2, p 249.

SUBVERSION, POLICE AND INTERNAL SECURITY

It was already becoming apparent in Portugal before the end of the 1780s that great change was afoot in France. Louis XVI had been forced to convene the States General in May 1789, and the Bastille was stormed that July. By the end of August the Declaration of the Rights of Man, with its resounding assertion that all are free and equal, had already been fully formulated. News of these happenings was at first welcomed by many among the Portuguese intelligentsia, who generally assumed France was moving towards some much-needed monarchical reform. But the central government in Lisbon viewed the situation with growing anxiety. Through the 1790s it waged a constant struggle to exclude from Portugal anything that smacked of subversion, real or imagined. At stake it saw the preservation of the Portuguese Old Regime as both a social and political system.

Marian Portugal had at its disposal an internal security apparatus inherited from the years of Pombal. In 1760, largely in response to intermittent unrest in the aftermath of the earthquake, Pombal had decided to establish an agency called the intendancy-general of police (*intendência geral da polícia*). This body was in part a civil constabulary and in part a security police. In the former capacity, broadly interpreted as the protector of the public from criminal activity, it had taken some strong but in certain respects quite progressive measures. For the first time in Portuguese policing a clear distinction had been made between executive and judicial law enforcement – between combating crime and apprehending offenders on the one hand, and legally convicting and punishing them on the other. Moreover, as well as pursuing a forceful policy of crime suppression the intendancy-general developed a keen interest in crime prevention.

However, the intendancy-general of police was also charged with ferreting out subversion – and it was in this capacity that it eventually evolved into a feared organ of state security. To protect himself and his immediate colleagues Pombal had extended the definition of *lèse-majesté* to apply not only to actions against the king but also to those against his ministers. The intendant-general of police was made responsible for guarding against all such actions and for combating anything else deemed subversive. For these purposes, he acquired a regular force of several hundred security police and built up an extensive network of spies and informers.[36] Furthermore, Pombal decided, probably following the Austrian precedent, to remove control of censorship from the inquisitorial and episcopal authorities and centralise it directly under the crown. Accordingly in 1768, he created the royal censorship board (*real mesa censória*) – an eight-man committee empowered to decide what could or could not be read. Under Pombal

---

[36] SHP vol 6, p 94; HP vol 4, pp 174–6; Maxwell K 1995, p 88; DIHP vol 2, p 116.

this board had cautiously permitted and in some instances even encouraged the circulation of approved progressive writings, mostly associated with the Moderate Enlightenment. But it also remained ostentatiously Catholic, with five of its original members being priests and one of them an inquisitor. Anything considered too radical or simply anti-Catholic continued to be banned outright. As a result Bayle's dictionary and various works of Hobbes, Spinoza, Voltaire and Rousseau among others were all prohibited.[37]

While under Pombal censorship was used by the state to keep out ideas considered inimical to the established order, it was only under Maria I that the royal censorship board and its associated institutions matured into well-directed instruments of state control. The man most responsible for this development was Diogo Inácio Pina Manique (1733–1805), intendant-general of police for twenty-three years between 1780 and 1803. Pina Manique has always been a somewhat controversial figure. He was without doubt a highly competent state functionary, a fact he had clearly demonstrated by his remarkable feat of significantly reducing contraband and correspondingly increasing revenue yields while administrator of customs. Over a long bureaucratic career he accumulated many offices – incidentally enriching himself much in the process.

As intendant-general, Pina Manique undertook a range of activities extending well beyond conventional police work, some of which were remarkably advanced and enlightened for his era. Motivated by strong convictions that prevention was better than cure, and that a contented population with self-respect was the best antidote for disorder, he undertook numerous public and charitable works. These included building roads and planting trees in the Lisbon area, providing the city with street lighting (and paying for it through a special charge on householders), establishing refuges for beggars and for homeless and delinquent children, setting up a pharmacy to provide free medicines to the poor, instituting health checks for prostitutes and sponsoring students studying in London, Edinburgh and Rome. But his best-known charitable enterprise was the *casa pia,* which he founded in Lisbon early in the 1780s as a home and school for street children.

Nevertheless, Pina Manique's core responsibility was to protect the status quo, and he soon acquired a formidable reputation for the efficient pursuit of dissenters and subversives. When the French monarchy was swept away in 1792 internal security concerns in Portugal naturally took on a new intensity. Pina Manique and his police responded by tightening vigilance, but found nothing seriously subversive – just a few individuals caught distributing objectionable pamphlets or talking indiscreetly in Lisbon cafes.[38] Genuinely

---

[37] SHP vol 6, pp 261–3; Maxwell K 1995, p 93.
[38] Silbert A 1977, pp 47–8.

revolutionary sentiment had few adherents at any level in Portuguese society in the 1790s, nor was there any significant undercurrent of social discontent for revolutionaries to exploit. As Albert Silbert succinctly expressed it, the Portuguese nobility was 'domesticated', the bourgeoisie was 'tied to the state' and the prevailing order was 'generally accepted'.[39] Jacobinism hardly elicited more enthusiasm in Portugal than had Protestantism nearly 300 years before. Nevertheless, there was a growing interest in secret societies – and Pina Manique now embarked on an energetic campaign to suppress them, paying particular attention to freemasonry.

Modern freemasonry, which probably reached Portugal from England in about the 1730s, steadily consolidated its Portuguese following during the mid- and late years of the century. Pombal may himself have been a freemason; certainly he had close contact with various lodge members while in England. He apparently considered them moderate progressives who adhered to the Christian tradition and were therefore acceptable. By Marian times Portuguese freemasonry was rapidly gaining numbers among both the elite and the intelligentsia and had become an important channel for the dissemination of liberal thinking.[40] However, the movement had been condemned by the pope as early as 1738, and Catholics were formally forbidden to join lodges. Now, under the exceptionally pious Maria I, freemasons found themselves the objects of growing official hostility, both lay and ecclesiastical.[41]

For Pina Manique in the early 1790s the principal concerns with freemasonry were its suspicious secrecy, its association with foreigners, its perceived 'liberal' orientation and its evident capacity to disseminate revolutionary ideas. Moreover, though Portuguese freemasonry had its origins in England it had subsequently established links with France, and the two traditions had different and often competing emphases. English freemasonry tended to stress rationalism and was also associated to some extent with liberalism. Freemasons in France were more likely to sympathise with the Radical Enlightenment; they were welcomed first by the Directory and later by Napoleon as useful agents for propagating revolutionary principles.[42]

Pina Manique's campaign against freemasonry led to the denunciation of several prominent persons, including a son of Pombal and also Dom Martinho de Melo e Castro, the secretary of state for naval and colonial affairs. But the campaign was not in the end very successful and eventually had to be abandoned. It may even have been sabotaged from within by elements of the

[39] Ibid, p 46.
[40] Marques A H de O 1990, pp 37–9, 48–9.
[41] Gonçalves A M n.d., pp 2–4; Marques A H de O 1990, pp 51–2.
[42] Gonçalves A M n.d., p 6; Pereira A 1953–8 vol 4, pp 17–18; SHP vol 6, p 434.

armed forces. Be that as it may, in 1801 the Portuguese freemasons received assurance from the government that they would no longer be harried provided they came together to form their own national grand lodge. The result was the creation of the *grande oriente lusitano* in 1802–6.[43] However, by that time Pina Manique's long tenure in office had already come to an end. This was not because of any shortcomings in the performance of his duties, but rather because he had become objectionable to the French, who applied intense diplomatic pressure to have him dismissed – as will emerge shortly.[44]

PRINCE JOÃO AND A WORLD IN TURMOIL

Despite her lack of political experience, Maria I carried out her queenly responsibilities conscientiously during the early years of her reign, even displaying a certain unsuspected adroitness. However, she was anxious and highly strung, and the death in 1786 of her husband Pedro left her greatly distraught. Two years later her promising elder son, Prince José, contracted smallpox and also died. This proved too much for Maria, who began to display alarming symptoms of mental breakdown. Her condition gradually worsened until by February 1792 she was to all intents and purposes clinically insane. Her doctors had no alternative but to declare her unfit to rule, and her surviving son, Prince João, was obliged to assume regal duties.[45]

Prince João, who later became King João VI, administered Portugal for seven years in his incapacitated mother's name before eventually assuming the title of prince regent in 1799. During these years, the overriding preoccupation of his government was the international situation, particularly the state of affairs in France. In September 1792, the Revolutionary Convention in Paris formally abolished the French monarchy. Emigrés including many nobles fled France in ever growing numbers, raising the level of hostility against the young republic throughout Europe and in some cases spreading subversive propaganda. News of Louis XVI's execution reached Lisbon in early February 1793. It caused the Portuguese government great dismay and plunged the court into immediate mourning.

At first the Portuguese crown and the new republican regime in France, despite their obvious ideological differences, both considered it desirable to maintain mutual diplomatic relations. However, by the time Paris despatched a representative to Lisbon in March 1793 to replace the now redundant

---

[43] Pereira A 1953–8 vol 4, p 17; Gonçalves A M n.d., p 5; Marques A H de O 1990, pp 61–2, 73–91.

[44] PDH vol 5, pp 738–40; MHP, p 395; HP vol 6, pp 175–6.

[45] Pereira A 1953–8 vol 1, p 57.

Bourbon ambassador, the Portuguese attitude had hardened. The would-be French envoy found himself denied access to the secretary of state for foreign affairs and war, and ignominiously expelled.[46] It was therefore Portugal, rather than France, that made the first hostile move between the two. Later, in 1793, the Portuguese government took matters much further, agreeing to participate in an invasion of France, in alliance with the British and the Spaniards.

For Portugal to take up arms in this way against another European power – particularly one that was not at the time posing any immediate threat to its territorial integrity – was a major policy departure. It can only be explained in terms of the unprecedented international situation and heavy pressure from Britain and Spain. Under the circumstances João felt compelled to show solidarity with his fellow monarchs – the new regime in France, which had not yet demonstrated its formidable military credentials, being totally abhorrent to him. In any event, a Luso-Spanish expedition was gathered together and duly invaded southern France, through Roussillon. With the benefit of surprise it achieved some initial success; but then the allies quickly discovered they were no match for a better-organised and more determined enemy.

The French, after defeating the Luso-Spanish expeditionaries in Roussillon, were keen to detach Spain from Britain. They therefore negotiated a separate peace with Madrid that was duly signed at Basle in June 1795. For Portugal, this was an alarming turn of events – for it meant its two erstwhile allies, Britain and Spain, were now on opposite sides of the European struggle. Indeed, from 1796 they were actually at war.[47] Portugal's first and only attempt at pre-emptive action against the French revolutionaries had proved not only a military humiliation; it had ended in diplomatic nightmare. The British alliance remained intact, more or less securing Portugal's seaboard and its maritime communications. But, within continental Europe, Portugal was now isolated and perilously exposed.

After the debacle of the Roussillon campaign, the Portuguese government's political priorities changed. There was no more thought of trying to influence the political scene within France – and even Portuguese internal security became a lesser concern. The first priority was henceforth to employ every possible means to deflect the growing external threat to Portugal's survival as a separate, independent kingdom. This threat was inherent in the hegemonic struggle that was unfolding between France, now supported by Spain, and Britain, placing Portugal in greater danger than at any other time since the Restoration War of 1640–68. Portugal was strategically and commercially important to the British on the one hand, but also of political interest to the

---

[46] Ibid, pp 65–6; Alexandre V 1993, pp 98–9.
[47] SHP vol 6, pp 316–18; Alexandre V 1993, p 101.

French and Spaniards on the other – and the seriousness of its predicament could therefore hardly be exaggerated.

In the 1790s Portugal's best guarantee of keeping its sprawling empire intact was still its alliance with Britain. It was also vital that Portugal avoid doing anything to attract active British hostility, because of the disastrous impact this could have on the country's international trade – and, more particularly, on crucial wheat imports. At the same time, Britain wanted to maintain the flow of Anglo-Portuguese trade and needed access to Portuguese ports for its naval ships. On the other hand, Portugal was, during these years, of more marginal importance to France; but Paris nevertheless had a keen interest in detaching Prince João's government from its close ties to Britain.

Through the late 1790s the French left direct dealings with Portugal largely in the hands of their Spanish allies. This meant in practice that as long as the Portuguese espoused a position of respectful de facto neutrality, and avoided attracting too much attention to themselves, they could reasonably expect to avoid invasion. However, the Portuguese government's repeated protestations that in Roussillon it had acted merely as a non-belligerent ally, not as an active participant, were rejected by the French.[48] It suited Paris to insist that, since the Roussillon campaign, a state of war had existed between France and Portugal. French privateers, often sailing out of Spanish ports, could then legitimately wreak havoc on Portuguese shipping.

During these years, the Spanish government did act as an intermediary in the protracted peace negotiations between Paris and Lisbon; but there were many obstacles. The French required that Portugal close its ports to the British, while the Portuguese were wary of offending their old ally. Discussions dragged on – until finally in 1799 Paris lost patience and began pressing Madrid to allow French troops passage through Spain to invade Portugal.[49] The Spaniards, meanwhile, had their own grounds for complaint against Lisbon. The Portuguese were trading profitably with the British and succouring British warships, while those same ships were inflicting significant losses on Spain. Yet how could Portugal contrive to satisfy French and Spanish demands without attracting a hostile reaction from Britain? Despite strenuous diplomatic activity, and judicious distribution of bribes, this question still remained unresolved when Bonaparte seized power in Paris in November 1799.[50]

Bonaparte's Portuguese policy was similar in principle to that of the Directory. With the collaboration of Spain, he intended to force Portugal to detach

---

[48] Alexandre V 1993, pp 100–1, 104.
[49] Ibid, pp 106–7, 110–17; Silbert A 1977, p 49.
[50] SHP vol 6, pp 322–3; Iams T M 1977, pp 33–4; Alexandre V 1993, pp 102–3.

itself from the British alliance and become instead a satellite of France.[51] In January 1801, he sent Lisbon a blunt ultimatum: Portugal had just two weeks to disavow the Anglo-Portuguese alliance, close its ports to British ships, pay a large indemnity and allow Spanish forces to occupy a quarter of its territory peacefully. Otherwise it would face invasion. Portugal failed to comply, seeking further compromise – so Spanish forces duly marched into Alentejo, at Bonaparte's behest. The outcome was the brief so-called 'War of the Oranges' in May and June 1801. This saw the occupation by Spanish troops of several Portuguese border towns, including Olivença.

To Valentim Alexandre the War of the Oranges amounted to little more than an intensification of Spanish diplomatic pressure. There is circumstantial evidence to support this view, for such fighting as there was seems to have been for appearances only, the two sides remaining in regular contact throughout.[52] Peace negotiations were quickly commenced at Badajoz, and an agreement was soon thrashed out. However, when Bonaparte learned of this deal he promptly rejected it, pronouncing its terms too lenient to Portugal. A revised treaty, imposing harsher conditions on Lisbon, was then drawn up – and duly signed, in Madrid, on 29 September 1801. This second treaty obliged Prince João to grant the French most-favoured nation status, close Portuguese ports to the British, pay France an indemnity of twenty-five million livres and make territorial concessions to the French in Guiana. Portugal was also required to indemnify the Spaniards, who were meanwhile to retain Olivença as surety. In return, other occupied Portuguese towns would be handed back and Portugal's neutral status recognised. Although the terms were harsh, Prince João had little choice but to accept them. Portugal had minimal capacity to resist a French invasion – particularly given that its British allies had failed to come up with any significant military aid.[53]

After Prince João had ratified the Madrid agreement of September 1801, Bonaparte despatched as his ambassador to Portugal General Jean Lannes. As it happened, Lannes arrived in Lisbon shortly after the Anglo-French peace of Amiens came into force on 25 March 1802. This development allowed Portugal, with much relief, not to proceed with closing its ports to the British. Nevertheless, in the months that followed, barely disguised animosity between the French and British in Lisbon made life difficult for the prince regent and his government. Lannes, who possessed a distinguished military record but little diplomatic finesse, was soon ruffling Portuguese feathers with his abrasive

[51] Pereira A 1953–8 vol 1, p 70; Silbert A 1977, p 49.
[52] Alexandre V 1993, pp 121–6.
[53] Ibid, pp 115–16; Pereira A 1953–8 vol 1, p 70; SHP vol 6, pp 325–6; Silbert A 1977, pp 50–2.

behaviour – although this was perhaps as much a consequence of the instructions he had received from Bonaparte as it was an expression of his own temperament.[54]

During 1802 Lannes challenged British influence in Portugal at every possible turn. He deemed particularly provocative the presence of numerous royalist émigrés, of whom several thousand had been brought into Portugal by the British in 1797 and organised into a military force. Before long, he also found himself drawn into conflict with various Portuguese ministers and senior officials.[55] His most serious brushes were with Pina Manique, and with that formidable intendant-general's police commander in Lisbon, the marquis of Novion, a French émigré nobleman. At one point, Pina Manique's customs officials confiscated a shipload of goods Lannes believed he had the right to import duty free. On another occasion one of Lannes' aides was arrested and roughed up by Novion's men. Possibly Pina Manique was deliberately trying to make difficulties for the ambassador. Be that as it may, Lannes raised the stakes by demanding the dismissal of not only the intendant-general, but also of the pro-British secretary of state for foreign affairs and war, João de Almeida Melo e Castro. When these demands were rejected, Lannes departed for Paris, without taking formal leave, in May 1802.[56]

Back in Paris, Lannes' demands for the dismissals of Pina Manique and Almeida were swiftly endorsed by Bonaparte. But Prince João did not comply – at least, not immediately. Meanwhile, Lannes returned to Lisbon in March 1803, promptly commencing what has been aptly described as a 'vitriolic pas-de-deux' with the British ambassador, Lord Robert Fitzgerald.[57] Within barely two months, war had resumed between France and Britain (May 1803) – and Lannes was soon demanding that the prince regent sign another treaty with Paris. Essentially, the terms would be the same as those imposed on Portugal in September 1801, but with the added requirement that Portugal pay France a subsidy of sixteen million francs. Fitzgerald warned that any such payment would be interpreted by London as aiding the enemy. So, once again, Portugal found itself uncomfortably wedged between the maritime power of Britain and the continental power of France.

During these crucial months of 1803 Lannes' handling of the Portuguese was more adroit and better targeted than it had been previously. As far as possible by-passing ministers, he sought to deal directly with the prince regent. In response, João began treating him with more solicitous attention, even

[54] Alexandre V 1993, p 128.
[55] Ibid, p 109; Pereira A 1953–8 vol 1, pp 98–9; Chrisawn M 1998, pp 1–4.
[56] Pereira A 1953–8 vol 1, pp 102, 104; SHP vol 6, pp 329–30; Chrisawn M 1998, pp 5–6.
[57] Chrisawn M 1998, p 9.

consenting to be godfather to his infant son. Eventually, in August 1803, there came a decisive break-through. Responding to pressure from Lannes – but also more crucially to those at court who believed it was preferable, if a choice had to be made, to alienate London rather than Paris – João changed his ministry.

First, the prince regent dismissed several ministers known to be pro-British, including Dom Rodrigo de Sousa Coutinho and João de Almeida Melo e Castro. Later, António de Araújo e Azevedo, count of Barca (1754–1811) – an exceptionally erudite and cultured nobleman, who was also mildly pro-French – was appointed secretary of state for foreign affairs and war.[58] Meanwhile, Pina Manique had been relieved of responsibility for customs – and then, on the insistence of Bonaparte, was dismissed as intendant-general of police. Finally, in March 1804, acting on the advice of the majority of his ministers, Prince João ratified the new Franco-Portuguese treaty, though efforts were made at the same time to placate the British.[59] Lannes was thereupon recalled to Paris, where Bonaparte had just proclaimed himself emperor.

The Franco-Portuguese treaty of March 1804 was acceded to fundamentally because the then ministry in Lisbon – and, in particular, its most influential member, António de Araújo e Azevedo – convinced Prince João that Portugal had no hope of successfully resisting a full-scale French invasion, even if British aid were forthcoming. After the treaty had been signed, one immediate consequence was a notable surge in trade between France and Portugal: the Portuguese imported mainly French manufactures, especially silks, while Portuguese exports to France, which were mostly of Brazilian origin, included cotton, sugar, tobacco and hides. These goods were transported in Portuguese or neutral ships, and, by the end of 1804, the French were importing more Brazilian-grown cotton than were the British.[60] Overall, the balance of trade with France was firmly in Portugal's favour, and the new treaty clearly delivered the Portuguese some tangible economic benefits. However, the crucial questions remained, how long and to what extent could Portugal adhere to the treaty's terms without fatally compromising relations with Britain? Not surprisingly, Portugal sought by every possible means to postpone, or evade fully implementing, those clauses of the treaty to which Britain most objected.

Over the next two years Portugal's international relations became ever more difficult to manage. In December 1804 Spain re-entered the war on the side of France – and Spanish political pressure on Portugal was added to that of the French. It was during this period that Manuel de Godoy, Carlos IV of Spain's chief minister, conceived a self-serving plan to invade, occupy and then

---

[58] Ibid, p 10; Pereira A 1953–8 vol 1, p 101; Alexandre V 1993, pp 133–5.
[59] Pereira A 1953–8 vol 1, pp 106–7; Alexandre V 1993, pp 129–30; Chrisawn M 1998, p 13.
[60] Silbert A 1977, pp 55–7; Alexandre V 1993, p 35.

partition Portugal.[61] Although this plan at the time received only lukewarm support from Napoleon, he subsequently took up its main features, adapting them to his own purposes – as we shall shortly see.

During the course of 1805–6, the threats to Portugal posed by Britain on the one hand, and France on the other, were revealed with ever more frightening clarity – and walking the tightrope became for Prince João increasingly difficult. Britain's dominance of the seas was now indisputable, as Nelson's destruction of the French and Spanish fleets at Trafalgar in October 1805 demonstrated. But Napoleon, with his smashing victories at Austerlitz, Jena and Friedland, was supreme on land. The stalemate drew both antagonists into placing more emphasis on economic struggle. In November 1806, Napoleon announced his imposition of the continental system, requiring all ports on the European continent to be closed to British ships and British trade. Britain responded with a series of orders-in-council that placed France, her colonies and her continental allies under naval blockade. This intensification of economic warfare meant that from the end of 1806, from Napoleon's standpoint, it became still more imperative to bring Portugal definitively under French control. Action to accomplish this was delayed for a while by French entanglements in northeastern Europe; but it was not delayed for very long.

1807: THE *ANO TORMENTOSO*

In July 1807, Napoleon signed the treaty of Tilsit with Tsar Alexander, effectively bringing Russia into the continental system. Portugal, on the southwestern flank of Europe, was now that system's last remaining breach. Prince João had already given in to French demands to the extent of formally closing his ports to the British; but he had baulked at arresting British citizens, or seizing their possessions – and had in practice continued to allow British ships, including naval vessels, to visit Portuguese ports. Indeed, it is difficult to see how he could have done otherwise.

Meanwhile, Napoleon had already decided in the summer of 1807 to proceed with the invasion of Portugal, dethrone the Braganças and establish a puppet regime in Lisbon. After the treaty of Tilsit, adequate French forces were available for the necessary operations, and in August 1807 a final ultimatum was accordingly delivered to Prince João. By 1 September, he must declare war on the British, genuinely close his ports to their ships, arrest all Britons resident in his kingdom and confiscate their property. Failure to comply in every respect would result in immediate French occupation.[62] General Jean Andoche Junot

---

[61] Alexandre V 1993, pp 141–2.
[62] Manchester A K 1969, p 149.

had already been ordered to move with his army to Bayonne, in southwestern France, to await the order to march on Lisbon.

Despite the seriousness of the situation, Araújo e Azevedo and his colleagues remained remarkably calm, apparently still convinced that Portugal could maintain its neutrality. It was even proposed that Portugal contrive a nominal state of war with Britain, in which neither side actually fought or harmed the other; but, when put to them, this idea was rejected out of hand by the British.[63] Eventually, after prolonged debate and divided advice from his council, the prince regent announced on 20 October his decision to adhere to the continental system and close all ports to the British. He hesitated a little longer over arresting Britons and sequestering their property, before on 5 November giving way on these issues also. The British ambassador, Lord Strangford, then duly took his leave – and a British naval squadron under Admiral Sir Sidney Smith moved in to blockade the Tagus.[64]

João's concessions to Paris meant he had acceded to all the crucial French demands – and Napoleon's logical policy objectives regarding Portugal were therefore well on the way to being achieved. Nevertheless, Lisbon's effective submission proved of no avail to the Braganças. On 27 October 1807, France and Spain signed a secret treaty at Fontainebleau, in essence agreeing to an adaptation of the scheme conceived in late 1804 by Godoy. Portugal was to be occupied militarily, and then split up into three principalities. The country's south would be assigned to Godoy, as his personal fiefdom. The central region was to be occupied and placed under military rule until the end of the European war, after which its permanent fate would be decided. Northern Portugal would go to the king of Etruria, a minor Italian potentate. This last provision was because Napoleon wanted to annex Etruria himself. Accordingly, he needed something to give, in exchange, to its current rulers – who, being Spanish Bourbons, were of interest to France's allies in Madrid.[65] It is evident therefore that Napoleon did not decide to occupy Portugal because the Portuguese had failed to adhere to the continental system – for on that, in response to repeated threats, they had already conceded everything. In reality, the decision was made merely to accommodate the emperor's momentary political agenda in Italy.[66]

But Prince João and his government still had another card to play. On the opposite side of the Atlantic in Brazil, the Braganças possessed territories

[63] Manchester A K 1933, pp 60–1 and 1969, pp 149–50, 174.
[64] Manchester A K 1969, pp 151–2; Alexandre V 1993, pp 150–1, 156–9.
[65] MHP, p 427; Silbert A 1977, pp 62–3; SHP vol 6, p 334; Esdaile C 2003, pp 7–8; Gotteri N 2006, pp 158–9.
[66] Alexandre V 1993, pp 141, 162–3.

far larger, and potentially much richer, than metropolitan Portugal itself. Therefore, the court always had the option of effecting an evacuation to the New World, if its position in the Old World became untenable. The idea of such a transfer was by no means new, having been aired and seriously contemplated several times during earlier crises. In 1580 the followers of the pretender António, prior of Crato, had toyed with the possibility, as had the advisers of João IV at the start of the 1660s.[67] It had also been raised a number of times in the eighteenth century, though by then more in response to growing economic reality, and beckoning opportunity, than to any particular crisis.

One of those to speak out in favour of the court moving to Brazil had been the progressive diplomat and statesman Dom Luís da Cunha, in 1738. Dom Rodrigo de Sousa Coutinho did likewise in 1798 – followed by the marquis of Alorna and José Manuel de Sousa, *morgado* of Mateus, in 1801. All these prominent persons recognised that Brazil, by virtue of its vastly greater size and resources, ultimately had more to offer the Braganças in material terms than did Portugal.[68] As the *morgado* of Mateus expressed it, in Brazil João would star as the first monarch in the New World – and the equal of any in Europe.[69] Dom Rodrigo thought that in the event of a French invasion Portugal should mount a campaign of resistance, directed by a government in Brazilian exile. The British supported this view, and in 1803 Ambassador Strangford had urged Prince João to proceed forthwith to Rio de Janeiro, under British naval escort.[70]

Of course, proposals of this kind, however enticing, were unlikely under normal circumstances to be implemented – if only because of the immense upheaval such a move would entail for the royal family, the court and the nobility. In the late eighteenth century the powerful Portugal-based merchant oligarchy that had come to dominate the Brazil trade also opposed any thought of a trans-Atlantic shift.[71] It was therefore only when French invasion loomed as a serious threat that practical contingency planning for an evacuation began. The challenge was formidable, for to relocate the court physically to Brazil would require a massive and unprecedented seaborne operation. Hundreds of elite Portuguese, including many women and children, their attendants and their baggage, would have to be transported across the Atlantic at a single stroke, most likely at very short notice. Nevertheless, contingency plans were drawn up, in consultation with the British, and by as early as May 1803 were given the prince regent's

---

[67] Boxer C R 1962, p 324; SHP vol 6, p 337.
[68] Boxer C R 1962, pp 324–5; Maxwell K 1973, p 211, 232–4; SHP vol 6, p 337.
[69] Pereira A 1953–8 vol 1, p 91.
[70] Alexandre V 1993, p 136.
[71] Cf. Maxwell K 1973, p 235.

personal approval. Detailed diagrams of the space available on each vessel in the Portuguese fleet were prepared.[72]

After Strangford's departure and the imposition of a British naval blockade in early November 1807, a decision regarding evacuation could not long be delayed. All now depended on whether the French actually invaded – and the turning-point came when news reached Lisbon on 23 November that Napoleon had decreed the dethronement of the Braganças and that Junot, having entered Portugal, was advancing rapidly down the Tagus valley. Ironically, Portugal's military forces were at this point heavily concentrated along the coast, and particularly at the mouth of the Tagus – for Araújo e Azevedo, mindful of what had happened to the Danes at Copenhagen, considered an attack more likely by the British than by the French.[73] The consequence was that Junot's army met almost no resistance. Meanwhile Strangford, who had returned to Lisbon, warned the prince regent that Britain would indeed commence action against Portuguese naval and merchant shipping if the Anglo-Portuguese treaties were not immediately reaffirmed. It was under these dramatic circumstances that on 24 November 1807 Prince João and his council finally decided to implement the Brazil option.[74]

Speed was essential – and it is said that, within five hours of the signal to move being given, some 700 heavily laden carts bearing 'effects' were already rumbling down from the Mafra palace to the Lisbon docks.[75] Government records, furniture, works of art, personal possessions, provisions and most of the contents of the royal treasury were all loaded with frantic haste aboard a fleet of thirty-six Portuguese ships anchored in the Tagus. The embarkation of perhaps 15,000 evacuees, including fourteen members of the royal family, began on 27 November. There was understandably much confusion – and not all the ships were adequately provisioned. Nor could everyone who wished to leave be accommodated, not even the papal nuncio.[76] One account claims that General Junot, whose first priority was to prevent the escape of the Braganças, reached Lisbon on 28 November with a small advance guard and proceeded straight to the flagship for an audience with the prince regent. But his efforts to dissuade João from leaving were icily rejected.[77] However, the more generally accepted version of events has Junot arriving only on 30 November. By then the fleet was already well on its way to Brazil, having weighed anchor

---

[72] Manchester A K 1969, p 153; Chrisawn M 1998, p 10.
[73] Alexandre V 1993, pp 156, 59–61.
[74] Manchester A K 1969, pp 150–3.
[75] O'Neill T 1809, pp 19–20.
[76] Ibid, pp 24–5; Rossi C L de 1944, p 11.
[77] O'Neill T 1809, pp 27–33.

on the previous morning and duly departed the Tagus, along with its escort of British warships. To govern Portugal in his absence the prince regent appointed a five-man committee chaired by the marquis of Abrantes. He left behind him a populace desperately anxious and fearful for the future.[78]

Serious questions have inevitably been raised about how the Portuguese government handled the crisis of the *ano tormentoso* – and especially about the personal behaviour of the prince regent. Did João desert his people in their hour of greatest need? It may well have seemed so to some. But what else could he reasonably have done, given unanimous advice from his council, and from the British, to leave? Then again, did his actions – not just in 1807, but throughout the whole preceding decade – show him to have been a vacillating prince, possessed of little intellectual capacity and quite unsuited to lead? This is all too often the ungenerous image presented of him. Even so meticulous a historian as Alan Manchester originally chose to sneer at João as, 'an obese royal prince', who 'suffered from a chronic case of indecision' and presided over a 'decadent' court.[79] To his credit, Manchester later retracted this view. In doing so he was presumably influenced by historians like Ângelo Pereira, to whom the decision to go to Rio was neither a desertion nor a disorganised flight, but 'an intelligent resolve long contemplated'. Likewise, Araújo e Azevedo's conviction, almost to the last moment, that a French invasion could be avoided was based on a careful and thoroughly rational evaluation of the situation. It just happened that Napoleon's decision-making in this instance followed a different, quite unpredictable logic.[80] Moreover, by escaping to Brazil, Prince João ultimately succeeded in frustrating Napoleon's plans to destroy his kingdom. Sailing off to Rio de Janeiro was a considered move – and, given the difficult circumstances prevailing, remarkably well executed.[81] Nevertheless, the notion that João was 'notoriously dull-witted' is still routinely – and quite unjustifiably – parroted to this day.[82]

The fact that Portugal's rulers controlled a substantial empire in the western Atlantic to which they could repair when seriously threatened gave them an option that no other victim of Napoleon in Europe possessed. Spain obviously had a transatlantic empire too; but for various reasons, particularly its ongoing war with Britain, transferring the Spanish court to America was not practicable. The option was always available to Portugal because the British favoured it – and because Prince João, despite all his concessions to the French,

[78] SHP vol 6, p 338.
[79] Manchester A K 1933, p 54.
[80] See Alexandre V 1993, p 161.
[81] In introduction to Rossi C L 1944, pp v–vi; see also SHP vol 6, p 338.
[82] Esdaile C 2003, p 5.

was careful to keep it in reserve as a final resort. Of course, at a more fundamental level, the Brazil option was there because the Portuguese had themselves, from the start, played a central role in the process of European global
expansion. Without that participation, and the trade and wealth it generated,
the Portuguese would most probably have long since lost their separate political identity – and Portugal would have become, in the words of the *morgado*
of Mateus, 'a slave of Spain'.[83]

The departure of the Prince Regent Dom João on his unprecedented voyage
across the Atlantic to the New World at the end of 1807 symbolises the demise
of Portugal's Old Regime. Moreover, the old mercantilist structures that fun-
nelled exclusively through Portugal the intercontinental trade of Brazil – and, in
varying degrees, that of other Portuguese possessions – effectively collapsed in
the aftermath of the *ano tormentoso* of 1807. Portugal was cut off from its
empire, was starved of Brazilian re-exports and lost its monopoly in the Brazilian
market. Brazil was Portugal's only significant overseas outlet for industrial goods –
and, as such, clearly fundamental to its progress towards industrialisation.[84]

The *ano tormentoso* marks the chronological end-point of this history. But
there nevertheless remains much more to tell and to explain. So far, we have
concentrated only on what happened within metropolitan Portugal itself,
Portuguese expansion beyond Europe featuring only incidentally. Yet the
Portuguese are better known in the world at large for their role in the process
of Western global discovery and expansion, than for their contribution to the
internal history of Europe. Beginning with a first tentative sally into North
Africa in 1415, Portugal was to accumulate, in the three centuries that followed, an empire as improbable as any the world has seen. Far-flung and
varied, this empire was accumulated with remarkable individual enterprise –
and then held together by notable loyalty to certain basic institutions, particularly the crown and a specifically Portuguese brand of Catholicism. Portugal's
empire beyond Europe will be the subject of the volume that follows.

[83] Pereira A 1953–8 vol 1, p 85.
[84] Alexandre V 1993, pp 163–4, 167, 795, 797–9; Arruda J J de A 2000, pp 869, 873–4.

Glossary

albergaria:	a charitable institution that provided poor relief
alcaçova:	citadel
alcaide-mor:	governor; Castellan
alçaprema:	here, a hand-press used for crushing cane
aldeia:	village
alfandega:	customs house
amante:	girl-friend; sex-partner
amma:	in al-Andalus, the common people
ano tormentoso:	'tempestuous year' – the year 1807, when Napoleonic forces invaded Portugal and the royal family withdrew to Brazil
arroba:	a measure of weight – Portuguese equivalent of a quarter
asiento:	commercial or financial contract; used here especially in relation to (1) contract to provide loans to Habsburg crown, (2) contract to supply slaves to Spanish America
atalaia:	detached watch-tower
auditor:	presiding judicial officer or magistrate, usually in a special jurisdiction
aula de comércio:	school of commerce
azulejo:	decorative tile
bacaudae:	in late Roman times, rebellious peasants
câmara:	town council
cantiga:	ballad

capela:	entailed estate with a charge or encumbrance to support a religious foundation
capitão:	captain
carta de foro:	certificate of tenancy
casa:	house
casa da Índia:	crown agency in Lisbon that supervised trade and communications with Asia
casa pia:	'holy house'; a home and school for poor children, founded in the late eighteenth century
casal (pl. *casais*):	family farm
castro:	a hillfort or other fortified site often of prehistoric origin
cavaleiro:	lesser nobleman approximating to a banneret or knight bachelor; mounted gentleman-soldier
cavaleiro-mercador:	gentleman-merchant; nobleman who engaged in trade
cavaleiro-vilão:	commoner knight; non-noble who fought as a knight maintaining necessary horse and equipment, and enjoyed appropriate noble privileges
cidadão honrado:	in a town, a commoner of high status; member of the upper bourgeoisie
colégio:	secondary school; Jesuit college for advanced studies
comarca:	judicial district
comenda:	benefice attached to a military order
comissários volantes:	itinerant traders or commission agents, especially in Portugal-Brazil trade
concelho:	a community with its own council to administer internal affairs; a municipality; a council
condado portucalense:	earldom of Portugal that immediately preceded the kingdom
confraria:	brotherhood
conselho da fazenda:	treasury council; advisory council on economic affairs
conselho de estado:	council of state
conselho de guerra:	war council
conselho del rei:	king's council
conselho ultramarino:	council for the overseas colonies
constable:	from the late fourteenth century, king's general-in-chief
consulado:	in Spain, a merchants' guild
continental system:	Napoleonic policy proclaimed in 1806 of closing European ports to British trade

converso:	Jew converted to Catholicism
corregedor:	superior crown magistrate exercising judicial and administrative oversight of a *comarca*
corso:	privateering; corsair activity
cortes:	representative assembly of the kingdom
couto:	seigneury and its associated immunities and concessions
criado:	dependent or employee, often attached to a great household
cristão novo:	New Christian – Jewish convert to Catholicism, or descendant of same
cruzado:	name of a succession of gold coins minted in Portugal from 1457; from late sixteenth century a unit of account worth 400 *reais*
cúria:	early kings' advisory council – forerunner of *cortes*
décimo militar:	a tax on property, originally imposed to help fund seventeenth-century war of independence against Spain
degredado:	a criminal condemned to exile
desembargador:	high court judge
desembargo do paço:	Portuguese supreme advisory council for judicial affairs
dízimos:	tithes
doação (pl. *doações*):	endowment
dobra:	a high-value eighteenth-century Luso-Brazilian gold coin
donataria:	seigneury; concession of lordship granted by Portuguese crown to an individual as means of developing a colonial territory at minimal cost
donatário:	seigneur; recipient of a *donataria*
donativo:	'gift' to state levied on property and/or income; effectively a tax
emphyteusis:	form of land tenure fixed for life or specified period
encoberto:	imagined king-in-hiding, especially Sebastião
erário régio:	state treasury created during Pombaline reforms
ermamento:	partly deserted frontier region separating Christian and Muslim territory in northern Portugal
escrivão:	secretary
escrivão da puridade:	the king's confidential secretary
escudo:	gold coin first minted in reign of King Duarte
estado da Índia:	Portuguese empire east of Cape of Good Hope

estrangeirado:	'foreign-influenced'; person who sought to learn from or imitate foreigners and maintain friendship with them
fama:	reputation
familiar:	attendant of the Inquisition who made arrests on its behalf
fazenda:	plantation or other landed property; treasury
feira:	fair or market
feitoria:	official Portuguese trading station or 'factory' established overseas
fidalgo:	nobleman, usually of middling or lesser rank
fidalgo da casa del rei:	gentleman of the king's household
fidalgo filosófico:	eighteenth-century 'Enlightened' nobleman – particularly a colonial administrator
fidalguia:	traditional nobility
fitna:	in al-Andalus, confused period between collapse of caliphate and emergence of *taifas*
foedarati:	autonomous barbarian allies of Rome settled in Roman territory in return for providing military service
foro:	legal immunity or privilege
forro:	emancipated former slave
freirático:	an admirer of religious; more particularly, a man who has affairs with nuns
garum:	sauce made from fermented fish
grande:	peer of the realm
grange:	isolated sub-centre of a Cistercian monastery, staffed by lay brothers
hadith:	traditions concerning the Prophet Muhammad
haraj:	land-tax
hassa:	Muslim aristocracy
infanção (pl. *infanções*):	nobleman by birth of middle or lower rank
infante:	title given to king's sons other than first born
intendência geral da polícia:	intendancy general of police
jihad:	Muslim holy war
jornaleiro:	journeyman; day-labourer
judaize:	observe Jewish rites and traditions while ostensibly Christian
juiz ordinário:	local magistrate

junta:	board or committee
junta de providência literária:	board for educational affairs
junta do comércio:	board of trade
juros:	treasury bonds
kura (pl. *kuwar*):	in Muslim era, administrative region governed by a *wali*
Lei Mental:	law of 1434 defining royal patrimony as inalienable and grants from it as always conditional, and inheritable only by grantee's oldest son or grandson
letrado:	graduate, usually a lawyer
liberdades:	duty-free allowances
limpeza de sangue:	ethnic purity; 'untainted' by Jewish blood
literatura de cordel:	literally 'string literature'; cheap printed booklets or pamphlets produced for the general public
malado:	in al-Andalus, a convert from Christianity to Islam
Manuelino:	architectural style current in Portugal in the early sixteenth century
mare clausum:	'closed sea'; exclusive jurisdiction over designated waters
mercê:	grant of office or other income-producing benefit
mesteiral (pl. mesteirais):	craft-master or artisan; skilled worker
Misericórdia:	brotherhood that fulfilled many vital social and charitable functions throughout the Portuguese world
moeda:	standard eighteenth-century Portuguese gold coin of medium value; in contemporary English, a *moidore*
morabitino:	*maravedí* – Medieval gold coin, originally Moroccan; later money of account
mordomo-mor:	head, or steward-in-chief, of a royal or noble household
morgadio:	entailed estate
morgado:	entailed estate; heir to entailed estate
morisco:	In Spain, Muslim convert to Christianity
mozarab:	Christians in al-Andalus living under Muslim rule and adopting much from Arab culture
mudéjar:	peninsular Muslim living under Christian rule
muwallad:	Muslim of native peninsular origin
New Christian:	Jew converted to Catholicism, or descendant of such
nobre:	noble

nobreza simples:	lower-ranking nobility
oppidum:	a large pre-Roman settlement or a Roman town
ordenações:	statutes; codified laws
ouvidor:	judge
párias:	tribute payments made by Muslim rulers to Christian ruler in al-Andalus, and later by Asian rulers to Portuguese king
peão (pl. *peões*):	foot-soldier
Physiocrats:	group of late-eighteenth-century French thinkers who believed 'natural' economic laws should be left to operate without government interference, stressed agriculture was the sole source of wealth and advocated free trade
poderoso:	a locally prominent person, usually a landowner, with power and influence in his area or sphere
portos secos:	inland customs posts
povo:	the third estate; the common people
praça:	town square
presúria:	title to land gained through occupying it, then seeking formal approval later
principe:	usually royal prince, but sometimes applied to any great magnate
procurador:	deputy or agent; representative of a municipality in the *cortes*
professor régio:	licensed secondary school teacher
provedoria:	office of a *provedor*
provedor-mor:	senior official with financial and/or supply responsibilities; purveyor in chief
puritano:	in later years of Old Regime, member of exclusive inner group of the nobility
qadi:	Islamic judge
quinta:	country house; in Medieval times, a seigneurial demesne or large rural property, usually with house attached
quinto:	royal fifth; a traditional 20 percent tax, imposed particularly on precious metals extracted in Portuguese territory
razia:	raid
real (pl. *reais*):	after monetary reforms of 1435–6, the basic Portuguese unit of account
real mesa censória:	royal censorship board

reconciliado:	Inquisition prisoner reconciled to church after due punishment
reguengos:	crown lands
Rei Sol:	'Sun King'
reinol (pl. *reinóis*):	European-born Portuguese
relação:	high court
relaxado:	Inquisition prisoner handed over to secular authorities for execution
regimento:	standing orders
rico homem (pl. *ricos homens*):	Medieval nobleman of higher rank
sanbenito:	garment of sack-cloth worn by the condemned at autos da fé
secretário de estado:	secretary of state
sesmaria:	in Portugal, uncultivated land
sharif:	courtesy title of Muslim ruler claiming descent from Muhammad's daughter Fatima
sisas:	excise duties
socorro:	subsidy
sufi:	member of an ascetic or mystic Muslim brotherhood
tabelião:	notary
taifa:	an independent petty princedom in al-Andalus after collapse of the caliphate
talha dourada:	ornamental gilt wood
terço:	sixteenth-seventeenth century military unit, equivalent to a regiment, theoretically composed of integrated elements of arquebusiers, pikemen and swordsmen
trova:	traditional ballad
valido:	favourite or chief minister running the country on behalf of the king
vedor da fazenda:	superintendent of revenue
vereador:	town councillor
vila:	town or suburb
villa:	in Roman times, a country estate with associated large residence
viradeira:	turnaround; fundamental change of policy direction, especially that after the fall of Pombal
VOC:	Dutch East India Company
WIC:	Dutch West India Company

Bibliography

Printed Sources

Abun-Nasr J M 1987 *A history of the Maghrib in the Islamic period*. Cambridge University Press, Cambridge.

Ackerland S R 1990 *King Dinis of Portugal and the Alfonsine heritage*. Peter Lang, New York.

Ahmad A 1991 *Indo-Portuguese trade in seventeenth century (1600–1663)*. Gian Publishing House, New Delhi.

Alarcão J de 1988 *Roman Portugal* (2 vols). Aris and Phillips, Warminster, vol 1.

Albuquerque L de 1989 *Introdução a história dos descobrimentos portugueses*. 4th edn Publicações Europa-América, Lisbon.

Albuquerque L de (dir) 1994 *Dicionário de história dos descobrimentos portugueses* (2 vols). Caminho, Lisbon.

Alden D 1968 *Royal government in colonial Brazil with special reference to the administration of the marquis of Lavradio, viceroy, 1769–1779*. University of California Press, Berkeley and Los Angeles.

Alden D 1984 Sugar planters by necessity, not choice: the role of the Jesuits in the cane sugar industry of colonial Brazil, 1601–1759. In J A Cole (ed) *The church and society in Latin America*. Center for Latin American Studies, Tulane University, New Orleans, pp 139–70.

Alden D 1996 *The making of an enterprise. The Society of Jesus in Portugal, its empire, and beyond, 1540–1750*. Stanford University Press, Stanford.

Alden D 2000 The suppression of the Society of Jesus in the Portuguese assistancy in Asia: the fate of survivors, 1760–77. In *VGL*, pp 361–86.

Alexandre V 1993 *Os sentidos do império: questão nacional e questão colonial na crise do antigo regime*. Edições Afrontamento, Porto.

Almeida F de 1967 *História da igreja em Portugal* (4 vols). 2nd edn Portucalense Editora, Porto.

Almeida J F de and Albuquerque M M B de 2003 *Os painéis de Nuno Gonçalves*. Verbo, Lisbon.

Alves A M 1984 A etiqueta de corte no período Manuelino. *Nova história* 1: 5–26.

Alves A M 1985 *Iconologia do poder real no período Manuelino*. Imprensa Nacional-Casa da Moeda, Lisbon.

Ameal J 1962 *História de Portugal. Das origens até 1940*. 5th edn Livraria Tavares Martins, Porto.

Andrade e Silva J de (ed) 1855 *Collecção chronológica de legislação portuguesa 1627–1633*. F X de Souza, Lisbon.

Antunes M 1983 Como interpretar Pombal? In *CIP*, pp 9–12.

Antunes M (ed) 1983 *Como interpretar Pombal? No bicentenário de sua morte*. Edições Brotéria, Lisbon.

Appian 1912–13 *Appian's Roman history* (4 vols). Heinemann, London.

Arnaud J M 1993 O mesolítico e o neolitização, Balanço e perspectivas. In Carvalho G S de, Ferreira A de B and Senna-Martinez J C de (eds) *O quaternário em Portugal. Balanço e perspectivas*. Edições Calibri, Lisbon, pp 173–84.

Arruda J J de A 1991 Colonies as mercantile investments: the Luso-Brazilian empire, 1500–1808. In *PEME*, pp 360–420.

Arruda J J de A 2000 Decadence or crisis in the Luso-Brazilian empire: a new model of colonization in the eighteenth century. *HAHR* 80/4: 865–78.

Azevedo J L de 1922 *História dos christãos novos portugueses*. Livraria Clássica Editora, Lisbon.

Azevedo J L de 1922a *O marquês de Pombal e a sua época*. 2nd edn O annuário do Brasil, Rio de Janeiro.

Azevedo J L de 1947 *Épocas de Portugal económico. Esboços de história*. Livraria Clássica Editora, Lisbon.

Azevedo P de 1921 *O processo dos Távoras*. Biblioteca Nacional, Lisbon.

Baião A, Cidade H and Múrias M (eds) 1937–40 *História da expansão portuguesa no mundo* (3 vols). Editorial Ática, Lisbon.

Barlow C W 1969 *Iberian fathers* (2 vols). Catholic University of America Press, Washington, DC, vol 1.

Baroja J C 1974 *Inquisicíon, brujería y cryptojudaísmo*. Editorial Ariel, Barcelona.

Barrett W 1990 World bullion flows, 1450–1800. In Tracy J D (ed) *The rise of merchant empires*. Cambridge University Press, Cambridge, pp 224–54.

Beckford W 1834 *Italy; with sketches of Spain and Portugal* (2 vols). Richard Bentley, London.

Beckford W 1972 *Recollections of an excursion to the monasteries of Alcobaça and Batalha* ed B Alexander. Centaur Press, Fontwell, Sussex.

Beloff M 1954 *The age of absolutism, 1660–1815*. Hutchinson, London.

Bethencourt F 2000 *História das inquisições. Portugal, Espanha e Itália séculos XV–XIX*. Companhia das Letras, São Paulo.

Bethencourt F and Chaudhuri K (dir) 1998 *História da expansão portuguesa* (5 vols). Círculo de Leitores, Lisbon.

Bicho N F 1993 Late glacial prehistory of central and southern Portugal. *Antiquity* 67: 345–51.

Bishko C J 1975 The Spanish and Portuguese reconquest, 1095–1492. In Setton K M (ed) *A history of the crusades* (6 vols). University of Wisconsin Press, Madison, vol 3, pp 396–456.

Blance B 1961 Early Bronze Age colonists in Iberia. *Antiquity* 35: 192–202.

Blanning T C W 2002 *The culture of power and the power of culture. Old regime Europe 1660–1789*. Oxford University Press, Oxford.

Blot J-Y and Lizé P (eds) 2000 *Le naufrage des Portugais sur les côtes de Saint-Jean-de-Luz et d'Arcachon (1627)*. Éditions Chandeigne, Paris.

Blussé l and Winius G 1985 The origin and rhythm of Dutch aggression against the Estado da India, 1601–1661. In Souza T R de (ed) *Indo-Portuguese history. Old issues, new questions*. Concept, New Delhi.

Borges C J 1994 *The economics of the Goa Jesuits, 1542–1759*. Concept, New Delhi.

Bouchon G and Thomaz L F R 1988 *Voyage dan les deltas du Gange et de l'Irraouddy 1521*. Fondation Calouste Gulbenkian, Centre Culturel Portugais, Paris.

Bouza Álvarez F J 1992 Portugal en la politica flamenca de Felipe II: sal, pimienta y rebelion en los Paises Bajos. *Hispania* 181: 689–702.

Bouza Álvarez F J 1998 Maria 'Planeta Lusitana', Felipe II y Portugal. In *Felipe II un monarca y su época. La Monarquia Hispanica*. Patrimonio Nacional, pp 105–15.

Bouza Álvarez F 2000 *Portugal no tempo dos Filipes. Política, cultura, representações (1580–1668)*. Edições Cosmos, Lisbon.

Boxer C R 1955 Pombal's dictatorship and the great Lisbon earthquake, 1755. In *CRB OM* vol 3, pp 225–33.

Boxer C R 1956 Some contemporary reactions to the Lisbon earthquake of 1755. *In CRB OM* vol 3, pp 235–48.

Boxer C R 1957 *The Dutch in Brazil 1624–1654*. Clarendon Press, Oxford.

Boxer C R 1957a *A great Luso-Brazilian figure. Padre António Vieira, S.J., 1608–1697*. Hispanic and Luso-Brazilian Councils, London.

Boxer C R 1962 *The golden age of Brazil. Growing pains of a colonial society*. University of California Press, Berkeley and Los Angeles.

Boxer C R 1963 *Two pioneers of tropical medicine: Garcia d'Orta and Nicolás Monardes*. Hispanic and Luso-Brazilian Councils, London.

Boxer C R 1965 *Portuguese society in the tropics. The municipal councils of Goa, Macao, Bahia, and Luanda, 1510–1800*. University of Wisconsin Press, Madison.

Boxer C R 1969 *The Portuguese seaborne empire 1415–1825*. Hutchinson, London.

Boxer C R 1969a Brazilian gold and British traders in the first half of the eighteenth century. *Hispanic American Historical Review* 49/3: 454–72.

Boxer C R 1978 *The church militant and Iberian expansion 1440–1770*. John Hopkins University Press, Baltimore.

Boxer C R 1981 *The English and the Portuguese Brazil trade, 1660–1780: some problems and personalities*. Institute of Latin American Studies, La Trobe University, Bundoora.

Boxer C R 1984 *Seventeenth century Macao in contemporary documents and illustrations*. Heinemann, Hongkong.

Boxer C R 2002 *Opera minora* ed D R Curto (3 vols). Fundação Oriente, Lisbon.

Boyajian J C 1983 *Portuguese bankers at the court of Spain 1626–1650*. Rutgers University Press, New Brunswick, NJ.

Boyajian J C 1993 *Portuguese trade in Asia under the Habsburgs, 1580–1640*. John Hopkins University Press, Baltimore.

Braga I M D 1998 *Entre a cristandade e o islão (século XV–XVII). Cativos e renegados nas franjas de duas sociedades em confronto*. Instituto de Estudios Ceutíes, Ceuta.

Braga P D 2002 *Dom João III*. Hugin, Lisbon.

Braudel F 1972–73 *The Mediterranean and the Mediterranean world in the age of Philip II* (2 vols). Collins, London.

Braudel F 1981 *The structures of everyday life.* Collins, London.

Bulliet R 1979 *Conversion to Islam in the medieval period. An essay on quantitative history.* Harvard University Press, Cambridge, MA.

Caetano M 1965 Recepção e execução dos decretos do concílio de Trento em Portugal. *Revista da faculdade de direito da universidade de Lisboa* 19: 7–87.

Cardim P 1998 *Cortes e cultura política no Portugal do antigo regime.* Edições Cosmos, Lisbon.

Carvalho A F de, Zilhão J and Aubrey T 1996 *Vale do Côa. Arte rupestre e pré-história.* Parque Arqueológico do Vale do Côa, Lisbon.

Carvalho R de 1983 As ciências exactas no tempo de Pombal. In *CIP*, pp 215–32.

Cavallo G and Chartier R (eds) 1999 *A history of reading in the West.* Polity Press, Cambridge.

Chadwick H 1976 *Priscillian of Avila. The occult and the charismatic in the early church.* Clarendon Press, Oxford.

Checa F 1992 *Felipe II. Mecenas de las artes* Editorial Nerea, Madrid.

Cheke M 1938 *Dictator of Portugal. A life of the marquis of Pombal 1699–1782.* Sidgwick and Jackson, London.

Chicó M et al. 1942–53 *História da arte em Portugal* (3 vols). Portucalense Editora, Porto.

Chrisawn M 1998 A military bull in a diplomatic China shop: General Jean Lannes's mission to Lisbon 1802–1804. www.NapoleonSeries.org, pp 1–16.

Christensen S T (ed) 1990 *Violence and the absolutist state: studies in European and Ottoman history.* Academisk Forlag, Copenhagen.

Claude D 1980 Freedmen in the Visigothic kingdom. In James E (ed) *Visigothic Spain: new approaches.* Clarendon Press, Oxford, pp 159–88.

Coelho M H da C 1983 Apontamentos sobre a comida e a bebida do campesinato coimbrão em tempos medievos. *Revista de história económica e social* 12: 91–101.

Coelho M H da C 1987 A mulher e o trabalho nas cidades medievais Portuguesas. *Revista de história económica e social* 20: 45–63.

Coles J M 1982 The bronze age in northwestern Europe. In *Advances in world archaeology*, Academic Press, New York, vol 1, 266–321.

Coles J M and Harding A F 1979 *The bronze age in Europe. An introduction to the prehistory of Europe c. 2000–700 BC.* Methuen, London.

Collins R 1989 *The Arab conquest of Spain 710–797.* Blackwell, Oxford.

Collins R 1995 *Early medieval Spain. Unity in diversity, 400–1000.* 2nd edn Macmillan, London.

Collis J 1984 *The European iron age.* Batsford, London.

Conquista de Lisboa aos Mouros em 1147 1989. Trans J A de Oliveira. Livros Horizonte, Lisbon.

Cook W F 1994 *The hundred years war for Morocco: Gunpowder and the military revolution in the early modern Muslim world.* Westview Press, Boulder, CO.

Cortesão J 1984 *Alexandre de Gusmão e o tratado de Madrid* (4 vols). 2nd edn Livros Horizonte, Lisbon.

Costa J P O 1991 Do sonho manuelino ao realismo joanino. Novos documentos sobre as relações luso-chinesas na terceira década do século XVI. *Studia* 50: 121–56.

Costa J P O 2002 O Império português em meados do século XVI. *Anais de história de além-mar* 3: 87–121.

Costa J P O 2005 *D. Manuel I 1469–1521. Um príncipe do Renascimento.* Círculo de Leitores, Lisbon.

Couto D S 2000 Some observations on Portuguese renegades in Asia in the sixteenth century. In *VGL*, pp 178–201.

Crossley N and Roberts J M (eds) 2004 *After Habermas: New perspectives on the public sphere*. Blackwell Publishing/ Sociological Review, Oxford.

Davidson D M 1973 How the Brazilian west was won: freelance and state on the Mato Grosso frontier. In D Alden (ed) *Colonial roots of Modern Brazil. Papers of the Newberry Library conference*, University of California Press, Berkeley and Los Angeles, pp 61–106.

Delaforce A 2002 *Art and patronage in eighteenth-century Portugal*. Cambridge University Press, Cambridge.

Dias J J A 1988 *Ensaios de história moderna*. Editorial Presença, Lisbon.

Dias J J A 1996 *Gentes e espaços (em torno da população portuguesa na primeira metade do século XVI)*. Fundação Calouste Gulbenkian – JNICT, Lisbon, vol 1.

Dias J J A 2000 From the west to the east: the return of the printed word. In *VGL*, pp 295–306.

Dias J S da S 1973 *Os descobrimentos e a problemática cultural do século XVI*. Universidade de Coimbra, Coimbra.

Dicionário ilustrado da história de Portugal 1985. (2 vols). Publicações Alfa, Lisbon.

Diffie B W 1960 *Prelude to empire: Portugal overseas before Henry the navigator*. University of Nebraska Press, Lincoln.

Disney A R 1978 *Twilight of the pepper empire. Portuguese trade in southwest India in the early seventeenth century*. Harvard University Press, Cambridge, MA.

Disney A R 2001 From viceroy of India to viceroy of Brazil? The count of Linhares at court (1636–39). *Portuguese Studies* 17: 114–29.

Disney A R and Booth E (eds) 2000 *Vasco da Gama and the linking of Europe and Asia*. Oxford University Press, New Delhi.

Duarte C 1999 The early paleolithic human skeleton from the Abrigo do Lagar Velho (Portugal) and modern human emergence in Iberia. *Proceedings of the National Academy of Sciences USA* 96: 7604–9.

Dutra F A 1998 The wounding of King José I. Accident or assassination attempt? *Journal of Mediterranean Studies* 7: 221–9.

Edmondson J C 1987 *Two Roman industries in Lusitania. Mining and garum production*. BAR international series no. 362. BAR, Oxford.

Elliott J H 1963 *Imperial Spain 1469–1716*. Edward Arnold, London.

Elliott J H 1986 *The count-duke of Olivares. The statesman in an age of decline*. Yale University Press, New Haven, CT.

Elliott J H 1991 The Spanish monarchy and the kingdom of Portugal, 1580–1640. In Greenglass M (ed) *Conquest and coalescence. The shaping of the state in early modern Europe*. Edward Arnold, London, pp 48–67.

Esdaile C 2003 *The peninsular war. A new history*. Penguin, London.

Fagan B M 1992 *People of the earth. An introduction to world prehistory*. 7th edn Harper Collins, New York.

Fernández-Armesto F 1992 The survival of a notion of Reconquista in late tenth and eleventh century León. In Reuter T (ed) *Warriors and churchmen in the Middle Ages: Essays presented to Karl Leyser*, Hambledon Press, pp 123–43.

Ferreira A 1987 *The tragedy of Ines de Castro*. Trans and ed J R C Martyn. Coimbra University Press, Coimbra.

Fisher H E S 1971 *The Portugal trade. A study of Anglo-Portuguese commerce 1700–1770.* Methuen, London.

Fletcher R 1992 *Moorish Spain.* University of California Press, Berkeley and Los Angeles.

Flynn D 1991 Comparing the Tokugawa shogunate with Habsburg Spain: two silver-based empires in a global setting. In Tracy D (ed) *The political economy of merchant empires,* Cambridge University Press, Cambridge, pp 332–59.

Freeman L G 1975 Acheulian sites and stratigraphy in Iberia and the Maghreb. In Butzer K W and Isaac G LL (eds) *After the australopithecines. Stratigraphy, ecology and culture change in the middle Pleistocene.* Mouton, the Hague, pp 661–743.

Furber H 1976 *Rival empires of trade in the orient, 1600–1800.* University of Minnesota Press, Minneapolis.

Gamito T J 1988 *Social complexity in southwest Iberia 800–300 BC. The case of Tartessos.* BAR international series no. 439. BAR, Oxford.

Gibb H A R et al. (eds) 1960 *Encyclopaedia of Islam* (9 vols). Brill, Leiden and Luzac, London.

Glick T F 1979 *Islamic and Christian Spain in the early middle ages.* Princeton University Press, Princeton, NJ.

Godinho V M 1962 *A economia dos descobrimentos Henriquinos.* Livraria Sá da Costa, Lisbon.

Godinho V M 1968 *Ensaios* (3 vols). Livraria Sá da Costa, Lisbon.

Godinho V M 1978 L'Emigration Portugaise (xve–xxe siècles) une constante structurales et les répouses aux changements du monde. *Revista de história económica e social* 1: 5–32.

Godinho V M 1980 *Estrutura da antiga sociedade Portuguesa.* 4th edn Arcádia, Lisbon.

Godinho V M 1981–83 *Os descobrimentos e a economia mundial* (4 vols). 2nd edn Editorial Presença, Lisbon.

Godinho V M 1990 *Mito e mercadoria, Utopia e prática de navegar séculos XIII–XVIII.* Difel, Lisbon.

Goffart W 1980 *Barbarians and Romans, AD 418–584. The techniques of accommodation.* Princeton University Press, Princeton, NJ.

Goís D de 1790 *Chronica do serenissimo senhor rei D. Emanuel* (2 vols). Real Officina da Universidade, Coimbra.

Gomes A J and Trigueiros A M 1992 *Moedas Portuguesas na época dos descobrimentos 1385–1580. Portuguese coins in the age of discovery 1385–1580.* Antonio Gomes, Lisbon.

Gomes J F 1983 Pombal e a reforma da universidade. In *CIP,* pp 235–51.

Gomes R C 1995 *A corte dos reis de Portugal no final de idade média.* Difel, Linda-a-Velha.

Gonçalves A M n.d. *A shortened history of freemasonry in Portugal* www.freemasons-freemasonry.

Gotteri N 2006 *Napoleão e Portugal.* trans P Reis. Editorial Teorema, Lisbon.

Gottfried R S 1983 *The black death. Natural and human disaster in medieval Europe.* Free Press, New York.

Gracias F da S 2000 *Beyond the self. Santa Casa da Misericórdia de Goa.* Surya, Panjim.

Gracias F da S, Pinto C and Borges C (eds) 2005 *Indo-Portuguese history – global trends.* Maureen and Camvet, Panjim.

Grande enciclopédia portuguesa e brasileira 1935–60. (40 vols). Editorial Enciclopédia, Lisbon and Rio de Janeiro.

Guedes M J 1990–93 *História naval brasileira* (2 vols). Ministério de Marinha, Rio de Janeiro.

Habermas J 1989 *The structural transformation of the public sphere. An inquiry into a category of bourgeois society.* Trans T Burger. 2nd edn MIT Press, Cambridge, MA.

Hanson C A 1981 *Economy and society in baroque Portugal, 1668–1703.* University of Minnesota Press, Minneapolis.

Hanson C A 1981a D. Luís da Cunha and Portuguese mercantilist thought. *Journal of the American Portuguese Society* 15: 15–23.

Harrison R J 1980 *The beaker folk. Copper age archaeology in western Europe.* Thames and Hudson, London.

Harrison R J 1988 *Spain at the dawn of history. Iberians, Phoenicians and Greeks.* Thames and Hudson, London.

Hemming J 1978 *Red gold. The conquest of the Brazilian Indians.* Macmillan, London.

Henshall N 1992 *The myth of absolutism: Change and continuity in early modern European monarchy.* Longman, New York.

Herculano A 1972 *History of the origin and establishment of the inquisition in Portugal.* Ktav Publishing House, New York.

Hespanha A M 1993 A 'Restauração' Portuguesa nos capítulos das cortes de Lisboa de 1641. *Penélope* 9–10: 29–62.

Hespanha A M 1994 *As vésperas do Leviathan. Instituições e poder político, Portugal – séc. XVII.* Livraria Almedina, Coimbra.

Higgs D 1979 The Portuguese church. In W J Callahan and D Higgs (eds) *Church and society in Catholic Europe of the eighteenth century.* Cambridge University Press, Cambridge, pp 51–65.

Hilgarth J N 1980 Popular religion in Visigothic Spain. In James E (ed) *Visigothic Spain: New approaches.* Clarendon Press, Oxford, pp 3–60.

Hirsch E F 1967 *Damião de Góis. The life and thought of a Portuguese humanist, 1502–1574.* Martinus Nijhoff, the Hague.

Hobsbaum E J 1954 General crisis of the European economy in the seventeenth century. *Past and Present* 5: 33–49.

Homem A L de C, Andrade A A, Amaral L C 1988 Por onde vem o medievismo em Portugal? *Revista de história económica e social* 22: 115–38.

Humble S 2000 Prestige, ideology and social politics. The place of the Portuguese overseas expansion in the politics of Dom Manuel (1495–1521) *Itinerario* 24: 21–43.

Hydace 1974 *Chronique* ed A Tranoy (2 vols). Les Éditions du Cerf, Paris.

Iams T M 1977 Braganza diplomacy in the crucible of the French Revolution, 1775–1807. *Journal of the American Portuguese Society* 11/1: 30–40.

Israel J I 1985 *European Jewry in the age of mercantilism 1550–1750.* Clarendon Press, Oxford.

Israel J I 1990 *Empires and entrepots. The Dutch, the Spanish monarchy and the Jews, 1585–1713.* Hambledon Press, London.

Israel J 2001 *Radical enlightenment: Philosophy and the making of modernity, 1650–1750.* Oxford University Press, Oxford.

Jayyusi S K et al (eds) 1992 *The legacy of Muslim Spain.* Brill, Leiden.

Johnstone P 1980 *The sea-craft of prehistory.* Harvard University Press, Cambridge, MA.

Jordan A 1994 *Retrato de corte em Portugal. O legado de António Moro (1552–1572)*. Quetzal Editores, Lisbon.
Jordan W C 1996 *The great famine. Northern Europe in the early fourteenth century*. Princeton University Press, Princeton, NJ.
Kamen H 1969 *The war of the Spanish succession 1700–15*. Weidenfeld and Nicolson, London.
Kamen H 1997 *Philip II of Spain*. Yale University Press, New Haven, CT.
Keay S J 1988 *Roman Spain*. British Museum Publications, London.
Keeler M F (ed) 1981 *Sir Francis Drake's West India voyage 1585–86*. Hakluyt Society, London.
Kendrick T D 1956 *The Lisbon earthquake*. Methuen, London.
Kennedy H 1996 *Muslim Spain and Portugal. A political history of al-Andalus*. Longman, London.
Laroui A 1977 *The history of the Maghrib*. Princeton University Press, Princeton, NJ.
Leite A 1983 A ideologia pombalina, despotismo esclarecido e regalismo. In *CIP*, pp 27–54.
Leite A 1983a Pombal e o ensino secundário. In *CIP*, pp 165–81.
Lévi-Provençal E 1950–53 *Histoire de l'Espagne musulmane* (3 vols). G-P Maisonneuve, Paris, and Brill, Leiden.
Lima D P de 1993 Crónica do Principe D João III 1537–1554, Esboço de uma biografia. *Anais. Academia Portuguesa de história 2nd ser* 33: 231–81.
Livermore H V 1966 *A new history of Portugal*. Cambridge University Press, London.
Livermore H V 1971 *The origins of Spain and Portugal*. Allen and Unwin, London.
Livy 1919–35 *Livy with an English translation* trans B O Foster (14 vols). Heinemann, London.
Loades D 1989 *Mary Tudor. A life*. Blackwell, Oxford.
Lomax D W 1978 *The reconquest of Spain*. Longman, London.
Lopes F 1990 *Crónica de D. João I* ed A Sérgio (2 vols). Livraria Civilização, Porto.
Lopes F 1994 *Crónica de D. Pedro I* ed D Peres. Livraria Civilização, Porto.
Loureiro F S 1989 *D. Sebastião e Alcácer Quibir*. Publicações Alfa, Lisbon.
Luz F P M da 1952 *O conselho da Índia*. Agência Geral do Ultramar, Lisbon.
Lynch J 1964–9 *Spain under the Habsburgs* (2 vols). Blackwell, Oxford.
Macaulay R 1946 *They went to Portugal*. Jonathan Cape, London.
Macedo J B de 1982 *A situação económico no tempo de Pombal*. 2nd edn Morães Editores, Lisbon.
Macedo J B de 1982a *Problemas de história da indústria portuguesa no século XVIII*. 2nd edn Querco, Lisbon.
Mackay A 1977 *Spain in the middle ages: from frontier to empire, 1000–1500*. Macmillan, London.
Magalhães J C de 1977 The first reactions of the Portuguese government to American independence. *Journal of the American Portuguese Society* 11/1:1–12.
Magalhães J R 1993 *O Algarve económico 1600–1773*. Editorial Estampa, Lisbon.
Manchester A K 1933 *British preeminence in Brazil. Its rise and decline: a study in European expansion*. University of North Carolina Press, Chapel Hill.
Manchester A K 1969 The transfer of the Portuguese court to Rio de Janeiro. In H H Keith and S F Edwards (eds) *Conflict and continuity in Brazilian society*. University of South Carolina Press, Columbia, pp 148–90.

Marques A H de O 1971 *Daily life in Portugal in the late middle ages.* University of Wisconsin Press, Madison.
Marques A H de O 1972 *History of Portugal* (2 vols). Columbia University Press, New York, vol 1.
Marques A H de O 1990 *História da maçonaria em Portugal.* vol 1 *Das origens ao triumpho.* Editorial Presença, Lisbon.
Marques A H de O (ed) 1990–2 *Chancelarias portuguesas. D. Afonso IV* (3 vols). INIC, Lisbon.
Marques A H de O 2000 Travelling with the fifteenth century discoverers: their daily life. In *VGL*, pp 30–47.
Marques A H de O and Dias J J A 1994 A população Portuguesa nos séculos XV e XVI. *Biblos* 70: 171–96.
Marques A P 1994 *A maldição da memória do infante Dom Pedro e as origens dos descobrimentos portugueses.* Centro de Estudos da Mar, Figueira da Foz.
Marques A P 1994a L'atlas Miller: un problème resolu. L'art dans la cartographe portugaise. *Revue de la Bibliotheque Nationale de France* 4: 53–7.
Marques A P 1994b *A cartografia dos descobrimentos.* Edição ELO, Lisbon.
Martins J P de O 1958 *Os filhos de D. João I* (2 vols). Guimarães Editores, Lisbon.
Mattoso J 1985 *Ricos-homens, infanções e cavaleiros. A nobreza medieval Portuguesa nos séculos XI e XII.* Guimarães Editores, Lisbon.
Mattoso J 1992 *Portugal medieval. Novas interpretações* 2nd edn Imprensa Nacional-Casa da Moeda, Lisbon.
Mattoso J (dir) 1993 *História de Portugal* (8 vols). Editorial Estampa, Lisbon. vol 1 Mattoso J (ed) Antes de Portugal. vol 2 Mattoso J (ed) A monarquia feudal (1096–1480). vol 3 Magalhães J R (ed) No alvorecer de modernidade (1480–1620). vol 4 Hespanha A M (ed) O antigo regime (1620–1807).
Mattoso J 1995 *Identificação de um país. Ensaio sobre as origens de Portugal 1096–1325* (2 vols). 5th edn Editorial Estampa, Lisbon.
Mattoso J 1998 *A identidade nacional.* Edição Gradiva, Lisbon.
Mauro F 1960 *Le Portugal et l'Atlantique au XVIIe siècle 1570–1670. Étude economique,* S.E.V.P.E.N., Paris.
Maxwell K 1973 *Conflicts and conspiracies: Brazil and Portugal 1750–1808.* Cambridge University Press, Cambridge.
Maxwell K 1995 *Pombal, paradox of the enlightenment.* Cambridge University Press, Cambridge.
Maxwell K 2001 The spark: Pombal, the Amazon and the Jesuits. *Portuguese Studies* 17: 168–83.
Maxwell K 2002 Lisbon. The earthquake of 1755 and urban recovery under the marquês de Pombal. In J Ockman (ed) *Out of ground zero. Case studies in urban reinvention.* Temple Hoyne Buell Center for the Study of American Architecture, Columbia University, New York.
Medina J (dir) 1995 *História de Portugal dos tempos pre- históricos aos nossos dias* (15 vols). Clube Internacional do Livro, Amadora.
Meléndez S de L 1992 El control de la hacienda Portuguesa desde el poder central: la junta de hacienda de Portugal 1602–1608. *Revista da Faculdade de Letras* (Porto) 2nd ser 9: 119–35.
Melo F M de 1967 *Alterações de Évora (1637)* ed J Serrão. Portugália Editora, Lisbon.

Melo F M de 1977 *Epanáforas da vária história portuguesa* ed J Serrão. Imprensa Nacional-Casa da Moeda, Lisbon.

Mendonça M 1991 *D. João II. Um percurso humano e político nas origens da modernidade em Portugal.* Editorial Estampa, Lisbon.

Mendonça M 1991a *D. Jorge da Costa, Cardeal de Alpedrinha.* Colibri, Lisbon.

Meneses L de (Conde de Ericeira) 1945 *História de Portugal restaurado* (4 vols). Livraria Civilização, Lisbon.

Miller S J 1978 *Portugal and Rome c. 1748–1830. An aspect of the Catholic enlightenment.* Università Gregoriana Editrice, Rome.

Monteiro N G 2003 Seventeenth and eighteenth century Portuguese nobilities in the European context: a historiographical overview. *e-journal of Portuguese History* 1/ 1: 1–17.

Moreno H B 1970 A conspiração contra D João II: o julgamento do duque de Bragança. *Arquivos do Centro Cultural Português* 2: 47–103.

Moreno H B 1979–80 *A batalha de Alfarrobeira* (2 vols) 2nd edn Biblioteca geral da Universidade, Coimbra.

Moreno H B 1988 Contestação e oposição da nobreza portuguesa ao poder público nas finais da idade média. *Ler história* 13: 3–14.

Nevins L 1971 Enlightening Portugal: the jornal encyclopédico, 1779–1806. *Journal of the American Portuguese Cultural Society* 5/3–4: 1–12.

O Sebastianismo 1978. Terra Livre, Lisbon.

Oliveira A de 1990 *Poder e oposição política em Portugal no período filipino (1580– 1640).* Difel, Lisbon.

Oliveira M de 1968 *História ecclesiástica de Portugal.* 4th edn União Gráfica, Lisbon.

O'Neill T 1809 *A concise and accurate account of the proceedings of the squadron under the command of Rear Admiral Sir Will. Sidney Smith, K.G., in effecting the escape and escorting the royal family of Portugal to the Brazils.* O'Neill T, London.

Orosius P 1964 *The seven books of history against the pagans* trans R J Deferrari. Catholic University Press of America, Washington, DC.

Parker G 1978 *Philip II.* Little Brown, Boston.

Parker G 1995 David or Goliath? Philip II and his world in the 1580s. In Kagan R and Parker G (eds) *Spain, Europe and the Atlantic world. Essays in honour of John H Elliott,* Cambridge University Press, Cambridge, pp 245–66.

Pereira A 1953–8 *D. João VI príncipe e rei* (4 vols). Empresa Nacional de Publicidade, Lisbon.

Pereira I da R 1984 O desacato na capela real em 1552 e o processo do Calvinista Inglês perante o ordinário de Lisboa. *Anais. Academia Portuguesa de história* 2nd ser 29: 597–605.

Pereira M H 1986 Portugal and the structure of the world market in the eighteenth and nineteenth centuries. In W Fischer, R Marvin McInnis and J Schneider (eds) *The emergence of the world economy 1500–1914.* Franz Steiner Verlag, Wiesbaden, vol 1, pp 279–300.

Peres D 1928–35 *História de Portugal. Edição monumental* (7 vols). Portucalense Editora, Barcelos.

Peres D 1992 *Como nasceu Portugal.* 10th edn Vertente, Porto.

Perez R M (coord) 1997 *Arab-Islamic Memories in Portugal.* CNCDP, Lisbon.

Pike R 1972 *Aristocrats and traders. Sevillian society in the sixteenth century.* Cornell University Press, Ithaca.

Pimenta A 1936 *D. João III.* Livraria Tavares Martins, Porto.

Pina R de 1950 *Crónica de el-Rei D. João II.* Atlantida, Coimbra.

Pinto V N 1979 *O ouro brasileiro e o comércio anglo-português. (Uma contribuição aos estudos da economia atlântica no século XVIII).* Companhia Editora Nacional, São Paulo.

Portugal – Dicionário histórico, corográfico, heráldico, biográfico, bibliográfico, numismático e artístico 2000–5 [1904–15, 7 vols] ed M Amaral electronic edn. www.arqnet.pt/dicionario.

Prestage E 1928 *As relações diplomáticos de Portugal com a França, Inglaterra e Holanda de 1640 a 1668.* Imprensa da Universidade, Coimbra.

Prestage E 1935 The treaties of 1642, 1654 and 1661. In E Prestage (ed) *Chapters in Anglo-Portuguese relations.* Voss and Michael, Watford, pp 130–51.

Queirós Veloso J M de 1940 A perda da independência. Factores internos e externos, que para ela contribuiram. In *Congresso do mundo Português. Publicações.* Comisão Executiva das Centenários, Lisbon, vol 6, pp 11–30.

Queirós Veloso, J M de 1946 *O reinado do Cardeal D. Henrique* (2 vols). Empresa Nacional, Lisbon, vol 1.

Raposo L 1989 *Portugal from its origins through the Roman era.* Mosaico, Lisbon.

Rau V 1968 *Estudos de história. 1. Mercadores, mercadorias, pensamento económico.* Editorial Verbo, Porto.

Raynal G-T 1780 *Histoire philosophique et politique des établissemens et du commerce des Européens dans les deux Indes* (10 vols). Jean-Leonard Pellet, Geneva, 1780.

Rego A da S 1940 *O padroado português do oriente. Esboço histórico.* Agência Geral das Colónias, Lisbon.

Reilly B F 1992 *The contest of Christian and Muslim in Spain 1031–1157.* Blackwell, Oxford.

Renfrew C 1978 *Before civilization. The radiocarbon revolution and prehistoric Europe.* Pelican, London.

Resende G de 1973 *Crónica de D. João II e miscelânea* (ed) J V Serrão. Imprensa Nacional-Casa da Moeda, Lisbon.

Ribeiro O 1967 *Portugal, o Mediterrâneo e o Atlântico.* 3rd edn. Livraria Sá da Costa, Lisbon.

Ribeiro O 1992 *Geografia e civilização: temas Portugesas.* 3rd edn. Livros Horizonte, Lisbon.

Rodrigues F 1931–50 *História da companhia de Jesus na assistência de Portugal* (7 vols). Apostolado da Imprensa, Porto.

Rogers F M 1961 *The travels of the infante Dom Pedro of Portugal.* Harvard University Press, Cambridge, MA.

Roque M de C 1982 A 'peste grande' de 1569 em Lisboa. *Anais. Academia Portuguesa de história 2nd ser* 28: 73–90.

Rooney P T 1994 Habsburg fiscal policies in Portugal 1580–1640. *Journal of European Economic History* 23: 545–62.

Rossi C L de 1944 *Diario dos acontecimentos de Lisboa, por ocasião da entrada das tropas de Junot* ed A Pereira. Casa Portuguesa, Lisbon.

Rouillard P 1991 *Les Grecs et la peninsule Iberique du VIIIe au IVe siècle avant Jésus-Christ*. Boccard, Paris.

Russell P E 1955 *The English intervention in Spain and Portugal in the time of Edward III and Richard II*. Clarendon Press, Oxford.

Russell-Wood A J R 1968 *Fidalgos and philanthropists. The Santa Casa da Misericórdia of Bahia, 1550–1755*. Macmillan, London.

Sanceau E 1959 *The Perfect Prince. A Biography of the King Dom João II*. Livraria Civilização, Porto.

Santos M E M and Torrão M M 1989 *Subsídios para a história geral do Cabo Verde: a legitimidade da utilização de fontes escritas portugueses através da análise de um documento do início do século XVI* CEHCA/IICT.

Saraiva A J 1969 *Inquisição e cristãos-novos*. Editorial Nova, Porto.

Saraiva A J 1979 A 'ideia de Portugal' pode remontar ao século IX. *História* 3: 14–21.

Saramago J 2002 *Journey to Portugal*. Harvill Press, London.

Saunders A C de C M 1982 *A social history of black slaves and freedmen in Portugal 1441–1555*. Cambridge University Press, Cambridge.

Savory H N 1968 *Spain and Portugal. The prehistory of the Iberian peninsula*. Thames and Hudson, London.

Schneider S 1971 *The General Company of the Cultivation of the Vine of the Upper Douro, 1756–1777: A case study of the marquis of Pombal's economic reform program*. University Microfilms, Ann Arbor, MI, 1971.

Schurhammer G 1973–82 *Francis Xavier. His life, his times* (4 vols). Jesuit Historical Institute, Rome.

Schwartz S B 1973 *Sovereignty and society. The high court of Bahia and its judges, 1609–1751*. University of California Press, Berkeley and Los Angeles.

Scott S and Duncan C J 2001 *Biology of plagues: evidence from historical populations*. Cambridge University Press, Cambridge.

Scott S and Duncan C 2005 *Return of the Black Death. The world's greatest serial killer*. Wiley, Chichester.

Segurado J 1984 Um livro para a ensinança do Principe Dom Sebastião com iluminuras do tempo de Camões. *Anais. Academia Portuguesa de história* 2nd ser 29: 1–17.

Sérgio A 1979 *Breve interpretação da história de Portugal*. 9th edn. Livraria Sá da Costa, Lisbon.

Serrão J (ed) 1961–71 *Dicionário de história de Portugal* (4 vols). Iniciativas Editoriais, Lisbon.

Serrão J 1981 *O Carácter social da revolução de 1383*. 4th edn. Livros Horizonte, Lisbon.

Serrão J and Marques A H de O (dirs) 1986– *Nova história da expansão portuguesa* (12 vols planned). Editorial Estampa, Lisbon. vol 2 Marques A H de O (ed) 1998 *A expansão quatrocentista*. vol 3 pt 1 Matos A T de (ed) 2005 *A colonização atlântica*. vol 3 pt 2 Matos A T de (ed) 2005 *A colonização atlântica*. vol 5 pt 1 Lopes M de J dos M (ed) 2006 *O império oriental. 1660–1820*. vol 5 pt 2 Lopes M de J dos M (ed) 2006 *O império oriental 1660–1820*. vol 6 Johnson H and Silva M B N da (ed) 1992 *O império luso-brasileiro 1500–1620*. vol 7 Mauro F (ed) 1991 *O império luso-brasileiro 1620–1750*. vol 8 Silva M B N da (ed) 1986 *O império luso-brasileiro 1750–1822*.

Serrão J and Marques A H de O (dirs) 1986– *Nova história de Portugal* (13 vols planned). Editorial Presença, Lisbon. vol 1 Alarcão J de (ed) 1990 *Portugal das origens à Romanização*. vol 2 Marques A H de O (ed) 1993 *Portugal das invasões Germânicas à 'reconquista'*. vol 3 Coelho M H da C and Homem A L de C (eds) 1996 *Portugal em definição de fronteiras*. vol 4 Marques A H de O 1987 *Portugal na crise dos séculos XIV e XV*. vol 5 Dias J J A (ed) 1999 *Portugal do renascimento à crise dinástica*. vol 7 Meneses A de F de 2001 *Portugal da paz da Restauração ao ouro do Brasil*.

Serrão J V 1977–2001 *História de Portugal* (14 vols). Editorial Verbo, Lisbon.

Shatzmiller M 2000 *The Berbers and the Islamic state. The Merinid experience in pre-protectorate Morocco*. Marcus Weiner Publishers, Princeton, NJ.

Shaw L M E 1989 The inquisition and the Portuguese economy. *Journal of European Economic History* 18: pp 415–31.

Shaw L M E 1998 *The Anglo-Portuguese alliance and the English merchants in Portugal 1654–1810*. Ashgate, Aldershot.

Sherratt A 1981 Plough and pastoralism: aspects of the secondary products revolution. In Hodder I et al (eds) *Pattern of the past. Studies in honour of David Clarke*. Cambridge University Press, Cambridge, pp 261–305.

Sideri S 1970 *Trade and power. Informal colonialism in Anglo- Portuguese relations*. Rotterdam University Press, Rotterdam.

Silbert A 1977 *Do Portugal de antigo regime ao Portugal oitocentista*. 2nd edn Livros Horizonte, Lisbon.

Silva I F de (et al.) 1858–1923 *Diccionario bibliographico Portuguez* (23 vols). Imprensa Nacional, Lisbon.

Silva L A R da 1971–2 *História de Portugal nos séculos XVII e XVIII* 2nd edn (6 vols). Imprensa Nacional, Lisbon.

Smith J [conde de Carnota] 1843 *Memoirs of the marquis of Pombal* (2 vols). Longman, Brown, Green and Longmans, London.

Smith R C 1968 *The art of Portugal 1500–1800*. Meredith Press, New York.

Sousa A de 1990 *As cortes medievais portuguesas (1385–1490)* (2 vols). Instituto Nacional de Investigação Científica, Porto.

Sousa A C de 1946–55 *História genealógica da casa real portuguesa* (9 vols). 2nd edn *Atlantîda*, Coimbra.

Strabo 1917–32 *The geography of Strabo* (8 vols). Heinemann, London.

Subrahmanyam S 1993 *The Portuguese empire in Asia 1500–1700: A political and economic history*. Longman, London.

Subrahmanyam S 1997 *The career and legend of Vasco da Gama*. Cambridge University Press, Cambridge.

Taha A D 1989 *The Muslim conquest and settlement of North Africa and Spain*. Routledge, London.

Tavares M J P F 1982 Judeus e Mouros no Portugal dos séculos XIV e XV (tentativa de estudo comparativo). *Revista de história económica e social* 9: 75–89.

Tavares M J P F 1983 Para o estudo do pobre em Portugal na idade média. *Revista de história económica e social* 11: 29–54.

Tavares M J P F 1983a A nobreza no reinado de D. Fernando e a sua actuação em 1383–1385. *Revista de história económica e social* 12: 45–84.

Tavares M J P F 1992 *Los Judíos en Portugal*. Editorial Mapfre, Madrid.

Thomaz L F R 1989 Le Portugal et l'Afrique au XVe siècle: les debuts de l'expansion. *Arquivos do Centro Cultural Português* 26: 161–256.

Thomaz L F R 1990 *L'idee imperiale manueline*. Fondation Calouste Gulbenkian, Centre Culturel Portugais, Paris.

Thomaz L F R 1991 Factions, interests and messianism: the politics of Portuguese expansion in the east, 1500–1521. *Indian social and economic history review* 28: 97–109.

Thomaz L F R 1994 *De Ceuta a Timor*. Difel, Linda-a-Velha.

Thomaz L F R 1995 A crise de 1565–1575 na história do Estado da Índia *Mare Liberum* 9: 481–519.

Thompson E A 1965 *The early Germans*. Clarendon Press, Oxford.

Thompson E A 1969 *The Goths in Spain*. Clarendon Press, Oxford.

Thompson E A 1976 The end of Roman Spain. *Nottingham Medieval Studies* 20: 3–28; 1977 ibid 21: 3–31; 1978 ibid 22: 3–22; 1979 ibid 23: 1–21.

Torgal L R 1984 Acerca do significado sociopolítico de 'Revolução de 1640'. *Revista de história das ideias* 6: 301–19.

Torres J V 1978 Uma longa guerra social: os ritos de repressão inquisitorial em Portugal. *Revista de história económica e social* 1: 55–68.

Tracy J D (ed) 1991 *The political economy of merchant empires*. Cambridge University Press, Cambridge.

Tranoy A 1981 *La Galice Romaine. Recherches sur le nord-ouest de la péninsule iberique dans l'Antiquité* Diffusion de Boccard, Paris.

Turner J (ed) 1996 *The dictionary of art* (34 vols). Macmillan, London.

Twigg G 1984 *The black death: a biological reappraisal*. Batsford, London.

Twohig E S 1981 *The megalithic art of western Europe*. Clarendon Press, Oxford.

Valladares R 1998 *La rebelión de Portugal 1640–1680: guerra, conflicto y poderes en la monarquía hispánica*. Junta de Castilla y León, Consejeria de Educación y Cultura.

Vasconcelos e Sousa B 1990 *A propriedade das albergarias de Évora nos finais da idade média*. Instituto Nacional de Investigação Científica, Lisbon.

Velasco J A S 1994 City and state in pre-Roman Spain: the example of Ilici. *Antiquity* 68: 289–99.

Vilar P 1984 *A history of gold and money 1450–1920* trans J White. Verso, London.

Villar F 1990 Indo-Européens et pré-Indo-Européens dans la péninsule Iberique. In Markey T L and Greppin A A C (eds) *When worlds collide. Indo-Europeans and pre-Indo-Europeans*. Karoma, Ann Arbor, MI, pp 363–94.

Wenke R J 1980 *Patterns in Prehistory. Humankind's first three million years* 3rd edn Oxford University Press, New York.

White L 2003 Guerra y revolución militar en la Iberia del siglo XVII. *Manuscrits* 21: 63–93.

Wolf K B (ed) 1990 *Conquerors and chroniclers of early medieval Spain*. Liverpool University Press, Liverpool.

Yerushalmi Y H 1971 *From Spanish court to Italian ghetto. Isaac Cardoso: a study in seventeenth century marranism and Jewish apologetics*. Columbia University Press, New York.

Yogev G 1978 *Diamonds and coral. Anglo-Dutch Jews and eighteenth century trade*. Leicester University Press, Leicester.

Zilhão J 1988 The early upper paleolithic of Portugal. In Hoffecker J F, Wolf C A (eds) *The early upper paleolithic. Evidence from Europe and the Near East*, pp 135–55.

Zilhão J 1990 The Portuguese Estremadura at 18,000 BP: the Salutrian. In Seffer O and Gamble C (eds) *The world at 18,000 BP* (2 vols). Unwin Hyman, vol 1, pp 109–26.

Zvelebil M and Rowley-Conwy P 1986 Foragers and farmers in Atlantic Europe. In Zvelebil M (ed) *Hunters in transition: Mesolithic societies of temperate Eurasia and their transition to farming*. Cambridge University Press, Cambridge, pp 67–93.

Index